OMAN SINCE 1856

OMAN
SINCE 1856

Disruptive Modernization
in a Traditional
Arab Society

BY ROBERT GERAN LANDEN

PRINCETON UNIVERSITY PRESS

PRINCETON, NEW JERSEY

1967

Copyright © 1967 by Princeton University Press
L.C. Card No.: 66-21835

Printed in the United States of America
by Princeton University Press, Princeton, New Jersey

To my Mother and Father,
Evelyn Geran Landen and
Harry James Landen

PREFACE

COMPARED to most other regions in the Middle East little has been written concerning the history of the Persian Gulf or of the districts surrounding it. Most of what has appeared touches upon the period since World War I and concentrates on questions related to the exploitation of the oil resources of the locality. There is also a lesser amount of historical writing that deals with the golden age of Persian Gulf commercial and maritime activity between the eighth and sixteenth centuries as well as with the time of initial European contact with the Gulf between the sixteenth and early nineteenth centuries. But the years between 1850 and 1914, insofar as they have attracted scholars, have been treated mainly in the context of the growth of European—especially British—imperial involvement in the region. There is nothing wrong with this approach as far as it goes, but one result of this orientation is that we know very little about the indigenous history of the Gulf's people themselves during the period from the late eighteenth to the early twentieth century, nor much about the way they reacted to the probes of a modern civilization that was destined to disrupt their ancient ways.

During my research I reached the conclusion that the late nineteenth century—especially after the penetration of modern steamer and telegraphic communications into the Persian Gulf beginning in 1862—was the time of crisis when the region's ancient culture was changed irrevocably. It was also my conclusion that an understanding of this relatively unknown upheaval could do much to clarify the region's present situation and also might illustrate that in some societies the process of modernization can be more destructive than constructive in its effects.

The Persian Gulf, however, while it is a homogeneous area in a number of respects, is also a region of several clearly identifiable subunits each of which has a distinct history and subculture. This book concentrates on one of these subunits—Oman—and attempts to analyze the events and trends within that single Persian Gulf principality during the crucial time when its ancient maritime and tribal society was buffeted by changes beyond the control and even the understanding of most of its indigenous population. I have made it my task to provide not only a factual narrative but also an interpretation of why things happened as they did in Oman after 1862. While primary attention is devoted to the 1862-1903 period, when the various accommodations to the new economic, international, and internal political realities were reached in their essentials, the book's final chapter also sketches Oman's twentieth century history down to the early 1960s. It is interesting that the 1862-1962 century constitutes an identifiable historical unit because in 1963 a major oil strike was made in Oman, and a new era in the country's history is already dawning.

A glimpse of the bibliography will reveal that this study is an exploratory one based primarily upon Omani chronicles and official archival materials. I am conscious of the inadequacy of some of my explanations, but I am afraid such inadequacies are in the nature of any pioneering work. I also expect that some will not agree with various parts of my analysis and perhaps even with the book's basic argument. This is to be expected. Middle Eastern history is a vast field, and there is a need at this time to offer many interpretations of it. I will be happy if this book is accepted generally but satisfied if it provokes more work on the questions I raise even if later writers disagree substantially with my answers.

I have not attempted to set down an encyclopedic coverage of all events; rather, I have made a factual selection. Also, there is much material included in the maps and charts that is not a part of the narrative, and these should be treated as integral to the text. As for the ever-present difficulties of transliterations from the Arabic, normally I have used generally accepted Western versions of the spelling of local places when such are available, the main exception to this rule is my use of "Masqat" instead of "Muscat." If, as is most often the case, there is no accepted Western spelling, then in the text I have used a simple transliteration but have not indicated all the various Arabic letters and long vowels. In the index a full transliteration is provided after each entry of a person or place whose name is taken from the Arabic. Finally, I have modified all Arabic personal names appearing in the text or footnotes, to conform to a standard transliteration system.

Many individuals and organizations have had a part in creating this work, and while I am responsible for the book's faults, I acknowledge that many of its virtues are the product of a great deal of help and advice that has been extended to me. I wish especially to thank all of my teachers including the earliest and best—my parents. Miss Mary Boyle, Miss Ruth Appel, Mr. John McNealy, and Mr. A. Robert Kelman among my teachers at Watertown High School in Massachusetts had far more influence on my subsequent work than I expect they realized in those years when I sat in their classes. Also, Professors Douglass Adair and R. Bruce McCully, under whom I studied history at the College of William and Mary, were most influential in teaching me a respect for the discipline and imagination that goes into any historical production. Professor George Hourani of the University of Michigan initiated me into the mysteries of Middle Eastern history and oriental maritime studies. I have yet to meet a more dedicated and knowledgeable scholar of the area than he. At Princeton I was particularly fortunate to be a student of Professor Cyril E. Black, who first suggested to me that the modernization of the Persian Gulf was a subject that needed investigation and whose lively, thought-provoking classes were a model of what good graduate seminars should be. Also at Princeton Professors T. Cuyler Young and the late Lewis V. Thomas provided much knowledge, advice, and—most valuable—friendship. I owe a special debt to two former members of the Princeton faculty: Professor Farhat Ziadeh of the University of Washington, who generously spent much of his time helping me during a period when he was heavily committed to other work, and Professor R. Bayly Winder of New York University, whose imposing store of knowledge of things Arabian as well as his thoughtful,

Preface

friendly advice was always at my disposal. Others I wish to single out for thanks include Professor Gordon Craig of Stanford University and formerly of Princeton; Mr. Ahmad Abu Hakimah, now of the University of Jordan in Amman; Mr. Douglas Matthews, Deputy Librarian of the London Library and formerly with the India Office Library; Mr. and Mrs. Alfred Vincent of New Barnet, England; Mr. Richard Chambers; Mr. Jon Mandaville; Miss Hind Abu Su'ud of the American University at Cairo; the three typists who have seen this work through various stages—Miss Sharon Kay Marshall, Mrs. L. Wren, and Mrs. Alice Weymouth; Mr. Roy Grisham of the Princeton University Press, this book's editor; also my mother- and father-in-law, Mr. and Mrs. Clark V. Kizzia, who put up with me one entire summer as this work was being finished.

I owe a very substantial debt to several organizations which provided financial support or research help during the preparation of this book. These include Princeton University, the India Office Library, the Arabian American Oil Company, the American University at Cairo, the Imamate of Oman Office in Cairo, the Arab League Secretariat, the Ford Foundation and the Social Science Research Council, both of which awarded me generous fellowships for periods of research and travel in the Middle East, and Dartmouth College.

My Princeton roommate, Mr. Robert B. R. Haller, now of the Department of English at the University of California at Berkeley, read practically this entire work at one stage, and it is only fair to thank or blame him for much of its grammatical structure. Too, I must acknowledge the presence of Michael, Bobby, and Jill, without whose efforts this book would have appeared either years sooner or more probably not at all. Finally, I must thank my wife, who shared in the production of this monograph to the extent of taking notes, typing the entire manuscript at least once, sharing my wanderings, and listening to my ideas, my fears, and my hopes.

Hanover, New Hampshire   R. G. L.

July 1966

CONTENTS

LIST OF TABLES AND MAPS

ABBREVIATED TITLES OF OFTEN-QUOTED WORKS

Admin. Rpt. (*year*)	Government of India, Foreign Department, *Report on the Administration of the Persian Gulf Political Residency and the Maskat Political Agency* (Calcutta, annual, 1873-1904).
Aitchison—year	Government of India, Foreign Department, *A Collection of Treaties, Engagements, and Sanads Relating to India and Neighboring Countries*, C. V. Aitchison, ed., 3rd ed. (Calcutta, 1892), 4th ed. (Calcutta, 1909), 5th ed. (New Delhi, 1933).
Al-Salimi	'Abdallāh ibn-Ḥumayd al-Sālimi, *Tuḥfat al-A'yān bi-Sīrat Ahl 'Umān*, 2nd ed. (Cairo, 1931).
Bombay Records—1856	Government of Bombay, R. H. Thomas, ed., *Selections from the Records of the Bombay Government. Historical and other Information Connected with the Province of Oman, Muscat, Bahrein, and other Places in the Persian Gulf*, new series, no. xxiv (Bombay, 1856).
EI–1	*Encyclopaedia of Islam, 1st ed.* (Leiden, 1913ff.).
EI–2	*Encyclopaedia of Islam, new ed.* (Leiden, 1960ff.).
French Records	The Archives of the Ministry of Foreign Affairs, Paris, "Correspondance Commerciale—Muscate 1894-1901."
Ibn-Ruzayq	Ḥumayd ibn-Muḥammad ibn-Ruzayq, *Al-Fatḥ al-Mubīn fī Sīrat al-Sādāt Āl-Bū-Sa'idīyīn*, trans., ed. and annotated by G. P. Badger, as *History of the Imāms and Seyyids of 'Omān by Salîl-Ibn-Razîk, from A.D. 661-1856* (London, 1871).
India Mss.–1	India Office Library, European Manuscripts, "Wood (Halifax) Collection, India Office Correspondence, Box 5, Correspondence of Sir Charles Wood with Sir Bartle Frere, 1859-1865."
India Mss.–2	India Office Library, European Manuscripts, "Hamilton Collection, Private Correspondence India, Lord George Hamilton to Lord Curzon, no. C 126."
India Mss.–3	India Office Library, European Manuscripts, "Hamilton Collection, Private Correspondence India, Lord Curzon to Lord George Hamilton, no. D 510."
India Mss.–4	India Office Library, European Manuscripts, "Lansdowne Correspondence, Selection of Despatches to Her Majesty's Secretary of State for India, D 558."
India Mss.–5	India Office Library, European Manuscripts, "Lansdowne Correspondence, Correspondence of Lord Lansdowne to and from the Secretary of State for India, D 558."

Abbreviated Titles

India Mss.–6	India Office Library, European Manuscripts, "Elgin Collection, Papers of the Ninth Earl of Elgin and Kincardine, Letters from and to the Secretary of State for India."
India Records–1	India Office Library, Records, "Factory Records—Persia and the Persian Gulf."
India Records–2	India Office Library, Records, "Political and Secret Department Records, Secret Letters Received, Various."
India Records–3	India Office Library, Records, "Political and Secret Department Records, Letters from the Persian Gulf."
India Records–4	India Office Library, Records, "Political and Secret Department Records, Secret Letters from India."
India Records–5	India Office Library, "Political and Secret Department Memoranda."
India Records–6	India Office Library, "Political and Secret Department Files."
Lorimer	Government of India, Foreign Department, J. G. Lorimer, compiler, *Gazetteer of the Persian Gulf, 'Omân, and Central Arabia* (Calcutta, 1908-15).
Précis Commerce	Government of India, Political and Secret Department, J. A. Saldanha, ed., *Précis of Commerce and Communications in the Persian Gulf, 1801-1905* (Simla, 1906).
Précis Gulf	Government of India, Political and Secret Department, J. A. Saldanha, ed., *Précis of Correspondence Regarding the Affairs of the Persian Gulf, 1801-1853* (Simla, 1906).
Précis Int'l. Rivalry	Government of India, Political and Secret Department, *Précis of Correspondence on International Rivalry and British Policy in the Persian Gulf, 1872-1905* (Simla, 1906).
Précis Makran	Government of India, Political and Secret Department, J. A. Saldanha, ed., *Précis of Makran Affairs* (Simla, 1906).
Précis Maskat	Government of India, Political and Secret Department, J. A. Saldanha, ed., *Précis of Maskat Affairs, 1892-1902* (Simla, 1906).
Précis Naval	Government of India, Political and Secret Department, J. A. Saldanha, ed., *Précis of Naval Arrangements in the Persian Gulf, 1862-1905* (Simla, 1906).
Précis Nejd	Government of India, Political and Secret Department, *Précis of Nejd Affairs, 1804-1904* (Simla, 1904).
Précis Persian Coast	Government of India, Political and Secret Department, *Précis of the Affairs of the Persian Coast and Islands, 1854-1905* (Simla, 1906).

Abbreviated Titles

Précis Slave   Government of India, Political and Secret Department, J. A. Saldanha, ed., *Précis on the Slave Trade in the Gulf of Oman and the Persian Gulf, 1873-1905* (Simla, 1906).

Précis Trucial Chiefs Government of India, Political and Secret Department, *Précis of Correspondence Regarding the Trucial Chiefs* (Calcutta, 1906).

Précis Turkish Expansion Government of India, Political and Secret Department, J. A. Saldanha, ed., *Précis of Turkish Expansion on the Arab Littoral of the Persian Gulf and Hasa and Katif Affairs* (Simla, 1906).

PART I

Introduction: Oman and the Old Order
in the Persian Gulf

CHAPTER 1

The Premodern Persian Gulf

FROM the second half of the seventeenth century to the middle of the nineteenth Oman and its chief city, Masqat, were numbered among the important locales of the East and of the Indian Ocean region. This renown derived mainly from the maritime and commercial activity of Oman's ports and was reinforced by the country's status as a regional political power of no small repute.

Since the early days of Islam one or another of a succession of such port cities as Masqat, located on the shores of the Persian Gulf, had served as a major commercial entrepôt, trade distribution point, and shipping center. The Gulf, located at the center of a network of maritime routes connecting India, southeast Asia, and the Far East with the Middle East, Africa, and Europe, traditionally played a large role in the international business and shipping activities of the eastern hemisphere. But the "golden age" of the Persian Gulf's premodern history closed with the appearance of the Portuguese on its waters in the early sixteenth century and the subsequent diversion of much of the most lucrative of the east and south Asian trade with Europe away from the routes cutting through the Middle East and the Persian Gulf. Nevertheless, various Persian Gulf ports continued to enjoy the benefits of a "silver age" of commercial and maritime importance and prosperity until the mid-nineteenth century. These ports retained a more than local significance as regional distribution and shipping centers since they served the trade of Arabia, Iraq, and Iran in the Middle East as well as other districts bordering the western Indian Ocean and situated in East Africa and the Indian subcontinent. During most of the Persian Gulf's "silver age," Masqat in Oman was commercially, and usually politically as well, the leading city in the region. As the center of business and marine activity in the area, Oman—and Masqat—were

3

the heirs of an ancient regional paramountcy passed down for over a thousand years through a succession of Persian Gulf states.

As late as the 1830s Masqat was still important enough to prompt one European observer to write: "With all its barrenness and unpromising appearance, such is the advantage of position enjoyed by Muscat, commanding, as it does, the entrance to the Persian Gulf, that its harbours are filled with vessels from all ports of the East, and the busy din of commerce constantly enlivens its streets. In few parts of the world can the necessaries, nay even the luxuries, of life, be obtained in greater profusion."[1]

Very similar writings are found in the works of other, earlier travelers in their descriptions of the various Persian Gulf ports which preceded Masqat as bellwether of the region. The essential similarity in the functioning of these ports suggests the existence of a design or pattern distinctive of the traditional pre-nineteenth century civilization of the Persian Gulf, a pattern that was expressed in a number of characteristics which remained more or less constant despite the changes in personalties, peoples, fashions, and politics that occurred as the years passed. Certainly the most enduring constants were those imposed by geography.

The Persian Gulf region actually consists of the depths and surrounding shores of two bodies of water, the all but landlocked Persian Gulf proper and the Gulf of Oman, whose broad mouth merges into the Arabian Sea. Together, these two gulfs, extensions of the Indian Ocean, form a trough thrusting into the heart of the Middle East. They are a passage whose northern end meets the Mesopotamian valley and the land routes connecting with the Mediterranean basin, and whose southern end opens onto the oceanic approaches to India and East Africa. The fact that the Persian Gulf forms a junction where some of the most ancient and important com-

---

[1] J. R. Wellsted, *Travels to the City of the Caliphs, along the Shores of the Persian Gulf and the Mediterranean* (London, 1840), II, 47.

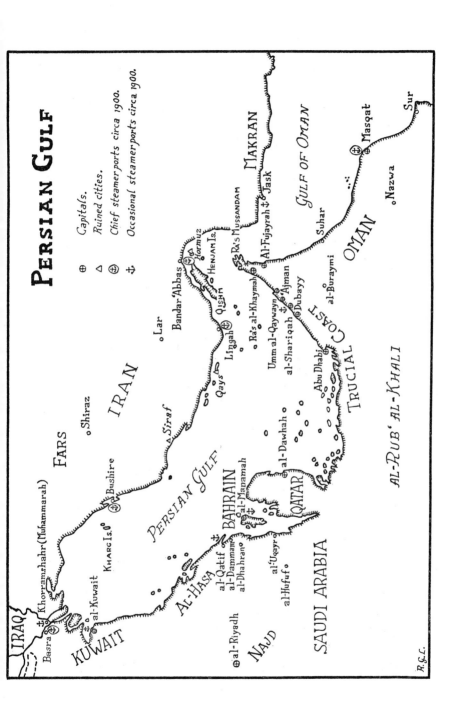

PERSIAN GULF

⊕ Capitals.
△ Ruined cities.
⊛ Chief steamer ports circa 1900.
⊹ Occasional steamer ports circa 1900.

IRAQ
Basra
Khorramshahr (Muhammarah)
al-Kuwait
KUWAIT

FARS
Shiraz
IRAN
Bushire
KHARG IS.
Lar
Siraf
PERSIAN GULF
Bandar 'Abbas
Hormuz
QISHM
Lingah
Qays
HENJAM IS.
Ra's MUSSANDAM

Al-HASA
al-Qatif
al-Dammam
al-Dhahran
al-'Uqayr
al-Hufuf
al-Riyadh
NAJD
SAUDI ARABIA

BAHRAIN
al-Manamah

QATAR
al-Dawhah

Ra's al-Khaymah
Umm al-Qaywayn
Ajman
al-Shariqah
Dubayy
Abu Dhabi
al-Buraymi
TRUCIAL COAST

MAKRAN
GULF OF OMAN
Al-Fujayrah Jask
Masqat
Sur
Suhar
OMAN
Nazwa

AL-RUB' AL-KHALI

R.G.C.

munications routes in the world cross one another, as well as the fact of the region's "corridor" configuration, have had immense influence on its history.

While geography decreed there would be considerable unity in the history of the various lands surrounding the Gulf's waters, it is also true that the details of events varied considerably in these different districts. The areas bordering the Persian and Oman gulfs can be conveniently divided into four territorial compartments which are further subdivided into distinct but lesser divisions. The compartments are: (1) the country touching the northern limits of the Gulf where the Tigris, Euphrates, and Karun Rivers unite and flow into the Gulf as the Shatt al-'Arab; this area of southern Iraq and the Iranian province of Khuzistan is fertile, with settled agriculture supporting a large population; (2) the Iranian shore of the Persian and Oman gulfs and the adjacent offshore islands; this inhospitable tract is backed by the long parallel ridges of the Zagros Mountains which are broken only by occasional passes which link Iran's Gulf coast with its relatively well-watered and heavily populated interior; throughout history the most important settlements along this coast have been situated convenient to one of the passes into the interior; (3) the low-lying, arid eastern coast of Arabia, stretching southward from Kuwait past the Qatar peninsula to include the lagoon-indented Trucial Coast; this section is flanked by a string of offshore islands most of which are insignificant but which also include the important island of Bahrain and a number of recently developed offshore oil sites; (4) the southeastern corner of Arabia, or Oman; this country, although part of the Arabian peninsula, possesses an insular character since it is bounded by the sea on one side and the desert on the other.

The waters of the Persian and Oman gulfs provide the strongest unifying link between the four compartments. Also tending to reinforce regional ties is the fact that these four primary divisions are each coastal areas, which, with the exception of southern Iraq and Khuzistan, are relatively isolated

6

from other centers of civilization. Mountains in Iran and deserts in Arabia prevent easy contact between the Gulf coast and the hinterland. Moreover, these coastal areas share the same general climate and are endowed with the same variety of resources and handicaps.

TRADITIONAL PERSIAN GULF CIVILIZATION

It is, of course, false to portray any premodern society and the history it recorded as something static. Change was no less a feature of former times than it is of our own day even if movement was not as rapid or frenzied then as is more often the case now. Still, it is possible to see that events that occurred during a distinct period of time and within a particular locality often developed within an identifiable context, were restricted within definite limits, and normally flowed along certain well-developed channels. So it was with the Persian Gulf in the years before the nineteenth century, when change, although continual, was less sweeping and happenings in the region normally unfolded within an unrevolutionary cultural context which remained relatively constant.

The presence of such constants is a feature of the history of the Persian Gulf from the pre-Christian era up to the nineteenth century. Even after the Gulf's culture began to be influenced and then altered by the impact on an alien, modern civilization born in Europe, many of the features which distinguished the traditional pattern of life in the Persian Gulf remained well into the late nineteenth century, and indeed, into our own day.

The influence of geography on the Gulf's history, especially the fact that the region lies squarely across the juncture of a number of natural communications routes, has already been noted. Another, essentially geographic, factor should also be stressed: the poverty of the area in the past. Although renowned as a source of pearls, in general the Gulf was poorly endowed with the basic resources, such as abundant water, necessary to the creating and maintaining of a high level of civilization. Traditionally, only a great deal of sustained effort —and a certain amount of luck—would allow any people, city or district within the Gulf to rise above a bare subsistence level of life. Competition for the available resources and means of livelihood was intense, a situation that was one of the basic causes for the continuing violence displayed in Gulf history until recent times. Piracy, for instance, was a fairly common "occupation" and a more or less accepted way of sustaining life or realizing certain political and economic ambitions in given districts. It can best be understood as war between the "haves" and the "have nots" rather than as an indication of some inherent flaw in the moral fiber of the Gulf's inhabitants. This latter belief is often encountered in the writings of nineteenth century European apologists for imperialism.[2] Indeed, many Gulf principalities were founded by successful marauders turned state-builders.

A third factor that characterized traditional Persian Gulf civilization was the continuing importance of commerce and maritime activity to the region. Although poor, the Gulf enjoyed a central position on what was traditionally one of the great highways along which trade and thought traveled between the civilizations of the premodern world. Competing communication lines were the "around-Africa" route (a track not used until the end of the fifteenth century), the Red Sea–Suez route, the trans-Iranian route, the Caspian–Black Sea

[2] See N. Tarling, *Piracy and Politics in the Malay World* (Melbourne, 1963), pp. 1-20, for a perceptive discussion of the nature of piracy among the Malay States, a situation which was comparable in many respects to the one encountered in the Persian Gulf before the mid-nineteenth century. Tarling points out that the political, economic, and social structure of the Malay world contributed to a situation in which robbery and violence on land and sea, activities dubbed as "piracy" by European observers, were established methods of effecting changes in the status quo and usually resulted from attempts by certain groups to realize their commercial and political goals and to enhance their general prestige. Such activities were not based simply on greed or moral turpitude. Tarling also warns of the dangers of indiscriminately applying irrelevant, modern Western standards of international law and morality to situations involving premodern Afro–Asian civilizations.

route, and the Central Asia–Caspian–Volga River route. Each of these communication lines has had its periods of dominance, and the history of many empires is linked with their rise, fall or rejuvenation. Each route was distinguished by a distinct and characteristic method of organizing the traffic that passed along it. In the case of the Persian Gulf, along its shores a chain of maritime city-states evolved which served, protected, and exploited the marine traffic moving by their harbor mouths. These ports also sheltered swarms of ships which carried cargo and men through the Gulf and the western Indian Ocean and engaged in activities of less widespread impact such as fishing and pearling. Generally, only considerable maritime and commercial activity by one or another group among the Gulf's population allowed a locality in the area to prosper. The welfare of the region was closely tied to finding employment for its vessels and seamen.

Given the importance of business and seafaring it is not surprising that the most significant political, economic or social activities carried on in the region were concentrated in the commercially oriented port cities. These usually maintained at least a de facto independence and served as collecting points for commerce that either originated in the area or, more important, originated elsewhere and passed through the Gulf on its way to destinations outside the region. Most of the city-states arose from a tribal base, and in the smaller cities there was never much distinction between tribal and city government or political aims. In the smaller ports it was normal to find that the local tribal *shaykh* was also the port's ruler. As a city grew larger and stronger, however, tribal links often lost much of their importance, and the city might well, in time, turn to rulers with at best tenuous tribal connections. Even when some formal political links between a commercially and politically important city and the surrounding tribal society were retained, the city normally gave precedence to policies designed to serve its peculiarly urban interests.

Normally, by using a system of flexible political relation-

9

ships, one or another of the larger city-states dominated the commercial and, many times, even the political life of the entire region. This domination was often obtained through economic manipulations but secured by naval power and stationing garrisons at strategic points. But political administrations were rather weak in the Gulf and few cities ever commanded the strength to prevent the rise of competing city-states or to pacify completely surrounding tribal lands. Competition among the city-states was ruthless and intense, as the histories of the cities of Siraf, Qays, and Hormuz show. Persistent disorders, wars with other cities or combinations of cities, maritime versions of the tribal troubles, and raids so characteristic of life everywhere in premodern Arabia crowd the annals of the various Gulf trading states. Too often Western observers have confused these upheavals with simple, criminal piracy. But even in the smaller ports many aspects of life differed rather markedly from those encountered in the surrounding rural and desert tribal areas. The economic, social, cultural, and in the larger ports political, elements that made up the basic civilization of a typical Gulf city-state revolved around commercial and maritime activity. Most ports depended on their trade or on pearling for their existence; activities that provided revenue which in turn afforded local prosperity and the means to maintain the state. Protecting trade and traders was a major function of any port. In a larger city the trade revenue derived from customs and taxes could be expended either directly on the military and naval establishment or on bribes and tribute to subsidize allies and buy off potential attackers. When a state's financial resources dwindled, however, its power quickly evaporated. With but a weak defense the way was open for raiders to attack and for another city to take over the commercial and political interests of the declining town.

Gulf society outside the seaport towns was organized on rather primitive lines. There rural tribal groups held sway and lived according to a different value system. However, a large percentage of the coastal tribes engaged in stable occupations and held more or less definite territory. At times there were fairly close political ties among the tribes surrounding a particular port. Moreover, there was a symbiotic relationship between the seaports and the surrounding tribes. The population of the city-state was drawn largely from its surrounding districts, and oftentimes rural dwellers would take up seasonal employment in the city. Conversely, the prosperity of the city seeped out to the hinterland, with the towns providing many goods and services to the countryside. If the city was large and powerful its ruler often held nominal authority over the nearby settled tribes, but such control was never as complete as that which he exercised within the walls of the city itself. Tribes situated inland or far from the cultural influences of the ports tended to be more self-sufficient than those on the coast and were almost out of the city-state's range of influence. Often the inland tribes consisted primarily of nomad bedouins and on occasion constituted a major security problem for the coastal city-states.

THE PERSIAN GULF'S HISTORY PRIOR TO THE NINETEENTH CENTURY

During the ascendancy of Oman and its capital, Masqat—that is, from the latter half of the seventeenth century to the early part of the nineteenth century—the country's history developed along the lines described above. Not until the British asserted themselves over the area did the old constants begin to fail. That Oman during its greatest years was the heir of many of the practices, attitudes, and limitations of the states it succeeded in the region's leadership can be illustrated by a look at Persian Gulf history prior to the nineteenth century.[3]

[3] Useful general accounts of large periods in the history of the Persian Gulf prior to the nineteenth century are found in A. T. Wilson, *The Persian Gulf* (Oxford, 1928); G. F. Hourani, *Arab Seafaring in the Indian Ocean in Ancient and Early Medieval Times* (Princeton, 1951); J. G. Lorimer, *Gazetteer of the Persian Gulf, 'Omán and Central Arabia* (Calcutta, 1908-1915); and C. F. Beckingham, "Baḥr Fāris," *EI-2*, I, 927-29. Also, H. W. Field, *Ancient and Modern Man in Southwestern Arabia* (Coral

The Old Order

This history is an old one. It is possible, for instance, that man initiated seaborne commerce upon the waters of the Persian Gulf. Certainly the Gulf has been used as a waterway for many thousands of years. Although lack of evidence about the period prior to Hellenistic times precludes the writing of an authoritative account of the region's ancient history, excavations in al-Hasa indicate the presence of a maritime civilization 6,000 years old. Moreover, a connection between the ancient civilizations of the Tigris–Euphrates and the Indus valleys via a water route traversing the Gulf of Oman and the Persian Gulf proper apparently has been discovered by archaeologists.[4] It is not certain when the Arabs occupied the coasts of the Gulf, but it appears that they entered the region as invaders who swept eastward out of the interior of Arabia and forced the Gulf's original inhabitants into the refuge areas, chiefly in the mountains of Oman and Dhofar, where they are still found to this day. Later, the Arabs moved across the Gulf, settling its islands and occupying much of its Iranian shores.[5] The region has continued to witness an endless tide of arrivals by both land and sea, coming as invaders, migrants, merchants, or slaves. Nevertheless, despite the fact that the Gulf's population is a mixture, the Arabs have remained in a decided majority, and their culture has been dominant ever since their initial conquest.

Even in ancient times it seemed that the Gulf's fortunes reflected the major trends in Asia's history. Recent scholarship shows that in the first century B.C. when great empires such as that of Rome flourished in Europe and in Asia, Arab mariners

---

Gables, Fla., 1956), contains a short account and detailed bibliography of the ethnology and early history of the region. A detailed bibliographical aid for the study of the Persian Gulf is provided by J. D. Pearson, *Index Islamicus, 1906-1955* (Cambridge, 1958) and *Index Islamicus, Supplement, 1956-1960* (Cambridge, 1962).

[4] M. Wheeler, *The Indus Civilization* (Cambridge, 1953), pp. 60, 93. See, too, R. Dougherty, *The Sealand of Arabia* (New Haven, 1932).

[5] G. Strenziok, "Azd," *EI-2*, I, 812.

served as middlemen in a brisk east-west trade.[6] In Roman times, however, the Red Sea route to India was favored over the Gulf route by Westerners because the head of the Persian Gulf, Iraq, was in the hands of Rome's enemies, the Persian empires of the Parthians and their successors, the Sassanids. The Persians, an inland people, for their part favored the trans-Iranian land caravan routes for trade. The Persian Gulf, which would not become a major trade route until Islamic times, was utilized by local Arab sailors engaged in maritime activities such as fishing and pearling.

The Persian Gulf's "golden age." The great years in Persian Gulf history were those from A.D. 750 to 1507, the so-called golden age of the region. But in fact, the gold began to tarnish as early as the eleventh century A.D. when the Gulf route was replaced by the Red Sea–Suez Isthmus route as the leading east-west seaborne trade corridor. Be that as it may, there is no doubt that, in relative terms, the Gulf's most prosperous time, with the possible exception of today's booming oil age, was that which began with the establishment of the 'Abbasid caliphate and ended with the fall of Hormuz to the Portuguese.

The birth of Islam in the seventh century followed a century and a half later by the establishment of the 'Abbasid caliphate in 750, signaled the beginning of this regional golden age. With the creation of a vast Muslim empire embracing all of southwestern Asia extending from the Atlantic to the Indus and with the building of a central political apparatus—the caliphate with its headquarters at Baghdad—to guide this empire, the circumstances were ripe for the Persian Gulf to prosper. Its waters thrust like an arrow virtually to the heart of the new economic, political, and intellectual center of the Islamic world. Moreover, at the very time that the universal Islamic empire of the 'Abbasids was reaching its height there was a coincident development of other strong states in other centers

6 G. W. Van Beek, "Frankincense and Myrrh in Ancient South Arabia," *Journal of the American Oriental Society*, LXXVIII (1958), 147-51; M. Wheeler, *Rome Beyond the Imperial Frontiers* (London, 1954), chap. 3.

of civilization. In China the brilliant T'ang dynasty was restoring that country's strength; the Byzantine Empire was reestablishing the prosperity of the northeastern Mediterranean area; and even western Europe was emerging under Carolingian aegis from the chaos that followed Rome's fall. Baghdad, a great economic hub in addition to being an imperial capital, lay directly in the path of major routes that tied together all these centers of civilization.

Because land routes between western Asia and eastern and southern Asia possessed only a limited capacity, the growth of the world's economic activity during the eighth century stimulated the use of water routes. Since the around-Africa route was not yet in use, the choice lay between using the Red Sea or the Persian Gulf as the main link for the sea trade moving through western Asia. Naturally, the use of either route depended to a large extent upon the size, prosperity, and political importance of the areas where they terminated—Egypt or Iraq —and the districts beyond with which these countries traded. Egypt during the height of the Ábbasids was only one of their many provinces; its trade with Europe and the Byzantine domains had fallen far below the high levels characteristic of Roman times. Iraq, on the other hand, was at the center of the empire, its population was increasing and its economy was booming. So the Persian Gulf route was favored and the Red Sea was relatively quiet for several centuries after 750.[7]

The trade of Iraq with the Far East was so extensive by the ninth century that settlements of Arab and Persian merchants were encountered in Canton. But Baghdad, although located at the very center of the world's trade routes as well as being the metropolis of a thriving Iraq, was too far upstream on the Tigris to serve as a terminal port for the large ships which sailed to India and East Asia. Consequently, Basra and its twin port, al-Uballah, served as the terminus for the ocean-going vessels used in the eastern trade. There, goods were

[7] Hourani, *Arab Seafaring*, pp. 59-61.

14

reloaded into river craft and sent upriver to Baghdad for distribution. The shores of the Persian Gulf were subject to the authorities at Baghdad, and numerous expeditions were dispatched from there to pacify unruly or rebellious districts such as Oman and Bahrain or to punish pirates who attacked ships passing through the Gulf. It was probably from Basra that the voyagers of the Sindbad legends sailed to their adventures, but it is also true that sailors from Oman were especially active on the ocean trade lanes.

It was not long before Basra, located on a river and thus subject to silting, began losing its status as a deep-water port. Even the building of lighthouses to warn ships away from the ever-moving river sandbars did not postpone for long the adoption of the practice of anchoring deep-draft vessels at a point down the Gulf on the Iranian coast where they transferred their cargoes to lighter-draft craft that could navigate the Iraqi rivers. One favorite site for these transfers was a desolate sandbank which eventually became the port of Siraf. The concentration of ships and trade at this place attracted the commerce of smaller Persian Gulf ports, and in time Siraf replaced Basra as the chief exchange, business, and shipping center for the Persian Gulf. Siraf was no small place; even today its ruins stretch for two miles along the shore.[8]

Siraf remained the leading emporium in the Persian Gulf and a major way station on the main east-west water route for most of the 900–1100 period. The city also became the main collecting place and outlet for sea shipments out of Persia. The port was situated near one of the gaps in the mountain wall which blocks Iran's coast from the country's interior; through this pass the silks of Iran were brought down from Shiraz. Siraf owed its existence solely to the fact that it was a necessity for commerce. Only the profits to be made in the city's exchanges, warehouses, and yards could have induced men to live in a place where most food and water had to be carried in

[8] Great Britain, Admiralty, *Iraq and the Persian Gulf* (London, 1944), p. 158.

from outside and where the heat was so horrific that little but thorn grew.

Siraf's fall began after a shift in the Middle East's political climate. With the decline of the authority of the 'Abbasids and the spread of political disorder in Iraq, raiders began attacking Siraf by both sea and land. During the century 1055 to 1155, coincident with the intrusion of the Saljuq Turks into Iran, Iraq, and other parts of the Middle East, Siraf's decay accelerated. Another factor that contributed not only to Siraf's bad fortune but also to a gradual shift of sea trade away from the Persian Gulf was the renascence of Egypt as a prosperous political, cultural, and economic community at the same time that Iraq was sinking into disorder. The new situation was crystallized by the establishment of the Fatimid caliphate in Egypt in opposition to the 'Abbasids in Iraq. By the eleventh century the Red Sea–Suez route had gained an advantage similar to that held by the Gulf during Iraq's ascendancy—it terminated in the midst of a thriving and powerful state. At the same time, Egypt was reclaiming a function it had performed in Roman times as middleman for traffic between Asia and Europe. The flight of trade and shipping to the Red Sea–Suez route was hastened as Iraq was rocked by revolutions and invasion. Moreover, as the 'Abbasid grip failed, the Gulf suffered as maritime disorder increased, trade decreased, and the region's ports fell to warring among themselves in frenzied attempts to corner the commerce that still flowed through the Persian Gulf.[9]

Siraf's successor as the Gulf's premier emporium was the city of Qays, located about 130 miles to the south and situated on an island about 10 miles off Iran's coast. Qays never enjoyed the renown of Siraf because of the rise of Egypt and the Red Sea–Suez route. Nevertheless, Qays was the chief collecting and distributing center for the bulk of goods which passed through the Persian Gulf between 1100 and 1300. The physical remains

---

[9] Wilson, *Persian Gulf*, chap. 7; C. Huart, "Sīrāf," *EI–1*, III, 444.

of Qays indicate that it was a smaller city than Siraf, for its ruins cover but a half mile of beach. Qays' preeminence was due not so much to the natural workings of economic factors as to the fact that an Arab dynasty from what is now the Trucial Coast took over the island and then sent its war fleet to appropriate Siraf's remaining commerce and force all ships and merchants to use Qays as a mart. By means of its seapower Qays extended its rule to include the larger Persian Gulf islands as well as districts on both the Arabian and Iranian sides of the Gulf. By 1170 Siraf became a dependency of Qays, and soon the older city withered to insignificance. The fact that Qays was on an island which could be protected by a fleet allowed the city to avoid the strife which vexed mainland Iran in post-'Abbasid days. Goods carried down the road from Shiraz could be lightered across to the island where they were safe from mainland disorder.[10]

Qays' position never became strong enough to prevent the rise of rivals. By the late thirteenth century the city of Hormuz, destined to become the most fabled of all the Persian Gulf emporiums, was ready to challenge Qays. Originally established in the eleventh century at a location on the Iranian mainland, Hormuz was strategically situated on the 40-mile-wide strait linking the Gulf of Oman to the Persian Gulf proper. The district surrounding Hormuz was relatively well watered and produced an abundance of crops, but the port for a long time was only of local importance as an outlet for goods from the Iranian provinces of Kirman and Sijistan. For many years the city was tributary to the various authorities who ruled in Kirman and other of Iran's inland capitals; its Arab rulers also maintained marriage ties with the lords of Qays. The disorders which accompanied the Mongol invasions of Iran during the thirteenth century provided the stimulus for the Hormuzi leaders to initiate major changes in this situation. A more and more independent line was adopted. For instance, if the authorities in Kirman tried to impose extraordinary taxes on the

[10] Wilson, *Persian Gulf*, chap. 7; M. Streck, "Ḳais," *EI-I*, II, 649-51.

city, the Hormuzi ruler adopted the tactic of quitting the port, crossing to Qalhat, a Hormuzi dependency on the Gulf of Oman, and from there directing his ships to halt seaborne commerce in and out of Iran. Eventually the Kirmani overlord would tire of losing revenue and come to terms with the Hormuzis. Finally, about 1300 the Hormuz merchants and rulers decided they had suffered enough inconvenience from the unsympathetic powers based in Iran's interior. They simply abandoned old Hormuz and proceeded to move its whole population to a small waterless island about five miles off the coast opposite the old town and there constructed a new city. Trade began to flock to new Hormuz, and as the town prospered it grew into a city of 40,000 inhabitants.

Qays did not give up its ascendancy in the Gulf easily. A long trade war, punctuated by armed clashes, ended only in 1330 when Hormuz, under the astute guidance of its king, Turan Shah (the name would indicate that some Turkish, Mongol or Persian blood and habits had been introduced into the Arab ruling house of Hormuz), reduced Qays to a subsidiary position. The wealth and power of new Hormuz were due in great part to the island's safe but commanding position in the straits leading into the inner waters of the Persian Gulf. Its position allowed the city to become a nodal point in the trade of India with Iraq, Iran, Arabia, and even Egypt; it was situated close enough to the main east-west sea route connecting India to Egypt and the growing markets of Europe that much of this long-distance commerce flowed through the city's warehouses. Moreover, with Hormuz's defeat of Qays the Persian trade—chiefly in silk—which concentrated at Shiraz as well as the local commerce of the Gulf region shifted to the new entrepôt.

During its heyday (1330 to 1507) Hormuz was nominally ruled by a king. But real power normally rested with the vizier, who represented an oligarchy of great merchants the king dared not resist if he wished to enjoy the honors and pleasures that accompanied his title. Rivalries among the males of the royal family were chronic in Hormuzi history, but some princes were allowed to serve as governors of outlying possessions. The royal council under the vizier's leadership appointed governors and maintained a well-subsidized navy and a mercenary army based at home which could be dispatched to threatened protectorates. Hormuz administered both shores of the Gulf of Oman and held many islands, such as Bahrain, as well as various mainland localities in a tributary status. Commonly, Hormuz herself paid tribute to the paramount power in interior Iran, a device which protected her business interests but did not interfere with essential independence. Commercially, Hormuzi merchants had connections in most of the major business centers of the Indian Ocean basin. Most important were their ties in India and in Egypt, which was the center of the sprawling Mamluk trade network.

Hormuz's safety from mainland disorder and the liberal trade policy followed by its government nurtured commerce. Port dues were very low, and in 1503 one observer counted some three hundred vessels lying off the port at one time. Most of the seamen were Arabs from Oman and Yemen, although some Indians and Africans were deep-sea sailors, too. Maritime activity was not highly organized. Individual captains sailed as they wished, where they wished, guided by their judgment of how the best profit could be made. The Hormuzi government only directed trade to the extent that Hormuz and its satellite ports were collecting points and that the city protected the goods and merchants gathered within its walls at a given time. While the king or other members of the royal family might own merchant vessels—which also could serve as warships—the state did not sponsor a state-owned merchant fleet. The city did, of course, war upon rivals who threatened its standing as a major trade center. The government and the merchants were more in a state of mutual dependence than in a relationship of master and subject. The wealth of Hormuz, judging from the enthusiastic reports of travelers, can only be described as "fabulous"; indeed in the literature of early mod-

The Old Order

ern Europe Hormuz often stood as the very symbol of Oriental opulence. Although the travelers' accounts may well have been extravagant, Hormuz at its height certainly was one of the great marketplaces of Asia.[11]

The Persian Gulf's "silver age." With the arrival of the Portuguese in the Indian Ocean the golden age of the Persian Gulf ended. But until the first half of the nineteenth century the Gulf continued to bask in its successor, silver age. The Portuguese were ejected from the Gulf in the mid-seventeenth century, and despite the appearance of an occasional English, Dutch or French ship upon its waters, the Persian Gulf essentially was controlled by indigenous states until the British finally established European supremacy there in the nineteenth century. During most of the "silver" period Oman and its leading port city, Masqat, dominated the Gulf region, particularly in an economic sense.

The new age began in 1498, when Vasco de Gama reached India. By 1530 the well-organized Portuguese, enjoying unified political and economic direction, benefiting from new designs in ships and arms, and driven by a religiously inspired crusading zeal, were masters of the Arabian seas. A series of devastating attacks on the most strategically located points in the Indian Ocean secured for Portugal the maritime dominion of virtually the entire East. Portugal's aim in taking over these strategic points (including Hormuz) was to control and monopolize the trade, especially the long-distance luxury trade, of the Indian seas. Local ships, including those of the Gulf

[11] There is a large bibliography on Hormuz. Especially useful are Ṭūrān Shāh, "Chronicle of the Kings of Hormuz," appendix to *The Travels of Pedro Teixeira*, W. F. Sinclair, trans. (London, 1902); Wilson, chaps. 7 and 8; Muḥammad ibn-Baṭṭuṭah, *Voyages d'ibn Batoutah*, Arabic text edited and translated by C. Defremery and B. R. Sanguinetti (Paris, 1854), Vol. II; D. Barbosa, *The Book of Duarte Barbosa*, M. L. Dames, trans. (London, 1918), pp. 41, 75-79, 90-100; R. Stübe, "Hormuz," *EI-1*, II, 325-26; P. Schwartz, "Hurmuz," *Zeitschrift der Deutschen Morgenländischen Gesellschaft*, LXVIII (1914), 531-43; J. Aubin, "Les Princes d'Ormuz du XIIIᵉ au XVᵉ siècles," *Journal Asiatique*, CDXLI (1953), 77-138; and Hourani, *Arab Seafaring*, pp. 87-122.

Arabs, supposedly had to sail with Portuguese passes or risk attack and seizure. The major result of this policy was to redirect the chief east-west maritime trade route from the Red Sea–Suez track to the up to then neglected course leading around the southern tip of Africa directly to Europe's Atlantic coast. Thus the vitalizing flow of trade was slowly choked off from the Middle East, and the area began to suffer an economic decline that developed into a wholesale disaster by the mid-sixteenth century, when shiploads of cheap gold and silver arriving from the New World upset the area's existing financial structure.

Both the Mamluks of Egypt and later the Ottomans, cognizant of the danger contained in the Portuguese bid to direct and monopolize Eastern trade, dispatched fleets and organized alliances in an effort to drive the Portuguese out of the Indian Ocean. The failure of these efforts was due largely to organizational troubles which prevented the great Muslim powers from maintaining a "fleet-in-being" on Eastern waters. The Portuguese penetration and subsequent conquest of Asian waters was one of the first concrete indications that the West was beginning to pass Asia in technique, equipment, and mastery of the various means by which man can control his environment. This situation developed, and although some trade continued to trickle through the old Middle Eastern routes, by 1626, roughly a century after the Portuguese took over the rule of the Indian Ocean, European vessels were often exporting products into the Levant that a hundred years earlier they had purchased there.[12]

The Portuguese took Hormuz in 1507, but after some initial fighting which secured the Persian Gulf flank of the new Portuguese trade route, the Gulf more or less settled back into its old patterns. Although the Portuguese constructed forts and bases in the region, their practice was to leave as much power as possible in the hands of local governments, to rule indirectly

[12] Great Britain, His Majesty's Stationery Office, *Calendar of State Papers, Venetian Series, 1625-1626* (London, 1913), XIX, 280.

through them, and consequently to avoid the expense, trouble, and manpower demands of a direct European administration. Hormuz, although reduced to the status of a Portuguese puppet state, kept her king through the sixteenth century. In fact, it seems that the main defect of Portugal's ascendancy in the Gulf was not that she ruled too harshly but that she neglected the region. For instance, the Portuguese did very little to encourage Persian Gulf trade. Immediately after its capture Hormuz was one of the wealthiest revenue producers in the Portuguese Viceroyalty of the Indies but by 1585 the authorities were complaining of its low yield.[13] Hormuz all but disappeared during the seventeenth century. However, since the commerce of the Gulf had started to decline as early as the eleventh century, it would be wrong to blame all the region's economic woes on Portugal.

The Portuguese, despite their initial blitzkrieg and their neglect of the region's commercial interests, did not seriously disturb the tempo or pattern of Gulf life. They never were able to entirely control Indian trade, while politically they played the role of titular overlord and generally left local administrators to their own methods. They did not interfere with local practices as long as the local officials did not openly oppose overall Portuguese imperium or seriously interfere with Portugal's shipping or trade monopoly of India-to-Europe commerce. By the beginning of the seventeenth century even these weak controls over Gulf life were openly challenged as Portugal's grip on the Eastern seas slipped noticeably. As it turned out, monopolistic control of an area as huge as the Indian Ocean basin was just too much for a small country of limited resources to maintain. Indeed, Portugal herself became a virtual Spanish province after Philip II of Spain fell heir to her crown. Under Philip the Portuguese empire in the East was neglected in favor of Spain's colonies in America.[14]

[13] Teixeira, *Travels*, pp. 265-66.

[14] *Ibid.*, pp. 18-24, 167-78. Ibn-Ruzayq, p. xxiii. F. Adamiyat, *Bahrein Islands* (New York, 1955), pp. 15-16.

In the early seventeenth century English and Dutch ships began to intrude on Portugal's weakly defended Indian Ocean preserve. Thus began 200 years of rivalry among the European powers for control of the Indian Ocean basin. In 1622 the Portuguese were finally expelled from Hormuz by the combined force of Shah 'Abbas, the Safavid ruler of Iran, and the English. But the day of exclusive European control in the Persian Gulf was not to dawn so early. Even during the period of Portuguese supremacy local shipping remained active and the maritime Arabs increasingly asserted themselves as Portugal's strength ebbed. After they were driven from Hormuz, the Portuguese retained other strongholds on the Gulf, but in time these were lost too. It is well to emphasize, however, that these ex-Portuguese strongholds passed first not into European but into local Arab hands during the seventeenth century.

From 1642 until the early eighteenth century the Omanis were foremost among the Gulf's peoples in attacking and annexing ports and forts once part of Portugal's empire, first driving the Portuguese from the port city of Masqat on the Oman coast and finally going so far as to reestablish Arab control over much of the East African coast. European writers often accuse the Omanis of practicing piracy during this time, but it would be more accurate to describe the Omani operations as a version of maritime warfare.

The Omanis enjoyed preponderance in the Gulf after Portugal's hold slipped. It is true that the English, the Dutch, and after the 1660s the French, too, sailed the Gulf and even maintained a factory here or there. The aims of the Europeans, however, were basically commercial rather than political, and the points the Europeans occupied in the Gulf, although fortified, were essentially business establishments which did not dominate the region in a military or political sense. The Gulf was, after all, not one of the main arenas where the great European imperial powers fought for the mastery of the Indian Ocean during the seventeenth and eighteenth centuries. The Europeans were too occupied with contesting the overall mastery of the East to worry about Oman's dominion over a small part of it.

Oman's and Masqat's preeminence in the Gulf was never conclusive. Many local rivals came forward from time to time to challenge it. In the eighteenth century Nadir Shah (1732–1747) of Iran, pursuing his expansionist policy and taking advantage of political squabbles inside Oman, temporarily occupied Oman's coast and assumed the leadership of the Persian Gulf. Although Oman's position was restored after Nadir's death, other Persian-based maritime forces loyal to Karim Khan Zand (1750–1773) continued to be serious rivals. The "Persian" fleets of Nadir and Karim Khan, however, were manned and captained mainly by Arabs who dwelt on the Iranian shore, and in a real sense the Persian interest in Gulf affairs in the eighteenth century was an expression of the desire of Iranian-coast Arabs to realize their own leadership in the Gulf.

After the expulsion of Nadir Shah's troops from the country, during the mid-eighteenth century the focus of Oman's political life shifted from the interior to the port of Masqat, a city which had already become the leading entrepôt and economic center in the Gulf. This move was symptomatic of the fact that Oman's political leaders were allowing the country to become a commercially oriented state in the tradition of Hormuz and Qays.

During the latter part of the eighteenth century the main challenge to Oman's predominance in the Gulf came from Arabia rather than Iran. Arabia during the eighteenth century experienced a tumultuous period of change, the effects of which remain visible to this day. Among the causes for this upheaval was the rise of a number of energetic maritime communities which still exist on the Arabian shore of the Gulf from Kuwait to the Trucial Coast.[15] The neophyte city-states,

---

[15] Lorimer, Vol. I, and the archives of the India Office, which contain material such as India Records–1, are excellent European sources for the rise of the Persian Gulf principalities in the eighteenth century. Also, A. Abu Hakima, *History of Eastern Asia, the Rise and Development of*

although profoundly influenced by their tribal beginnings, matured rapidly. By the late eighteenth century their sailors were ready to challenge Oman's dominance over Gulf trade and maritime activity. As usual in the Gulf, when new powers sought to realize their political and economic ambitions, a maritime war broke out. As this war slowly turned in Oman's favor, a factor developed that complicated matters—the spread of the Wahhabi religious revival, supported by the central Arabian ruling house of the Sa'udis, in the peninsula's interior and onto the shores of the Gulf. By 1800 most of eastern Arabia with the notable exception of Oman was infected with the beliefs of the new puritanical Wahhabi sect, and so a new ideological, religious dimension was added to the struggle between Oman and the Arabs of the upper Gulf. Wahhabi aid encouraged and revitalized Oman's maritime rivals, and the war was entering a new phase—one which might well have resulted in the overthrow of Oman's local preponderance or even loss of its independence—when the explosive politics of Napoleonic Europe was injected into the situation.[16]

The establishment of British preponderance in the Persian Gulf. By 1800 the contest among the European states for control of the Indian Ocean basin had evolved into a duel between Britain and Napoleon's France; between 1798 and 1810 the two powers competed for the support of various west Asian states in this struggle. Because Oman was at that time an important and strategic west Asian maritime power and because

---

Bahrain and Kuwait (Beirut, 1965), a work based primarily on Arabic chronicles, is especially valuable because it deals with Persian Gulf history from the point of view of indigenous sources.

[16] For the early history of Saudi Arabia, see Saudi Arabia, *Memorial of the Government of Saudi Arabia*, 1374/1955, Vol. I; G. S. Rentz, "Muhammad ibn 'Abd al-Wahhāb (1702/1703-92) and "The Beginnings of Unitarian Empire in Arabia," unpub. Ph.D. thesis, University of California (Berkeley, 1948); R. B. Winder, "A History of the Su'ūdi State from 1233/1818 until 1308/1891," unpub. Ph.D. thesis (Princeton, 1951), revised and republished as *Saudi Arabia in the Nineteenth Century* (New York, 1965).

it was heavily involved in India's maritime trade, the British anxiously bid for its support. Britain's efforts succeeded in 1798. An Anglo–Omani commercial and political treaty was concluded, and the threat to the flank of Britain's sea route to the East was considerably eased.[17] But at this very moment when Britain was engrossed in securing her imperial communications, some of her ships became involved in incidents arising from the Persian Gulf maritime war that had been raging for several years between the Omanis and the emerging Arab principalities of the upper Gulf. To the British and to Europeans in general the cause of these incidents appeared to be no more than the "predatory habits" of the maritime Arabs. They had little comprehension of why such disorder was common in the Gulf or indeed that they had blundered into the middle of a local naval and trade war. To the British the unrest was caused by "piracy" pure and simple, and they accused the Wahhabis of instigating attacks on British shipping. To guarantee their communications lines, the British, with the ready cooperation of the Omanis, attacked the "pirates"—who also happened to be Oman's rivals—three times between 1805 and 1820. After the insurgents were more or less finally pacified the British established an armed watch over the Gulf which originally involved land as well as naval units. Later they decreed a "maritime peace" which in effect forbade the Arab states in the Gulf to war with one another at sea without the express permission of British authorities. The "maritime peace," first declared formally in 1835, was originally intended as a temporary thing. However, the truce agreements were periodically renewed until 1853, when a permanent maritime peace was agreed to by the British and most of the maritime Arab shaykhdoms. During the mid-nineteenth century other treaties and less formal arrangements established a regime of special privileges for the subjects of various Western powers

[17] Lorimer, I, 169-210; A. Auzoux, "La France et Mascate au xviii° et xix° siècles," *Revue d'Histoire Diplomatique*, XXIII (1909), 518-40, XXIV (1910), 234-65.

resident or trading in the Gulf, import duty limits, and restrictions on the participation of Gulf mariners in the slave trade.

By these moves, which were undertaken with the best intentions, the British inadvertently struck the first real blows against the established system of Persian Gulf life. Officially, Britain declared her policy to be one of "noninterference" in the internal affairs of the various Gulf principalities. In actuality, her policy interfered as nothing had before in upsetting the context and dynamics of traditional life in the Gulf. Certain Western norms of conduct were imposed at the expense of the Gulf's traditional political mores in many situations involving relationships between states. Modified, qualified or abolished altogether were many of the old practices by which one local city-state used to dominate another or achieve preponderance in the Gulf. (It is significant that the Gulf, traditionally a scene of chronic political change, still has much the same political geography that the British found when they began their supervision of the region.)

Between 1820 and 1862 British activities in the Gulf began to alter the traditional context in which political events, and to a far lesser extent, economic and social movement, occurred. Britain's activities up to 1862 were mainly negative ones such as the prevention of "piracy," the prevention of slave trading, or the prevention of maritime war. True to the dominant English imperial philosophy of the time, Britain conceived of her role in the Gulf as that of a laissez-faire "policeman."[18] It was not until the second half of the nineteenth century that Britons in general developed the notion they had a positive

[18] Lorimer, Vol. 1; *Précis Gulf*; Aitchison—1933; *Bombay Records— 1856*, Winder, "Su'ūdi State"; H. Hoskins, *British Routes to India* (New York, 1929). Each of these works contains useful information on the growth of British power in the Persian Gulf during the early nineteenth century. But two works by J. B. Kelly, "British Policy in the Persian Gulf, 1813-1843," unpub. Ph.D. thesis (London, 1956) and "The Legal and Historical Basis of the British Position in the Persian Gulf," Middle Eastern Affairs, St. *Antony's Papers, Number IV* (London, 1958), pp. 119ff. offer probably the best guides to British conduct in the region during the period.

duty to spread the benefits of "progress" and "civilization" (in the nineteenth century European sense) in the Gulf. Thus it was that the traditional nexus of life in the Gulf was bent irreversibly during the first half of the nineteenth century although the old context did not begin to disintegrate very noticeably until after 1862.

CHAPTER 2

Oman Before the Late Nineteenth Century

THE COUNTRY, ITS RESOURCES AND PEOPLE

BEFORE the British established their preponderance in the Persian Gulf during the early nineteenth century Oman had dominated the Gulf's maritime, commercial, and political affairs for most of the preceding century and a half. Indeed, it was not until the 1860s that Oman's relative importance among the various states of the Persian Gulf noticeably declined. Since a main concern of this book is to offer an explanation of the destruction of the old order of things in Oman that took place during the later nineteenth century, a short description of the country in premodern times is necessary.

In Oman a distinct version of Persian Gulf civilization evolved quite early in history. The sea, the interior mountains, and the desert each influenced the character and development of the country in a fundamental way. Of the four territorial compartments surrounding the Persian and Oman gulfs, Oman is the most isolated. With the sea enclosing the country on three sides and with the forbidding sandy wastes of al-Rub' al-Khali (The Empty Quarter) on the fourth Oman is in effect almost an island. The country's contacts with the rest of the world have been, with few exceptions, via the sea. Besides providing a highway to the outside world, the sea has linked Oman's coastal towns and provided a source of livelihood for many of its people. The desert, although it can be crossed, has been primarily a barrier cutting off Oman from intimate contact with the interior of the Arabian peninsula. Finally, Oman's ultimate refuge against foreign encroachments, be they invading armies or unwelcome ideas, has been the lofty slopes and valleys of the country's interior mountain chain—the Hajar.

The name "Oman" probably means "the abode" or "the land" although there are local traditions which assert that the region was named for 'Uman ibn-Qahtan, Oman's legendary first inhabitant.[1] The country is approximately the size of Britain and is cut up into several distinct districts. The names of these districts are quite descriptive in that they simply state the location or a primary characteristic of the area in question. Thus we have: *al-Gharbiyah*—"the West"; *al-Shamal*—"the North" (known in the Western world as Trucial Oman or the Trucial Coast) ; *al-Batinah*—"the Inside" or the lowland; *al-Zahirah*—the "Outside" or the highland; *'Uman*—"the Abode" (often called Inner Oman and the central province which gave its name to the whole of southeastern Arabia) ; *al-Sharqiyah*—"the East"; *Ja'lan*—probably taken from the name of its ancient inhabitants, the people of the "Water Beetle"; *al-Hajar*—"the Rock," the Oman mountain massif which forms two districts, the Western Hajar (al-Hajar al-Gharbi) and the Eastern Hajar (al-Hajar al-Sharqi) ; these two parts of the Hajar chain were separated by a great cleft, the *Wadi Sama'il* which became a main route between Oman's coast and its interior; *al-Jabal al-Akhdar*—"the Green Mountain" (considered a separate district but geographically that part of Oman containing the Western Hajar's tallest peaks such as Jabal Wisham which is 10,000 feet high and may be seen a hundred miles at sea). Another district included in Oman is *Rus al-Jibal,* the mountainous continuation of the Western Hajar which forms a peninsula separating the Gulf of Oman from the Persian Gulf proper and which ends in the *Ra's Musandam* promontory. Traditional dependencies of Oman are *Masirah,* a barren 40-mile-long island off the Ja'lan coast, and Dhofar, a district on the southern coast of Arabia adjacent to the Hadramaut.

While the sea has provided effective communication among Oman's coastal towns, travel in the interior has been far more difficult. Since antiquity three main tracks have linked Oman's coast with its inner districts. Certainly the easiest and most

[1] Al-Salimi, I, 4.

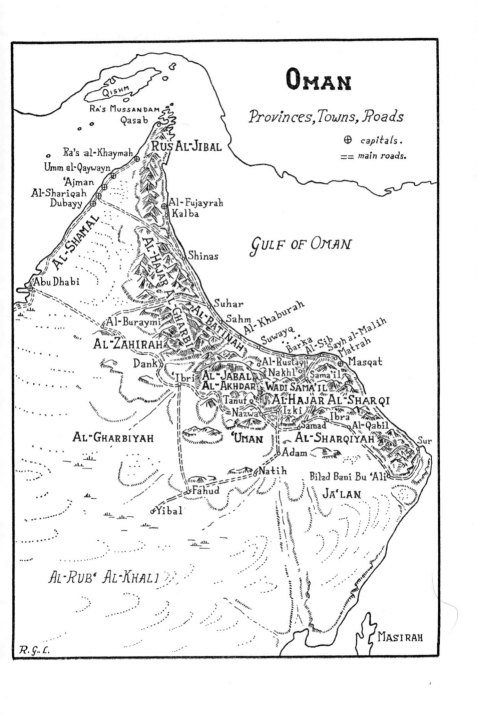

OMAN

Provinces, Towns, Roads

⊕ *capitals.*
== *main roads.*

QISHM

Ra's MUSSANDAM
Qasab

Ra's al-Khaymah
Umm al-Qaywayn
'Ajman
Al-Shariqah
Dubayy

RUS AL-JIBAL

Al-Fujayrah
Kalba

GULF OF OMAN

Shinas

AL-SHAMAL

Abu Dhabi

Suhar
Sahm
Al-Khaburah
Suwayq
Barka
Al-Sib
Sayh al-Malih
Matrah

Al-Buraymi

AL-HAJAR AL-GHARBI
AL-BATINAH

AL-ZAHIRAH

Danki

Al-Rustaq
Nakhl
Sama'il

Masqat

Ibri

AL-JABAL
AL-AKHDAR

WADI SAMA'IL

Tanuf
Nazwa

AL-HAJAR AL-SHARQI

Izki
Samad
Ibra
Al-Qabil

AL-GHARBIYAH

'UMAN

AL-SHARQIYAH

Sur

Adam

Natih

Bilad Bani Bu 'Ali

Fahud

JA'LAN

Yibal

AL-RUB' AL-KHALI

MASIRAH

R.G.L.

important of these has been the central track running from
the vicinity of Masqat up Wadi Sama'il where it branches—
one fork heading straight into inner 'Uman province and the
other leading to al-Sharqiyah. The northern path, second in
importance to the central route, starts at the port of Suhar
and follows a line through the Western Hajar to al-Zahirah,
al-Buraymi oasis, and ultimately to al-Shamal (Trucial Oman).
A southern road runs from the harbor of Sur into Ja'lan. There
are roads winding along the inland slopes of the Hajar massif
which link the interior terminals of these three tracks coming
from the coast. Recently (1955) a land route between inner
'Uman and Dhofar was pioneered and roads have been built to
the oil sites on the verge of al-Rub' al-Khali. In the Hajar, roads
are few, narrow, and usually consist of nothing more than the
dry, rocky stream beds of one of the numberless wadis which
cascade down the mountainside. Donkeys and camels rather
than wheeled vehicles are still the only practical carriers in
many parts of the country.

Oman may be better endowed than the rest of the Gulf
littoral in its water and other natural resources but by most
objective standards one would have to judge the country's
environment to be a harsh one. Living in Masqat in the summer is like existing in a Turkish bath; temperatures commonly climb to 100 degrees or more, coupled with a steaming
humidity. Typical of areas of marginal rainfall, Oman suffers
periodically from long lasting droughts. During a normal winter some parts of the Hajar receive more than 10 inches of
rainfall, thus some nonirrigated agriculture is possible in a few
mountain valleys. More important, however, is the fact that
much of this rainfall percolates down into the ground where
it provides the source for numerous wells and underground
irrigation channels—*aflaj*—along al-Batinah's coast and in inland oases. Nevertheless, for the most part and except where
irrigation is practical, natural vegetation and forage are scarce.
As in the rest of the Gulf region, the date palm is the most
important crop cultivated. Its fruit, along with fish, is the staff

of life in Oman. Extensive date palm plantations are found in al-Batinah, Wadi Sama'il, and al-Sharqiyah while smaller groves grow in various oases. Subtropical fruits such as figs, limes, mangos, pomegranates, olives, and walnuts are abundant; like dates, these fruits have provided Oman with an export crop at various times in the past. Grapes, some of which reputedly are transformed surreptitiously into wine—Islamic injunctions to the contrary—grow in al-Jabal al-Akhdar; the Portuguese supposedly used graftings from these Omani grapes to make a wine, Muscatel, whose very name seems to betray an Omani origin. A little grain—chiefly wheat, barley, and millet—is grown among the date groves but rice imports from India customarily have supplied the country's basic cereal needs. Camels, considered the best in Arabia, are raised in al-Sharqiyah, al-Batinah, and by the tribes that roam the edge of al-Rub' al-Khali. Donkeys and sheep are common in the mountains, while Indian cattle are used as work animals in the coastal province of al-Batinah. Goats are encountered everywhere. Until the 1860s Oman was an exporter of fine Arabian horses although many of them originated in Iran. For the most part, mineral resources either have been scarce or at best unexploited although the country was reputedly the site of the ancient copper and silver mines of Magan. Since the 1950s Oman has been the scene of extensive oil explorations. Test wells drilled along its undefined al-Rub' al-Khali border with Saudi Arabia indicate the presence of three large oil fields in the Fahud vicinity and other deposits in the Omani dependency of Dhofar.[2]

2 Materials describing Oman's geography and its resources are scattered. Although it was compiled during 1900-10 Lorimer, Vol. II still contains the most exhaustive treatment of the subject. See also H. Hazard, *Eastern Arabia* (New Haven, 1956); Arabian American Oil Company, *Oman and the Southern Shore of the Persian Gulf* (Cairo, 1952); W. Thesiger, *Arabian Sands* (New York, 1953); J. R. Wellsted, "Narrative of a Journey into the interior of Oman," *Journal of the Royal Geographical Society*, VII (1837), 102-13; G. L. Eccles, "The Sultanate of Muscat and 'Oman, with a Description of a Journey into the Interior

These resources have supported a population which today is estimated to be approximately the same as that of the island of Cyprus or somewhat in excess of 500,000, and which, according to observers of a century ago, numbered about the same then. The people are overwhelmingly Arab although considerable racial mixture, especially of Baluchi, Persian, and Negro elements, is apparent, especially among the coastal inhabitants. The traditions that recall the story of the Arab settlement (or conquest) of Oman are still current lore among its people. It seems that the ancestors of most Omanis arrived in two waves as part of the general movement of Arabs onto the Gulf littoral in prehistoric times. Although it is not certain when the first Arabs came to Oman, they probably filtered into the region over a long period and were descended from South Arab stock originating in Yemen. The descendants of these first arrivals have been identified by many designations including Yamaniyah, Azdi, Qahtani, and Hinawi. It is believed that the second wave of Arab settlers pushed into Oman from north and central Arabia beginning a few centuries before the birth of Islam. The scions of this second migration also bear various labels such as Nizari, 'Adnani, and most recently, Ghafiri. The feud between the two groups has sputtered for almost two thousand years, or ever since the second wave invaded Oman and is still a factor in the country's internal politics. The Ghafiriyah predominate in northwest Oman while the Hinawiyah are preponderant in the southeast, but there has been considerable intermingling of these groups, so the situation just described does not always hold true. The first wave—Hinawis—generally have been closely identified with Omani particularism; they have staunchly upheld the Ibadi version of Islam, which is the closest thing to a "national"

Undertaken in 1925," *Journal of the [Royal] Central Asian Society*, XIV (1927), 19-42. A fine bibliographical tool is American Geographical Society, *Bibliography of the Arabian Peninsula*, H. Hazard, ed. (New Haven, 1956).

Omani ideology that exists. The Ghafiris, on the other hand, traditionally have been more prone to outside influences. There are several Ghafiri tribes whose Islam is of the orthodox Sunni variety or who follow the Wahhabi practices which are closely identified with Saudi Arabia. The names "Hinawi" and "Ghafiri" which distinguish the two factions today have been in use since the eighteenth century. At that time serious internal strife occurred which ended only after every one of the more than 200 separate tribes in Oman attached itself to one of two great alliances of approximately equal strength. Muhammad ibn-Nasir al-Ghafiri, a member of the Bani-Ghafir tribe, led the faction which attracted most of the North Arab, Nizari tribes while the South Arab, Yemeni tribes gathered under the banner of Khalaf ibn-Mubarak al-Hina'i of the Bani-Hina tribe. Since the eighteenth century the popular labels of the two factions—Ghafiri and Hinawi—have honored their two erstwhile chieftains.

Tribes and tribal politics have played a powerful role in Oman's history since most of the country's people live under tribal authority or at least have tribal connections. Besides their Hinawi or Ghafiri adherence, the tribes may also be differentiated on the basis of whether they are settled or nomadic. Nomadic tribes are most numerous along the inland desert limits of Oman in al-Zahirah, 'Uman, and Ja'lan provinces. In the highlands and on the coastal lowlands the more populous settled tribes predominate. In general, the organization of Omani tribes is rather loose. A few tribes have a head shaykh, the *tamimah*, who presides at the tribal seat and whose influence, especially in times of unrest, extends in greater or lesser degree to all the subdivisions of the tribe. The office of tamimah, although nominally elective, is generally passed down among the leading shaykhs of the senior branch of the tribe. At one time the two great factions, the Ghafiris and the Hinawis, had tamimahs but this practice did not effectively survive the early nineteenth century. It is not rare among Omani tribes to find that the clans or *fukhudh* into which all tribes

OMAN

Major Tribes

Hinawi tribes underlined
Ghafiri tribes unmarked

Gulf of Oman

BANI QITAB

BANI KA'B

NU'AYM   o Al-Buraymi

BANI YAS

AL-MANASIR

NU'AYM

BANI QITAB

AL-'AWAMIR

AL-WASHAHAT

BANI GHAYTH o Suhar

AL-MARAZIQ

AL-SHAMMAS

BANI KULAYB

AL-BURAYK

AL-ZU'AH

BANI 'ISA

AL-BIDAH

BANI 'ALI

AL-BALUSH

o Ibri

AL-YAQIB

AL-'IBRIYIN

AL-DURU'

AL-HAWASINAH

BANI 'AMR

BANI KALBAN

BANI GHAFIR

BANI RIYAM

BANI HINA

BANI SHUKAYL

AL-JANABAH

Suwayq

A L Bu Rushayd

Al Sa'd

Al-Sib

AL-GHAWARIB

AL-HADADIBAH

Masqat

AL-MA'AWIL

BANI RUWAHAH

BANI KHARUS

o Sama'il

AL-NIDABIYIN

AL-SIYABIYIN

BANI RUWAHAH

BANI JABIR

BANI HINA

o Nazwa

AL-HUBUS

AL-'AWAMIR

AL-MAHARIQ

AL-BU SA'ID

AL WAHIBAH

BANI BATTASH

AL-MISAKIR

BANI JA'R

AL-HAJARIYIN

AL-HIRTH

o Al-Qabil

AL-HAJARIYIN

BANI BU HASAN

BANI BU 'ALI

Sur

BANI JABIR

AL-JANABAH

R.G.C.

are divided consider themselves autonomous of other branches of the tribe and follow the lead of their individual shaykhs. The clans themselves subdivide into households or *buyut* under a head man. Such shredded authority limits a tribe's potential power to the extent that those tribes which have a tamimah wield far more influence than those tribes which, although they may be larger, lack much in the way of political unity. Because of this fragmentation, the number of Omani tribes enjoying more than immediate influence has been small although the effects of prevailing tribal disunity have been temporarily overcome at times by an ever-changing network of local alliances, leagues, and client relationships.[3]

Until the present time most of Oman's people have lived in a rural, tribal environment. But the towns of the region have played a large role not only in the history of the immediate area but in the events of the Persian Gulf and even the Indian Ocean region as well. Omani towns have generally served one or a combination of three functions: seaport, tribal center and market town, or fortress. Some of the larger seaports have developed into "city-states" typical of the Gulf region. Masqat, because of its splendid harbor and easily defended position, developed into one of these city-states and has long been dominant among Oman's port towns. The inland towns are usually situated in the midst of an oasis and often contain strong castles which dominate the surrounding countryside. Some fortress towns guard strategic locations or control lines of communications and often serve as tribal seats.

It is apparent from the description above that Oman is a country of diversity especially in the characteristics that distinguish its coastal and interior regions. Nevertheless, it would

---

[3] Authoritative information on Omani tribes and the sociology of the country is scarce. Useful are Al-Salimi, I, 4, 10, 15-26, II, 121-29; Lorimer, II, 1,389-90, 1,414-17; S. B. Miles, "Notes on the Tribes of Oman," *Admin. Rpt.: 1880-1881*, pp. 19-34 and *The Countries and Tribes of the Persian Gulf* (London, 1919); Arabian American Oil Company, *Oman*; G. Rentz, "Djazīrat al-'Arab," *EI-2*, I, 533-56; C. Coon, "Badw," *EI-2*, I, 873-92; G. Strenzick, "Azd," *EI-2*, I, 811-13; Ibn-Ruzayq, pp. v-x.

be wrong to emphasize this diversity to the point where the community of conditions and interests that binds Oman together is obscured. Even commentators who have emphasized the uniqueness and separateness of coastal and interior Oman admit that the two parts of the country share important economic, social, and political characteristics. More important, most in the country recognize one religious and ideological ideal even if this unifying factor is sometimes obscured in practice. Certainly, most travelers who have set down their impressions have distinguished more similarities than differences among Omanis.

But the differences among Omanis are important, too. Comparing coast and interior one sees that coastal agriculture, characterized by the hundred-mile-long date palm groves of al-Batinah, has produced enough in most years so that dates and certain fruits can be exported. In the interior, on the other hand, agriculture has, with a few exceptions, been of the subsistence type with little surplus ever available. Neither section has ever been particularly strong industrially; manufacturing has always been on a handicraft basis in both areas but has been more widespread and better developed in coastal towns. The sea has obviously contributed much to the character of coastal Oman. Fishing has always been a steady occupation thriving even when other maritime-based activities have been in decline. Today, a hundred years after Oman lost the bulk of its seaborn trade and most of its commercial importance, large quantities of seafood are still exported. Before the 1860s trade on a relatively important scale and the shipping activity that accompanied it enriched coastal ports. Nothing like this maritime activity has ever stimulated the interior. On the coast social practices have grown up which reflect a society that has customarily been open to outside influences, a fact still attested to by the presence of so many Indian connections and influences there. The coastal population has been more tolerant of foreigners and their differing habits and beliefs than have the isolated interior dwellers. It is true, of course, that there is a core of common beliefs to which practically all Omanis—those of the coast as well as those of the interior—subscribe. Many of these are enshrined in the creed of Ibadi Islam which since the seventh century has been an epitome of Omani faith, thought, and philosophy—a summary of the country's ideology. Also, the same religious teachers have been respected in all parts of Oman. But even in religious matters we can recognize diversity amidst unity, for the Ibadism of the coast in practice has been more moderate than the reserved, isolationist, conservative Ibadism of the interior. Generally, then, coastal Oman has always been more affected by the current of world affairs and has been willing to take an active part in these affairs, while interior Oman has a tradition of isolation and inward looking reliance upon its own meager resources. The details of Oman's history, particularly its domestic history, have often emphasized the continuing tension between the elements of unity and diversity which for so long have tended to tie together or to push apart the country's coastal and interior halves. It is to those details and that tension we now turn.

THE CITY OF GOD ON EARTH—THE CONSERVATIVE IDEAL AND
THE MEDIEVAL IMAMATE

By the nineteenth century the tension between coast and interior, between unity and diversity, between a moderate and a conservative view of the world, was expressed most clearly in two themes which had been animating Oman's history since the country embraced Islam in the seventh century. The first theme concerned the efforts of certain Omanis to create an ideal Islamic society. In the main, these efforts were concentrated in the conservative interior and were most successfully realized by the imamate which governed much of Oman during medieval times. The second theme concerns Oman's continuing importance as a factor in the maritime and commercial activity of the Indian Ocean. Quite naturally, such activity had considerable influence on the development of the moderate, tolerant view of the world that characterized Oman's port cities. At times the two themes moved in harmony but more often the austere idealism of the first clashed with the relatively easygoing materialism produced by the second.

To a modern Westerner a knowledge of the nuances of classical Islamic theology might not seem the most vital prerequisite if one is to understand the modernization of a Middle Eastern country. Yet the traditional Islamic system embodied the ideology, the value structure, and the aspirations that for centuries prompted men to think and act in certain ways. If one is to have any comprehension of the movement of modernization in the Middle East—a movement which above all else involves changes or new directions in ideology, values, and aspirations—then a knowledge of the traditional Islamic religious system is most necessary.[4]

Since the seventh century Oman's history has been permeated with the story of the fortunes of the Ibadi sect of Islam. Omani Ibadism aimed at nothing less than establishing an ideal society—the City of God on earth—which would provide an environment in which man could assure himself of eternal salvation. Such was the main purpose of Islam itself according to the prophet Muhammad who preached that his mission was to proclaim and implement God's divine law and to establish a society where the divinely ordained rules of conduct could be lived and be preserved for all time. Muslims believe that the earthly community which would implement the divine law was established in A.D. 622 (the Muslim year one) when Muhammad led his small group of followers out of Mecca to establish a politically independent community in Medina. To be a Muslim necessitated that one be a member of this group and live under the order of its all-inclusive social and political code.

As long as Muhammad lived dissent over how the commu-

---

[4] The following discussion of Islam, the Khawarij, and Ibadism is particularly influenced by W. C. Smith, *Islam in Modern History* (Princeton, 1957).

nity of Muslims should be organized and governed never arose. After he died, however, serious disagreement began to cause rifts and ultimately to open splits within the Muslim community. These disputes did not concern the nature of ultimate truth or of the vision of an ideal earthly society revealed by Muhammad; rather, they turned on the practical tactics and organization needed to realize that truth on earth. The discord turned on the question of how the Muslim community was to be governed, and more specifically on what should be the qualifications of the men who would succeed Muhammad as leaders of the Muslim community. The question of the nature of the political leadership of their community was vital to Muslims because only a properly selected leader could be trusted to uphold divine law, to strive to retain Muhammad's vision, and to provide the proper Islamic environment which would allow a man to live in the way that would ensure his eternal salvation in the life to come. Only the leader of the Muslim state was empowered to resolve differences in interpreting the divine law and only if this divine law were properly carried out could man be saved. Thus in a society such as that of classical Islam, which strove to realize a complete fusion of religion and politics, any dispute concerning political tactics and organization necessarily became a religious as well as a political disagreement.

As a result of tactical and organizational differences, within 30 years of Muhammad's death the Islamic community had split into three competing parties which in turn soon developed into three competing sects. The most important and powerful of these divisions was that of Sunni or "orthodox" Islam. The Sunni claimed that the *khalifah* (caliph) or "successor" to Muhammad, should be elected from among Muhammad's tribe of Quraysh and should be a man acceptable to the Muslim community at large. This concept seems analogous to the procedures commonly used in an Arabian bedouin tribe whereby the tribal shaykh was selected from among the best men available in the senior branch of the tribe. Those of

41

Quraysh then, according to Sunni practice, occupied a position among the mass of Muslims analogous to that which those of the senior branch of an Arab tribe occupied among those other members of the tribe who were members of junior divisions. A second major unit within the Muslim community was that of the *Shi'ah* (the party), which claimed that the caliphate should be hereditary in the house of Muhammad. They traced the "royal" line through the descendants of 'Ali, the prophet's cousin and son-in-law (by his marriage to Muhammad's daughter, Fatimah) and asserted that the designation of the caliph was the prerogative of God alone and should not be diluted by any elective process. At the opposite extreme were the Khawarij or "seceders" whose basic premise was that any pious Muslim regardless of his tribe or race could be elected caliph by the vote of the Muslim community. It is from this group that the Ibadis of Oman trace their descent.

Initially, the Khawarij derived their strength from an alliance of certain tribal groups attracted by Kharijism's primitive democracy, with a group of fundamentalist intellectuals, the *qurra'* or "readers," who were fired by a determination to keep Islam simple, free from alien or sophisticated innovation, and close to the Muslim masses. To the Khawarij the Koran was their spiritual guide, their political constitution, and their social philosophy in practice as well as theory. This guide was supplemented only by the example of Muhammad's life and by certain traditions sanctioned by a few very respected scholars. Rejecting *ijma'* (consensus) and *qiyas* (analogy) as means for amending the law, the Khawarij were more limited than the other major Islamic sects in the sources from which they could or would draw legal sanctions to meet changing situations. This rigidity also dominated the Kharijite theory of state organization in that they insisted the basic structure of the state and the basic law code must remain unchanged since it was believed that the only purpose of the state was to regulate society in such a way as to save men's souls and that sufficient guidance in these matters was provided by the Koran.

Oman Before the Late 19th Century

Little room was left for adjustment and development of the law as Islamic society changed from a primitive into a highly complex organism. A thoroughgoing Khariji community was always a very static community, and it is not surprising that such communities were able to survive almost without exception only in isolated refuge areas.[5]

Content to remain a faction within the Muslim community under the first caliphs, the Khawarij did not break away from the main body of Islam until 'Ali's caliphate (A.D. 656–61) when that unfortunate ruler was accused by the Khawarij of deviating from divine law by accepting arbitration at the Battle of Siffin. The Khawarij then seceded (hence their name) and proceeded to elect a caliph of their own, referred to as the *imam* or the "leader" who pledged to maintain Islam's pristine purity and organization in their community. The Khawarij never referred to themselves as "seceders"; rather they styled themselves "the Muslims" since they thought that it was the other followers of Muhammad rather than themselves who had forfeited through ignorance and backsliding their right to be called Muslims. They claimed the right to attack any erring or innovating Muslims or their so-called caliphs and to replace these unfit rulers with their own virtuous leader who had remained faithful to the ideals of primitive Islam.[6]

The Khawarij were harsh judges of mankind in general because they did not have much use for this world; their thoughts, actions, and ideals were directed toward the next. They were a cheerless people who rejected music, dancing, singing, smoking, and rich clothing. Color itself was absent from their lives. In such a puritanical community with intense ideas of right and wrong it was inevitable that internal disputes break out. These, plus the failure of Khawarij attempts to upend the central caliphate, resulted in the disintegration of the Khawarij community into a myriad of squabbling inde-

[5] E. Salem, *Political Theory and Institutions of the Khawarij* (Baltimore, 1956), pp. 14-18, 67-68.
[6] Al-Salimi, I, 65, 68; Salem, *Khawarij*, p. 61.

43

pendent sects each claiming that theirs was the one, true path that all Muslims must follow in order to be saved. These sects, many of which originated in Iraq, ranged from the very fanatic —advocating death for all who refused to join them—to the fairly moderate. Among the moderate Khariji sects was one established by an Iraqi theologian, 'Abdallah ibn-Ibad (ca. 661-705). Apparently the Ibadi sect was named for him, although some claim that the term Ibadi is derived from the Arabic word for "white" or "pure."[7]

The medieval Ibadi imamate in Oman. Ibadi Islam was solidly established in Oman as the result of a number of coincidences. Ibn-Ibad, the sect's founder, lived in Iraq at the same time that al-Hajjaj ibn-Yusuf was serving in that country as the viceroy for the Umayyad caliphs. Al-Hajjaj was particularly concerned with suppressing divisive elements such as the Khawarij inside Iraq proper and also with tightening Umayyad authority throughout the Persian Gulf region. Driven by al-Hajjaj's persecution, numbers of learned Ibadis fled Iraq and scattered to places as distant from one another as north Africa and Oman. These Ibadi refugees were particularly welcomed by the Omanis because of tribal ties and because the latter, too, were victims of al-Hajjaj's drive to consolidate Umayyad power in the Gulf area. Until al-Hajjaj began his attacks on the country, Oman had enjoyed the status of being an autonomous part of the Islamic empire and was ruled by the same Julandid dynasty that had governed there before Oman's nominal acceptance of Islam in the early seventh century. Al-Hajjaj temporarily succeeded in dominating Oman and in driving its Julandid defenders into a short east African exile, aided as he

[7] Muṣṭafa ibn-Ismā'īl al-Miṣri, *Kitāb al-Hadīyah al-ūlā al-Islāmīyah lil-Mulūk wa-al-Umarā' fī al-Dā' wa-al-Dawā'* (Cairo, ca. 1903), pp. 79-88. Al-Salimi says nothing about the sect being named for ibn-Ibad and refers to his brethren only as "the Muslims." Ibn-Ruzayq, pp. 385-86, supports the view that the sect is named for ibn-Ibad but disclaims any significance of the color white for Ibadism. Nevertheless, conservative Ibadis used a white flag, wore white turbans and outer clothing, and considered white doves special omens of good fortune.

was by civil war inside the country between the Yemeni (Hinawi) and northern (Ghafiri) Arabs. In the process of this struggle, however, the Ibadis drew very close to the Julandids and the Yemeni tribes who were the champions of Omani autonomy. Since both Ibadis and Omanis—at least those of Yemeni stock—were enemies of the Umayyads their causes tended to merge and it was not long before Ibadi Islam became one of the key elements in Omani particularism.[8]

Umayyad dominance of Oman did not last long, however, for in the mid-eighth century the 'Abbasids led a successful revolution which ended with their usurpation of the caliphate in 750. The disorders that broke out throughout the Islamic world coincident with the 'Abbasid takeover gave the Omanis a chance to reassert their independence. Moreover, Omani particularism was joined with Ibadi Islam in 749 when Julanda ibn-Mas'ud, a scion of Oman's recently displaced ruling family, was elected to serve as the first Ibadi Imam of Oman. Thereafter, support of this Omani imamate could be justified as a defense of the true Muslim community against heretic attack.[9]

Once they consolidated their rule over the central apparatus of the Islamic empire the 'Abbasids set out to assert control over all the provinces once governed by the Umayyads. Oman, however, situated as it was on the fringe of the 'Abbasid empire, was able to resist resubjugation. The fighting was sporadic. Generally the 'Abbasids were able to hold only the coastal ports while the imamate controlled the interior. The imamate became the focus of Oman's resistance to the 'Abbasids, a tradition established by the first imam, Julanda ibn-Mas'ud, who was killed in battle only two years after his election. During the tenth century the 'Abbasids, occupied by more serious threats than the one posed by a sputtering war in a

[8] Al-Salimi, I, 61-71; Ibn-Ruzayq, pp. 2-5. Al-Salimi writes that the Omanis recognized Abu-Bakr and 'Umar as imam, or caliph, but gave their allegiance to 'Abdallah ibn-Wahb al-Rasbi, an early Khariji leader, after the Battle of Siffin.

[9] G. Strenziok, "Azd," EI-2, I, 812-13; Al-Salimi, I, 72-76; Ibn-Ruzayq, pp. 7-8.

border province, withdrew from Oman, leaving the country to the locals. With the removal of the external threat the vitality of the imamate and the solidarity which nurtured its strength declined. Finally, by 1150 tribal particularism asserted itself and the focus of power in the country passed into the hands of a loosely organized tribal alliance led by the Bani-Nabhan. Occasionally a Nabhanid shaykh was raised to the imamate but usually political power rested on a simple secular basis during many of the years up to the seventeenth century.

Nevertheless, throughout the medieval period an imamate was regarded as the ideal form of government for Oman, even if it was difficult to find a man who possessed the qualifications to fill the office of imam. Also, the imamate is an institution which, at least in parochial Omani terms, must still be reckoned with today. Between 1913 and 1955 an imam dominated the provinces of inner 'Uman, al-Jabal al-Akhdar and al-Sharqiyah until he was displaced by British-backed forces of the Sultan of Muscat and Oman. An imam still claims his right to rule in Oman and maintains a government in exile while his rather incongruous involvement in the politics of Arab nationalism and international oil rivalries is often attested to by debates within the halls of the United Nations. In few other areas of the Middle East is the issue of providing for a religiously sanctioned ruler entrusted with realizing the classical Islamic ideal of maintaining the kingdom of God on earth still such an important question. No caliph rules today in Baghdad, Cairo or Istanbul but in Oman the ancient vision—some might say the ancient anachronism—still inspires men to deeds.

What was the nature of the medieval imamate? Basically it was an institution designed to preserve a society and an environment in which the Ibadi version of God's law might be lived by man. The Ibadis shared, in theory at least, the Khawarij unwillingness to change their philosophy of proper political, social, and religious behavior. It was the imam's duty to defend and guide the community, as well as to prevent the encroachment of innovation. Specifically, he had to organize and command the army, appoint local governors and subsidiary military commanders, supervise the collection of taxes, enforce the laws, protect the poor, and lead the congregational prayers each Friday at his seat of government. Revenue at the disposal of the imam came from the *zakat* (a religious tax), the *sadaqat* (alms), *waqf* (charitable and pious endowments), derelict or heirless property, rent from state property, and, in later times, customs. This revenue could be used by the imam only for public purposes such as defensive war, *jihad* (war or missionary endeavor to spread the Ibadi faith), building fortresses and mosques, and providing for orphans, the aged, the infirm, and the poor. For his personal use the imam received only a pittance on which he was supposed to live without any ostentatious display.[10]

The concept of the ideal imam changed little over the centuries. He was supposed to be a humble, truthful, just, and pious man with a good knowledge of his faith and the ability to defend it from all dangers. Imams were primarily either soldiers or scholars, with the latter predominating. An imam was regarded as God's viceroy on earth and as the "chosen of God"; God's choice was manifested when the proper electoral procedures were used in selecting an imam.[11]

The election of an imam followed a set pattern. The leading political and religious shaykhs of the Ibadi community gathered at a central spot—usually Nazwa in inner 'Uman province —under the presidency of a respected, learned shaykh to discuss the candidates. If the members of this distinguished conclave agreed on a choice they gave the nominee their allegiance. This acceptance of a nominee by the notables was the first part of the *bay'ah* (investiture) ceremony. The second half of the bay'ah was preceded by the elector's choice being proclaimed to the people. The mass of the people could then indicate their

10 Al-Salimi, II, 237; Ibn-Ruzayq, pp. 31-32, 383-84; Salem, *Khawarij*, pp. 59-60.

11 Ibn-Battutah, *Voyages*, II, 227-29; Arabian American Oil Company, *Oman*, p. 71; Al-Salimi, I, 239-40, II, 218; Salem, *Khawarij*, pp. 59-60.

acceptance or rejection of the imam elect. The part played by the people in the bay'ah was not an empty formality, for many of those nominated in the conclave of the notables failed to receive the necessary public accolade and so never took office. An interesting feature of Omani Ibadism was the fact that an imam might have to agree to abide by certain conditions or restrictions at the time of his election. This went as far as the designation of some imams as "weak imams" who had to rule in close consultation with the sect's religious and political leaders. Other imams were not encumbered by such restrictions and ruled with more self-discretion.[12]

If an imam failed to perform his duties he could be deposed. In addition, since the imam's office was dependent upon the goodwill and elective mandate of the faithful, there was no hard rule that the community had to have an imam at all times. What was important to the community was that "God's law" must be enforced; it was possible that a group of notables acting in consultation and concert with one another could rule in place of an imam although such a body was not empowered to pronounce judgments that would appreciably add or change anything in the body of Ibadi law. The presence of an imam in the Ibadi community depended, in the final analysis, on the need for central direction at a given time.[13]

It is apparent that the intellectual and religious leaders of the Ibadis played an important role in Oman. Religious learning was deeply respected there, as in other Muslim areas. This respect contributed to the considerable political power enjoyed by the *ulema*—the religious teacher–scholar–legists. The authority of the ulema was often of a "power behind the throne" variety, but sometimes it was expressed in threats to depose an imam or to instigate a popular revolt if the suggestion of the ulema were not heeded by those executing the laws of the community. A most important prerogative of the ulema tac-

---

12 Al-Salimi, I, 239-40; II, 237, 289; Ibn-Ruzayq, pp. 30-32, 380-82; Salem, *Khawarij*, pp. 53-54.

13 Al-Salimi, I, 67-68, II, 217; Salem, *Khawarij*, note 51.

itly agreed to by the community was that leading ulema should act as an unofficial supreme court which would constantly review the conduct of both political leaders and people alike. It is significant that most of the upheavals in Omani history that led to the downfall of imams or drawn-out civil wars were instigated by some powerful faction among the ulema. A favorite ulema technique against leaders considered to be "innovators" or "deviationists" was to charge such leaders with propagating error among the Ibadis and to remind the community of its duty to depose a bad ruler unless he mended his ways. An imam or ruler who deviated from the norms imposed by the ulema was branded a *malik* (king), and it was an article of belief with the Ibadis that "we do not allow kings."[14]

In a system where politics and religion were thought of as indivisible it was natural for the ulema to enjoy an important place within the structure of government while they were at the same time its main critics. For instance, the law was enforced not only by the imam but also by ulema acting as local *qadis* (judges). Each locality selected its own qadi, usually after consultation with the imam. Since the qadis decided ordinary cases according to Ibadi interpretations of the Koran, religious learning was a necessity for the office. Often, more important cases were submitted to a noted religious scholar, to a council of qadis, or to the imam himself for a decision. In fact, the study of law was the most popular discipline among Oman's intellectuals and the country's most respected intellectual figure would often be the realm's leading qadi, historian, and philosopher at one and the same time, for most learning was embraced by legal study.[15]

---

[14] Al-Salimi, I, 66-68.

[15] Salem, *Khawarij*, pp. 79-80; Ibn-Ruzayq, p. 384. In general, Ibadi law is similar to Sunni law; see J. N. D. Anderson, *Islamic Law in Africa* (London, 1954), p. 358. There is a considerable body of Ibadi writing relatively unknown in the West and most of it deals with law. French scholars who have concerned themselves mainly with the Ibadi communities in North Africa (Mzab, etc.) have done the most to clarify Ibadi doctrines (see the bibliography in Salem, *Khawarij*). Three of the most important

The convinced Ibadis were confident that their vision of truth was entirely correct and that the rest of the world lived in error. In their writings they always refer to themselves as "the Muslims." In their view, other so-called Muslims actually had abandoned or were ignorant of the true path of God but the Ibadis were anxious to reconvert them and did not believe in killing them as did some extreme Kharijite sects. Their general rule toward all peoples not a part of their sect was that they would not fight non-Ibadis if they were not first attacked and that they would welcome anyone who wished to join their community. Even if they were drawn into battle they would first address an invitation to their enemies to mend their ways, make peace, and return to true Muslim (i.e., Ibadi) practices. Ibadi writers were very conscious of the fact that other Muslims lumped them together with the rest of the Khawarij but they stubbornly asserted their individuality. The Ibadis were moderate enough to respect even the legal testimony of a non-Ibadi against an Ibadi. Marriage with non-Ibadis and inheritance by non-Ibadis were also allowed. Christians were regarded with unusual tolerance, it being said that God had called them to their particular belief just as God had called the Muslims to theirs. This tolerant attitude was particularly strong in coastal Oman where there was more contact with foreigners.[16]

For those within their own sect, the Ibadis demanded strict adherence to the laws of the group. These laws were not concerned with the material well-being of an individual as much as they were with the salvation of his soul. The Koran and the *sunnah* (the "way" or the example of Muhammad's life), as interpreted by the Ibadi theologians, were regarded as sufficient knowledge for man. Indeed, it was commonly asserted and be-

---

products of Omani scholars have also been legal works; in the eleventh century two of these appeared—Muḥammad ibn-Sulaymān, *Bayān al-Shar'*, Vols. I-xx; and Aḥmad ibn-Mūsa, *Al-Muṣannaf*, Vols. I-xI. In the mid-nineteenth century came Jamīl ibn-Khamīs al-Sa'di, *Qāmūs al-Sharī'ah*, Vols. I-xc (see Al-Salimi, II, 209).

[16] Al-Salimi, I, 4, 64-68; Ibn-Ruzayq, p. 310.

lieved that there was no other or no new knowledge worth discovering. This attitude toward intellectual curiosity was well summarized by one learned Ibadi shaykh who warned his coreligionists "to leave the doubtful alone." The Ibadis, like the other Khawarij sects, rejected the idea of "justification by faith alone" and taught that a man's good works proved his inner worth. Some scholars have claimed that this complete integration of the ideal with the practical is the greatest contribution of the Khawarij to Muslim theology in general. Corollary to the insistence that all Ibadis must follow set norms of conduct was a conviction that the rules of the faith should be constantly preached so that ignorance of the law would not lead to error. The Ibadis emphasized, therefore, the importance of all praying together and listening to the sermons of the congregational services each Friday. Most Ibadis regarded these demands as quite moderate and the assertion "we don't exaggerate our religion nor do we allow ignorance to rule us" probably could still stand as an accurate statement of how a convinced Ibadi views his faith.[17]

It is characteristic of Oman that even in expressing its Ibadi political–religious ideology a tension between conservative and moderate interpretations has existed since medieval times. The moderate view of the world differed from that of the conservatives or fundamentalists in that the moderates were not willing to admit that man had to turn his back on the rest of mankind in order to achieve a truly Muslim society; they were, consciously or not, for a compromise between the demands of the flesh and the demands of the spirit. The moderates did not graft any significantly new practices onto the main stem of the Ibadi creed. Their practices differed from those of the conservatives more in what they neglected to do rather than in what they did do. One cannot say that the moderates departed from the true spirit of Ibadi Islam for the sect began as a reaction against the extreme conservatism and fanaticism in other

17 Salem, *Khawarij*, p. 33; Al-Salimi, 1, 64-70.

Khawarij groups and the Ibadis always prided themselves on the moderation they claimed for their group. On the other hand, numbers of moderate Ibadis appeared lax in their faith, a situation which added weight to the conservative argument that only a narrow path could be followed if one was not to deviate from "truth." This typically Khariji split between two viewpoints within Omani Ibadism has been one that has vexed the country's history until this century. It is not a split between religion and nonreligion but rather a difference in emphasis between two factions within the same sect. Conservative Ibadism, of course, was strong in Oman's interior since in that harsh quarter conservative goals did not clash with any other strongly vested interests. Moderate Ibadism was dominant in Oman's coastal cities where the inhabitants had to compromise with outside influences. The balance between the two wings shifted constantly, but usually the periods of the greatest strength in the institution of the imamate and of the ulema's greatest influence were also times of conservative domination in Oman. Periods of pronounced maritime and commercial prosperity and of overseas expansion generally were times of moderate supremacy. One can also say that until the seventeenth century Oman was, more often than not, under conservative dominance, while the moderates have normally been in control since that time.

THE GROWTH OF OMAN'S MARITIME AND COMMERCIAL IMPORTANCE AND THE RISE OF MODERATE IBADISM

Long before Islam spread into Oman the country's ports were thriving seafaring and trade centers. Until modern times Oman's continuing eminence in the maritime and commercial life of the Indian Ocean was, along with the story of Ibadism's efforts to create an ideal Islamic society, one of the two major threads running through Omani history. During the Persian Gulf's "golden age" before the coming of the Portuguese in the early sixteenth century Oman's seamen and merchants, notably those of Suhar, had major roles in Oriental commercial life. They were among the first Muslims who traveled the sea route to China, and they played a prominent part in creating a string of commercial city-states along the shores of East Africa which were modeled on those of the Persian Gulf. Close links between Oman and Indian's ports were also forged at this time, a situation accompanied by the settling of many Indian merchants in Omani and Persian Gulf port towns. During most of the Middle Ages the evolution of coastal Oman's maritime civilization and the development of the section's commercial interests continued; coastal Omanis were not vexed with the problems of accommodating themselves to the more conservative measures and ideals championed by the Ibadi imamate. This was the case because the imamate's power was largely restricted to Oman's interior by the various non-Omani powers which held the country's major ports. For instance, we have already noted Umayyad and 'Abbasid efforts to control Oman's coast; Hormuz held the ports from 1300 to 1500 until replaced as suzerain on the coast by the Portuguese who exercised sovereignty until the mid-seventeenth century.[18]

The Ya'aribah imamate and Omani imperial expansion. Portugal's last foothold in Oman, the city of Masqat, was taken by an Omani army in 1650, a date which marked the beginning of a 200-year span of Omani predominance among the Persian Gulf states. The expulsion of the Portuguese from Masqat was one of the climactic events which accompanied the rise of a power in Oman which, by regional standards, was to gain considerable maritime, commercial, and even political

[18] For the development of Oman's commercial and maritime interests during the medieval period see Hourani, *Arab Seafaring*, pp. 63ff.; Ibn-Ruzayq, pp. xix-xx, 5, who tells of Julandid princes from Oman who fled to "the land of the Zanj"—east Africa—to escape the Umayyads, and implies the existence of Arab communities there during the seventh century. Also see Ibn-Battutah, *Voyages*, ii, 214-28; Barbosa, *Book*, pp. 68-71, passim, who describes the Arab city-states of east Africa as they were in the fifteenth century; T. Lewicki, "Les Premiers Commerçants Arabes en Chine," *Rocznik Orientalistyczny*, xi (1935), 173-86, a work by one of the world's leading scholars of Ibadism; Wilson, *Persian Gulf*, chap. 4.

strength. Oman's star began to rise in the early seventeenth century after the Ibadi imamate was revived in the country's interior under the energetic prod of leaders from the Ya'aribah tribe. Unlike most of the medieval imams, who were content to restrict their rule to Oman's interior, the Ya'aribah imams pushed an aggressive policy designed to unite all Omani Ibadis under their banners. Inevitably, then, the Ya'aribah clashed with the Portuguese on Oman's coast. As Portugal's strength ebbed her holdings were compressed to the point where her power did not extend beyond Masqat's walls by the 1640s. Such was the energy behind the Ya'aribah thrust that after they secured Masqat in the early 1650s, the Omanis were not content merely to drive the Portuguese out of the country. With an imam ruling an Oman united for the first time in hundreds of years, and with Oman's maritime and merchant classes liberated from Portuguese restrictions, the Omanis began to extend their economic and political influence overseas. The Omani–Portuguese war did not cease; rather, it spilled over into the rest of the western Indian Ocean. In this fighting the Omanis were aided by their adoption of new-style ships and artillery. For example, they abandoned the use of ships with sewn hulls, the traditional method of ship construction used in the Persian Gulf. They began using copies of large, Western-style square-rigged vessels, and even those craft constructed according to traditional designs were built with nailed hulls. By the eighteenth century all of the Persian Gulf's indigenous naval powers possessed numbers of Western-style ships, often built in India and armed with modern artillery.[19]

Initially, the Omanis, like the Hormuzis three centuries earlier, took control of both shores of the Gulf of Oman and

[19] R. A. Wadia, *The Bombay Dockyard and the Wadia Master Builders* (Bombay, 1955), indicates the widespread sale of Indian-built, European-style ships to Arabs. Hourani, *Arab Seafaring*, pp. 88ff.; A. Moore, "Notes on Dhows," *Mariner's Mirror*, Vol. XXVI (1940); J. Hornell, "A Tentative Classification of Arab Seacraft," *Mariner's Mirror*, Vol. XXVII (1942). Wilson, *Persian Gulf*, chaps. 9-11, provides a convenient summary of the Portuguese expulsion from the Persian Gulf.

established themselves at strong points in the southern part of the Persian Gulf proper. This expansion was followed up by the reestablishment of Arab domination over much of the east African coast, an action undertaken at Portugal's expense. Even more significant than the expansion of Omani political power was the rapid rise of Masqat to the position of chief entrepôt of the Persian Gulf area and major Indian Ocean port. Thus by the start of the eighteenth century the Ya'aribah imams ruled a state whose political influence extended throughout the lower Persian Gulf, as well as to the coasts of east Africa and southern Arabia in the west and to the coastal approaches to the Indus valley in the east. The economic influence of this state reached out from the shores of the Gulf into interior Iran, Iraq, and Arabia; at its western limits this influence extended to the central African lakes, and in the east it touched the Ganges delta. Despite the fact that European ships occasionally plied the waters of the Gulf none of the areas where the Omanis were politically strong were regions then coveted by the strong Western maritime empires of Britain and France. During the eighteenth century the Indian subcontinent was to monopolize the attention of the great Western imperial powers to the extent that there still was time and room for local Indian Ocean states such as Oman to aspire to and maneuver for empire.

The Omanis never achieved the monopoly of political power in the Gulf that some of the states that had dominated the region in earlier times enjoyed. Omani dominance was challenged often and, during occasional short intervals, successfully. One of the underlying reasons was the fact that the very success of the Ya'aribah imams in guiding the expansion of Oman's economic and political interests meant that the institution of the imamate was forced to cope with a myriad of problems never faced by an Omani imam before. The old conservative imamate had worked well enough in its native environment in the austere highlands of interior Oman. But at the very core of this conservative institution was the fact that traditionally one of its chief functions had been the prevention of all change and innovation within the Ibadi community. Such a philosophy could not work as a practical guide for the government of a rapidly expanding commercial empire and a cosmopolitican merchant society. Grudgingly but surely the character of the imamate changed after the Ya'aribah took Oman's coast. The leadership of the state became more occupied with purely secular matters and less concerned with the state of men's souls. By 1700 the Ya'aribah imams had, in effect, created a dynasty. Practices grew up whereby imams commonly designated their own successors while even infants were sometimes "elected" to the office of imam. Such, of course, was a negation of basic Ibadi and Khawarij principles; the tension between the new reality and the old dogmas created a serious dilemma. By the early eighteenth century most imams were little more than pawns in the hands of competing factions who sought to realize their interests by capturing and then utilizing the machinery of a puppet imamate. The wealthy coastal merchants were adept at this game and the imams increasingly aligned their interests alongside those of Oman's trade and maritime leaders. In time, the imam himself became a leading shipowner and businessman as the once austerely religious imamate was transformed into an instrument for reaping profits and encouraging the aspirations of coastal business leaders. So by 1700 the imam of Oman had become the ruler of a strong economic and naval power which exercised hegemony over many thousands of miles of Indian Ocean coastline, a leader having more in common with the merchant kings of Hormuz than with the Julandid imams who had established Ibadism in southeastern Arabia.[20]

Accompanying these developments was the gradual conver-

[20] Al-Salimi, II, 2-90; Ibn-Ruzayq, pp. xxi-xxxi, 53-100; L. Lockhart, "The Menace of Muscat and its Consequences in the late Seventeenth and early Eighteenth Centuries," *Asiatic Review*, new series, Vol. XLII (1952), no. 152, pp. 363-69; India Records-1, Vol. XIX; Lorimer, I, chap. 1; Wilson, *Persian Gulf*, chaps. 9-11.

sion of the imamate into a stronghold of moderate Ibadism and a consequent decline in conservative influence. But the fundamentalists refused to give up their ideals and supremacy easily, so that by the 1720s serious internal disorders involving the sect's two branches had broken out and were sapping the country's strength. This situation was compounded by the outbreak of tribal warfare between the Hinawi and Ghafiri factions, disorders that were destined to last into the latter half of the eighteenth century. Finally a desperate imam, destined to be the last of his dynasty, foolishly called upon Nadir Shah (1732–47), the ruler of Iran, to aid him in pacifying his realm. The wily Nadir, a conqueror who had built up a huge Persian empire stretching from Iraq to the Punjab, was searching for an opportunity to expand in the Persian Gulf. He eagerly dispatched his newly constructed fleet and an army to Oman. Intervention by the Persians resulted, predictably enough, in the occupation of Oman's coast, the fall of the Ya'aribah dynasty, and the temporary supremacy of Iran in the Persian Gulf during much of the 1730s and 40s.[21]

In a sense, the attitudes and conditions that caused the downfall of the Khawarij in the earliest days of Oman seemed to present themselves again in the eighteenth century, and did lead to the fall of the Ya'aribah imams. In both periods the more conservative Khawarij faced a situation where they had to come to terms with a world containing peoples of differing backgrounds, values, and ideals—or fail. The limited perspective of these Khawarij, who saw things only in the fundamentalist terms of an ideal single society, led them to clash with others within their own sect willing to make accommodations. The way was now open for outsiders to defeat the divided Khawarij. When the Ya'aribah failed to resolve the split be-

---

[21] Al-Salimi, II, 90-190; Ibn-Ruzayq, pp. 100-55; L. Lockhart, "Nadir Shah's Campaigns in 'Omān, 1737-1744," *Bulletin of the School of Oriental Studies*, Vol. VIII (1935), part 1, pp. 157-71; A. Hamilton, *A New Account of the East Indies* (Edinburgh, 1727), Vol. I, a work that contains material on Oman between 1688 and 1725.

tween an ancient religious ideal and the demands of an expanding commercial society its rule was doomed.

The Al Bu Sa'id dynasty and the height of the moderate Ibadi state, 1749–1856. The Iranian occupation created a reaction in Oman which produced a remarkable leader who rose to revive the country's independence, restore her empire and supremacy in the Persian Gulf, and reassert the realm's unity. This leader, Ahmad ibn-Sa'id, was the scion of a small Hinawi tribe of inner 'Uman, the Al Bu Sa'id. Ahmad rose to prominence in the al-Batinah port of Suhar where he became a successful merchant and eventually was appointed the port's governor by the Ya'aribah government. When the Iranians moved into Oman, Ahmad refused to surrender Suhar. Instead he organized an anti-Persian coalition supported by several Hinawi tribes, moderate Ibadi commercial and maritime groups, and conservative Ibadi ulema. Sometime between 1744 and 1749 Ahmad ibn-Sa'id expelled the last Iranian invaders and was rewarded for his resolution, energy, and success by being elected imam, an event which established the still-reigning Al Bu Sa'id family as Oman's ruling dynasty.

Ahmad proved to be a strong-willed ruler who imposed unity on Oman without undue worry over the methods he used to realize his policies. The Ghafiri tribes of the interior never gave this Hinawi imam anything more than grudging allegiance, so that through many of his years of rule Ahmad was forced to wage constant campaigns against them and their allies, the Qawasim of Ra's al-Khaymah. As imam he tried to unify the moderate and conservative wings of Ibadism, but in the long run succeeded only in temporarily papering over the wide split between the two factions. In the final analysis it seems Imam Ahmad embraced the secular concept of the imamate that had marked the latter period of Ya'aribah rule. To support his government Ahmad relied on the traditional prerogatives of his office, his close alliance with the Hinawi tribes, the wealth derived from his trading interests, and his ruthless will. He was known to employ such tactics as inviting troublesome enemies to dine with him, only to slaughter them before the last course was served. He was also an innovator, establishing new precedents in his administration. Upon the structure of the institution of the imamate he grafted new offices such as "collector of customs" and "commander of the navy." Furthermore, he organized a small standing army manned by slaves and mercenaries. He raised his sons to positions of responsibility either in his central administration or as *walis* (governors) of important towns and their surrounding districts. He encouraged his family's dynastic tendencies by giving each of his sons a title, that of *sayyid* (lord).[22] Nevertheless, his reign was disturbed by rebellions led by his more ambitious sons and relatives.

Once he consolidated his supremacy within Oman, Ahmad carried on a successful struggle to restore Oman's dominance on the Persian Gulf. His chief adversary in that quarter was Karim Khan Zand (1750–79), the founder of a southern Iranian successor state to Nadir Shah's empire. Karim Khan retained Nadir's actively expansionist Persian Gulf policy although he operated through vassals such as the Shaykh of Bushire who had fallen heir to much of Nadir Shah's fleet. Nevertheless, profiting from temporary alliances, war, the gradual debilitation of his enemies, and, most of all, Karim Khan's death, Imam Ahmad, by the time of his death early in the 1780s, had definitely reestablished Omani preponderance in the Persian Gulf, strengthened the supremacy of Masqat as the Gulf's leading entrepôt, and had even concluded an alliance with the Ottomans which netted his treasury a handsome sum each year in return for providing Omani naval protection for southern Iraq.[23]

[22] While in most Muslim countries the title "sayyid" signifies that its holder is a descendant of the prophet Muhammad, in Oman it means only that the possessor is a member of the ruling Al Bu Sa'id family, a lineage with no blood ties to the family of Muhammad.

[23] Al-Salimi, II, 161-66; Ibn-Ruzayq, pp. 156-88; Miles, *Countries and Tribes of the Persian Gulf*, Vol. II, passim; Lorimer, I, 400-17; India Records–1, Vols. xx-xxi. The Ottoman–Omani alliance was still operative as late as 1826.

During Ahmad's old age a conservative Ibadi reaction against his innovations began to gather strength, although a fearful respect for the old imam discouraged open calls for his deposition. This opposition was centered in Nazwa in inner 'Uman, the capital of the medieval imamate, and traditionally a conservative stronghold. With the death of the old imam (probably in 1783) Ahmad's son, Sa'id ibn-Ahmad, succeeded to the prestige of the imamate but was not destined to enjoy many of the fruits of his office. Sa'id, even if he had inherited his father's political sagacity, doubtless could not have avoided the challenges of family rivals nor suppressed the conservative resentments which exploded into violent revolt in 1784. The conservatives accused Sa'id of being an "innovator" who had turned his back on true Muslim practices, then declared the new imam deposed. Also in 1784 Sa'id's son, Hamid, who was administering Masqat for his father, received the title of *wakil* or "regent" from the harried imam, an action which, in practical terms, surrendered the rule of coastal Oman to a succession of Al Bu Sa'id sayyids (or "sultans" after 1861) who ruled as secular monarchs without religious sanction. Sa'id clung to the title of imam until his death but it was a position virtually devoid of political or religious significance in both coast and interior. Thus the split between "moderate" Ibadis who dominated the commercial/maritime-oriented coastal state and the "conservative" Ibadis of interior Oman who clung to the hope of reinstituting a medieval-style imamate was virtually complete by the late eighteenth century. It is interesting that many of the families identified with the conservative movement of that period have continued to provide leadership for conservative Ibadism in Oman until present times.[24]

Despite the political tensions which disturbed Oman during the century following the establishment of Al Bu Sa'id rule, the country—especially the coastal half—prospered economi-

24 Al-Salimi, II, 168-85; Ibn-Ruzayq, pp. 188-213.

cally during the period. This prosperity was based on three main factors: the activity of the country's seamen whose ships sailed the length of the Indian Ocean from Indonesia to east Africa; the energetic contribution of the Omani merchant classes who were able to take advantage of the decline of Iran's ports to enhance Masqat's status as the primary trade center in the Persian Gulf, as well as one of the most important ports on the Indian Ocean littoral; the Al Bu Sa'id rulers of Oman using the resources of their government to encourage trade and shipping.

During the half-century 1750 and 1800, Masqat's trade and shipping activity increased to the point where it stood at levels substantially higher at the beginning of the nineteenth century than it had in Imam Ahmad's time. This increase was stimulated in large part by the protection and favorable treatment extended to all merchants, sailors, and strangers by the Masqat authorities. A uniform 6½ percent customs duty, later reduced to five percent, was charged on imports loaded in the city, and traders knew they need fear no further demands for payments. Naval patrols lessened the danger of piracy in the sea lanes approaching the port while the walls of Masqat protected both merchants and their goods from sudden raids.

Omani merchants for their part energetically sought out business. Masqat's trade benefited from the shift to her harbor of business that once collected at the British factory at Gombroon (Bandar 'Abbas) before that trading station was abandoned by the Europeans in 1763 as political anarchy spread in Iran. Also, the Masqati custom of buying and selling with hard cash attracted and protected smaller merchants while the larger business houses enjoyed the benefits of established credit procedures and contacts with agent firms in other Indian Ocean ports. It is estimated that in the last decade of the eighteenth century about five-eighths of the total long-distance trade of the Persian Gulf passed through Masqat, the port monopolized the lucrative coffee trade into Iran and Iraq, and a considerable portion of the region's local trade was organized there as well. Virtually every type of business was carried on in the city's *suqs* and landing places, transactions ranging from the exchange of luxury goods such as pearls to the buying and selling of slaves, to the import and export of staples such as grain, coffee, fish, and fruit. Indian-manufactured goods—cotton cloth in particular—were major items of trade; the few European-produced articles exchanged usually arrived in the Gulf via India, although some came by way of the Levant-to-Iraq caravan road. In the 1790s Basra, near the mouth of the Tigris and Euphrates rivers, was the second-ranking Gulf port, while Bushire was the only considerable port on the Iranian shore. In the last years of the eighteenth century newly established principalities in Bahrain, Kuwait, and the ports of the Trucial Coast mounted an aggressive challenge to Oman's preeminence in Gulf trade, a situation destined to spark a naval war between these states and the Omani Arabs. But in 1790 two English observers reported that Masqat was "a more rich and a more flourishing seaport than any of those bordering the Persian Gulph," a place where "commerce must ever flourish."[25]

This rosy view was substantiated by the healthy development of Oman's shipping industry during 1750 to 1800. Masqat alone was the home port of some 15 Western-model, square-rigged ships, three brigs, and some 250 dhows, many of which were cargo carriers of large size and tonnage. Over 100 vessels of various sizes operated out of Sur, while other Omani ports such as Suhar counted large fleets, too. Besides the traditional voyages to India's west coast, to Yemen and the Red Sea, to east Africa, and to other Persian Gulf ports, the largest vessels sailed as far afield as Calcutta, Malacca, and Batavia (Jakarta).[26]

[25] S. Manesty and H. Jones, "Report on British Trade with Persia and Arabia, 18 December 1790," India Records–1, Vol. XXI.

[26] *Bombay Records—1856*, pp. 300-12; D. Carruthers, ed., *The Desert Route to India* (London, 1929); Lorimer, I, 163-66, 435-36; *Précis Commerce*, pp. 42-59.

Oman Before the Late 19th Century

Oman's commercial and shipping activities reached their peak at the end of the eighteenth century. In terms of worldwide trade, Masqat at that time was an important secondary trade center where goods originating in or bound to a wide area of southwest and south Asia, as well as east Africa, were exchanged. The three primary Indian Ocean trade centers of the time were Calcutta, Malacca, and Batavia, which were served by European vessels and tied directly to the other primary commercial centers of the world, cities such as London, Amsterdam, or New York. Omani-based ships and merchants played a significant role in Indian Ocean commerce as distributors and organizers of the regional trade that fanned out from Calcutta, Malacca, and Batavia, as well as in the local trade from Masqat and the Omani-controlled east African port of Zanzibar.

Zanzibar was destined to enjoy a great boom during the first half of the nineteenth century. Indeed, it began to eclipse Masqat itself as the leading commercial city of the Omani empire. From 1803 to 1856 Masqat retained its position as the leading entrepôt in the Persian Gulf, but by the late 1820s Oman's ruler, Sayyid Sa'id ibn-Sultan (1804–56), began to divert much of his energy away from Omani affairs in an effort to consolidate his hold over Africa's east coast. Absenting himself from Masqat for long periods Sa'id virtually moved the capital of his empire to Zanzibar. After 1832 Zanzibar and the mainland opposite that island began to enjoy the benefits of a boom founded upon Sa'id's planting of highly profitable clove and coconut palm plantations there, as well as from a great quickening of the slave trade and its accompanying business. Zanzibar harbor became the commercial hub of east Africa and the city attracted great numbers of Arab, Indian, European, and American traders. In time, the Indians, through their financial manipulations, took control of much of this increasing economic activity. The ancient slave trade which received new impetus from the Zanzibar boom contributed to the spread of a shadowy Omani political influence that followed on the heels of the Arab slave traders penetrating into the interior of east and central Africa. Even after British efforts to halt the slave trade began to strike at the profits from this commerce, Zanzibar's prosperity continued to grow. By the end of Sa'id's reign in 1856 his African dominions were contributing twice as much to his exchequer as were his Asiatic possessions.[27]

In Oman, Sa'id's reign witnessed the beginnings of a long, slow business slide which rapidly accelerated during the 1860s and which progressed so far by the end of the nineteenth century that the country became little more than a stagnating economic backwater. Sa'id's preoccupation with prospering Zanzibar contributed to the start of this slide; obviously, he did not give as much time and thought to encouraging Oman's less spectacular trade as did his predecessors. Moreover, as his reign progressed, Sa'id was increasingly vexed by conservative Ibadi challenges to his rule which contributed to a breakdown of order in some areas of the country. His political troubles in Oman were compounded by Wahhabi incursions out of central Arabia and, naturally, all of this political uncertainty had a decidedly adverse effect on the economy. On the larger scene, Western intervention became a very real factor in the politics and, indirectly, the economic life of the states surrounding the Persian Gulf during the first half of the nineteenth century. We will return to a discussion of the political implications of this intervention below but it would be well to point out that the economy of the whole Gulf region began to suffer as European-manufactured goods were introduced into the region. For instance, in Iran in the 1840s the local weaving industry was ruined as cheap British cottons began to flood the

[27] For the emergence of Zanzibar as a major trade hub under the aegis of Sayyid Sa'id ibn-Sultan, consult R. Coupland, *East Africa and Its Invaders from Earliest Times to the Death of Seyyid Said in 1856* (Oxford, 1938); R. Burton, *Zanzibar* (London, 1872); H. Hart, "A Visit to Zanzibar in 1834," *Bombay Records—1856*; C. P. Rigby, "Report on the Zanzibar Dominions," *Selections from the Records of the Bombay Government*, new series, no. LIX (Bombay, 1861).

country. Iranian cities and towns went into a deep depression, a situation which must have cut into the trade of Iran's old commercial partners such as Oman.[28] By the 1840s the British had forced Sa'id into restricting the slave trade within his dominions and by the 1850s it was estimated that the export of slaves from Zanzibar had been reduced to one-fifth its previous levels.[29] Oman's ships and merchants naturally suffered from all these developments. Indicative of the business slump was the fact that Sa'id could sell the Masqat customs concession for only $MT 80,000 (Maria Theresa dollars) in 1854, whereas it was worth $MT 105,000 in 1835.[30] But if Masqat's business and shipping interests were not as healthy as in the pre-1800 days, during Sa'id's reign the city remained the leading port and exchange place in the Persian Gulf and still functioned as a major cog in the workings of Indian Ocean commerce, with over half of the Gulf trade still carried in Masqati-owned ships.[31] So although a slow recession had set in, a depression had not developed and it would be wrong to overstate the effects of the slowdown of business activity in Masqat.

Observers who visited the city during Sa'id's reign described it as a picturesque and thriving place. The city was built around its busy harbor, a cliff-bound inlet whose narrow entrance was flanked on either side by two massive Portuguese-built forts. The port's whitewashed houses made a neat picture when viewed from the sea, but on closer inspection the town —to Europeans at least—seemed hot, dirty, full of foul odors, and crowded. Masqat was surrounded on all but its harbor side

[28] Although it is written strictly according to Marxist class warfare theories, the best treatment of the economic dislocations in Iran during the 1840s and 1850s is M. S. Ivanov, *Babidskie Vosstaniya v Irane* (Leningrad, 1939).

[29] Coupland, *East Africa and its Invaders*, p. 509.

[30] J. B. F. Osgood, *Notes of Travel or Recollections of Majunga, Zanzibar, Muscat, Aden, Mocha, and Other Eastern Ports* (Salem, 1854), p. 53; J. R. Wellsted, *Travels in Arabia* (London, 1838), I, 22.

[31] Osgood, *Notes*, pp. 82-83.

by a 15-foot-high wall which was pierced by two gates and protected by a dry moat. Much of the space within the walls was filled by the port's numerous bazaars. Most streets in the city were about 10 feet wide and shaded from the pitiless sun by mat coverings. In the suqs the various trades each occupied a particular quarter. The usual shop was a dark, 10-foot-square hole inside which merchants and artisans labored and displayed their wares on the small platforms that separated the shops from the street. The houses of the rich were of two or three stories built around a galleried court and had interior walls of cane and whitewashed ceilings decorated with geometrical designs; the floors were covered with mats and carpets. The city's poor were concentrated in flimsy cane huts outside the walls. In addition to Omani Arabs, Masqat was peopled by Indian, Persian, and Jewish merchants and artisans, plus laborers from Baluchistan and slaves from Africa. The material condition of this melange was "far better," according to knowledgeable observers, than that of most Asian cities—the city had its rich but even more poor and public beggars were common. In the 1830s, probably 50 to 60,000 people lived in the Masqat vicinity because it was a place of wealth and trade where, despite a business slowdown, fortunes could still be made.[32]

The uneasy economic climate in Oman between 1820 and 1856 was paralleled by the country's uncomfortable political situation during these years. This unrest was due to the continuation of the friction among Omani factions, in particular to the troubles between conservative Ibadis and the moderate Al Bu Sa'id government that broke out after Imam Ahmad's death and which were compounded by dissension within the ruling house, to the disquiet that resulted from Wahhabi incursions into southeastern Arabia, and to growing British intervention in Persian Gulf affairs.

We have noted the conservatives' reaction against what they considered to be the irreligious policies of the Al Bu Sa'id rulers.

[32] *Ibid.*, pp. 74, 89-93, 105-107; Wellsted, *Travels in Arabia*, I, 13, 22, 318-22, 347-48.

The latter, however, powerfully situated as they were upon Oman's prospering coast, were too strong to be unseated. As the nineteenth century lengthened the Al Bu Sa'id regime became more and more identified with the coast whose fortunes the dynasty fostered and protected. The first important Al Bu Sa'id ruler after Imam Ahmad was another of his sons, Sultan ibn-Ahmad (1793–1804), whose reign in many ways marked the height of Al Bu Sa'id power, prestige, and prosperity in Oman. It was Sayyid Sultan's aim to develop the Omani state into a tightly supervised maritime empire embracing both shores of the Gulf of Oman, the major Persian Gulf islands, strategic points on the Arabian coast of the Persian Gulf proper, as well as Oman's east African possessions. Thitherto, Omani preponderance in the Persian Gulf was of a loose variety designed to dominate but not absolutely control maritime and commercial activity in the Gulf. Sultan ibn-Ahmad, however, initiated practices such as charging tolls on all Arab ships entering or leaving the Gulf. Attempts to implement such schemes intensified the already violent rivalry between Oman and the rising maritime states on the Arabian coast of the Persian Gulf proper and ultimately contributed to the outbreak of open warfare. At first this struggle went well for Sayyid Sultan but its complexion changed after the Gulf Arab states gained the assistance of a powerful ally, the Wahhabi Sa'udis of central Arabia. In return for their adherence to Wahhabi Islam and their acceptance of nominal Sa'udi political overlordship, the Gulf principalities received powerful military support which even included Sa'udi land attacks against Oman itself. In the midst of this war Sayyid Sultan was killed in a naval action against the Qawasim of Ra's al-Khaymah, one of the Arab shaykhdoms challenging Oman in the Gulf. Leaderless, divided by factionalism, and beset by powerful enemies on both land and sea it appeared for a time that Oman would fall into the Wahhabi sphere.[33]

---

[33] S. Miles, "Sketch of the Life of Seyyid Sultan bin Ahmad," *Admin. Rpt.: 1887-1888*; Ibn-Ruzayq, pp. 230-39; Al-Salimi, II, 184-86. Lorimer, I, 420-35. Saudi Arabia, *Memorial*, Vol. I, 100-41.

Disaster was averted by three events. First, Sultan ibn-Ahmad's energetic young son, the aforementioned Sa'id ibn-Sultan, filled the leadership void in 1807 by intriguing his way to supremacy in Oman, which ended four years of civil strife following Sayyid Sultan's death. One of Sa'id's first moves was to bribe the Wahhabis to cease their attacks. Second, Britain, allied to Oman since 1798, answered attacks on her shipping in the Gulf by intervening with armed force against the Wahhabi-backed Arab "pirates" of the "Pirate Coast," actions which by 1820 brought the submission of Oman's maritime rivals. Third, the power of the Sa'udi Wahhabis slowly waned as they were forced to divert their strength in order to resist aroused counterattacks by other Middle Eastern states; invaded by the armies of Muhammad 'Ali's Egypt in 1811, the Sa'udi state itself was temporarily crushed by 1818.[34]

Of the factors that contributed to Oman's unsettled political situation between 1800 and 1856 the intrusion of the West in the form of British intervention was destined to have the most revolutionary long-term effects. Although the Western presence was to become far more pervasive in the second half of the nineteenth century, British intervention was transformed into a permanent supervision of the Gulf during the first part of the century. This supervision, exercised through the maritime truce system and backed up by naval patrols and political surveillance, was most influential initially in bringing political changes. But ultimately it went so far as to overturn the context within which Gulf civilization had traditionally operated, and established the prerequisites for the penetration of modern culture into the region. Oman, because it was Britain's ally, originally had a great deal of freedom vis-à-vis the new British supervisory system in the Gulf and was not bound by any of the "truces" that fettered the upper Gulf Arabs. Nevertheless, by the mid-nineteenth century it was clear that Britain had replaced Oman as the arbiter of

[34] Ibn-Ruzayq, pp. 259ff., contains an account of Sa'id ibn-Sultan's early reign.

68

Persian Gulf affairs and that the latter had been increasingly restricted in her actions and independence especially in respect to maritime war, the slave trade, and economic affairs. The failure of an attempt to take Bahrain in 1828 marked the end of Omani attempts to implement an aggressive, independent foreign policy in the Gulf. By the 1840s a new treaty with Britain, along with other treaties with France and the United States, ratified the Western presence as well as special Western privileges in Omani territories. Westerners and their subjects were exempt from local law, and a five percent limit was placed on the import duties that Oman could levy on Western commerce. Moreover, the British, starting with the 1822 "Moresby treaty," pressured Sa'id into restricting the lucrative slave trade within his dominions, an action universally unpopular with all classes of Omanis and thus contributive to internal unrest within the country.[35]

Intervention from another quarter—the Sa'udi Wahhabis —also contributed to Oman's unease. In addition to posing a recurrent political threat to Oman's independence, it is apparent that Wahhabi intervention shook the Ibadis in a religious and ideological sense as well. Indeed, some Ghafiri tribes along Oman's desert border adopted Wahhabi Islam. Even more important, Ibadi intellectuals began a "stock taking" process which resulted in a reemphasis of the fundamentals of the conservative Ibadi creed. Although the Wahhabi threat was temporarily eclipsed between 1818 and 1833 it was not until 1870 that it was lifted from Oman.[36]

It is not surprising that in the face of economic uncertainty, war, foreign intervention, and ideological ferment the Al Bu Sa'id sayyids faced rising opposition to their rule within Oman.

[35] The growth of British influence and Anglo–Omani relations during the early nineteenth century are covered in *Précis Gulf*; Kelly, "British Policy, 1813-1843" and "British Position in the Persian Gulf," *St. Antony's Papers, Number IV*; Aitchison—1933; see also chap. 5.

[36] Sa'udi intervention in Oman is treated in Winder, "Su'ūdi State"; Saudi Arabia, *Memorial*, I, 104-236; J. B. Kelly, *Eastern Arabian Frontiers* (London, 1964), pp. 51-90.

Mention of the conservative opposition has already been made, but another facet of this opposition was the appearance of dynastic rivalries among the Al Bu Sa'id sayyids themselves. By the early nineteenth century the struggle for supremacy among Al Bu Sa'id factions had settled down into a contest between the scions of two of Imam Ahmad's sons, the above-mentioned Sultan ibn-Ahmad and Qays ibn-Ahmad, the lord of Suhar and al-Batinah. When Sultan's son, Sayyid Sa'id ibn-Sultan, succeeded in winning his father's position in 1807 he left his uncle Qays an extremely disgruntled, if defeated, rival. The enmity between Sultan's and Qays' descendants was destined to be a feature of Omani history through the entire nineteenth century. Generally, the line of Sultan, Sa'id, and their heirs supported "moderate" Ibadism, whereas in time the children of Qays combined with the "conservative" Ibadis. Indeed, in the 1830s and 1840s the conservative ulema, led by a figure we shall learn more of later—Sa'id ibn-Khalfan al-Khalili—a major influence in the mid-nineteenth century, conservative Ibadi intellectual revival, conspired to restore a medieval-style imamate in Oman with the leader of the Qays branch of Al Bu Sa'id, Hamud ibn-'Azzan, as imam. The movement was initially successful when Hamud ibn-'Azzan, asserting the de facto independence of his patrimony, Suhar and the northern al-Batinah coast, threatened to expel Sayyid Sa'id from Oman. Sa'id, preoccupied with his prospering east African schemes to the extent that by the 1840s he spent most of his time at Zanzibar, reacted slowly to the danger. Only in 1851 after the British, fearful of possible trouble if the conservatives took over in Oman, influenced Sa'id to return from Africa, was the Qays branch ejected from al-Batinah, their movement contained, and some semblance of stability restored to Oman's coast if not to her interior.[37]

[37] The rise of conservative Ibadi opposition to Sayyid Sa'id, which reached its height in 1846 when Hamud ibn-'Azzan was elected but declined to serve as imam, is outlined in Al-Salimi, II, 186-220. See also Ibn-Ruzayq, pp. 259-371; E. Ross, "An Outline History of Oman," *Admin.*

Oman Before the Late 19th Century

Oman in 1856—the end of an era. Sayyid Sa'id's death in 1856 marked the end of an era. He was the last ruler of any importance in the Persian Gulf whose career was successful in the context of the region's traditional civilization and its ancient system of political dynamics, for the impact of Western imperialism and modernization was to destroy the overall structure, if not each individual characteristic, of the old order in the Gulf within a few years of Sa'id's passing. But in 1856 the Gulf still reflected, for the most part, the civilization of its post-sixteenth century "silver age." Oman was still the leading political power among the Gulf states and Masqat still retained its place as the region's leading commercial and shipping center.

The Omani state continued to be a maritime empire whose possessions were strung out over thousands of miles of the western Indian Ocean and whose ships sailed the length of that sea. The firmly attached parts of this domain included the Omani east coast from Sur north to Suhar, the port of Gwadar in Makran, the islands of Zanzibar and Pemba off the east African coast, and the African mainland around Mombasa and Dar as-Salaam. A far more precarious claim was asserted over interior Oman, the Makran coast outside of Gwadar, the south Arabian coast west of Ra's al-Hadd to Dhofar, and the east coast of Africa north of Mozambique to Somaliland and inland to the great central African lakes. Bandar 'Abbas on the Iranian mainland, and the Iranian offshore islands of Qishm and Hormuz were leased from Persia. The capital of this spider-like realm, held together by sea communications, was Masqat, although Zanzibar, Sayyid Sa'id's favorite residence, had risen to virtually equal status. There were some strong commercial

Rpt.: 1882-1883; S. Miles, "A Biography of the late Seyyid Said," *Admin. Rpt.: 1883-1884*; R. Said-Ruete, *Said bin Sultan (1791-1856) Ruler of Oman and Zanzibar* (London, 1929); *Précis Gulf*; for accounts of Sa'id ibn-Sultan's rule in Oman. British attitudes toward Sayyid Sa'id's neglect of Omani affairs after 1828 are stated in *Bombay Records—1856*, pp. 205, 217-19.

ties within this empire whereby Oman's seamen and merchants exploited the prospering African possessions while the latter area provided trade, wealth, slaves, and opportunity to the Omanis.

The cohesion of the Omani domain in 1936 should not be overemphasized, however. The central authority was strong only in a few towns such as Masqat or Zanzibar and in many places it was exercised in only the most shadowy fashion. In Oman itself, tribal unrest, coupled with conservative Ibadi religious opposition, and recurrent Wahhabi inroads, occasionally threatened to overwhelm the moderate Al Bu Sa'id rule on the coast. But Sayyid Sa'id's deft use of his resources always saved the situation during his lifetime. Diplomacy, tribute, and bribes held off the dangerous Wahhabis after their revival in the 1830s. These devices, plus rent payments, also discouraged the Persians from outright annexation of Oman's Iranian footholds. In fact, the maintenance of Sa'id's hold over his sprawling possessions depended in large measure on the liberal use of his revenues, which were derived primarily from his empire's commerce. These revenues provided for tribute payments, tribal subsidies, presents and bribe payments, as well as for more orthodox military and naval expenditures. In 1840 state revenues were estimated at $MT 610,000, or £120,000. The only sure revenues of the state were derived from the Masqat–Matrah and Zanzibar customs, royal lands, and slave trade duties. The exchequer was augmented by profits from Sa'id's trading and his private estates, over $MT 200,000 coming from his Zanzibar clove plantations alone. Almost two-thirds of this money originated in Oman's African possessions.[38]

Sa'id ibn-Sultan did not claim religious sanction for his rule, although not a few European travelers referred to him as "the imam." Rather, Sayyid Sa'id governed as a secular monarch in a style similar to that displayed by the rulers of past Persian Gulf commercial states. Indeed, the openly secular nature of

[38] Ibn-Ruzayq, p. ci; *Bombay Records—1856*, pp. 238, 276-77, 287-88, 631; Osgood, *Notes*, pp. 23-24.

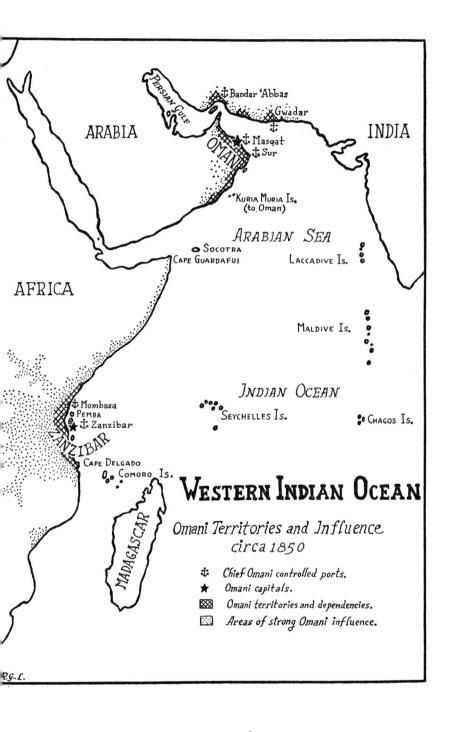

PERSIAN GULF

ARABIA

INDIA

⚓ Bandar 'Abbas

⚓ Gwadar

OMAN

★ ⚓ Masqat
⚓ Sur

•• KURIA MURIA Is.
(to Oman)

ARABIAN SEA

Socotra
CAPE GUARDAFUI

LACCADIVE Is.

AFRICA

MALDIVE Is.

INDIAN OCEAN

⚓ Mombasa
PEMBA
★ ⚓ Zanzibar

SEYCHELLES Is.

CHAGOS Is.

ZANZIBAR

CAPE DELGADO
COMORO Is.

WESTERN INDIAN OCEAN

MADAGASCAR

Omani Territories and Influence
circa 1850

⚓ Chief Omani controlled ports.
★ Omani capitals.
▩ Omani territories and dependencies.
▦ Areas of strong Omani influence.

P.G.L.

his regime was held against him by conservative Ibadi propagandists who charged him with being a deceitful *malik* (king) who had no use for true religion.[39] As an administrator, Sa'id divided his time between Zanzibar and Masqat; he left local authority in the hands of one of his sons when he was absent from one or another of these favorite residences. A large portion of his time and money was spent in maintaining Oman's fleet which at its period of greatest strength consisted of about 15 Western-style warships, including a 74-gun ship-of-the-line and five frigates, as well as numerous Arab-style vessels. In times of peace, this fleet might serve as cargo carriers and revenue earners. British naval experts did not hold a high opinion of this assemblage's martial effectiveness but estimated that Sa'id could assemble a transport fleet capable of carrying 20,000 men. Sa'id, like his contemporary William IV of Great Britain, was a "sailor king" who enjoyed life at sea, and his fleet provided the bonds that tied together the separate parts of his realm. Although a small mercenary army, largely dispersed for garrison duty, was also maintained, Sa'id was always more adept at nurturing commerce than at playing power politics with Oman's factions.[40]

The influence of the foreigners—particularly the British—on the conduct of affairs within Sa'id's domain was important

---

[39] Al-Salimi, II, 186, 217-20; Ibn-Ruzayq, pp. 368-70.

[40] Wellsted, *Travels in Arabia*, I, 400; Rigby, "Report on Zanzibar," *Records of the Bombay Government*, new series, no. LIX (1861), pp. 18-19; Wadia, *Bombay Dockyard*, pp. 334-37. Practically all of Sayyid Sa'id's navy was constructed in India after European designs. The largest ship in this fleet, the 74-gun, 1,889-ton ship-of-the-line, *Liverpool*, was launched in Bombay in 1826. But Sayyid Sa'id found he could not maintain this dreadnaught, so he saved money and gained some diplomatic capital as well by presenting the vessel to William IV as a gift in 1836. The *Liverpool*, renamed *Imaum* in honor of its donor, was broken up in 1852 after spending its final years as a receiving hulk in Jamaica. During the 1830s this navy was triple the size of the British East India squadron, according to Wellsted. Estimates on the size of Sayyid Sa'id's army vary; probably he maintained a mercenary force of some 1,500 men in Oman, 1,300 men in Zanzibar, and he could raise an additional 5,000 to 10,000 men among the Omani tribes in emergency situations.

in 1856 but it should not be overestimated. The main fact of Oman's foreign relations was the alliance with Britain. The alliance proved invaluable to the Al Bu Sa'id government on several occasions, particularly in discouraging Wahhabi incursions into Oman. However, it also proved to be a handicap when British humanitarianism forced Sayyid Sa'id to tamper with the lucrative and religiously sanctioned slave trade. Britain and other Western countries also built up their influence in Oman by means other than political alliances during the first half of the nineteenth century. An increasing percentage of Oman's trade was involved in exchange with British India, a fact underlined by the presence of hundreds of British Indian merchants in Omani territories. The boom in Zanzibar attracted Arab, Indian, European and American traders and resulted in commercial treaties between Oman and the United States (1833), Great Britain (1839) —in addition to a series of political treaties, and France (1844). These engagements gave the Westerners special trading rights and set import duties at a five percent limit. Because these treaties established a Western-administered extraterritorial regime within the Omani empire, eventually a large part of the merchant community working in Omani territory was excluded from local jurisdiction.[41]

In summary, when he died in 1856 Sayyid Sa'id held an essentially independent position although he ruled in an environment characterized by a strong foreign presence, much internal unrest, and an uneasy economic climate.

[41] For texts of these, as well as the other treaties between Oman and the Western powers concluded before 1930, see Aitchison—1933, XI, xxvii-xxxiv, 287-301. In the Persian Gulf extraterritoriality was usually a practice sanctioned by custom and usage before it was included in specific treaty provisions.

PART II

The Impact of Early Economic and Technological Modernization

CHAPTER 3

The Beginnings of Modernization
in the Persian Gulf

WHEN the British set up their maritime supervisory system in 1820 it was an event that augured the eventual transformation not only of the Persian Gulf's established political system but of the entire complex which formed the rest of the area's traditional civilization, as well. Nevertheless, from 1820 until the 1860s British influence in the region was exercised in such a way that its effects were felt mainly by the political elite, and less so by the mass of the population. Also, this influence was lightly exercised; it was designed more to prevent Gulf rulers from undertaking certain warlike and destructive actions than to aggrandize British profits, prestige, and power. Not until the 1840s when Britain's humanitarian ideals compelled her to restrict slave trading did the interests of the merchant and seafaring classes of the Gulf clash with British restrictions. But in the main, although the prerequisites for a more active, visible, and disruptive imperialism were prepared in the 1820–60 period, ordinary life in the Persian Gulf seemed little affected by the birth of the new era.

The first really profound and widespread alteration in the Gulf's economic environment occurred in the 1860s as a consequence of the initial large-scale penetration into the Gulf of Western-controlled economic enterprises and the modern technological paraphernalia accompanying these moves. It is sometimes argued that it was not until the eve of World War I, with the coming of the oil industry to the Gulf, that the region began to modernize in an economic sense. This assertion is not strictly true, for in 1862 steamer service between Indian, Persian Gulf, and other western Indian Ocean ports began, and during the mid-1860s telegraphic communication was introduced to the Gulf region. By the end of that decade the commerce of the region was falling into the hands of Indians and other merchants who were agents of modern business concerns, with their headquarters in India or Europe. The effect of this intrusion by Western economic interests and modern technology into the Gulf was the disruption of the area's shipping and commercial community, the undermining of the traditional economy, and the dislocation of the society and the entire congeries of activities that for so long had been dependent on the Gulf's traditional seafaring and business operations. Gulf seamen, for instance, found their ancient carrying trade usurped by the new steamers. With the steamers stopping at several ports of call Masqat could no longer function as a commercial entrepôt for the entire Gulf region, so that city—and coastal Oman, also—lost a 200-year-old status as the region's economic leader. What is more, it was nearly impossible for any inhabitant of the Gulf littoral to escape the effects of the new situation. By the beginning of this century even the cotton cloth used in a rural tribesman's garments was often manufactured in Lancashire and carried into the region in steamships.

It might be said that the coming of the oil industry to the Gulf region in the early twentieth century was essentially a constructive action that, even if it hastened the fall of traditionalism, resulted in a start being made in building a solid economic framework upon which other modernizing activity could be based in the future. The coming of the steamers, however, had a largely destructive initial effect on the Gulf's ancient maritime civilization. Still, modernization is often a most destructive process in that old ways are swept away in a flood of change.[1] In any event, it seems that the history of the

[1] The term "modernization" is used in this work to describe the process by which a society confronts or adapts to the complex of revolutionary ideas and techniques first developed in Western Europe, starting in the twelfth century, which enhanced man's ability to understand and control his environment and radically changed his relationship to this environment. The process may be viewed as a two-sided one—an implied

80

The Beginnings of Modernization

Middle East and many other areas of Afro–Asia during the nineteenth century was more often a case study in the disruptive effects of the penetration of modern influences than it was of the construction of valid, strong, modern institutions. The Persian Gulf, then, like Iran, Anatolia, Egypt, and Syria–Lebanon also endured a discouraging time when old institutions, values, and aspirations were torn down before a new civilization began to rise.

Although the entire late nineteenth century was a time of revolutionary change in the Persian Gulf, the decade 1862–72 was a time of particular upheaval. During these years rapid and radical alterations in customary political and economic practices and relationships took place and were followed by the appearance of social variations only slightly less significant. Oman, the leading seafaring and commercial state and an important though no longer dominating political power in the Persian Gulf at the time of Sayyid Saʿid's death in 1856, was particularly hard hit by the upheavals of this period. Oman's sudden fall to utter political insignificance and economic stagnation remains a particularly striking example of just how destructive the process of modernization has been in some societies.

INDIAN INFLUENCES ON EARLY ECONOMIC AND TECHNOLOGICAL MODERNIZATION

Traditionally, India enjoyed a place as one of the oldest and most important of the commercial and seafaring partners of the Persian Gulf's inhabitants. The exchange of Indian grain, spices, cloth, hardware, and luxury goods had for centuries prior to the nineteenth century been the foundation of a large percentage of the business and maritime activity carried on by Gulf merchants and seamen. Certainly the strongest element in the trade of the Omanis was commerce and traffic originat-

---

destruction as well as *construction* of institutions, attitudes, and practices. Indeed, this work is more concerned with the destructive aspects of modernization.

ing in India. This had been the case for the two centuries prior to the 1860s during which Masqat dominated the business activity of the Persian Gulf and controlled the interregional seaborne carrying trade of much of the western Indian Ocean as well. Before European manufactures and traders finally captured the economic supremacy of the region during the nineteenth century, Indian manufacturing, distributing, and marketing activities were the key elements in the economic life of a great expanse of Asia and Africa adjacent to the Indian Ocean. Before modern times most Indian Ocean littoral peoples supported themselves by exploiting a fairly limited number of occupations and products. India, almost alone in the area, enjoyed a wealth of resources and so exported her excess food, raw materials, manufactures, capital, and even her organizational know-how to less endowed neighbors. If one had visited Masqat in the 1780s, for instance, he would have encountered numbers of Indian businessmen; he would have seen that the bulk of the goods being exchanged—including the cloth for the garments most Masqatis wore—were either produced in India or bound for that subcontinent, and probably he would have eaten a dinner consisting in large part of Indian-grown rice.

During most of their long period of close relationship with India the Persian Gulf trading states occupied a subsidiary but important position vis-à-vis the Indian economy. Gulf seamen owned and sailed a large segment of the shipping that carried India's products throughout the Indian Ocean. One of the cities of the Gulf usually served as an entrepôt for the trade of the region and as a secondary distribution center which transferred the cargos of the western Indian Ocean to and from the Indian subcontinent—the primary economic center for the entire Indian Ocean basin. This was essentially the relationship of Sayyid Sa'id's Oman to India during the first half of the nineteenth century. The Omani state was the center of a western Indian Ocean distribution system that was in turn tied to India's commercial system which, since the sixteenth century, was itself bound to a Europe-dominated worldwide economic system.

It is not surprising, given these ancient ties, that the Persian Gulf's first contacts with the West and with modern civilization occurred via India. When the Portuguese entered the Gulf after they had established themselves in the subcontinent they came to divert Gulf trade into the ports they had seized on India's coast and to defend the sea lanes leading to their new possessions. When the British intervened forcibly in Persian Gulf politics and set up what became the "truce system" in 1820 they too acted primarily to protect the flanks and sea routes of their newly conquered Indian empire. Indeed, it was the side effects of various British projects designed to spur the modernization of their Indian domain that eventually led to the first large-scale invasion of the Gulf by modern technology and economic enterprise in the 1860s. In the light of history, it was only natural that basic changes in India's economic condition would in time spill over into the Gulf.[2]

The modernization of India's transportation system and its extension into the Persian Gulf. It was noted above that prior to the nineteenth century Indian manufacturing, distributing, and marketing activities dominated the markets of southern Asia and eastern Africa; Indian cottons even captured a large European market during the eighteenth century. In the early nineteenth century, however, Indian manufactures began to lose these markets when the products of newly mechanized British mills began to invade the East. These goods were carried directly to India in European ships (an increasing number were steamships after 1840). From India they were distributed throughout the Indian Ocean basin by local carriers such as the Omani mariners. The impact of these European imports

[2] See J. Auber, *Histoire de l'Océan Indien* (Tananarive, Madagascar, 1955), pp. 229-60, for one impression of India's place in the Indian Ocean basin, and S. C. Kuchhal, *The Industrial Economy of India* (Allahabad, 1963); V. Anstey, *The Trade of the Indian Ocean* (London, 1929), introd., for remarks on India's premodern economy and trade.

was devastating to India as well as to other regional manufacturing centers such as Iran; by the mid-nineteenth century India's old handicraft industries—especially the important one of cloth weaving—were prostrate. Only by becoming handlers of European as well as local goods could Indian traders adapt to the new situation.[3]

At first the destructive changes which took place within the Indian economic structure did not affect the secondary distribution patterns of the Indian Ocean. Omani and other Persian Gulf ships continued to carry goods from India—even if these goods might be increasingly of European rather than Indian manufacture—to other areas in the Indian Ocean throughout Sayyid Sa'id's reign. Not until the 1860s did the progress of technological modernization disastrously affect the secondary distributive system and the place of Persian Gulf and Omani shipping and commerce in the Indian Ocean.

As early as the 1830s, however, the handwriting had appeared on the wall. By that date the volume and organization of world commerce was primed for a period of rapid development: Europe was developing steamboats, railroads, telegraphs, and engineering skills, all of which fundamentally advanced the efficiency and speed of transport. As a result of these advances, stimulated by a desire to raise trade profits and goaded by international rivalries and conflicts such as the Napoleonic Wars, European powers—especially the British—developed an acute interest in establishing a short, fast route between Europe and the Orient. Most of this interest focused on developing routes which would traverse the Middle East and bypass the lengthy around-Africa route that had been supreme as the main route between the East and the West since Portugal pioneered it in the sixteenth century. In the 1820s the British began to consider the use of steamships and steam locomotives on the Levant coast, in Mesopotamia, and along the Persian Gulf route to India; in the 1830s actual experiments using

[3] V. A. Smith, *Oxford History of India*, 3rd ed., P. Spear, ed. (Oxford, 1958), pp. 641-42.

steamboats on these routes were tried. The projected plan of this enterprise was to link two projected steamer services, Britain–Levant and India–Persian Gulf–Iraq, via a Levant–Iraq river steamer–railroad combination and in this way afford quick communication between East and West. Several variations on this scheme were put forward but failed to come off because the British government would not guarantee the ventures' finances. It was only in 1861 that the Messrs. Lynch began to employ steamboats on the Iraqi rivers, and even this service merely provided a link among the Iraqi river towns or fed the trade of ships sailing the Persian Gulf; it was not part of a through connection.[4]

In the 1840s attention turned to Egypt as a possible location for the proposed East–West connection. During Napoleon's time France had developed plans to pierce the Suez isthmus with a canal but these had been shelved after the failure of Napoleon's Egyptian campaign. In the 1840s, however, the old design was revived by the French but opposed by the British who feared that such a canal would only become a gateway into the Indian Ocean for the French and other of Britain's rivals. The British proposed an alternative: a railroad from Alexandria to Suez via Cairo which would facilitate travel but still keep the Mediterranean safely plugged at its eastern limits. In 1840 the Peninsula and Oriental Line started steamer service between England and Alexandria and followed this up by initiating service on a Suez to India route in 1844. The British plan was entirely realized in 1858 when the Alexandria-to-Suez railroad was completed and the two steamer runs were joined. Nevertheless, this accomplishment was soon overshadowed as a result of the efforts of Ferdinand de Lesseps who in 1854 persuaded the francophile ruler of Egypt, Sa'id Pasha, to allow the construction of a Suez canal, a work finally completed in 1869. Although they were later frustrated by their defeat in the

---

[4] Hoskins, *Routes to India*, chaps. 6-7, 17; Lorimer, I, 226-27; Wilson, *Persian Gulf*, chap. 16; J. C. Hurewitz, *Diplomacy in the Near and Middle East* (Princeton, 1956), I, 109-10.

Franco–Prussian War, the French anticipated the opening of the Suez Canal by evolving elaborate plans to push their political and commercial interests in the Indian Ocean. In the Persian Gulf, the French envisioned establishing an agricultural colony near Basra, consulates in the larger ports, and a coaling station at Masqat that would supplement one planned for the Aden–Djibouti area.[5]

During the 20-year period between 1840 and 1860 most of the effort and capital devoted to building up modern communications in the Indian Ocean basin was spent in strengthening the Peninsular and Oriental Line's Suez-to-India direct connection. It was too soon to try to set up subsidiary feeder steamer services in the Indian Ocean given the economic and technological factors which limited such a development until the main trade route was strongly established. Within India itself, however, the period witnessed the climax of a comprehensive modernization movement which had started in 1828 with Lord William Bentinck's arrival as governor-general. The liberal, evangelical reformers from Britain attempted to change everything from Hindu ethics and India's educational system to the subcontinent's material environment. A high point in this westernization movement was reached between 1848 and 1856 when Lord Dalhousie served as governor-general in India. Dalhousie initiated a rigorous, often ruthless, centralizing policy aimed at creating a single, homogeneous, British-controlled, modern Indian state. Fundamental to Dalhousie's plan was the development of an efficient communications net to bind India's separate provinces together into one integrated unit. Projects for trunk roads, railroads, and postal services were begun which, although they were undertaken mainly for political ends, became basic ingredients in the more general process of India's modernization.

Ironically enough, after Dalhousie retired from India one

[5] Hoskins, *Routes to India*, chaps. 12-14; Hurewitz, *Diplomacy*, I, 146-49; "Atkinson to Gonne, 9 Dec. 1868, no. 555: Masqat," India Records–2, Vol. L; "Frere to Wood, 10 Dec. 1862," "22 May 1863," "12 Oct. 1865," India Mss.–1.

of the men most responsible for the extension of his ideas on communications was a person who strongly disapproved of the departed governor-general's reformist political program. This was Sir Bartle Frere, who began his service in India in 1834 after graduating from the East India Company's college at Haileybury. As his career progressed, Frere developed a passionate belief that it was Great Britain's destiny and moral duty to bring modern civilization to India and the non-Western world. In this goal Frere and Dalhousie were not far apart. But Frere felt that such an end could be achieved only through adroit, tactful diplomacy; he disliked Dalhousie's arrogant tactics aimed at forcing Indians to adopt Western practices. Frere believed that Britain would have the most success in the long run if she respected India's various cultures, ruled through existing local Indian governments, and spread "civilization" by subtle education and indirect influence. Such a course he reasoned would eventually, and in orderly fashion, convert India to basically Western standards yet preserve the best of the local culture. Nevertheless, Frere, like other "conservative," anti-reformist British administrators, thought it right to push schemes that would increase India's share of the material benefits of "civilization" and warmly supported technological modernization. To men like Frere, modern civilization could best be spread through economic rather than political and cultural means."[6]

Much of Frere's career was spent in western India in the regions around Bombay and in the province of Sind, the territory surrounding the mouths of the Indus river. During the 1840s and 50s he urged that the transportation facilities of these vast regions be improved and argued that the construction of railways and roads would contribute to India's defenses and at the same time open up the more inaccessible areas to

[6] *Oxford History of India*, 3rd ed., pp. 643, 654-62; J. Martineau, *The Life and Correspondence of the Right Honorable Sir Bartle Frere* (London, 1895), I, 168-69; P. Mason, Philip Woodruff (pseud.), *The Men who Ruled India—the Guardians* (London, 1954), pp. 37-41.

commerce. Two of his pet projects included the linking of Bombay with the railroads pushing westward from Calcutta and also the connecting of the Punjab with the port of Karachi on Sind's coast. His improvements of Karachi harbor, which prior to the 1850s was limited to light-draft vessels, were completed to the degree that the port was used as a troop debarkation point when the Great Indian Mutiny erupted in 1857.

After the Mutiny was suppressed, as a result of Frere's foresight concerning India's transport needs and the new prestige of antireformist, conservative thinking, Sir Bartle and his ideas received an ample hearing in the highest councils of the Indian government. By 1861 the railroad between the Punjab and Karachi was completed and the city began its rise to its modern status as one of the major ports of South Asia. An integral part of Frere's communication plans was the building of feeder roads fanning out from the new railway lines. By such projects Frere hoped that India could be crisscrossed with routes that would give the interior quick access to coastal ports.[7]

Frere's ideas on transportation were broadcast throughout India after his appointment to the Governor-General's Council by Lord Canning who served as India's governor-general and viceroy from 1856 to 1862. While in his post Frere's sphere of friends and contacts was enlarged, particularly among the European business community resident in Calcutta, a group Frere was not well acquainted with before his move to the then capital of British India. Among Frere's new friends was William (later Sir William) Mackinnon, a man destined to win fame as one of the architects of Britain's expansion into east Africa and fortune as a founder of the British India Steam Navigation Company. It was as a steamship company magnate that Mackinnon was to inadvertently spark a revolution in the Persian Gulf.

William Mackinnon was a Scot who migrated to Calcutta from Glasgow in 1847 in order to join an old schoolmate, Robert Mackenzie, in administering a general merchandising con-

---

[7] Martineau, *Life of Frere*, I, 45, 93-103, 468.

cern. By 1854 the partners had become involved in the Bay of Bengal coasting traffic and in that year the imaginative and energetic pair accepted a contract to carry mail, passengers, and general cargo between Calcutta and Rangoon. With borrowed capital Mackinnon and Mackenzie purchased two small steamers and established a business that would eventually grow into a shipping giant spanning the breadth of the Indian Ocean. In 1856 the company became the "Calcutta and Burmah Steam Navigation Company." The mail subsidy and the lucrative charters that resulted from the Indian Mutiny were enough to tide the concern over early growing pains and in 1862 Mackinnon returned from a business trip to England with new capital, new steamers, and a new plan to push the Calcutta and Burmah into three new routes: a round-India coasting service, an eastward extension to Singapore, and a westward extension into the Persian Gulf that would connect with Lynch's new river-steamer line operating in Iraq.[8]

These were bold plans. Mackinnon and Mackenzie had the knowledge and drive to succeed in them but originally they did not have the necessary money. It was at this point that Sir Bartle Frere, still on the governor-general's Council, intervened to push Mackinnon's scheme. It was characteristic of Frere to be attracted when he learned of Mackinnon's expansion plans. After all, Frere's vision of Britain's civilizing mission was not limited to India. He was enthusiastic about opening any area that could possibly be reached by modern influences. Frere believed Mackinnon's ships could serve as emissaries of "civilization" as well as commercial pioneers. Thus, by helping Mackinnon he saw a chance to realize his own vision of Britain's role in the world.

[8] For an outline of the life of Sir William Mackinnon see E. Carlyle, "Sir William Mackinnon," *Dictionary of National Biography, Supplement*, III, 127-28; "Obituary, Sir W. Mackinnon," *The Times*, London, 30 June 1893. For an account of the early history of the British India Steam Navigation Company consult, E. A. Ewart, Boyd Cable (pseud.), *A Hundred Year History of the P. & O. Peninsular and Oriental Steam Navigation Company* (London, 1937), pp. 202-07.

The crux of the matter was that Mackinnon needed a subsidy to begin and then sustain his venture. Although "subsidy thinking" was not then popular in England, the Anglo–Indian government had shown some sympathy to the concept and especially so when considering communications ventures. India's railroads, for instance, were constructed largely with funds raised from Indian government tax revenues and were described in official sources as necessities for Indian defense rather than as potentially profitable commercial ventures. Frere used similar arguments when he presented the case for giving Mackinnon's projected new marine service a subsidy. The subsidy was to be granted in return for carrying mails and for a promise that Mackinnon's steamers could be used as troop transports in times of emergency, a stipulation that would save the Indian government the expense of maintaining its own transport fleet. The Bombay government had been urging the need for regular steamer service to the Gulf for years, so when Lord Canning and Whitehall gave the venture their blessing the "Calcutta and Burmah Line" was reorganized as the "British India Steam Navigation Company" and service on the new routes began in 1862.[9]

The scheduling of regular steamer service to the Persian Gulf was regarded by some as something of a risk. But happily for Mackinnon, the new route's opening coincided with a worldwide cotton boom that began after the availability of American cotton supplies was curtailed drastically by the American Civil War. The willingness of Lancashire to pay inflated prices for cotton encouraged an increase in planting in Egypt, India, and other countries.

The cotton boom hit India at approximately the same time Sir Bartle Frere became governor of the great Indian presidency of Bombay. Frere's term from 1862 to 1867 in what was considered the second most important post in British India, ranking only after that held by the viceroy himself, was a conspicuous success. Soon after taking up his post, Frere moved

[9] *Précis Turkish Arabia*, p. 199; Martineau, *Life of Frere*, I, 297-98.

to take advantage of the impetus built up by the cotton boom by pushing irrigation, transport, and communications improvements. As vast, newly irrigated tracts were brought under cultivation a huge public works program of port facilities and transportation was inaugurated. Bombay became the center of a dizzy boom as investors fought to back Indian cotton; by the end of the 1860s the city was the busiest port in India.

The boom was a fortunate event for the new British India Steam Navigation Company, too. Not only did the new round-India coasting route profit but the infant Persian Gulf service was bolstered by the fact that the cotton madness infected Iran. There, as in India and Egypt, land was planted in the new wonder crop. When Mackinnon's ships sailed back to Bombay from the Gulf their holds were stuffed with Iranian cotton which was snapped up by buyers for the English mills.[10]

So the line prospered during the 1860s. Its sailings were coordinated with the Peninsula and Oriental Britain–Suez–India routes. Although there was some disturbance following the opening of the Suez Canal in 1869, in the long run this development stimulated the company's business immensely. By 1895 the line owned 85 steamers, employed agents scattered over south Asia, east Africa, and Australia, and had started a direct service to London. But to the Persian Gulf the coming of the British India steamers marked the beginning of a disruptive material and economic modernization that would eventually distort in some respects and destroy in others the traditional context of life in the region.

Anglo–Indian governmental support for Persian Gulf modernization. The beginning of voyages by British India steamers was only part of the story of Indian influence on early economic and technological modernization in the Gulf. Another facet was that the Anglo–Indian government—or more specifi-

[10] *Ibid.*, pp. 398-414, II, 1-27; "Frere to Wood, 12 May 1863," India Mss.–1; V. Anstey, *Economic Development of India*, 4th ed. (London, 1952), pp. 208, 261; C. Mackenzie, *Realms of Silver* (London, 1954), pp. 28-40; *Précis Commerce*, p. 107.

cally, the Bombay government under Frere—began a policy of spreading Western concepts of "civilization" in the Gulf after 1862. The vehicle of this policy was the British Political Residency in the Persian Gulf. During 1862 to 1872, a period of momentous change in the Gulf, the residency was served by a remarkable man, Lewis Pelly. Frere handpicked Pelly, with a reputation of being an adventurous, energetic, and capable cavalry officer, to supervise Britain's and India's interests in the Gulf. In Pelly Frere knew he had a man who sympathized with his vision of what the Gulf could become under the prod of Western civilization. The inspiration for this vision may have been Frere's, but Pelly was the man who applied the new concept—a "new concept" that was, in reality, an early variety of the "white man's burden" school of imperialism first stirring in the 1860s. Frere must rank alongside Livingstone and Froud as a founder of this philosophy which lies at the heart of the "New Imperialism" of the late nineteenth century, while Pelly and Mackinnon were early disciples of this creed.

Between 1822 and 1862 the British Residency in the Persian Gulf generally limited its role to that of a policeman concerned with maintaining order. Under Pelly, Britain's Gulf residency entered a new era; as Frere's protégé and subordinate, he played a positive and active, although not always an adroit or successful, role in Gulf events. In administering his residency, Pelly stood ready to cooperate with British merchants or businessmen such as Mackinnon who wished to begin or expand their activities in the Gulf. It would be difficult to say where or if Pelly drew a line between furthering political and economic ends. He developed and asserted Britain's extraterritorial privilege in the Gulf as much to assure freedom of business operations as to advance British political influence. In 1866 he did not hesitate to use gunboat diplomacy when the Wahhabis attacked British–Indian merchants in the Omani port of Sur. Moreover, if resident British–Indian merchants were molested he would force the punishment of the malefactors, usually in the form of stiff indemnities.

The Beginnings of Modernization

During his tour of service in the Gulf, Pelly, working within the general context of Frere's ideas on how Western civilization could best be spread, developed a number of specific ideas —some unrealistic—for the modernization of the Gulf and Britain's position there. He favored the extension of Mackinnon's or other British steamer services within the region, even if it meant the disruption of native shipping or maritime industries. To Pelly, the area's best hope lay in quickly adopting and unhesitatingly accommodating modern Western civilization rather than in clinging to traditional ways which appeared to be doomed. Secondly, the resident naively believed that the volume and variety of commerce in the region would quickly and inevitably increase if trade was not unreasonably interfered with by local governments. He favored improving communications and trade routes, such as the Karun valley in Iran, which opened onto the Gulf; but he underestimated the difficulty of achieving these ends. He publicized regional resources that might be exploited. He even thought it possible the Gulf region could once again become a major route for world trade if the plan first popular in the late 1830s—to build a railroad across the deserts separating the Levant and upper Gulf coasts—were revived.[11]

The capstone of Pelly's design for the modernization of the Gulf was his scheme to create a small British-ruled colony on Cape Musandam where the Gulf of Oman meets the Persian Gulf. Ignoring the location's oppressive climate, he argued that its centrality would make it superior to Bushire (the Iranian coastal city, then the location of Britain's Residency in the Persian Gulf) for overseeing the affairs of the region. Also, Pelly hoped the proposed colony would become a "free port," a new center of the area's trade, and a sort of modern-day ver-

[11] "Trade Report on the Persian Gulf, 1863," *Précis Commerce*, pp. 31-37; "Pelly to W. Nichol & Co., 13 June 1872, no. 896-378: Residency," India Records-2, Vol. xx; "Pelly to Duke of Argyll, 18 Oct. 1871, despatch no. 1,195-136: Residency," India Records-2, Vol. xix. In the 1860s the British practice of encouraging Arab shipping was abandoned.

93

sion of the traditional Persian Gulf entrepôt. But this city, like Bombay, Singapore, or other European-founded cities in the East, would also be what Pelly called "a beacon of civilization" that would display to the locals the advantages of modern civilization and ultimately become a major stimulus to the Gulf's westernization. In addition, because the colony would be under British sovereignty, Pelly believed it could serve as a Persian Gulf "Gibraltar" without any vexing legal problems. Pelly assumed that the Sultan of Masqat and Oman would be willing to sell the land needed for the colony. Although Frere was interested in Pelly's proposal the Calcutta authorities turned down the idea because they feared overinvolvement in local Arabian politics, and shied away from the expense of such an undertaking.[12]

As in Frere's case, Pelly's ideas on the material and economic modernization of the Gulf were part and parcel of his larger philosophy. Pelly was an untiring publicist of the Persian Gulf's potential economic importance. As early as 1863, in official reports and in publicized articles, he called on Britain to take advantage of the changes dawning in the Gulf area as a result of "the probe of European civilization." He believed and argued that the Gulf littoral was capable of great economic growth if the region's potential was properly nurtured. But he warned that there was a distinct possibility that other European powers might develop this potential and achieve economic predominance in the trade area drained by the Gulf unless the British consolidated their political and economic positions there. It was natural that Pelly should warn of possible competition in the Gulf. During the 1860s there were various French plans to develop the Gulf—an outgrowth of their plans to move into the Indian Ocean area in force after the opening of the Suez Canal. But Pelly's warnings, though seconded by Frere, fell on deaf ears, not only in the highest councils of the

12 "Pelly to Anderson, 12 Jan. 1863," "1 Feb. 1863," *Précis Int'l Rivalry*, pp. 25-30.

Anglo–Indian government in Calcutta, but among the leaders of the British government in London.[13]

Still, it is indicative of Pelly's energy and dedication to his ideals that he accomplished much during his 10-year term as resident despite the limited resources and influence at his disposal. Frere, as long as he was Bombay's governor, supported Pelly and, even if neither man could convince the central Anglo–Indian government of the need for such schemes as Pelly's colony, in a very real sense Calcutta policy—inadvertently perhaps—supported the thrust of modernization into the Gulf. Despite an official creed supporting free trade and political "masterly inactivity," the major elements involved in the modernization activity going on in the Gulf in the 1860s —the British India Steam Navigation Company's steamers, the resident merchant colony of British–Indians in the Gulf, the British residency under Pelly, and the Europe-to-India "Indo–European" telegraph and cable line constructed through the Gulf at that time—were all supported directly or indirectly by both Calcutta and London governments. Usually this support was viewed only in terms of being a necessity for India's defense or as an expression of the government's duty to protect and uphold the rights of all of Her Majesty's subjects, be they European or Indian. But the repercussions of this support, especially as far as traditional Gulf civilization was concerned, went far beyond the realm of Indian defense policy. The changes that occurred in the Persian Gulf region as a result of the activities of Frere, Mackinnon, and Pelly illustrate how the aspirations of certain Anglo–Indian officials and businessmen outgrew the limits of India and how India's modernization spilled out over its borders to affect neighboring regions.

[13] "Pelly to Anderson, 16 Feb. 1863," *Précis Int'l Rivalry*, p. 29; "Pelly to Bombay Govt., 12 May 1866," *Précis Commerce*, pp. 29-30. Pelly wrote many articles publicizing the economic possibilities of the Gulf region, the most important of which was, "Remarks on the Tribes, Trade, and Resources around the Shore Line of the Persian Gulf," *Transactions of the Bombay Geographical Society*, XVI (1863), 32-113.

Early Economic–Technological Modernization

By the 1860s India had become a source from which modernizing influences were spreading into other Indian Ocean areas.

ECONOMIC REVOLUTION AND STAGNATION IN THE PERSIAN GULF, 1862–1914

1862 marks the start of economic and technological modernization in the Persian Gulf. The main development of the period between 1862 and World War I was the dislocation of the traditional pattern and tempo of economic life within the region. The years since World War I have been characterized by the increasing spread of modern industrial society in the region as an adjunct of oil exploitation. The post-World War I years are most vital ones in the area's economic modernization. But the 1862 to World War I period is highly significant as well; in terms of regional economic developments the period subdivides at 1872. Between 1862 and 1872 an economic revolution occurred as modern communications penetrated the region. The consequent growth of European-directed or controlled enterprise in the Gulf obscured the fact that established patterns of economic activity indigenous to the Gulf were seriously disturbed or even destroyed in many instances. Between 1872 and the First World War, however, it became painfully clear even to Europeans that the apparent promise of the 1860s would not be realized. The shock that resulted from the revolutionary changes accompanying the birth of the modern era in the Gulf smashed many of the old economic relationships and left much of the region's indigenous economy in a moribund state, unable to respond in any positive fashion to the challenges and possibilities of the new situation. Until foreign-directed oil exploitation created a new economic context and oil royalties afforded capital the region remained too poor in money and modern skills and too disorganized to stimulate or support a healthy growth in trade and the general economy.

Economic revolution: 1862–1872. In absolute terms there was a large jump in the volume of trade and the tempo of economic activity within the Gulf in the decade 1862 to 1872. Unfortunately for many in the area, most of the new profits accrued to Europeans and their agents, the resident Indian merchants, while the Arab business and seafaring interests that traditionally dominated much of the region's economy found their position undercut. Particularly disastrous to local interests was the alternating boom-recession-recovery that distinguished the trade climate of the 1860s. Estimated long-distance commerce of the Persian Gulf was worth roughly £3,500,000 in the 1830s; virtually all was in the hands of local merchants and seamen.[14] By 1866 Gulf long-distance commerce was valued at an estimated £5,000,000. Most of the increase took place during the 1860s.[15] More specifically, there was a sharp rise in Gulf trade between 1862 and 1865, coincident with the start of the British India Line steamer service and the cotton boom. The spurt in Gulf trade depended principally on the demand at inflated prices for cotton at Bombay. Also, it was supported by heavy-wool exports to Bombay, opium exports, bound for east Asia, and the import of sugar from India and Indonesia. Large profits were earned despite the high freight charges; the resulting flow of wealth into the Gulf stimulated increased imports of goods there. The result of all this prosperous activity was that Gulf-owned shipping, as well as the British

[14] It must be emphasized that this figure is a very rough estimate reached after an evaluation of the scattered, sparse, and probably none too accurate information contained in various sources and especially in Wellsted, *Travels in Arabia*, 1, 22-24; and F. R. Chesney, *The Expedition for the Survey of the Rivers Euphrates and Tigris* (London, 1850), 1, 237, 569. The estimate is composed of the following judgments: value of Masqat trade, £1,800,000; value of Bahrain pearl exports, £400,000; value of Bushire trade, £800,000; value of trade of other Persian Gulf ports (Kuwait, Basra, Muhammarah, etc.), £500,000. This last figure is an educated guess based mainly on the supposition that about five-eighths of the total long-distance trade of the Persian Gulf passed through Masqat during the late eighteenth, early nineteenth century period. The accuracy of Persian Gulf trade statistics in general must be suspected until the post-World War I years. Still, they at the very least provide a sound indication of overall trends.

[15] *Précis Commerce*, pp. 29, 32-37, 107.

97

steamers, were profitable and constantly occupied during the early sixties. These were the final years of glory and steady prosperity for Persian Gulf seamen, however, because the trade and shipping boom in the Gulf collapsed with the end of the American Civil War and the reappearance of United States-grown cotton on the world market. With the end of the boom Gulf trade from 1865 and 1868 dipped to nearly half of its 1864 totals.[16]

Local shipping was one of the first victims of the recession. With the coming of the recession, British steamers slashed their freight rates, an action which helped to revive Gulf commerce by 1869 because local merchants could afford to trade in the Indian market again. Meanwhile, however, numbers of Gulf captains had abandoned their ships and businesses during the recession because they could not compete with the cut-rate steamer freight rates and there was not enough carrying trade available for both the steamers (which had increased their Persian Gulf sailings to twice a month in 1866) and local sailing ships. Therefore, when trade in the Gulf began to revive it was the dependable steamer service that profited from the recovery. After 1865 local shipping could no longer compete seriously against the steamers on the ancient and vital India–Gulf trade routes and increasingly the dhows were relegated to minor coasting operations, irregular ocean voyages, or illicit trade including smuggling.[17]

Despite the leveling off of trade in the Gulf after the economic recovery of 1868–69 steamer service there continued to grow during the late nineteenth century. Table 1 illustrates the steady increase in steamer sailings to the Gulf from 1862 until 1904 and also indicates the continuing domination of this service by British interests. Although several other countries op-

---

[16] "Pelly to Anderson, 23 Aug. 1864, no. 41: Residency," *Précis Commerce*, pp. 27-28; "Pelly to Gonne, 25 Apr. 1870, no. 86-34: Residency," *ibid.*, pp. 35-37.

[17] *Ibid.*, pp. 32, 37-38; *Admin. Rpt.: 1877-1878*, p. 129; Lorimer, I, 2,319-32. As late as 1854 only three British ships sailed from Bombay to Bushire.

erated occasional vessels in the Gulf and some even established special Gulf services, they were unsuccessful in challenging Britain's near monopoly of steam freight and passenger service until the 1906–14 period when the Hamburg–Amerika Line offered serious competition. By 1897, 84 percent of the steamers entering and clearing Gulf ports were under British registration. Most of them flew the house flag of the British India Steam Navigation Company. It is also true that, with the very large exception of the oil tanker trade, the British India Line continues today to be a major carrier of cargo and passengers in the Gulf. By the start of the twentieth century practically every port of size in the region was visited periodically by steamers. Most of these sailed from Bombay, a smaller number from other Indian and Indian Ocean ports, but an increasing total arrived directly from Europe—especially between 1890 and 1912 when the importation and smuggling of arms into Persian Gulf ports was a large factor in local commerce. The steamer business in the Gulf was intensely competitive largely because of the limited trade potential in the market served. Freight rates fluctuated rather violently at times, although there was a general fall in the rates throughout the later nineteenth century. This situation may have worked to the advantage of local Gulf merchants but on the other hand it helped to undermine both the competitive position of local mariners as well as the prospects of weakly established steamer lines that tried to break into the Persian Gulf trade.[18]

Besides the local shipping industry, another citadel of the Gulf's traditional economic structure that fell before the revolutionary changes of the 1860s was the entrepôt system. Before 1862, Masqat had been unquestionably the most important center of Gulf trade. But the decade 1862 to 1872 witnessed the demise of the ancient entrepôt system, by which one port controlled the region's commerce; consequently, Masqat declined rapidly as a port and business center. The introduction of

---

[18] Hurewitz, *Diplomacy*, I, 227ff.; *Admin. Rpt.: 1881-1882*, p. 21; *Admin. Rpt.: 1882-1883*, pp. 18-21.

Early Economic–Technological Modernization

TABLE 1

Development of Steamer Service in the Persian Gulf, 1862-1904

YEAR	COMPANY	REGISTRY	SERVICE	HOME PORT
1862	British India	U.K.	eight annual voyages	Bombay
1866	British India	U.K.	twice each month	Bombay
1868	British India	U.K.	fortnightly	Bombay
1869-79	Persian Mail	U.K.	irregular	Bombay
1870	Bombay & Persia	U.K.	irregular	Bombay
1870	Oman & Ottoman	Ottm.	irregular	Istanbul
1870	Anglo-Arabian & Persian Gulf	U.K.	monthly by 1879	London
1874	British India	U.K.	weekly	Bombay
1883-85	Messageries Maritime	Fr.	irregular	Marseilles
1896-97	Messageries Maritime	Fr.	monthly	Bombay
1901	Russian Gulf & Persian	Rsn.	monthly	Odessa
1904	British India	U.K.	weekly, fast and slow services	Bombay

Note: Compiled from *Admin. Rpts: 1876-1901*; Lorimer, 1, 2,468-69.

steamers was the basic cause of this decline, although the process was intensified by the varied consequences of the political division of the Omani state in 1861 into an African sultanate with its capital at Zanzibar and an Arabian sultanate with its capital at Masqat. The traditional marine technology upon which Oman's maritime importance had been founded was obviously obsolete after 1862; Omani seamen had neither the knowledge, the capital, or the organization to shift over to the use of steamers. Not only did the steamships take business away from Omani seamen but also the position of Masqat as an entrepôt for Persian Gulf trade was undermined as the steamers began sailing from India directly to all the larger Persian Gulf ports. Thus, the foundation of Masqat's prosperity and much of her business was destroyed when the port was in effect bypassed. Masqat's wealth and importance had been based largely on the fact that she was a trans-shipment point where goods were transferred to vessels bound to and from other Gulf and western Indian Ocean ports; relatively little trade originated in strictly Omani commerce.[19]

Concurrent with the fall of the entrepôt system was the rise of other Gulf harbors as steamer ports of call. None of the new steamer ports achieved anything like the commercial dominance in the area enjoyed by pre-1862 Masqat. Until World War I probably the most important of the growing steamer ports was Bushire, the gateway to the south-central interior of Iran and the seat of the British Persian Gulf residency. For a time Bandar 'Abbas on the southern Iranian coast of the straits of Hormuz showed some signs of becoming an exchange hub for a large expanse of south-central Asia but the port declined in the 1890s after which it served only the trade of southeast Iran. This occurrence was due in large part to changes in central Asia's political climate. Russia's annexation of central Asia quite naturally was followed by a large increase in the volume of Russian goods imported into that area, as well as by the penetration of Russian products into northern and eastern Iran. These were both situations which curtailed the import of British goods via Bandar 'Abbas. Finally, the completion of the Quetta–Sijistan railroad in the 1890s provided an alternate route from India into eastern Iran, Baluchistan, and Afghanistan. Another port on the Iranian coast that enjoyed a limited period of prosperity was Lingah, which became for a few decades a trans-shipment center for traffic to and from Bahrain and the various Trucial Coast ports. After 1902, however, Lingah declined, because of trade-suffocating customs restrictions imposed by the Iranian government, a situation which also contributed to Bandar 'Abbas's troubles. As a result, the steamers began direct though irregular service to both the Trucial Coast and Bahrain. Basra in Iraq, after a dip during the first half of the nineteenth century, recovered as a port under the double stimulus of the introduction of river steamers in Iraq in 1861 and the start of the British India Line steamer

[19] "Pelly to Anderson, 23 Aug. 1864, no. 41: Residency," *Précis Commerce*, pp. 27-29.

calls in 1862. Another growing port of the upper Gulf in the late nineteenth century was Muhammarah (Khurramshahr), situated near the confluence of the Shatt al-Arab and the Karun. Muhammarah profited from the opening of steamer routes on the Karun River in 1888 and the building of the "Lynch Road" between the Karun port of Ahwaz and Isfahan in 1900. The city attracted an increasing volume of trade until it became for a time after World War I the Gulf's leading port. Kuwait, the doorway to central Arabia, by 1900 had become the principal haven for what remained of the Persian Gulf's long-distance dhow fleet, but it was only an occasional steamer port at that time.[20]

One more legacy of the economic upheaval of 1862–72 was the capture of most of the business activity in the Gulf cities by Indian merchants. The Indians had for hundreds of years been important cogs in the region's economic machinery but they gained a near monopoly of local commercial leadership after the 1860s. The Arab and Persian merchants were too enmeshed in the Gulf's pre-1862 system of distribution, lacking the knowledge, resources, and flexibility to cope with the new situation. The Indians, on the other hand, through their commercial connections with the subcontinent and their access to credit sources there, were able to weather the initial storm and then were quick to seize advantages afforded by the modernization of business methods and communications. In essence, the Indians became intermediaries between the Gulf Arabs and the Europeans who were modernizing India itself and who were the ultimate directors of the world's commerce.

The steamship was not the only innovation in communications to come to the Gulf in the 1860s, since telegraphic communication was introduced during the decade. The building of overland and undersea telegraph lines was one concrete accomplishment whose inspiration derived from the 1830–50s Euphrates communications schemes. Their construction in the

[20] Anstey, *Trade*, pp. 24-25; *Précis Commerce*, pp. 44-57; *Admin. Rpt.: 1900-1901*, pp. 98-99.

1860s in the wake of the Indian Mutiny assured the quick transfer of information between Britain, Europe, and India just as the Suez Canal guaranteed the rapid passage of passengers, troops, and freight. There were two phases in the building of the India–Europe telegraph, the political negotiations that preceded the lines and the actual construction.

The first attempt to connect India and Europe by telegraph was made in 1859–60 by the "Telegraph to India Company," which tried to lay an undersea cable along a route passing through the Red Sea and the Arabian Sea to India, with stations at Aden, the Kuria Muria Islands, Masqat, and Monze (near Karachi). Unfortunately, neither the technical competence nor the finances of the company were equal to the task, and after numerous cable breaks the concern failed. Nevertheless, the British government, convinced of the need for the Indo-European telegraph, decided to try another route that would utilize a combination land and undersea line. The most feasible path for such a line ran through the Persian Gulf. Between 1861 and 1865 negotiations were carried out between Britain and the various governments and chieftains through whose territory the telegraph would have to pass. Agreements were eventually signed with the Ottoman, Omani, and Iranian governments, while an additional group of treaties were concluded with the petty chieftains of the coasts of Makran and Baluchistan. Usually in these agreements British subsidy payments were granted to the minor princelings in return for their promise to provide labor and armed protection for the lines passing through their territories. Ultimately, British political control was extended into Baluchistan partly to guarantee the security of overland portions of the telegraph system. British political interests in the Persian Gulf generally were stimulated by the construction there of a major artery of imperial communication.

Most of the actual building of the various lines in the Gulf was accomplished between 1863 and 1865. These links joined an existing Ottoman line at Baghdad which in turn was tied to the expanding European network by way of Istanbul. By 1865, Teheran and other Iranian cities were bound to the Indo–European system via connections at Bushire and Baghdad. These Iranian lines were eventually extended to Europe by way of the Russian telegraph network.

Although the Indo–European Telegraph's primary importance was to bind the British Empire closer together it also had its effects on purely Persian Gulf affairs. The policy of Britain's residents in the Gulf was more tightly supervised by their superiors in India. Also, in Iran the Qajar government's hold over the empire—including the previously lightly administered Iranian ports on the Gulf coast—was strengthened. On the Arabian side of the Gulf there were no permanent telegraph facilities until the laying of the Jask–Masqat cable in 1901, so the rulers of the region's Arabian states could not rely upon such facilities to aid in the control of their realms. On the other hand, Gulf merchants, notably the Indians, employed the new means of communication to conduct business activities that could benefit particularly from speed.[21]

Another innovation in Gulf communications, an outgrowth of the expansion of steamer traffic, was the establishment of a postal service. Before 1862 a letter sent from Baghdad to India ordinarily went by way of Syria, Egypt, and then by ship across the Red and Arabian Seas. Often mail bound for India from Bushire would be sent by the same route after first being dispatched to Baghdad via Teheran. This situation existed because of the infrequency, irregularity, but mainly the unreliability of sailings between India and the Gulf before the period of scheduled steamer sailings. Naturally, it took letters several months at least to travel in such a manner. After 1864, how-

[21] The most complete account of the construction of the Indo-European telegraph is Sir F. J. Goldsmid, *Telegraph and Travel, a Narrative of the Formation and Development of Telegraphic Communication between England and India* (London, 1874). See too *Précis Commerce*, pp. 27, 67-68; Wilson, *Persian Gulf*, pp. 266-69; *Précis Makran, Précis Persian Coast.* For telegraph treaties see Aitchison–1892, IX, 74, 394-95, 401-406, X, 76, 80-93, 137, XI, 26-30.

ever, the British Indian government established and operated post offices in conjunction with existing diplomatic stations such as those as Masqat, Bushire, and Basra. The new postal service reduced the time it took for a letter to travel between the Gulf and India to a matter of a few weeks. During the late nineteenth century this Anglo–Indian postal system was the sole organized mail service in the Gulf; like the telegraph it had its political and economic repercussions.[22]

It has been asserted that despite a growth in the total trade of the Gulf between 1862 and 1872 the most revolutionary of the events of that decade was the overturning of the established system of economic organization in the Gulf. The destruction of the entrepôt system, the decline of Masqat, and the dislocation of the local shipping industry were products of this revolution. Unfortunately for the region, the start of a new era in its history was not accompanied by a general and sustained quickening of its economic life. Originally, it had been supposed by men such as Frere and Pelly that the economic revolution of the 1860s would be the overture to a long period of comprehensive, rapid economic development and modernization. Pelly, when he predicted such an eventuality, presumed that the countries surrounding the Gulf would be eager and able to adopt Western technology and procedures. He had little appreciation of the complex and interrelated circumstances operating in the area that would frustrate the realization of his vision. Most of all, he was not aware that most of the Gulf's inhabitants had no particular wish to embrace modern life and that, indeed, they preferred holding on to as much as they could of their familiar and customary values, attitudes, and modes of action.

Economic stagnation: 1872–1914. Unfortunately for all concerned, the economic development of the Gulf region was neither rapid nor comprehensive during the years between 1872 and World War I; certainly the hopes of 1862–72 were not realized. In fact, with a few exceptions, practically every

[22] Lorimer, I, 238; Wilson, *Persian Gulf*, pp. 264-66.

quarter of the Gulf endured a prolonged period of economic stagnation or even decline down to World War I, a situation that continued through World War II and even to our own day in these parts not touched by the myriad results of oil exploitation. The unsettled political climate of the late nineteenth century in the lands surrounding the Persian Gulf certainly contributed to this situation. Internal dislocation or political uncertainty was the rule in interior Arabia which was the scene of bitter strife among tribes and particularly between the Sa'udis and the forces of Ibn-Rashid. The attitude and ineffectiveness of the Ottoman authorities discouraged foreign investment in Iraq. Iran, where over half the Gulf's trade was concentrated, was vexed by the demoralizing results of rule by a weak yet corrupt and grasping central government coupled with near anarchy in tribal and rural areas. Complicating the entire picture was the presence and growth of European imperial interest in the Gulf and the countries surrounding it. In Iran, for instance, British and Russian political rivalry seriously compounded the economic ills of the Qajar empire. Neither power wanted the other to establish its preponderance in Persia. Hence, they continually blocked each other's schemes to open up trade routes or to develop mineral rights. This went so far that in 1890, because of fears that a rival might gain an advantage, the two powers decided that they would block the building of any long-distance railroads in Iran.[23] The chief loser in their game was of course Iran, while the potential growth of Persian Gulf trade, too, was discouraged by such machinations. An example of what improvements in communications could have meant to the development of the entire Gulf region is afforded by the picture of the rise of Muhammarah as a prosperous port after steamer service started in 1888 on the Karun river. Certainly, the low capacity and the lack of improvements on the trade routes connecting Gulf ports with the hinterland impeded the growth of commerce

[23] Hurewitz, *Diplomacy*, I, 207.

and was one basic reason for the region's disappointing economic posture after 1872.

It has been stated that the estimated value of the seaborne long-distance commerce of the Gulf was approximately £5,000,000 in 1866. By 1869, after the recovery from the 1865–68 trade recession, the region's long-distance trade was valued at £6,000,000. There is proof of the general stagnation of Gulf trade and economic life in the fact that in 1899 the total value of the area's long-distance commerce still hovered around the £6,000,000 mark.[24] The continued expansion of steamer service to the Gulf during the late nineteenth century in some ways only made the situation worse. By the early 1880s British and other European steamships were saturating the Gulf with imports. In 1883 goods were piled up in Iranian ports waiting their turn to be transported over the primitive caravan routes into the interior. Naturally, such glutted situations stimulated periodic slides in prices.[25] In the 1890s the notation, "the year under review has not been a favourable one for trade operations," is often encountered in official British governmental reviews of Persian Gulf trade.

Between 1872 and 1902 the total trade of Iran, south central Asia, Iraq, eastern Anatolia, and eastern Arabia—all areas served at one time or another by Persian Gulf ports—steadily if unspectacularly increased, but the Gulf's share of this trade did not rise appreciably. In 1890, for instance, Russia and Great Britain each controlled about 40 percent of Iran's foreign trade, whereas on the eve of World War I Russia's share of this commerce amounted to 60 percent, while Britain's part was only 21 percent. The fact that practically all British trade with Iran was conducted via the Persian Gulf, that the value of Gulf commerce was fairly constant throughout the period, but that this Gulf-directed trade figured as a significantly smaller percentage of Iran's total foreign trade in 1914 than in 1890 indicates that in a relative sense the Gulf's economic activity not only was stagnating but was declining. Certainly,

24 *Ibid.*, pp. 227ff.
25 *Admin. Rpt.: 1881-1882*, p. 21; *Admin. Rpt.: 1882-1883*, pp. 18-21.

there was some economic expansion in Iran's interior but a decreasing share of the enlarged trade filtered through Gulf ports. With the exception of occasional uncertain periods of localized prosperity due to causes such as unusual date, grain, or pearl harvests, or an extraordinary demand for commodities such as arms or gold, it was not until the coming of the oil era on the eve of World War I that trade really began to revive in the region.[26]

Although a few local ports and indigenous groups benefited from the upheaval that accompanied the change in the Gulf's economic situation the end of the old maritime and commercial system was not compensated for by the growth of other more modernly oriented economic activities. Neither large-scale plantations nor extensive mineral extraction activities, both of which were the foundation of much modernization in tropical and subtropical regions during the late nineteenth century, were initiated in the Gulf before the oil era. Whatever modern technology there was operating in the region during the period—the steamship and the telegraph mainly—was under the direction of Europeans. However, a number of prerequisites were established between 1862 and 1914 that would influence the course of future, more constructive modernization in the region, a movement that began when the local oil resources began to be exploited just before World War I. The old order, dominated by one great regional trade entrepôt and by the movements and calculations of Arab seamen and merchants, was destroyed and the Gulf was reduced to the status of a dependency of Western, notably British, business interests. Many of these generalizations will be more specifically treated in the next chapter where the changes that took place in the economic structure of Oman during the late nineteenth century will be reviewed.

[26] Anstey, *Trade*, pp. 22-24; Iran, Ministry of Customs and Posts, *Tableau Général de Commerce avec les Pays Étrangers* (Teheran, 1902); H. Sotoudeh, *L'Evolution Economique de l'Iran et ses Problèmes* (Paris 1936). The best picture of the sluggish commercial climate in the Persian Gulf during the late nineteenth century is afforded by an investigation of the various *Admin. Rpts.*: 1876 to 1904, and *Précis Commerce*.

CHAPTER 4

Economic Change in Oman During the Late Nineteenth Century

THE disruptive impact of early economic and technological modernization in the Persian Gulf can be observed in microcosm by events in Oman in the late nineteenth century. During that period, although Oman and the rest of the Persian Gulf area endured a situation of profound economic change, the country did not experience any significant economic development. Nowhere in the Persian Gulf did the economic movements of the late nineteenth century have more disturbing results than in Oman. The intrusion of modern communications in particular destroyed the established economic environment of the country's coast. Even in the midst of the cotton boom of the early 1860s, while the rest of the Gulf was prospering, Oman plummeted into a depression from which it has yet to recover. From its ancient place of economic and commercial importance in the western Indian Ocean, Oman dropped into insignificance within the span of a few years. Now that commercial deposits of oil have been discovered in Oman and plans have been set in motion to exploit this rich find, the country undoubtedly will regain some measure of its old prosperity and importance. But until the economic development that inevitably accompanies the exploitation of a large oil field begins to transform Oman, the country will exist as a prime example of a locale which has suffered but has not benefited from the effects of modernization.

THE OMANI ECONOMY IN 1856

It was stated earlier in this work that the details of Omani life and history have often reflected the tension between various elements of unity and diversity which have alternately separated or united the country's interior and coastal sections. This condition of tension, unity, and diversity certainly characterized the Omani economy at the time of Sayyid Sa'id's death. In a very real sense there were two subeconomies operating within Oman at that time, one in the interior and one in the coastal regions centered around the port of Masqat. The economy of Masqat and her dependent seaports and coastal areas was to change radically as a result of the spread of modern technology and economic enterprises in the Persian Gulf during the years after 1862. The economy of Oman's interior, however, was to remain relatively unaffected by the new situation.

In the interior, economic activity in 1856 was conditioned by a number of factors which had combined to produce a self-sufficient agricultural economy geared to the sharing of what was viewed as a constant but very scarce supply of commodities. The geographic barriers—the Hajar mountains and the Rub' al-Khali, chiefly—that isolate interior Oman discouraged the development of outward-looking economic responses and imposed formidable boundaries on the world view of interior Oman's inhabitants. The mobility of the region's people was severely restricted by these geographic barriers and by poor communications dictating that practically all trade between Oman's coast and the interior depend on camel caravans. The interior populace's restricted view of the world was reinforced by the conservative ideology that was supreme in the locale. There a highly static society organized to preserve a fundamentalist, conservative Ibadi environment held sway. There was a general consensus in the area that life's activities were better directed toward achieving eternal salvation than toward acquiring worldly goods or enjoying worldly pleasures. An interior Omani's idea of wealth was limited to such things as the number of date palm trees, camels, goats, wives, or slaves a man might possess. Even these material belongings would have to rank behind the spiritual virtues and knowledge of the Koran and Ibadi law in the hierarchy of desired possessions; ostentatious display was, of course, forbidden. Consequently, most of the creative energy of Oman's interior dwellers was devoted to spiritual, local political, and family affairs. The energy devoted to economic enterprise was primarily restricted to occasional trips to local markets, or to even rarer trips to the emporiums of Masqat in search of those necessities which could not be produced in the immediate vicinity. Moreover, the tribal shaykhs and other leaders of Oman's interior, although they would go to great lengths to enhance their tribes' political prestige and at times would pledge their swords to uphold the Ibadi faith, would seldom move to advance anything but the most necessary economic ventures. The conservative Ibadi tradition had much to say about assuring an equitable distribution of goods but it was silent on the subject of how to correct a situation of chronic scarcity. Economic activity in Oman's interior was viewed more as a means to sustain life, learning, and spiritual contemplation than as an end in itself. The contrast of this situation with that which characterized economic activity in coastal Masqat and her dependent seaports and coastal areas was striking.

The coastal economy was governed by more complex requirements than those that influenced the economic practices characteristic of Oman's inland provinces. The fact that the waters of the Gulf of Oman were a highway linking Masqat and Oman's other ports to the various Indian Ocean countries meant that coastal Omanis had many opportunities to trade and to observe other peoples and civilizations. The coastal Omani often considered the entire western Indian Ocean his world; his vision was not restricted by the rim rocks of a narrow mountain valley as was so often the case with an inhabitant of Oman's interior. In terms of his marine technology the coastal Omani of 1856 enjoyed a high degree of mobility. When the wind was fair he could sail from Zanzibar to Masqat in two weeks, or from Masqat to Aden or Masqat to Bombay in 12 days. Because of coastal Oman's intimate ties with India, events there often influenced happenings in Oman—especially economic events. In contrast to the inward directed agricultural subsistence economy of the interior, Oman's coastal economy in 1856 was one oriented toward competitive, long-distance commerce and entrepôt exchange; it was a middleman economy whose health depended on the transfer of goods produced or procurable in one part of the Indian Ocean basin to other areas bordering that same ocean.

Socially, Masqat nurtured a relatively open society geared to business activity. The city attracted and tolerated not only local Ibadi merchants and seamen but also Hindu traders, Jewish artisans, Baluchi laborers, and Shi'ah Persian salesmen and craftsmen. Still, Masqat was an Omani city and therefore an Ibadi city. Ibadism in Masqat, as in the rest of Oman, was a conservative force, albeit on the coast it was a creed moderated by foreign influences. Ibadi Masqatis in 1856 clung to narrow and traditional ideas concerning science and the nature of the world; they generally acknowledged the same religious authorities as did Oman's interior dwellers. Yet there seemed to be a certain tension and lack of consensus among coastal dwellers caused by the clash between Ibadi exclusivism and the practical concerns of running a society dependent on commercial activity and foreign trade. Consequently, the Ibadism practiced in Masqat was modified to the extent that it tried to accommodate two spheres of action, a spiritual sphere and a practical, worldly sphere. In the interior these two spheres meshed well because the primacy of spiritual values was generally recognized. On the coast the problems of accommodating materialistic concerns with a puritan faith caused difficulty.

The coastal dweller's concept of wealth was more all embracing than that of his cousin in the mountains. Date palm trees were considered the safest investment in both areas, but on the coast money, ships, shop inventories, and—among the Indian merchants, at least—connections with overseas trading houses were all considered valuable. Coastal Omanis were not embarrassed by the pursuit or the modest display of wealth.

There was a wide gap between coast and interior in the attitudes displayed in the two sections toward economic enterprise.

On the coast trade and business were respected. Indeed, Sayyid Saʻid, the ruler, was the country's leading capitalist and owned many ships and plantations. The government actively encouraged business to the point of welcoming and protecting the resident foreign merchants who were playing a more and more active role in the country's commerce. By 1856, however, the power of the rulers of Masqat to manipulate or control the economic and political environment of the Persian Gulf to Oman's advantage was declining, due to the rise of British power in the western Indian Ocean. Masqat had risen to commercial greatness in the seventeenth and eighteenth centuries because it was a fiercely competitive state that cannonaded its way to supremacy in the Gulf region. Intense competition to control the available trade was, of course, a major characteristic of traditional Persian Gulf powers. But after the British imposed the maritime peace system in the Gulf in the 1820s the old competitive system had in practice disappeared in the region. This was probably one reason why the energy of so many Omani merchants, including those of Sayyid Saʻid, had shifted toward Zanzibar and Africa after the 1820s; there, the old competitive methods still could be used in the absence of a powerful European presence.

ECONOMIC DEPRESSION AND STAGNATION, 1862–1900

The changes that took place in Oman's economy following the death of Sayyid Saʻid in 1856 occurred mainly in the coastal half of the country. After 1856 the area endured a severe depression which was then followed by a long period of economic stagnation. The rapidity of the decline of coastal Oman's economic strength and importance was due to a combination of causes.

Not the least of these were the political troubles that came to Oman after 1856. First, a ruinous war of succession among Saʻid's heirs threatened to bring disorder to all parts of the Omani empire. The danger of war evaporated only after the British in 1861 arranged a partition of the domain left by

Sa'id into an independent Asiatic sultanate with its capital
at Masqat and an independent African sultanate ruled from
Zanzibar. But the cure imposed by the British–Indian government in many ways was worse than the disease, for it broke
apart a state one British observer somewhat condescendingly
described as "a first-rate Asiatic maritime power," smashed
that power's economic as well as its political unity, and contributed to the choking off of much of the active trade of her
seafarers. Pelly noted that partition was second only to the
introduction of steamers as a cause for the economic depression
that hit Oman full force in the 1860s. The culmination of the
political disturbances which proved so destructive to Oman's
economic health was the capture of Masqat by conservative
fundamentalist Ibadis from Oman's interior. Their attempts
to recreate a medieval-style imamate at Masqat between 1868
and 1871 only aggravated the country's economic plight. The
zeal of the fundamentalists in enforcing the outward observ-
ances of Ibadi piety ignored the tolerant social arrangements
necessary in a port city and damaged Masqat's remaining trade
to the extent that it was feared that the city would become "a
mere fishing village."[1] During the period of conservative Ibadi
dominance in Masqat even the Indian merchants who enjoyed
British protection were in dire straits. Many began removing
their specie and goods; there were instances of some merchants
who had lived in Masqat for decades quitting the city for other
ports. The owner of the ship, *Calcutta Merchant,* an Indian
whose family had lived in Masqat for 50 years, put his house-
hold aboard his ship and moved his business to Zanzibar.
Other Indians, less wealthy or with their assets tied up in real
estate or shop inventories, could not afford to abandon their
property and appealed to the British government to intervene
against the "fanatics" from the hills who were ruining their
livelihoods. In 1871, when the moderate Sultan Turki drove

[1] "Disbrowe to Gonne, 9 Dec. 1869, no. 297: Masqat," India Records–2,
Vol. L.

the conservatives out of Masqat, the city returned to its traditional policy of fostering trade.[2]

But the economic climate of the western Indian Ocean and the Persian Gulf had changed radically during the 1860s. It seems clear no amount of encouragement by any Masqati government could have brought back the vanished trade. With the success of the steamers in the early 1860s and the opening of the Suez Canal in 1869 the concept of a central entrepôt for Persian Gulf trade was out of date. Thenceforth Masqat would have to be content with being only one of many Persian Gulf steamer ports. Even the shipping that remained to the port declined in time in the face of the overwhelming competition from steamers. As early as 1864 it was reported that little business was left for Masqati shippers except the export to India of salt from the Bandar 'Abbas districts, and dates from Oman. The loss of trade cut the customs revenues so important to the Masqati sultan, and the sultan only quickened the city's ruin by raising customs duties in an effort to make up his lost income. During the 1860s shipping fled Masqat, some captains moving to Sur to enjoy the relative freedom of trade available there.[3] By 1868 Masqat was described as "about half deserted" and "declining further still."[4] Between its political problems, the competition of steamers with Masqati shipping, and the decline of the port's entrepôt trade, Masqat plunged into a deep depression during the 1860s.

The decline of shipping and maritime activity. As has been emphasized, the shipping industry had been the keystone of Oman's coastal economy for thousands of years prior to the 1860s. Omani seamen, pioneers of the route to China in the Middle Ages, were the cement of a maritime empire in the eighteenth and nineteenth centuries. In medieval and early

[2] "Disbrowe to Gonne, 21 Aug. 1869, no. 464: Masqat," "25 Nov. 1869, No. 683: Masqat," India Records-2, Vol. L.

[3] "Pelly to Anderson, 16 Feb. 1862," "23 Aug. 1864, no. 41: Residency," *Précis Int'l Rivalry*, p. 27.

[4] "Atkinson to Gonne, 17 Sept. 1868, no. 412: Masqat," India Records-2, Vol. L.

modern times the technology of Oman included some of the most advanced maritime know-how in the world, but by 1800 its naval technology had long since ceased to develop. Consequently, the appearance of revolutionary steam-powered ships in the mid-nineteenth century found the Omanis unable to meet the challenge; Oman's shipping industry was ruined as a result. In the seventeenth century the Omanis had copied Western marine technology but Oman's seamen were not equal to learning the secrets of operating nineteenth century machine-driven steamers.

The problems facing Omani shipping in the 1860s were similar to those faced by other Persian Gulf shipowners during the period. As has been stated, because of the economic activity stimulated by the simultaneous arrival of steamers and the cotton boom in the Gulf there was enough business for both local ships and the steamers during the early sixties. However, increased economic activity also stimulated a rise in the general level of prices around the Gulf that lasted through 1869. This inevitably raised operating costs for local shippers. When the cotton boom played out in 1865 the combination of high operating costs, less available business, and decreased need for shipping prompted many local captains to sell off, beach, or abandon their ships. The steamers, however, were not so dependent on Persian Gulf price levels as were local ship operators; they countered the post-1865 recession by dropping their freight rates, a move which led local merchants to shift their business to the steamers and which helped to revive Gulf commerce by 1869. So successful was this tactic that the steamers actually increased their sailings to the Gulf in 1866. Local shippers, however, did not have the strength to endure both four years of recession and the competition of low cost, dependable steamers. So even in the fairly prosperous if agitated 1860s, when there was an overall rise in economic activity in the Persian Gulf, most of the profits to be made in shipping were taken by the steamers and there was a decrease in local shipping. Masqati shipping interests, coping as they were with

Economic Change in Oman

serious political problems as well as with the competition of steamers, were particularly hard hit.[5]

The ruin of the country's hitherto considerable navy also contributed to the decline of Omani maritime power in the 1860s. After Sayyid Sa'id's death in 1856 most of the navy was anchored at Zanzibar, a situation formalized in 1861 as part of the arbitration award that divided the Omani empire. Even those ships remaining in Masqat were sold during the 1860s, so the decade closed with Oman no longer possessing a navy of any consequence. This was significant economically as well as politically because Sayyid Sa'id had used his navy for merchant as well as military activity, and he was the leading shipowner of his realm. In the 1860s the Omani state, which for 150 years had been a major factor in the Persian Gulf's carrying trade and maritime enterprise, abandoned the shipping business. Due more to political than to economic circumstances, this development was nonetheless one more factor in the decline of Oman as an important maritime state.[6]

During the years 1868 to 1871, when a conservative Ibadi imam ruled at Masqat, a number of shipowners fled the port. In 1870, however, the puritanical measures of the conservatives were relaxed and trade in Masqat began to revive.[7] This revival was encouraged further by the restoration of the moderate sultanate in Masqat. In 1871 16 large ships, some of them old

[5] *Précis Commerce*, pp. 32-37.

[6] For the fate of Sayyid Sa'id's navy see Rigby, "Report on Zanzibar," *Records of the Bombay Government*, no. LIX (1861), pp. 18-19. "Disbrowe to Gonne, 4 Mar. 1869, no. 139: Mascat," India Records–2, Vol. L. Lorimer, I, 469, also has information concerning the Masqati government's withdrawal from shipping activity. In addition to his 15-warship navy, Sayyid Sa'id also owned 20 ships engaged in private trade; the profits from the sovereign's shipping business might benefit the government exchequer since there was no distinction between the public and private income of the ruler. Sir J. C. R. Columb, *Slave Catching in the Indian Ocean* (London, 1873), p. 117, states that the last of Sayyid Sa'id's navy was sunk in a cyclone at Zanzibar in 1872.

[7] "Pelly to Duke of Argyll. 7 May 1870, despatch no. 147-2: Residency," India Records–2, Vol. L.

British or American-built clippers, belonged to the port.[8] But by 1876, the difficulty of keeping old ships in seaworthy condition and the relentless competition of the steamers dictated that only six large ships continued to sail from Masqat; in succeeding years only one or two large vessels operated from the port. The last of the large ships, the Masqati clipper, *County of Forfa,* disappeared on a grain run to Calcutta in 1901. It is interesting that most of these large vessels were purchased originally from European shipping firms who were about to scrap them.[9]

By 1878 the shipping revival of the early 1870s ended in Masqat and native shipping of all types clearing the port dropped steadily from a total of 999 in 1875–76 to 716 in 1878–79 to 374 in 1893–94 to 238 in 1895–96.[10] Table 2 illustrates this steady decline in local Masqati shipping activity during the late nineteenth century and shows the coincident rise in the visits of European ships, especially steamers, to the port during the same period. For 1895 the total tonnage of steamers entering Masqat harbor was 194,000 tons, whereas the total tonnage of local Arab shipping was only 24,900 tons.[11] It is obvious that during the late nineteenth century European ships captured the bulk of the carrying trade once controlled by Omani mariners, that the number of Omani ships in operation dropped precipitously (for all Omani ports experienced drops), and that native shipping became insignificant except in local and coasting activity. This was a far cry from the Oman of the 1840s, with her 14 very large ships, at least 200 seagoing vessels of good size, and several hundred fishing boats of 50 tons burden owned in the Masqat region alone. Masqati-owned ships carried over half of the trade of the Persian Gulf as late as 1854 according to some Western observers.[12]

Between 1874 and 1894 there was a rise in total tonnage

---

[8] *Admin. Rpt.: 1876-1877*, p. 81.
[9] *Ibid.; Admin. Rpt.: 1901-1902*, p. 9; Lorimer, I, 2,319-32.
[10] *Précis Commerce*, p. 220; *Admin. Rpt.: 1895-1896*, p. 52.
[11] *Précis Commerce*, p. 221; *Admin. Rpt.: 1895-1896*, p. 52.
[12] *Bombay Records—1856*, pp. 631-32; Osgood, *Notes*, pp. 76, 82-83.

TABLE 2

Vessels Entering and Leaving Masqat, 1874-94

WESTERN VESSELS

Classification or destination	1874-75	1875-76	1876-77	1877-78	1878-79	1879-80	1880-81	1881-82	1882-83	1883-84	1884-85	1885-86	1886-87	1887-88	1888-89	1889-90	1890-91	1891-92	1892-93	1893-94
American	4	5	5	5	4	3	3	3	3	5	3	1	1					1		1
Coal Ships	1			3	1	1	1	1		3		1	3	1		2	3		2	
India	18	12	18	22	17	27	20	22	11	7	7	9	10	15	16	13	12	13	11	13
London Stmrs.										3			1	3	2	1		1	2	2
B.I.S.N. Co. Stmrs.	81	81	54	52	58	73	73	81	84	72	79	74	74	74	77	60	61	62	65	65
French Stmrs.										11	14	8	2	1					1	
Mauritius	5	3	8	12	5	5	3	4	1	3	6	3	2	2	1	4	4	1	2	2
Persian Gulf	5	7	13	15	13	6	4	6	4	7	5	4	4	6	10	8	10	6	9	16
Red Sea		1	4	7	3	3	1	1	1	1	3	5	2	2	3	3	3	3	4	5
Singapore	1		3	2	3	5	1	2												
Zanzibar		3	1	3	4	1	2	3	2	5	4	1								
Other Stmrs.	13		3	26	15	12	13	12	9		1		2	4	2	3	3	3	3	2
Total	128	89	107	153	138	136	130	138	99	121	117	107	103	108	111	94	96	90	99	106

ARAB VESSELS

Classification or destination	1874-75	1875-76	1876-77	1877-78	1878-79	1879-80	1880-81	1881-82	1882-83	1883-84	1884-85	1885-86	1886-87	1887-88	1888-89	1889-90	1890-91	1891-92	1892-93	1893-94
India	400	300	450	500	300	250	200	215	141	141	132	148	170	180	199	150	170	150	160	99
Persian Gulf	100	200	95	140	200	200	180	200	150	150	148	125	45	40	50	50	45	40	44	40
Makran	50	150	120	100	200	100	60	55	84	84	80	110	102	90	75	86	85	80	70	75
Yaman	60	200	50	20	40	40	40	40	46	46	37	25	25	30	22	21	20	18	20	34
Zanzibar	40	60	25	30	40	35	20	22	22	22	28	35	30	25	20	18	20	24	20	20
Total	650	910	740	790	780	625	500	532	443	443	423	358	371	365	365	325	340	312	318	268
Total All Vessels	778	999	847	943	918	716	630	670	542	544	560	465	475	473	476	419	436	402	413	374

Note: Compiled from *Précis Commerce*, pp. 219-21.

clearing the ports of the Persian Gulf, yet at the same time there was a drastic drop in the number of local ships. The number of European ships on the Gulf remained fairly constant, but were becoming larger. On the other hand, ships navigated by local sailors during the later nineteenth century were smaller than those used in former times; as early as 1877 it was noticed that the large, European-style square-rigged vessels that still traded between Masqat and India were being replaced by smaller craft.[13]

The disappearance of large sailing vessels and the decrease in number of smaller Arab craft inevitably had disastrous effects on Omani and other regional shipbuilding centers. Early in the nineteenth century "trankis" (large galleys) were encountered in the Gulf but disappeared during the century. Also an increasingly rare sight by the later years of the century were the large dhows called "baghalas." The British naval officer, Lieutenant Wellsted, described one of these ships that he encountered in Masqat harbor in the 1830s as "a huge misshapen vessel, of at least four hundred tons, with a long projecting prow, and an elevated and elaborately carved and ornamented stern, having but a single mast and single sail, the latter spread on a yard one hundred and fifty feet in length, and containing more canvas than the courses of the largest first rates in His Majesty's navy."[14] The ship Wellsted described carried a crew of about 150 men, many of them African Negroes. Other local-style ships could carry 400 men, were 200 feet long by 50 feet wide. By the late nineteenth century, however, the largest ships being built in Oman were of but 100 to 200 tons burden, while craft only 30 feet long and of 10-ton burden were in the largest demand. This underlines the fact that despite their continued practice of embarking on occasional long voyages to Africa and India, Omani seamen were increasingly restricted to short-haul coasting operations. The two centers of ship construction in Oman were Matrah (Masqat's twin port, five miles dis-

13 *Précis Commerce*, pp. 219-22; *Admin. Rpt.: 1877-1878*, p. 129.
14 Wellsted, *Travels in Arabia*, I, 28.

tant) and Sur, the latter even building some ships for export. But by 1900 Kuwait was the major shipbuilding center in the Gulf. Omani shipbuilding continued its slide and today is insignificant. Inevitably, the whole complex of port activities related to shipping and shipbuilding, once important to Oman's coast, suffered with the decline of the shipping industry.[15]

The disappearance of large ships, when it occurred, did not affect directly many Arab ship owners. In the 1860s one result of the concentration of wealth and business in the hands of Indian merchants resident in the Gulf was their increasing ownership of shipping, one of the principal investments open to a Gulf businessman. By the 1870s the large ships registered at Masqat-Matrah were all Indian owned. Arabs remained the sailors and owners of most smaller vessels.[16]

As pointed out, the activities open to Omani shipping after the 1860s were more and more constricted. Although shipments, chiefly of dates and rice, were still made to India, their number dropped sharply. Bombay and Calcutta were replaced by Karachi, a port considerably closer to Oman, as the main terminus of the India–Oman trade still in the hands of Arab captains. As might be expected, the number of voyages by local craft to areas served by steamers decreased. Although Indian traffic declined, harbors in areas such as Makran, where the steamers did not stop, retained their importance as ports of call for Omani ships. By 1900 Omani ships seldom sailed to the Red Sea, and the number of voyages to Zanzibar fell although some illegal slave voyages were made. Illicit trading —slaving, smuggling, and gunrunning, chiefly—became, in fact, a last refuge for many Omani sailors and was a major activity of the seamen of Sur. Coasting voyages, collecting goods at numerous tiny ports and bringing them to steamer ports, was along with fishing the major legitimate maritime activity

[15] Miles, *Countries and Tribes of the Persian Gulf*, II, 412; Lorimer, I, 2,320-26; Hazard, *Eastern Arabia*, p. 326.

[16] Lorimer, I, 1,181-86.

left in Oman by 1900. In 1902 even illegitimate seafaring was struck a hard blow when Portuguese forces surprised, captured, and subsequently destroyed much of the Suri fleet at anchor in a Mozambique cove in the act of loading slaves.

The fact that steamers still called at Masqat, however, meant the port lived on although in a depressed state. After 1874 a British India Steam Navigation Company steamer stopped at Masqat. The Bombay and Persia Steam Navigation Company ships called at irregular intervals, as did the ships of a number of other concerns. The only regular caller direct from Europe was the monthly Anglo–Arabian and Persian steamer which started its calls at Masqat in 1886 and took about four weeks to sail from London. The French operated subsidized steamer services which called at Masqat in the years 1883–85 and 1896–97. The Russians, too, started a short-lived, subsidized Gulf service from Odessa which initiated calls at Masqat in 1901.

The only prosperous Omani ports in the late nineteenth century were those that sheltered smugglers or slavers. Wudam, in 1840 a tiny al-Batinah settlement of palm frond huts with approximately 100 people, by 1900 had become a smuggling center counting 40 seagoing vessels which frequented other Gulf ports, India and the Yemen.[17] More important as a center of illicit commerce was Sur. The Masqati sultans even in their days of relative power never had much control over Sur. After the 1860s, with the virtual disappearance of the sultan's navy, Masqat's hold on the port became almost nonexistent. As seamen flocked there to escape taxes and supervision, Sur became the largest sail port in Oman during the late nineteenth century. Its population of 12,000 made it the largest single city in Oman in 1900, a rank it has since lost to Matrah. At the time over 100 seagoing ships were based at Sur, but even this figure represented a drop from the total of 300 baghalas reportedly operating out of the port in the 1830s. Except in Sur, Wudam, and a few other minor ports, the last 40 years of the nineteenth century were a time of depression on Oman's coast.

[17] *Bombay Records—1856*, p. 627; Lorimer, II, 285-86.

All port activity except for fishing was moribund. The old Arab merchant families retreated to their date palm groves, abandoning most of what was left of the seaports' business to Indian merchants.[18]

The decline of business and prosperity. A major consequence of the decline of Masqat's importance as a shipping center and the ruin of the port's entrepôt trade was a precipitous fall in the city's commercial importance, prosperity, and population. The decade following Sayyid Sa'id's death in 1856 was a terrible one for Masqat and her dependencies. In the 1840s about five-eights of the trade of the Persian Gulf touched at Masqat; by 1874 only one-twelfth passed through the port. That the percentage was no higher in 1900 illustrates the fact that the initial depression was followed by business stagnation.

Trade figures underline the extent of the depression and subsequent sluggishness that crippled the economy of Oman's coast. The total estimated value of Masqat's import and export trade was £1,800,000 in the 1830s. This was no insignificant sum in terms of premodern foreign trade activity in the Middle East; the Ottoman Empire's import–export commerce was valued at £11,000,000 in the mid-nineteenth century.[19] By 1874–75, however, the records of the British consulate at Masqat indicated the port's total trade had dropped to a value of £425,794. Also, the fact that Masqat's trade languished after depression struck is shown in Tables 3, 4, and 5 which list the value of Masqati imports, exports, and total trade. These tables illustrate a situation in which, with the exception of a few interim jumps and dips in trade earnings, the ports' foreign trade was virtually at the same level at the beginning of the twentieth century as in the mid-1870s. During the entire late nineteenth

[18] Wellsted, *Travels in Arabia*, I, 43-44; "Miles to Ross, 15 Sept. 1884, no. 253: Masqat," India Records–3, Vol. VI; *Admin. Rpt.: 1879-1880*, p. 134; Lorimer, II, 1,413-14, 1,847-50.

[19] Wellsted, *Travels in Arabia*, I, 22-24. For an estimate of Ottoman trade see, J. H. A. Ubicini, *Letters on Turkey: an account of the religious, political, social, and commercial condition of the Ottoman empire*, trans. from the French by Lady Easthope (London, 1856), I, 351-52.

century period imports exceeded exports; the difference between the value of imports and exports was undoubtedly made up by loans and by earnings from services such as those provided by shipping, and by such illicit activities as smuggling and gunrunning. Prior to the 1860s a great variety of products, including many fine luxury items, were exchanged in Masqat because of its entrepôt function. In the last quarter of the nineteenth century trading commodities were virtually all staples and necessities: rice, cloth, yarn, sugar, and coffee were the leading imports, while dates, fruit, fish, and pearls were the leading exports. Specie in varying amounts and, in the 1890s and the early twentieth century, arms imports destined to be smuggled into other Asian countries, were also important trade commodities.[20]

During the quarter century 1875 to 1900 the most pronounced drops in the value of Masqati commerce were invariably caused by political upheavals within Oman, which served to discourage exports. 1878, 1884, and 1895 all witnessed these politically instigated dips that occurred when caravan routes connecting Oman's interior with the ports were closed for a time.

The extent of the fall in business activity and prosperity along Oman's coast probably was revealed most dramatically in the marked decline of the country's port cities after 1862. Masqat in the early 1850s was estimated to have a population of 55,000, while the city's twin port, Matrah, numbered anywhere from 8,000 to 20,000 inhabitants, according to various observers.[21] The economic and political disorder that overtook the capital after Sayyid Saʻid's death apparently caused a considerable population flight, and in the early 1860s Masqat's population reportedly hovered slightly above the 40,000

[20] *Précis Commerce*, pp. 182-86, *Admin. Rpts: 1875-1876 to 1902-1903*, passim. The accuracy of Omani trade figures varied up to the 1920s, but the early statistics do indicate general trends.

[21] Osgood, *Notes*, p. 92; Wellsted, *Travels in Arabia*, I, 32.

Economic Change in Oman

TABLE 3
Value of Imports, Masqat, 1874-1903

	VALUE		
	Maria Theresa Dollars	Rupees	Pounds Sterling
1874-75	1,446,515	3,037,681	280,228
1879-80	1,736,300	3,646,230	303,852
1884-85	1,963,025	4,122,352	329,788
1889-90	1,997,726	4,195,224	288,529
1894-95	2,079,600	4,367,160	238,382
1899-1900	2,600,720	3,250,900	216,438
1902-1903	3,205,435	4,006,793	267,119

TABLE 4
Value of Exports, Masqat, 1874-1903

	VALUE		
	Maria Theresa Dollars	Rupees	Pounds Sterling
1874-75	750,400	1,577,940	145,566
1879-80	1,522,175	3,196,567	266,380
1884-85	1,641,555	3,447,265	275,781
1889-90	1,406,605	2,953,870	203,154
1894-95	1,628,580	3,420,018	186,682
1899-1900	1,533,300	1,916,625	127,604
1902-1903	2,506,515	3,133,143	208,876

TABLE 5
Total Value of Imports and Exports, Masqat, 1874-1903

	VALUE			
	Maria Theresa Dollars	Rupees	Pounds Sterling	(Exchange: rps. per £1)
1874-75	2,197,915	4,615,621	425,974	10.84
1879-80	3,258,475	6,842,797	570,232	12.00
1884-85	3,604,580	7,569,617	605,569	12.50
1889-90	3,404,331	7,149,094	491,683	14.54
1894-95	3,708,180	7,787,178	425,064	18.32
1899-1900	4,134,020	5,167,525	344,042	15.02
1902-1903	5,711,950	7,139,936	475,995	15.00

See *Précis Commerce*, pp. 182-86, 212-13; *Admin. Rpts: 1875-1903*, for statistics from which charts were compiled.

mark.[22] The near ruin of the city in the depression of the 1860s was reflected by a sharp drop in the city's permanent population to about 8,000 inhabitants, a figure reached in the 1870s.[23] Today, slightly more than a century after the disaster of the 1860s, Masqat is estimated to have a permanent population of between 5,000 and 6,000, with nearby Matrah a little larger.

The seriousness of Masqat's ordeal was reflected in changes in the city's physical appearance after 1856. In the late 1870s it was reported that the trade, prosperity, and population of Masqat were declining rapidly and the town was falling into ruins, a situation attributed to steamer competition, the demise of the city's entrepôt trade, and political disruptions. The British traveler, Theodore Bent, who visited Masqat in 1895, stated that the once wonderfully supplied bazaars no longer offered much to a curio hunter, that, indeed, a large part of the bazaar was in a ruined or dilapidated condition, and that Matrah had taken over as the commercial capital of Oman.[24]

Matrah in 1900 was a slightly larger place than Masqat, with about 10,000 permanent inhabitants and about 14,000 during seasons of peak employment. It was important because it was the main gateway to interior Oman. The number of ships of 30 to 300 tons using Matrah as home port fell from 50 to 27 during the last 40 years of the nineteenth century, and by 1900 all of them were Indian-owned.[25] Suhar, in 1840 a city of 9,000, and which possessed some 40 seagoing baghalas, by the 1880s had only eight vessels of a size so small that they

[22] W. G. Palgrave, *Narrative of a Year's Journey through Central and Eastern Arabia*, 3rd ed. (London, 1866), II, 369.

[23] Lorimer, II, 1,181-86. Estimating the population of a city such as Masqat always presents difficulties because of the fluctuations caused by seasonal employment and the rise and fall of port activity.

[24] *Admin. Rpt.: 1876-1877*, p. 81; Bent, *Southern Arabia* (London, 1900), pp. 63-68.

[25] *Bombay Records: 1856*, p. 629; Lorimer, II, 1,197-1201. By 1907 Matrah's seagoing fleet had decreased further to seven ships.

were used only to run down the coast to Masqat, plus a few fishing craft left to it; by 1900 the city's population was down to approximately 4,000.[26] Other al-Batinah towns that declined were Barka, Shinas, Sahm, al-Masna'ah and Suwayq, a town reputed to have supplied $MT 20,000 in taxes to Sayyid Sa'id but which afforded only $MT 2,000 to Sa'id's successor in 1904.[27] Some of al-Batinah's smaller hamlets maintained a fairly stable population since they depended on fishing and date palm cultivation rather than trade. It is not certain where the population displaced from the depressed ports migrated. A large percentage of Masqat's population in the years before 1856 were foreigners attracted to the city by its employment opportunities; thus it may be assumed that most of these people returned to their homeland. Native Omanis could always find a welcome in their home villages, and it is certain that there was a steady emigration to Zanzibar going on in the 1860s and 1870s.[28] Only places like Sur, which thrived on illicit commerce, escaped the full effects of the depression, stagnation, and loss of prosperity that vexed Oman's coast during the late nineteenth century.

The currency crisis. But neither Sur nor interior Oman could avoid the repercussions of another misfortune that struck the country between 1870 and 1900. This was a currency and coinage crisis that aggravated the other economic ills suffered by Oman during the period. The currency crisis was created by a long slide in the value of Oman's basic monetary unit, the silver Maria Theresa dollar (also called the German crown) during the last 30 years of the century. Traditionally—and after the 1870s, according to Omani law—the Maria Theresa dollar circulated at "par value," that is, the trade price of

[26] Wellsted, *Travels in Arabia*, I, 229; *Bombay Records—1856*, pp. 625-26; Lorimer, II, 1,828-40; S. W. Zwemer, *Arabia, Cradle of Islam* (New York, 1900), p. 84.

[27] *Bombay Records—1856*, pp. 624-28; Lorimer, II, 265-66, 285-86, 1,645, 1,810, 1,815.

[28] *Admin. Rpt.: 1877-1878*, pp. 126-29.

silver.[29] Also, various types of "bad" or low silver content dollars (a category which included "Basra dollars," debased or broken coins, and "copper" dollars) circulated at reduced value. In other words, Oman's currency was free to rise or fall with the world value of silver.

Because of her intimate commercial connections with India, Masqat's coinage had been unofficially pegged to the Indian rupee since 1835 at the rate of 2.11 rupees to the Maria Theresa dollar although exchange rates often fluctuated rather widely from the pegged figure. There was little difficulty in exchanging dollars for Indian currency because silver bullion could be coined into rupees upon presentation at the Calcutta and Bombay mints. The late nineteenth century, however, was a troublesome time for silver-based currencies all over the world, as witnessed by the fate of the American silver dollar. After 1873 the gold value of all silver currencies the world over began to fall because of a tremendous increase in the world supply of silver. An ounce of silver worth $60\frac{1}{2}$ pence in 1871–72 was valued at only $26\frac{15}{16}$ pence in 1898–99.[30] In the case of India the initial answer to this problem was to issue an excessive amount of rupees—also a silver-based coinage—in an effort to keep up trade payments to Britain whose pound currency based on gold was stable throughout the period. In time, India's inflationary issue of rupees threatened her financial stability and seriously disturbed her trade relationship with Britain. The logical next move for India seemed to be the adoption of a gold standard, if disaster were to be averted. Indeed, what appeared to be the first step toward this solution was taken in 1893 when India's mints were closed to the free coinage of silver in an attempt to reduce the number of rupees in circulation. By 1900, although the gold standard was never actually

[29] "Proclamation of Imam 'Azzan ibn-Qays, enclosure in, Pelly to Duke of Argyll, 14 Jan. 1871, despatch no. 81-7: Residency," India Records–2, Vol. xvii.

[30] B. E. Dadachanji, *The Monetary System of India* (Bombay, 1955?), p. 188; K. N. S. Nambudiripad, *A Short History of Indian Currency* (Poona, 1955), p. 50.

adopted, the decline in rupee value was halted. This stabilization was achieved by converting the rupee into a token coin equal to one shilling fourpence of 15 rupees to a pound sterling.[31]

The coinage of the Persian Gulf had drained eastward toward India for time immemorial; as long as the free coinage of silver was allowed in India this meant currency exchange could go on in the traditional way even if a single dollar brought less after the break in silver prices in 1873. Certainly prices might rise, but this problem was solved by exchanging more silver to cover the price increase. After 1893 and the closing of the Indian mints, however, Oman and other Gulf countries were affected by a serious drain in Indian rupees and copper *pice* (a local low value coin) which could not be replaced. At the same time the fall in silver prices dictated a drop in the value of the Maria Theresa dollar. While only 4.7 Maria Theresa dollars equalled a pound in 1861, it took 11 to equal a pound in 1902. In this situation a serious exchange and coinage shortage developed, particularly in the copper pice used by the poorer classes. It was complicated by the fact that the price of imports and prices generally went higher and higher and at the same time the value of silver fluctuated wildly, albeit in a generally downward direction. This situation in turn led to widespread merchant distress and stimulated ruinous currency speculation. Basically, the trouble revolved around the fact that after 1893 the Maria Theresa dollar occupied the same position vis-à-vis the stabilized rupee that the unstabilized rupee had in relation to the gold pound between 1873 and 1893. The two situations were different in that it was very difficult to replace the drained-off coinage in Masqat once the free minting of silver rupees was halted in India. Consequently, in the 1890s there was not enough coinage to make up the differences in the price of imports which seemed to get

[31] Anstey, *Economic Development of India*, pp. 409-10.

higher and higher as the Maria Theresa dollar fell in value.[32]

Everyone in Oman suffered to some extent because of the currency crisis, and especially so the inhabitants of the coastal towns. Political instability increased as the sultan was forced to borrow extensively to meet normal governmental expenses. The poor were squeezed between a situation of rising prices— one MT dollar to 110 to 130 pice in 1861, while in 1904 an MT dollar was worth anything from 220 to 270 pice—and the physical lack of enough coinage to make necessary purchases. Imports fell since there was not enough coin available to buy at prevailing price levels and there was an unsuccessful effort to increase exports in an attempt to bridge the currency gap. In this monetary climate merchants found it difficult to arrange for credit; conversely, outstanding credits fell in real value. For a time the sultan contemplated banning the export of specie, particularly copper pice, but avoided doing so when he became convinced that such a move would ruin what was left of Masqat's trade. Finally, he began to mint his own copper pice in an effort to make up for the lack of minor Indian coins in circulation, but the effort was not large enough to really dent the coin shortage. Before the MT dollar temporarily revived in 1904 in the wake of rupee stabilization, the sultan considered adopting Indian currency and abandoning Oman's "independent" monetary system.[33]

There are two aspects of the currency crisis of the post-1873 period which should be emphasized. First is the obvious fact that Oman was so tied to world economic movements after 1862 that even minor variations in world money and commodity price levels could affect the well-being of the country's entire population. In previous times, although the country was influenced by world trade trends, Oman's economy was more autonomous, flexible, and better cushioned against sudden shocks. The second aspect of the crisis is that published trade

---

[32] "Frere to Wood, 27 Feb. 1864," India Mss.–1; *Admin. Rpt.: 1893-1894*, p. 43; Lorimer, I, 586; *Précis Maskat*, p. 139.

[33] *Admin. Rpt.: 1894-1895*, p. 18; *Précis Maskat*, pp. 134, 139.

figures concerning Omani trade must be taken with a large grain of salt. In terms of MT dollars, Masqat's trade increased from a total value of $MT 2,197,915 in 1874–75 to $MT 5,711,-350 in 1902–1903. If these figures are converted into pounds sterling, however, Masqati trade, worth £425,794 in 1874–75, was valued at £475,395 in 1902–1903. So, in fact, Masqati trade stagnated, a situation which could not be effectively attacked for many reasons, among which was the late nineteenth century currency and coinage crisis.

The domination of commerce by Indian merchants. The Indian trader was a long established and familiar figure in Persian Gulf and western Indian Ocean cities. At least as early as the dawn of Islam Indian merchants were spread over the Indian Ocean littoral. When Da Gama penetrated the area he encountered thriving colonies of Indians in east Africa. The Indians in the Gulf were almost universally involved in commerce, being divided into two broad categories, Hindu "Banians" and Muslim "Khojas." The term "Banian," sometimes used in referring to all Indians, is evidently a corruption of the word "Bhattia"—the label for one of the Hindu commercial subcastes which was particularly identified with foreign trade. Members of this subcaste, plus those of the Lohana Wania subcaste constituted the bulk of the Hindu traders in the western Indian Ocean. Indian traders, both Banian and Khoja, were skilled in adapting their business techniques to the manners and mores of the country in which they were living, while at the same time preserving their own distinct identity and way of life.[34]

Although they had to readjust their commercial habits after the advent of the Europeans in the eastern seas, the Indian merchants were able to retain some of their old importance at least in a number of western Indian Ocean ports. Masqat always had a few Indian merchants in residence. In the seventeenth century the Banian merchant, Narutem, "one of the

[34] Sir B. Frere, "Memorandum regarding Banians or Natives of India in East Africa, October 1873," *Précis Slave*, pp. 7-8, 16.

worshippers of the cow," instigated the war that finally drove the Portuguese out of Masqat.[35] By the eighteenth century the Indians constituted a thriving commercial group in Masqat, but were only rarely settled in most of the other Persian Gulf towns or in East Africa. As late as 1820 Indians were seldom encountered in Zanzibar or in east Africa and those few found there boasted a settlement of less than 40 years. An Indian merchant required sufficient order in a port to assure his property before he settled there. East Africa between 1500 and 1820 did not meet this requirement.[36]

Ironically enough, after 1820 the commercial influence, as well as the number of Indian merchants, in the western Indian Ocean area increased at the very time when India's domestic economy was being subjugated to the modern economy of Britain. Sayyid Sa'id's development of Zanzibar and of East African trade was a major impetus to the spread of Indian merchants during the nineteenth century. Sa'id wanted the Indians to finance and market the products of his new clove and coconut plantations. The Indians also financed the revival of the east African slave trade. The rising tempo of commerce in Sayyid Sa'id's domain stimulated the settlement of Indians in the Asiatic part of his state and by 1840 some 2,000 Indian merchants reportedly were settled at Masqat–Matrah.[37]

The importance of the Indian merchant in the early nineteenth century Omani empire was due to the fact that he was the only one able and willing to manipulate certain sectors of the economy, particularly those involving finance. Thus it was in the interest of the Omani authorities to encourage his activities. The Indians possessed the necessary connections with associate firms in other cities within the Omani empire and in India itself to expedite business. They were content to

[35] Ibn-Ruzayq, p. 81.

[36] Frere, "Banians," *Précis Slave*, pp. 7-13; *Admin. Rpt.: 1887-1888*, p. 22.

[37] Coupland, *East Africa and its Invaders*, pp. 314ff.; *Bombay Records— 1856*, pp. 631-32; Ibn-Ruzayq, p. 81.

start business in small ventures, were politically innocuous, and were willing to live for years in a place and status which few other peoples of wealth and intelligence would endure. Prior to 1856 the Indians slowly reestablished the business hegemony they used to enjoy in the Indian Ocean before Da Gama's day. Business ventures passed up as unpromising by Arabs or as petty by Europeans were seized upon by the Indians and in a few years built into profitable ventures.[38]

The typical Indian merchant was a moneylender or broker, and Indians were generally the agents for any Western ships trading at Masqat. Some had considerable influence with Sayyid Sa'id, as shown by the fact that the Masqat and Zanzibar customs were administered on a concession basis by one or another of the resident Indian merchants. Before the economic revolution of the 1860s a pattern had emerged within the mercantile system of the Omani state. The Indians assumed the functions of financier, wholesale and retail merchant, and agent for Western business concerns. The Arabs concentrated on shipping, although not a few were also merchants. Sayyid Sa'id himself in his business operations was a shipping line operator and plantation owner rather than a merchant. While Indian capital tended to be invested in movable, easy to sell goods such as cloth or grain imports, Arab capital tended to concentrate in real estate or shipping. Some modification of this pattern occurred in the 1840s and 50s largely because the Arabs, including Sa'id himself, utilized the financial services of Indians and contracted short-term debts. Arab indebtedness to the Indians increased as the years passed; by the end of Sayyid Sa'id's reign Indians had become the owners if not the actual sailors of numbers of ships. Doubtless this was a situation which resulted from foreclosures of settlements of the debts of Arab borrowers who were unable to repay loans. As stated previously, by the late nineteenth century much of the

[38] Frere, "Banians," *Précis Slave*, pp. 7-13.

shipping of Oman fell into the hands of Indians as the Arabs were unable to cope with the prevailing hard times.[39]

By 1856 few products exchanged in the Omani empire could be bought for the European, American, Indian, or local market without an Indian merchant being involved in the transaction in some capacity. Conversely, few Western imports could be sold for local consumption except through the intermediary of an Indian agent. Some of the Indian firms operating in Omani commercial centers were long established, commanded large capital resources, and counted several partners assisted by troops of lesser clerks and apprentices. More often the merchant was a young ex-apprentice recently departed from an established firm starting his own business with an inventory or cash advanced by other Indian merchants on credit. At all times a close interlocking relationship was maintained among numbers of Indian concerns doing business all along the Indian Ocean littoral and in India itself. Thus a single Indian merchant in Masqat might represent, in actuality, a large combine with branches in places such as Zanzibar, Bahrain, Bushire, Karachi, Bombay, and Calcutta. Europeans trading in the area quickly adopted the practice of doing business only with the help and advice of resident Indian merchants. For his part, the Indian regarded Western, Arab, and African traders and mariners alike as links in the chain of a primarily Indian-oriented commercial establishment.[40]

It has been emphasized elsewhere that the entry of European-owned, trade-carrying steamships into the western Indian Ocean and Persian Gulf during the 1860s was the fundamental cause of an economic upheaval of the most profound type. Naturally the decline in Omani business activity and prosperity hurt the Indian merchants as well as the local Arab traders, a fact evidenced by the migration of numbers of In-

[39] *Ibid.*, Rigby, "Report on Zanzibar," *Records of the Bombay Government*, no. LIX: 1861, pp. 5-20; *Bombay Records—1856*, pp. 631-32.

[40] Frere, "Banians," *Précis Slave*, pp. 7-13; "Pelly to Duke of Argyll, 18 May 1872, despatch no. 764-57: Residency." India Records–2, Vol. xx.

dians away from Oman to more prosperous climes. On the other hand, in a curious way the Indian merchants that remained in Masqat and in Oman benefited from the new economic climate in the Persian Gulf. The general reordering of the business environment that occurred in the Gulf during the 1860s afforded numerous and profitable opportunities for merchants able to exploit the changing economic relationships. The Indian merchant in his capacity as an "on the spot" agent for European steamers and Western firms was more vital to the economy of the Persian Gulf than ever before and especially so in light of the abandonment of merchant activity by so many erstwhile Arab businessmen. By the 1870s the Indians were administering a large proportion of the locally established commercial machinery of the Gulf region.

The Indian merchant operating in Oman during the late nineteenth century was a member of neither the Western business world nor of the Arab society in which he did business. He stood as an intermediary between the modern Westerner and the still traditionally oriented Omani. Even after the post-1862 step-up in European involvement in the Persian Gulf's economic affairs only a few Western firms such as Grey, Mackenzie and Company Ltd. dealt directly with the local population. Most preferred to have their interests discharged by resident Indian merchants. That such an arrangement was possible was due to the existence of the "managing agent system," a key ingredient in the commercial organization of much of the East.

Indian commercial houses traditionally were characterized by their membership in complex associations of interlocking and allied business firms. With the end of the East India Company's foreign trade monopoly and its reorganization in 1833 native Indian business concerns were encouraged to formalize and strengthen their long established network of associated concerns, and so the managing agent system evolved to meet the needs of the new economic environment.[41]

41 Kuchhal, *Industrial Economy of India*, p. 421.

The major advantages that association with an agency combine could offer was know-how concerning unknown markets,
ready-made merchandising machinery, a division of business
risk among many partners, and, most important, long- and
short-term capital sources. In the case of a Western concern
that wanted to do business in Masqat, for instance, association
with a resident Indian merchant solved many problems. For one
thing the agent could provide expert knowledge and an entry
into the local economic system. In Masqat the Indian merchants, despite their ties with Western-oriented firms based in
India, operated according to traditional Masqati business procedures. Often these resident merchants had their own "agents"
scattered throughout Oman. In addition to being able to better
serve the local market, due to their familiarity with local practices and local conditions, agency firms solved the problem of
continuity of management for companies whose representatives did not or could not settle in an area. The parent firm
was saved the trouble and risk of establishing new branch enterprises in places where they wanted to do business yet had
few contacts. The use of the managing agent system meant that
the direction of the affairs of modern Western- or Indian-based
concerns in places like Oman was in the hands of people not
directly employed by the parent concern. Rather, firms already
operating in the locale where trade was to be carried on represented the parent company. Agency firms were usually well
known and respected in the locality in which they actually
operated. Most agency firms also carried on extensive trading
operations on their own account, which had nothing to do with
the interests of any of the other concerns within their combine.
Moreover, many agency firms conducted general merchandising
houses that did not specialize in one type of commerce, and
they often represented several European companies at one and
the same time. The position of many Indian agency firms was
more that of a resident partner than a subsidiary of the large
parent companies. The arrangement between parent and agent,
or between associated agents operating in different locations,

was normally handled on a straight fee or on a commission basis. A source of strength to an agency firm operating in a city like Masqat was the fact that it could usually secure money advances or loans from the large parent concerns when they were needed. In many ways the managing agency system reminds one of that used by the fire insurance business in the United States today with its large parent companies which are represented by thousands of local insurance agents who know neighborhod conditions and operate other activities, such as real estate sales, on the side.[42]

But the managing agent system had serious weaknesses, too, the chief of which were the dangers of fraud or mismanagement by the local agents. The income of the local firm depended on locally derived profits, not on the efficient management of the parent company's interests. Overstocking of local markets through the use of resources supplied by parent companies was a common device used by local firms to drive competitors out of business. Such techniques caused periodic business difficulties, often driving weak firms into bankruptcy, but did little to expand the economy or serve a parent concern's interests. Indeed, during the late nineteenth century the tendency was for business in Oman to concentrate in the hands of fewer and fewer merchants. Although the poorly organized and poorly financed Arab firms were the earliest victims of such trade practices, many Indian concerns also fell by the wayside. The managing agent system tended to overemphasize speculation, manipulation, and the dominance of short-term financial considerations in business management.[43]

It is obvious that a key to the success of the Indian merchants in achieving dominance over Oman's commerce was their willingness to lend and transfer capital back and forth through the various chains of interlocking firms, agencies, and parent concerns that crisscrossed the Indian Ocean region.

[42] *Ibid.*, pp. 421-33; Anstey, *Trade*, pp. 134-38.
[43] Kuchhal, *Industrial Economy of India*, pp. 433-36; Anstey, *Trade*, pp. 134-38.

While this capital may have been expensive, at least it was available. The use of cooperative practices by the Indians contrasted markedly with the individualistic "lone wolf" posture characteristic of local Arab merchants.

The events of the 1860s, both political and economic, extended the Indians' hold over the economic life of coastal Oman to the point where the Indians were clearly dominant there by 1871. The 1860s witnessed the destruction of the structure on which the commercial practices and prosperity of the Arabs were founded: the Masqat entrepôt trade was crippled, Arab shipping had difficulty finding cargoes, and the political breakup of the Omani empire made it difficult or impossible to maintain African connections. Constant political crises in Oman, culminating with the conservative Ibadi conquest of the country's coast in 1868, finished the Arab merchant, so that by 1869 Pelly estimated there were only two or three Arab businessmen of any consequence still doing business in Masqat. Although Arab merchants still operated in interior Oman and the smaller coastal towns after the 1870s most of those once active in the large coastal ports retired to their date groves or emigrated to Zanzibar. The field was left to the Indian traders.[44]

Nevertheless, the business depression that decimated the ranks of Arab businessmen did not entirely spare the Indians. While the Indian business community numbered some 2,000 in the 1840s, there were only 250 Hindu traders left in Masqat by 1869. There was still a Muslim Indian-Khoja community of about a thousand in Matrah, but of these only 250 were adult males.[45] The size of the Indian community in Masqat–Matrah remained virtually stationary for the rest of the century; interestingly enough, in 1902 there were still but three Arab mer-

[44] "Pelly to Anderson, 23 Aug. 1864, no. 41: Residency," "Pelly to Gonne, 19 June 1869, no. 140: Residency," *Précis Commerce*, pp. 28-32.
[45] "Disbrowe to Gonne, 14 May 1869, no. 285: Masqat," India Records–2, Vol. L; Lorimer, II, 1,188.

chants of consequence doing business in Masqat.[46] In a relative sense, Indian traders controlled a far larger share of Omani foreign trade and Masqati business activity in 1900 than they did in 1856. On an absolute scale, however, the Indian community resident in Oman apparently was smaller in 1900 than in 1856, and the depression and stagnation that adversely affected the Masqati economy also hurt the business prospects of Oman's Indian merchants.

Between 1870 and 1900 the Indian merchants in Oman functioned as importers, exporters, retailers, distributors, bankers, government officials, and shipowners. The Indians did not operate banks as such but instead carried out their financial activities largely by trading in drafts, called *hundis,* issued in India. Usually about one-half of the capital owned by Masqati Indians was invested in India and the other half was at work locally. The Indians provided most of the credit and money that powered Masqat's business. In 1900 normal interest rates in the city ranged anywhere from 1½ to 3 percent a month. Although loans and mortgages were a favorite investment, Indian businessmen also made money as merchants. In disposing of imports in Masqat a merchant usually realized 10 percent of the value of an article as profit; in Bombay an importer averaged only 2½ percent profit. Arms importing, a major item of Masqati commerce between 1890 and 1912, was a very lucrative pastime since weapons sales netted 20 to 30 percent. In 1900 most of the 80 moneylenders, 100 cloth sellers, 100 food merchants, and 20 arms dealers of Masqat were Hindus. Ten Hindu-owned firms in the city counted the 35 wealthiest merchants in Masqat. In fact, the most powerful merchant in late nineteenth century Masqat was invariably a Hindu. Typical of these very rich men was the shrewd Rattansi Purshotam, who in the 1890s was not only the largest importer and exporter in Masqat, but also one of the two leading arms merchants in the

[46] Lorimer, I, 2,382-83, II, 1,197-1201; "Ottavi, Commercial Report, 1901," French Records, Vol. II.

Gulf area. Purshotam owned a considerable part of the city of Masqat, and his loans to the sultan coupled with his position as director of port customs gave him considerable, if indirect, political influence.[47]

Most of the Hindu or Banian community of Masqat originated in western India. Usually the Hindus remained in Masqat only 15 or 20 years, interrupting their stay with long visits to their homes and families in India. They did not bring their families to live in Masqat, preferring to shield their loved ones from a harsh climate and the necessity of coping with an unfamiliar and often unsympathetic culture. While the Hindus had the reputation of being shrewd traders they kept to themselves as much as possible. They worshipped in their own temples, followed their particular caste regulations, and generally led an isolated social existence.[48]

The Muslim Indians, the Khojas, a larger community than the Hindus, were concentrated in Matrah. Khojas was mainly shopkeepers, carpenters, shipbuilders, artisans, and small merchants. While their community began with migrants from Gujarat, unlike the Hindus, the Khojas were more or less permanently settled in Oman. They owned land and raised families there. Originally the Khojas were Isma'ilis subject to the Agha Khan, but in the 1860s a schism split the community, with most of the group in Masqat renouncing the Agha Khan's authority to become Ithna 'Ashari Shi'ites. Actually, it seems that few in the Khoja community were particularly interested in the subtleties of religion; rather their thoughts turned to business. Similar to many other Indian Muslim groups, the Khojas were a close-knit community governed by an elaborate system of communal rules similar in many ways to Hindu caste

[47] Frere, "Banians," *Précis Slave*, pp. 7-13; Lorimer, I, 578, 2,629, II, 1,181-86, 1,425; M. A. Daud, "British Relations with the Persian Gulf 1890-1902," unpub. Ph.D. thesis (London, 1957), p. 348; "Ottavi, Commercial Report, 1901," French Records, Vol. II; A. S. Jayakar, "The Medical Topography of Muscat," *Admin. Rpt.: 1876-1877*, pp. 101-105.
[48] Osgood, *Notes*, pp. 35-39.

regulations, and they did not mix socially with other elements of the Omani population.[49]

There was a certain amount of economic rivalry between the two Masqat–Matrah Indian communities. Each numbered about 250 adult males. While the Hindus were the more powerful group economically—only about 12 Khojas being considered big businessmen in the local sense—they were also more vulnerable to social inconveniences and actual physical harm because some rigid Ibadis thought them idolators. An incident typifying the relations between the two Indian groups occurred in 1894 when the Hindu Banians succeeded in having the date scales at Matrah closed, an action that forced the Khojas to load their dates in small skiffs, sail to Masqat, and use the Hindu-controlled date scales there.

Khojas and Banians were found scattered throughout Oman's coastal towns. Most of these merchants were only small tradesmen. In 1900 there were approximately 380 Hindus in Oman, of whom 250 lived in Masqat, 37 in Matrah, 28 in Sur, and the rest in other coastal communities. Of the estimated thousand Khojas residents in Oman only about one-third were adult males. The largest Khoja settlements were those of Matrah, with 685 inhabitants, Masqat, 120, al-Khaburah, 107, Suwayq, 34, and Sur, 31. The entire Indian community in Oman, both Hindu and Muslim, was part of the commercial network controlled by the rich merchants of Masqat–Matrah. This network essentially repeated in miniature the managing agent systems to which the Indian merchants of Masqat–Matrah were themselves bound. The Muslim Khojas were generally more numerous than were the Banians in the outlying towns where law and order were periodically threatened and where a Hindu was more liable to be hurt than was a Muslim.[50]

---

[49] S. C. Misra, *Muslim Communities in Gujarat* (New York, 1964); Frere, "Banians," *Précis Slave*, pp. 7-13; Lorimer, II, 321-23, 1,034, 1,197-1,201; Martineau, *Life of Frere*, II, 105-106.

[50] *Précis Maskat*, p. 89; Lorimer, I, 2,351, II, 1,411-12, 1,425.

Early Economic–Technological Modernization

Typical of the pattern of activity and the mechanics developed by the Indian merchants to operate their Omani ventures were the methods they used to organize the country's date trade. Dates were Oman's most valuable export and source of exchange by the late 1890s, earning over $MT 750,000 in a typical year at that time. Dates for export were brought from interior groves—in Wadi Sama'il, 'Uman, and al-Sharqiyah, mainly—as well as from al-Batinah, and collected at Matrah by Indian date merchants. Most of these dates were actually purchased from the growers by local Arab date buyers or brokers who, using money advanced to them by Indian date merchants, scoured the date-growing areas, purchased crops, and brought in the dates. For his efforts an Arab broker earned about 2½ percent to 5 percent of the final price an Indian merchant collected on his date sales. On some occasions Khoja and even Hindu merchants themselves went into Wadi Sama'il as far as 'Uman to purchase dates. It was normal, however, for the Hindus in the business to remain in Masqat where they organized the export sale of the date crop. Masqat, the Hindu center, was still Oman's chief overseas exporting center since it was the country's only steamer port. The Khojas engaged in the date business dealt mainly with the collection and distribution of dates inside Oman and so, quite naturally, the center of their activity was Matrah, that city being a coasting rather than an exporting harbor and being the major trade distribution port for strictly Omani commerce. The pattern of business organization seen in the date business was typical of those used in other branches of Omani commerce: the Hindu merchants dominated overseas trade, the Khojas concentrated on the Omani distribution trade, and local Arab merchants, often backed by Indian money, served as agents for Indian concerns in out of the way spots, and as the masters of the caravans and ships that distributed goods throughout the country.[51]

51 Lorimer, II, 1,187-88.

The prevailing attitude of the Omani Arabs toward the Indians was one of arrogant toleration. While the Khojas had to endure less inconvenience, insult, and injury than did the Hindu Banians, murders of Indians were not uncommon both in outlying towns and in Masqat itself. Although the motives for such crimes could just as easily have been robbery as religious intolerance, one concludes that the Indian community within Oman did not command the same level of protection in the 1860s and after from the Omani authorities that it had enjoyed under Sayyid Sa'id. Nevertheless, only during the time of fundamentalist Ibadi domination of the coast (1868–71) did the Indians suffer much trouble, and events such as those in 1868–71 only hastened the institution of a system of British protection for the Indians.

In 1873 the details were worked out for administering extra-territorial protection for the Indians, most of whom claimed British–Indian citizenship. As subjects of Her Majesty, the Indian community was exempt from Omani law and was answerable only to British authority. The British consul in Masqat, or in more extreme circumstances, Her Majesty's gunboats, were quick to give threatened Indian merchants protection. Any merchant whose property was damaged by an Omani usually received compensation forced by the British either from the guilty party or, if the guilty one had escaped, from the sultan. It became clear during the last decades of the nineteenth century that the British government would not tolerate any interference with the Indians' commercial dealings or personal freedom in Oman. By 1903 the protected status of the Indian merchant was assured, understood, and invariably honored.[52]

Although their status as British subjects meant that the Indian community was outside the jurisdiction of the local authorities, this could not alter the fact that they were the most important commercial group in Oman. Their commercial importance and power, notably that derived from their finan-

[52] *Ibid.,* I, 2,629.

cial manipulations, meant that the Indian community was significant in local politics, since the finances of the Masqati sultanate depended largely on Indian-administered loans or port customs. As long as the business climate remained favorable the Masqati government was assured of a source of credit. The Indians shunned an active political role for the most part, preferring a safe niche behind the scenes. Moreover, all the open political actions of the Indians, even the control of the Masqati customs administration, had one end in view: assuring themselves profits.

The Indians were businessmen pure and simple, following commerce with devoted, single-minded concentration. They were the bridge connecting the traditional society of the Omani Arabs with the modernizing West and also with India which had during the nineteenth century become a secondary source of modernizing influences for the other nations bordering the Indian Ocean. But the resident Indian merchants served more as cultural insulators than as cultural conductors. They did little to introduce modern practices into Oman. They preferred to operate their businesses so as to attract as little attention as possible. They coordinated their activities with local manners and mores. They did not try to change these manners and mores, nor did they introduce elements and practices into the conduct of their businesses that might unduly disturb the stability of Oman and thus endanger their commercial predominance. Although many of those aspects of the modern world that Oman encountered filtered into the country through the intermediary of Indian business houses, in the main because (1) the Indian community of Oman was making profits, (2) it conducted its day-to-day business in the country using premodern methods, and (3) it was content with a limited place in Oman as it was, the Indian community was a poor agent of modernization.

The decline of handicraft industry. Oman never has been at any time in its history an important manufacturing center. The country did possess a number of handicraft industries of local importance; as in many other areas of Afro–Asia the vitality of many of these enterprises was destroyed after cheap Western manufactures invaded the local market during the nineteenth century.

In the 1840s and 50s Masqat and Matrah were the largest manufacturing centers in Oman although other towns such as Suhar and the interior villages of Wadi Sama'il, Nazwa, Bilad-Bani-Bu-Hasan, and 'Ibri also had important artisan colonies. Wellsted in the mid-1830s said the principal employment in Matrah was weaving cloth and fabricating the brown woolen outer cloaks universally worn by the Arabs. He added that one could scarcely find a hut in the city that did not contain a "spinning wheel, with a female busily employed before it."[53] Certainly, the weaving of cotton and woolen cloth, supplemented by silk weaving in a few places such as Bilad-Bani-Bu-Hasan, was the major handicraft industry in Oman at the time of Sayyid Sa'id's death. Blacksmiths operated in the larger towns, and only slightly less important than weaving was the fashioning of hardware items including copper pots, gold and silver ornaments, and such arms as spear heads, daggers, swords, matchlocks, and even cannon for the ruler's fleet. Sugar was refined at Masqat and Nazwa, while both places exported to Iran and India a confection, *halwa,* made of honey, ghee, almonds, and sugar. Those participating in manufacturing included Omanis, Khojas, Persians, and even a few Jews who arrived in Masqat and Suhar in 1828 after quitting Basra.[54]

In the 1860s Western manufactures began to invade Oman in large quantity. By the end of the century they had captured much of the local market. Even before the death of Sayyid Sa'id American and British cloth was filtering into the country. Following the 1860s cheap white cotton cloth and colored prints from the West—and after 1890, from India—were im-

[53] Wellsted, *Travels in Arabia,* I, 32.

[54] *Ibid.,* pp. 13, 22, 123, 315-22; Osgood, *Notes,* pp. 90-91; W. Ruschenberger, *Narrative of a Voyage round the World including an Embassy to Muscat and Siam* (Philadelphia, 1838), p. 85.

ported in such quantity that they reduced local cloth manufacturing to an activity of little consequence. Only the luxury
stuffs—Suhar-produced red, black, and brown-striped cloth;
Masqat–Matrah varicolored turbans; Wadi Sama'il brown wool
and cotton cloaks, and Suhar and Masqat canvas sails—retained enough of their market appeal at home and abroad to
justify continued weaving. In 1900 clothing was still produced
locally, in Masqat–Matrah and Suhar especially. But this manufacture, one of the few left to Oman by then, utilized foreign
machine-made cloth almost exclusively. Food processing—dry-
ing and packing of limes, dates, and fish—retained its place as
an important supplement to the income of several Omani
coastal towns; many people, including women, were employed
in such processing during slack seasons in date cultivation
and fishing. After 1862 the local hardware industry retreated
in the face of large-scale imports. While a few copper pots
were still banged out in Nazwa, the import of European firearms destroyed the local arms industry, an activity also affected
by the fact that cannon were no longer forged for use by an
Omani fleet. The fashioning of ornamental jewelry and daggers by Arab and Indian artisans in Masqat was one of the
few "art" handicrafts remaining in 1900. In 'Ibri cloth was still
dyed although the stuffs so embellished were foreign manufactured varieties. Nakhl in Wadi Sama'il remained a pottery-
producing center especially renowned for its porous water
cooling jugs. All in all, we may conclude that the invasion
of modern machine-produced products seriously damaged the
old standby handicraft industries of weaving and hardware
manufacture and contributed to the decline of Oman's towns
during the late nineteenth century. If the drop in shipbuilding
is also taken into account the decline in Omani manufacturing
after 1856 is even more pronounced.[55]

Unlike manufacturing, agriculture did not suffer. Dates, the

[55] "Ottavi, Commercial Report, 1901," "French Records, II; Lorimer,
II, 757-58, 1,181-86, 1,359-66, 1838-40; Great Britain, Board of Trade,
"Report on the Condition and Prospects of British Trade in Oman,
Bahrain, and Arab Ports of the Persian Gulf," cd. 2,281, *House of
Commons Sessional Papers, 1905,* LXXXV, 4.

staple Omani crop, remained along with fish a basic element in the local diet and food supply. The export of dates during the late nineteenth century increased in absolute value until they became Oman's single most valuable export. In terms of the general decline of Oman's economy the relative value of the date crop to the country rose to unprecedented levels. By 1880 Omani dates were exported in increasing quantities to India and the United States. (A variety known as the "fard," or black date, was favored by American importers.) The over-all demand for Omani dates was strong between 1875 and 1914; some growers as well as the Indian merchants who shared in the date export trade grew very rich. The export of dates to India was facilitated by the modernizing of India's transport system. Sales of wet dates were stimulated by dispatching date cargoes to Karachi where the fruit was unloaded and shipped into the populous Punjab via the new railroad lines. A con-servative estimate of the value of Omani date exports in an average year in the 1890s is $MT 750,000.

Other products of Omani agriculture retained their estab-lished domestic and external markets. Fruit continued to be sent to Iran and India and the level of domestic consumption of fruits and grains remained firm. There were a few casualties. Local cotton production, never very large, suffered with the decline of Oman's weaving industry. The export of horses to India and Mauritius and of asses to Mauritius, a thriving occu-pation in the early nineteenth century, was extinct by the 1870s. But since most of the horses were raised in Iran and the asses originated in Bahrain the demise of this trade was more a sign of the decline of Oman's entrepôt activities than of her domestic agriculture. Omani camels were still considered among the finest in Arabia; a few still found their way into other parts of Arabia during the years after Sayyid Sa'id's death.[56]

[56] *Admin. Rpt.: 1876-1877*, pp. 79-80; *Précis Commerce*, p. 212; "Ottavi, Commercial Report, 1901," French Records, Vol. II, *Bombay Records—1856*, pp. 238-39; Ruschenberger, *Embassy to Mascat and Siam*; "Report on Trade in Oman, cd. 2,281," *House of Commons Sessional Papers, 1905*, LXXXV, 4.

Early Economic–Technological Modernization

Western business enterprises did not establish plantations in Oman as they did in several other tropical and subtropical regions. Except for the increased export importance of the date crop Omani agriculture remained much the same as it had been for hundreds of years. Only in a few large date groves and extensive fruit orchards was there much "cash cropping"; most agricultural activity was still of the subsistence variety. Landholding, labor, production, and distribution methods all followed their time-worn grooves unaffected by modernization.

The relative significance of illicit trades. Due to the general decline of Omani commerce after 1862, illegal commerce—smuggling, slaving, and gunrunning—assumed a new position of relative importance within the economy of coastal Oman. Certainly there was a great deal of Omani trade that never came under the inspection of Masqat's customs authorities. Sur, the largest city in Oman and one of its busiest ports by 1900, contained no government customs agents. Specific information on the extent of most Omani smuggling operations is, practically speaking, nonexistent, so no major generalizations will be attempted. Suffice it to say that a probable factor working against the rise of a more general reliance on smuggling was the fact that after 1862 an ever larger share of the import–export trade of the Persian Gulf and Oman was carried in steamers. Since Masqat was the one steamer port in Oman such trade could be regulated. Two areas of illicit commerce on which some information is available are the slave trade and the arms trade. The import (but not the ownership) of slaves was illegal in Oman after 1873 and the arms trade, although legal in Oman, was not legal in many of the countries to which Masqati arms merchants transshipped their wares.

Slaves had traditionally been of more economic value as articles of commerce than as sources of labor in Oman. In the mid-1830s Masqat was a great marketplace for slaves, and supplied the entire Persian Gulf, Iraq, and Iran area. Sayyid Saʻid himself engaged in the traffic, realizing a profit of some

$MT 60,000 per year until he abandoned it in 1845 to satisfy the demands of his British allies. Prior to 1845 the Omani government itself collected a dollar on every slave landed in Zanzibar and half a dollar on every slave landed at Masqat. But in the 1840s the transport of slaves was a major item in the commerce of the Omani state, and the trade was even more profitable for slave merchants than for Sayyid Sa'id's government. In the 1830s about 4,000 slaves were sold annually in Masqat, and profits of 20 percent were realized there from slaves imported from east Africa; if the slaves were taken up to Basra there was a 50 percent profit. The cost of slaves was determined by their age, sex, appearance, and place of origin. Around 1840 eunuchs from Darfur in the Sudan were sold to Persian buyers for $MT 200 to $MT 300. An Ethiopian girl brought $MT 60 to $MT 200, an Ethiopian man $MT 50 to $MT 150. Other African adult males brought $MT 20 to $MT 60, while a boy would cost from $MT 15 to $MT 30. Once an African survived the terrors of transport to Masqat he was fairly well treated, and could even go to a qadi and demand public sale if he were badly treated. A necessary cog in the slave trade was the Indian merchant since the Indians financed the Arab slave brokers. Apparently more Khojas than Banians were involved in the traffic.[57]

In the 1860s the tempo of the slave trade in the Persian Gulf began to slow down noticeably, largely due to British navy patrols, although it was estimated that anywhere from 4,000 to 10,000 slaves still were sent to the Gulf from east Africa each year during the decade. A tighter supply meant that slave prices nearly doubled. Prodded by Whitehall, the Anglo–Indian government began to strike at Indian participation in slaving. During the 1860s Indians who held slaves or who aided slave trade activities were prosecuted, and in 1873 the government effectively halted Indian participation in the trade by

---

[57] Wellsted, *Travels in Arabia*, I, 387-90; *Bombay Records—1856*, pp. 648-49; Rigby, "Report on Zanzibar," *Records of the Bombay Government*, no. LIX (1861), pp. 9-12; Wilson, *Persian Gulf*, pp. 213-30.

decreeing that any British-protected Indian implicated would be sent back to Bombay for trial. In 1873, too, both the Masqati and Zanzibari governments made it unlawful for their subjects to either export or import slaves. Thus in one year two harsh blows were struck against slaving.[58]

But individual Arab captains continued to carry slaves, although their actions were illegal after 1873 and British cruisers were hunting down slave carriers. One reason for the persistence of the Arab seamen is well expressed in a letter of one Arab ruler to the sultan of Zanzibar: "We did warn them [to stop the trade] O my brother, and sent people to tell them, and made public your letter; but it will, I am afraid, have but little effect in keeping them back. The gains are so enormous that it is hopeless to think of stopping them. With ten baskets worth of dates that a man can get on credit, he can get 20 slaves at Zanzibar worth 1,000 dollars. . . ."[59] In 1872 a captured slaver sailor declared that any shipper could expect three MT dollars for each slave carried to the Gulf if he was not caught by "the Christians," while a Masqat slave dealer could sell for $MT 60 to $MT 100 a slave that could be purchased for $MT 20 at Zanzibar. After 1862 the slave trade was more important than ever to Arab seamen as they were squeezed out of more legitimate traffic by steamer competition.[60]

Between 1874 and 1884 British antislavery cruisers effectively throttled the slave trade; but between 1884 and 1902 traffic revived somewhat, partly because numbers of the slavers operated under the protection of the French flag which was being

---

[58] Frere, "Banians," *Précis Slave*, pp. 12-19; Lorimer, I, 2,498; Columb, *Slave Catching*, pp. 46-48, estimated that 13,000 slaves were shipped to Arabia from Zanzibar in the year 1870 alone; however, in 1866 only 400 slaves were landed at Masqat.

[59] "Shaykh of Abu-Dhabi to Sultan of Zanzibar, enclosure in East Africa Slave Trade Correspondence," c. 141, *House of Commons Sessional Papers, 1870*, LXI, 46.

[60] "Pelly to Duke of Argyll, 5 Oct. 1872, despatch no. 1621-161: Residency," India Records–2, Vol. XXI. Columb, *Slave Catching*, p. 59.

rather indiscriminately granted to various Indian Ocean captains. The large-scale transport of slaves on the Indian Ocean ended in 1902 when the Portuguese captured 114 Arabs of Sur, 12 ships, and 725 slaves at a base the slavers had established in a Mozambique cove. The slavers were sentenced to 25 years in prison in Angola—news which "converted Sur into a scene of wailing and lamentation." It was news which also marked the end of Sur's importance as a slave port.[61]

The sultan's decree of 1873 had banned only the traffic, not the holding of slaves by Omanis. Thanks to this exception, the sultan's weak if well-intentioned execution of his decree, and the nearly universal belief among Omanis that slavery was approved by the scriptures of their Muslim faith, the institution of slavery remained strong within Oman and a small but steady trickle of slaves continued to slip through the British naval patrols into the country. Most slaves landed in Oman were unloaded at Sur. Private markets inside the houses of slave dealers existed in the larger towns. During the 1870s the most notorious slave broker in Matrah was himself an African. There were an estimated 15,000 to 50,000 slaves in Oman during the late nineteenth century, while as many as 1,000 slaves were added to the total in some years.[62] Female slaves were servants and concubines. The males were usually house servants, field workers, and sailors. Often the relation between master and slave was purely a formality, the slave working where he pleased and returning to his master a portion of his earnings. It was not unusual to find slaves holding positions of trust and importance.

The demand for slaves varied in Oman. It was minimal in Ja'lan and al-Sharqiyah where the irrigation system did not

[61] Lorimer, I, 2,500-14; Great Britain, Foreign Office, *Counter Case, Muscat Dhows Arbitration in the Permanent Court of Arbitration of the Hague* (London, 1905), p. 5.

[62] "Ross to Duke of Argyll, 25 Jan. 1873, despatch no. 92-12: Residency," India Records-2, Vol. xxii; "Miles to Prideaux, 28 Apr. 1876, no. 165—57: Masqat," India Records-3, Vol. ii; "Ottavi, Commercial Report, 1901," French Records, Vol. ii.

demand much labor. It was higher in al-Batinah with its irrigation wells requiring constant upkeep. Most slaves landed in Oman were reexported to Iran and the Trucial Coast where they were used as sailors and pearl divers. The center in al-Batinah for slave reexport was Wudam. After 1902, when the supply of African slaves finally was choked off, Wudam began to import captives from Baluchistan who were sold into slavery. Oman slave prices in 1900 were steep: children brought $MT 120, male adults $MT 150, girls $MT 200 to $MT 300. The price in Africa remained a low three pounds sterling for a human being; ivory tusks cost more at the time.[63]

As the century closed the traffic finally declined in intensity, chiefly because of British efforts. But the decline of the trade was just another instance in Omani eyes of Western interference in a long-established maritime pursuit. Indeed, in 1866 one irate Saudi Arab told Colonel Pelly that the anti-slave trade drive branded the British as "successful pirates."[64]

The arms trade and gunrunning was another extralegal commercial activity carried on in Oman in the late nineteenth century. Between 1890 and 1912 Masqat became the center of a lucrative traffic in arms. Munitions, chiefly modern rifles and ammunition, were imported directly from Europe by steamers into Masqat without any legal barriers. But 95 percent of these arms were then reexported, usually illegally, to other parts of South Asia. In the late 1890s about 25,000 rifles, costing about $MT 30 to $MT 50 apiece, entered Masqat each year; by 1908 more than 85,000 rifles were being landed there. Profits of 20 to 30 percent commonly were earned in these transactions by Masqat arms dealers.[65]

The commerce bolstered Masqat's sagging foreign trade dur-

[63] Lorimer, I, 2,499-2,503, *Précis Maskat*, p. 53.

[64] Columb, *Slave Catching*, p. 50; Arabian American Oil Company, *Oman*, pp. 45-46, 63. The sultan received many protests about interference in the slave trade.

[65] Wilson, *Persian Gulf*, pp. 263-71; Daud, "British Relations with the Persian Gulf," p. 348; *Précis Maskat*, p. 135; "Arms Trade—1913," "Persian Gulf Trade—1909," India Records—5.

ing the uncertain economic climate of the 1890s and early twentieth century. In many years proceeds from arms imports alone accounted for over one quarter of Masqat's import income. During the 1890–1912 period the ups and downs in total trade closely corresponded to the fluctuations in the level of arms imports. This traffic alone prevented Masqat's foreign trade from falling to unprecedented and dangerous low levels during the time of Oman's currency crisis. Although the value of the arms trade fluctuated erratically from year to year, the figures for munitions imports advanced from a very modest total in the early 1890s, to £73,666 in 1897—98, £110, 993 in 1904–1905, a peak £279,050 in 1907–1908, and declined precipitously in 1910–11 after the British imposed a naval blockade to halt arms smuggling out of Masqat. The Masqati munitions trade collapsed in 1912 when the British induced the sultan to set up an arms warehouse and to impose strict controls on the business. To make up for large losses in his customs revenue the British gave the ruler a 100,000-rupee (£6,666) increase in his annual subsidy.[66]

As early as 1898 the British authorities initiated efforts to limit the Masqati arms trade because practically all of the arms imported into Oman were smuggled into other Asian nations, which was contributing to a deteriorating security climate in many Middle Eastern and south Asian countries; the threatening situation on India's northwest frontier, where by 1906 an estimated 94,000 modern rifles were held in tribal arsenals, especially alarmed the British. Until the intervention in 1898 the arms traffic was the creature of British manufacturers, shippers, and their Indian agents; after 1900, in the face of disapproval by their government, they surrendered much of their arms business only to see the void filled by French suppliers. For their part, the British-protected Indian merchants of Masqat, heavily involved in the arms traffic just as their earlier compatriots were involved in the slave trade, were gen-

[66] Lorimer, I, 2,587-88; "Arms Trade—1913," India Records–5.

erally exasperated with their government's attempts to limit the flow of arms, and many remained active in the commerce. Also, the French government repeatedly refused to cooperate with the British effort to restrict weapons imports into Oman. Only in 1914 when the British agreed to compensate the French arms merchants for their unsold munitions stocks did the French government abandon its opposition to control measures.[67]

The lack of technological modernization. During the late nineteenth century there was almost a total lack of locally inspired effort to introduce modern technology into Oman. What interest there was in modernization was evidenced mainly by the tiny group of Westerners in the country. The few isolated, sporadic attempts to introduce aspects of modern civilization were opposed and rejected by the population of both coastal and interior Oman. Even in Sayyid Sa'id's day it was rare to find an Omani with scientific knowledge or an informed curiosity concerning the modern world. The Koran, some Ibadi chronicles, and a few medieval theories about the nature of the world satisfied the intellectual appetites of most. Nor did this situation change substantially after 1856.

The modernization schemes specifically concerned with Oman do not make a long list. Britain's representative in Masqat supported efforts to introduce modern standards of public health and hygiene. Because cholera and plague periodically broke out into great epidemics that swept across Asia to endanger Europe, they were singled out for attack by British health authorities. But no Omanis supported any of the efforts to update health measures until a serious epidemic in 1900 in which 12,000—61 percent of those who fell ill—died. This prompted the sultan to build hospital sheds and hire a doctor from Bombay to carry on inoculations and disinfection, but not until 1903 did he agree to establish effective quarantine regulations. Generally, the people of Masqat, including the

[67] *Précis Maskat,* p. 135; "Memorandum D. 238, Dec. 1918," India Records–5.

resident Indian community, were averse to vaccination and preventive health measures. The "Civil Hospital" in Masqat, which was part of the British Political Agency and was staffed by a very knowledgeable Indian doctor, received only nine rupees in non-British financial support in 1899. By that year, however, an average of 58 patients a day, a quarter of the them Indian, sought help from the hospital. In 1900 the sultan began to consult the agency doctor when he or a member of his family was ill, but still he did not bring himself to support the expansion of medical facilities.[68]

When Protestant missionaries arrived in Masqat another source of modernization efforts began to operate in Oman. Missionary activity began in 1891, though it was another six years before the Arabian Mission of the Dutch Reformed Church in America permanently established itself at Masqat. In addition to its evangelistic work the Mission operated a dispensary and a school. In the early days most of these efforts were welcomed only among emancipated Negro slaves, a fairly considerable group in Masqat–Matrah. When Dr. Thoms arrived in 1898 medical work was extended to the interior. The mission school introduced a number of Masqatis to the modern world but the school's effects, still negligible today, were not visible until this century.[69]

In 1901 and 1902 it appeared that Oman might become the scene of a British mining enterprise. Some experts suspected there was a rich coal field located about 30 miles inland from Sur. Two field investigations by geologists were carried out

[68] Jayakar, "The Medical Topography of Muscat," *Admin. Rpt.: 1876-1877; Admin. Rpt.: 1898-1899*, pp. 28-29; *Admin. Rpt.: 1899-1900*, pp. 20-35. Lorimer, I, 573-78, 2,517-55; the steam yachts operated by the sultan starting in the early 1880s represent practically the only instance where modern machinery was utilized by Omanis during the late nineteenth century.

[69] Lorimer, I, 2,386-99; see also the journal, *Neglected Arabia*, and W. H. Storm, *Whither Arabia? A Survey of Missionary Opportunity* (New York, 1938). The missionary records of the Dutch Reformed Church in America are located in the library of the church's seminary at New Brunswick, New Jersey.

despite tribal harassment, but the vein proved too thin for profitable exploitation. Thus, no Western industry came to Oman at this time.[70]

The attitude of the Omanis did not grow noticeably more sophisticated during the last decades of the nineteenth century despite the changes modern communications and technology were bringing to the Gulf. The attitudes, beliefs, and actions of those Omanis who opposed the use of modern medicine in 1899 or those who fired on the British coal geologists in 1902 were a continuation of Ibadi aversion to innovation. In the country's interior, especially, there was little notion of or interest in modern or foreign things.

There was no indigenous group within the country interested in encouraging Oman's modernization. Conservative Ibadi opposition to innovation was as much a matter of instinct as it was the product of intellectual conviction. The sultan, dependent on British guns, was not encouraged to modernize his military means; thus his country escaped the manifold repercussions of an activity that brought so much change to other Middle Eastern countries. The resident Indian population were content with their profits and economic dominance. There was nothing in Oman that attracted large Western investments or technological improvements. Oman, with its premodern maritime culture in a shambles, developed nothing to take its place.

THE OMANI ECONOMY IN 1900

The last 40 years of the nineteenth century were ones of disruptive—and destructive—economic change in Oman. These changes were especially revolutionary on Oman's coast by bringing about a fundamental reordering of economic life there. Due to the spread of steamers and other aspects of modern technology into the Gulf, the pre-1856 "middleman" economy of Oman's coast and the long-distance carrying trade and entrepôt exchange that characterized it were all but destroyed.

---

[70] Aitchison—1909, XII, 244; Lorimer, I, 576-77.

Masqat lost the status of commercial leader of the Persian Gulf that she had enjoyed since the seventeenth century. The importance of Omani shipping in the Persian Gulf and Indian Ocean was reduced to near insignificance. Business activity in Omani ports declined precipitously and then remained at a low level. The doom of the carrying and entrepôt trade, as well as the complex of activities dependent upon them, prompted a shift to subsistence agriculture and fishing, local trade, and opportunistic or illicit commerce as the basis of Oman's coastal economy.

Coupled with the demise of the middleman economy was the rise of a pessimistic, bewildered attitude toward the world. Arabs who grew rich in shipping and business retreated to their date groves and surrendered what remained of Oman's commerce and even much of her shipping into the hands of Indian merchants, who by 1900 dominated the country's commercial life. Among the Arabs, the crisis of the 1860s seemed to produce a retreat to the citadel of the old Ibadi verities rather than an energetic attempt to cope with the new economic realities. Omani political leaders, a group who led the country to economic dominance in the Persian Gulf during the seventeenth and eighteenth centuries, were barred by the British from using the old strongarm methods of assuring economic prosperity. They could not manipulate the new situation in any effective way, so they contented themselves with trying to maintain the trappings if not the essence of power. Effective political power in the country devolved upon local tribal shaykhs, on the one hand, or the British on the other. The shaykhs, for their part, maintained their traditional lack of interest in encouraging local economic interests while the British were content if the country was peaceful enough to pose no threat to imperial communications or to the business of the British-protected Indian merchant community resident in Oman.

This depressing situation was rendered all the more difficult by the capture of the local markets once served by Omani handicraft industry by cheap European machine-produced imports. The country's monetary system, buffeted as it was by the winds of a late nineteenth century world monetary crisis, failed Oman. Indeed, the Omani monetary crisis of the 1890s is a particularly striking example of how the country's economy was at the mercy of forces entirely out of local control or understanding.

Unlike many other areas where the premodern economy was destroyed, the foundation for a modern economy was not substituted. In 1900 there seemed to be no rich mineral deposits in the country; no Western investment and technology were attracted. Oman did not even receive the dubious benefits which follow the establishment of modern agricultural plantations. Yet the elements of Oman's economy most disturbed by the economic revolution of the 1860s were those peculiarly identified with the coast. The interior remained essentially undisturbed. There, as on the coast, handicraft industry declined and the monetary crisis had some effects. The reliance of the inland districts on a self-sufficient agricultural economy, however, cushioned the disturbances that accompanied economic change.

The effects of the economic changes of the late nineteenth century on Oman's political climate were significant. The coast's decline in commercial strength meant a weakening of the economic undergirding that supported the political apparatus, controlled by the coast's moderate Ibadi rulers. With the curtailing of customs and other revenue sources the sultan had available far smaller monetary resources with which to influence the course of events than he did prior to 1856. While the Omani economy in general declined after 1856 the worst problems were on the coast. After the 1860s the coast, and moderate Ibadism, no longer possessed resources and wealth unquestionably superior to those controlled by interior conservatives. This fall in the coast's power in relation to that of the interior has reflected itself in the touch-and-go political situation in Oman during the century after Sayyid Sa'id's death in 1856.

Oman's pre-1856 position of importance in Indian Ocean trade depended on the economic activity of the country's coast. Therefore, her importance in the world declined to almost total insignificance in the years between 1856 and 1900 with the eclipse of her middleman function. After its fall in the 1860s Oman remained a sleepy backwater for another century —a situation that promised to change, however, after the Shell Oil Company late in 1963 asserted the inhospitable salt and sand wastes of Oman's Fahud region contain large commercially exploitable oil deposits. Fahud, close to Oman's Rub' al-Khali undemarcated desert border with Saudi Arabia, will be connected to tanker-loading facilities on the Gulf of Oman by a 200-mile pipeline to be built over the Hajar Mountains via Wadi Sama'il. Cautious estimates state that Oman's oil production probably will total some 10 million tons a year. This is approximately the same amount of oil pumped out of Qatar's fields in 1963, a production that earned Qatar some $56,000,000 in royalties during that year. Since the revenues of the Sultan of Masqat and Oman now total only $3,000,000 in an average year, it is obvious that oil royalties will produce major changes in the sultanate very soon. Probably within a few years Oman's century of economic stagnation will come to a close and the country finally will become a participant rather than victim in a modernizing world.

PART III

The Consolidation of British Political
Paramountcy in Oman and the Persian Gulf

CHAPTER 5

The Evolution of Indirect Rule, 1862-92

SOME assume that the techniques and apparatus Britain has used to supervise Persian Gulf affairs for the past 150 years were produced during the early nineteenth century. This is not strictly the case; the structure of British power in the region evolved over a long period of time. The nature of Britain's involvement in the Gulf changed often between the seventeenth century and the mid-twentieth century.

A salient development in the Persian Gulf region during the late nineteenth century was the consolidation of British political paramountcy. Britain's authority in the region, founded on a connection that extended back to the early seventeenth century and clearly established during the first half of the nineteenth century, was, nonetheless, exercised in a relatively relaxed manner until 1862. During the late nineteenth century, however, her grip tightened and the local effects of Britain's dominance grew more and more pronounced. The chief causes for the increase in British involvement in Gulf politics during the late nineteenth century were the need to enhance imperial and Indian security, the necessity to preserve the maritime truce system established in the region during the first half of the century, the desire to propagandize European standards of culture—particularly those associated with "humanitarianism," the drive to expand profitable economic contacts, and the predilection to spread modern concepts of political administration among the several Gulf principalities. Economic repercussions created by the penetration of modern Western communications and technology into the Gulf have been discussed. Hand in hand with this economic subjugation of the region went a thorough, albeit subtly administered, political subjugation. In 1862 the official—and usually the actual—policy of Britain in the Gulf was one of supervision of the foreign affairs, but one of noninterference in the internal affairs of the various local states. By 1900, however, although the official policy remained unchanged, few Gulf rulers could escape without consulting British representatives when they considered important decisions concerning their internal administrations.

THE GROWTH OF BRITISH POLITICAL CONTROL IN THE PERSIAN GULF BEFORE 1862

It is possible to distinguish five major stages in the development of the British position within the Persian Gulf and of the machinery by which her interests in the region have been assured.[1] The first stage, lasting from the establishment of the first British foothold in the vicinity of the Gulf, at Cape Jask on Iran's southern coast in 1616 until the late eighteenth century, was primarily a period of commercial rather than political involvement. East India Company merchants operating from ports in India came to the Gulf to tap the trade of Iraq, Persia, and central Asia. Therefore, Britain's participation in Gulf affairs was a derivative of her Indian connection; Indian interests were most influential in shaping the dimensions of this involvement. This circumstance was reflected by the fact that until 1947 the British government in India, rather than Whitehall, supervised most British activities in the region. Early British "factories" in the Gulf, such as Gombroon (present-day Bandar 'Abbas), although fortified, were more centers of trade than political influence. During this first stage, except for an occasional ship calling at Masqat or "Grane" (Kuwait), British interests in the region were not concerned with the Arabian coast but were concentrated in Iran and Iraq and particularly in the factories at Bushire and Basra, which were the sole bases of British activity in the region after the Gom-

[1] A thoughtful analysis of the development of Britain's political position in the Persian Gulf is Kelly, "British Position in the Persian Gulf, *St. Antony's Papers, Number IV*, pp. 119-40; also H. Liebesney, "International Relations of Arabia, the Dependent Areas," *Middle East Journal*, I (1947), 148-68; and J. Brinton, "The Arabian Peninsula: the Protectorates and Sheikhdoms," *Revue Egyptienne de Droit International*, III (1947), 5-38.

broon factory was abandoned in 1763. The two factories, as well as Britain's other concerns in the area, were supervised by "residents." While the residents at Basra and Baghdad watched over Britain's Iraqi interests, the resident at Bushire was charged after 1778 with overseeing her Persian Gulf and Iranian involvements. The Bushire resident continued, despite later shifts in function and power, and except for the years 1798–1810, when an independent Masqat residency was maintained, to be the vehicle by which British interests in the Gulf were administered down to 1946, when he shifted his headquarters to Bahrain.

The second stage in the development of Britain's position in the Gulf extended over the first half of the nineteenth century—more specifically from 1798 to 1862. During these years Britain's role in the Gulf shifted from one based on commercial activity to one that was concerned mainly with politics. These political interests revolved around imperial and Indian defense requirements, the maintenance of maritime order, and the preservation of the Gulf maritime states. Also, Britain became increasingly active in Arabian affairs to the point where her new interests on the peninsula became as important as her long-standing involvement in Iran and Iraq. These developments occurred as a consequence of the East India Company acquisition of extensive territorial holdings on the Indian subcontinent during the latter decades of the eighteenth century. As a result, the Company changed in nature from a trading concern to a sovereign political power which held India as trustee for the British government. With the establishment of a British empire in India the Persian Gulf inevitably assumed a predominantly strategic and political importance to Britain because its waters lay adjacent to the lines of communications which tied England to her new South Asian empire.

Napoleon's invasion of Egypt in 1798 and the discovery of his plans to attack India stimulated the British to assert their strategic interests in the Persian Gulf by moving to assure that the area remain in nonhostile hands. In the late 1790s an intensive Anglo–Indian diplomatic offensive forestalled French intrigues in western Asia and resulted in a number of British and Anglo–Indian treaties with various western Asian states. Among these agreements was Britain's first treaty with a Persian Gulf Arab state, the 1798 "alliance" between the East India Company's government of Bombay and the Omanis represented by Sultan ibn-Ahmad, the moderate Ibadi ruler of Masqat.[2] By 1810 the Napoleonic threat to India and the Middle East was contained, as a result of the British conquest of Mauritius from the French. In the meantime, the British had signaled their intention to deny use of the Persian Gulf to any power potentially dangerous to India or to imperial communications.

This intention was reinforced by British actions to counter another threat to empire communications from raiders based on a number of upper Gulf eastern Arabian ports. Since the 1780s maritime disorder had increased in the Gulf to the point where it involved the Omanis, eager to extend their predominance in Gulf trade, as well as the maritime Arabs of what we know today as the Trucial Coast, Bahrain, and Kuwait. These peoples were establishing new states and asserting their commercial independence at the same time. By 1800 the upheaval took on a new dimension. The Saudi Wahhabis were intruding onto the eastern Arabian coast and combining with Oman's enemies. Because of the general strife British vessels became involved in incidents and several were attacked. To the British these incidents were simple piracy, for there seemed to be little appreciation that their ships were sailing in the midst of what would have been described in a later day as a "war zone." Fears were expressed that corsairs might emerge from the Gulf to ravage the main Europe-to-India shipping lanes or even to raid the coast of India itself. Britain determined to crush this new threat to imperial communications and India's frontiers. In cooperation with their Omani allies, the Anglo–Indian authorities in Bombay dispatched expeditions in 1805–1806, 1809–10, and in 1819–20 which by the

2 Aitchison—1933, xi, 287-88.

last date succeeded in all but destroying the naval capability of the Qawasim of Ra's al-Khaymah and al-Shariqah, the most aggressive of the Wahhabi-supported maritime Arab states of the Trucial Coast—the "Pirate Coast" as it was labeled by Europeans of that day.[3]

In 1820 the Anglo–Indian government determined to begin a permanent surveillance of the Gulf's waters to prevent any recurrence of maritime disorder. The resident at Bushire was charged with overseeing this watch. At first, it was planned to station Indian troops in the Gulf to support the peace and a camp was established on Qishm Island, which commanded the strategic strait of Hormuz. Because of expense, climatic hardships, Persian protests, and fears of overinvolvement in the internal affairs of the Gulf states the troops were withdrawn in 1822 and British primacy in the region thereafter depended on warship patrols. The reluctance of the British to become involved in military adventures on the Arabian mainland or to make commitments that would force them to undertake land campaigns became a feature of British policy in the Gulf after 1822.[4]

To regulate Britain's newly assumed position in the Gulf a series of treaties and settlements were concluded with various Gulf principalities. The process was initiated by drawing up the "General Treaty for Suppressing Piracy and Slave Traffic" of 1820 to which the shaykhs of the Pirate Coast as well as the shaykh of Bahrain subscribed.[5] Although this treaty halted

[3] Wilson, *Persian Gulf*, chap. 13; *Bombay Records—1856*, passim; C. R. Low, *History of the Indian Navy, 1613-1863* (London, 1877), vol. I, chap. 10.

[4] Excerpts from original records and a comprehensive treatment of the growth of British involvement in the Persian Gulf in the early nineteenth century are provided in *Précis Gulf*. Probably the best secondary account of the period is Kelly, "British Policy, 1813-1843." More generally available than the works cited above, if not so detailed, is Kelly, "British Position in the Persian Gulf," *St. Antony's Papers, Number IV*. Anglo–Indian troops had been used in several actions on the Arabian mainland during the two decades prior to 1822.

[5] Aitchison—1933, XI, 245-47. In 1820 the "pirate shaykhs" proper in-

Consolidation of British Paramountcy

attacks on British shipping it did not completely end maritime disorders among the subjects of the several upper Gulf principalities. Finally, in 1835 the British induced the upper Gulf shaykhs to accept a truce of several months duration which outlawed attacks at sea on the shipping of each other's subjects during a period coinciding with the pearling season. Thus appeared the trucial system in the exact sense of the term. This truce was renewed each year until 1843 when a 10-year agreement banning hostilities at sea was concluded. The series of temporary engagements was crowned in 1853 by the "Perpetual Maritime Truce" which remains in effect to this day.[6] By subscribing to these treaties the participating Gulf rulers recognized Britain's right to prevent maritime disorders, police the

---

cluded that of Ra's al-Khaymah and al-Shariqah (Sharjah), a state first divided into two independent shaykhdoms in 1866 and finally separated in 1919, as well as the shaykh of Umm al-Qaywayn, and the shaykh of 'Ajman. Although they did not take part in the hostilities against Britain, Abu Dhabi and Dubayy (Dubai), Abu Dhabi's dependency until 1834, also signed the General Treaty of Peace of 1820 and all the later truce agreements. Bahrain, which followed Abu Dhabi's example in this regard, is, nonetheless, not usually counted as one of the "Trucial States" in the strict sense of the term, because it became a party to more complicated engagements later in the century. In 1868 the shaykh of al-Dawhah on the Qatar peninsula, although his ties to both Bahrain and the Sa'udis were such that he was not then an "independent" ruler in the same sense as were the trucial shaykhs, agreed to abstain from all warfare at sea and thus became personally associated with the trucial system. This association was not binding on the shaykh's successor, however, and Qatar did not formally join the trucial system until 1916; even today Qatar is not included among listings of the "Trucial States." Kuwait did not enter into an agreement with the British until 1899 and the engagement signed that year concerned itself mainly with Kuwait's international relations and not with the maritime peace. In a legal sense, then, Kuwait was not part of the trucial system but like Oman it observed its rules in practice. In 1952 al-Fujayrah (al-Fujairah), situated on the Gulf of Oman and once part of al-Shariqah, was recognized as a distinct shaykhdom and was incorporated officially into the trucial system; al-Fujayrah had been enjoying a de facto separate existence since 1902. Between 1936 and 1952 Kalba, now part of al-Shariqah, was recognized as an independent trucial shaykhdom.

6 Aitchison—1933, XI, 248-53.

Gulf, and mediate disputes among the Gulf states. Commerce, the legal position of European protégés, and the slave trade were also regulated by other treaties or understandings formulated during the same period. Although the practice was not then specifically sanctioned by treaties, Britain also assumed the role of advising Gulf rulers concerning their foreign relations.

Two important eastern Arabian powers, the Saudi state and Oman, never became signatories of the truce treaties, yet, in reality, their actions in the region increasingly were determined in large measure by the implications of the trucial system. For instance, the expansionist urges of the Saudis were curbed by the knowledge that in return for agreeing to abide by the maritime peace, the petty Gulf principalities had received from Britain an unspecified and tacit, but none the less real, pledge of support—a pledge which almost amounted to a de facto guarantee of the independence of the small littoral states. Finally, in 1866 the Saudis officially recognized this situation by signing an engagement in which they promised to respect the integrity of the other eastern Arabian states in treaty relationship with Great Britain.[7] Omani-British relations were formulated by the 1798 "alliance," as amended in 1800, a commercial engagement undertaken in 1839, and antislave trade agreements drawn up in 1822, 1839, and 1845.[8] The Omanis, like the Saudis, were expected to observe the spirit of the trucial system and to curb their old designs upon Bahrain and certain points on the Iranian coast. Although the British avoided giving a specific guarantee to support Oman's independence, in actuality they lent the Al Bu Sa'id authorities in Masqat both military and naval support on several occasions after 1806, as well as strong diplomatic assistance numerous other times when the state's independence seemed threatened. By such actions the British established precedents which underlined their intention to preserve the essential political status quo in the Gulf as a corollary of their efforts to

[7] *Ibid.*, p. 206.   [8] *Ibid.*, pp. 289-302.

maintain maritime order there. On the other hand, specific treaty commitments, predetermined responses, and ironclad guarantees of independence were shunned in favor of a policy which preserved Britain's flexibility to deal in various ways with individual problems as they arose.

In their totality these formal settlements and informal commitments created in the Persian Gulf a political climate similar to that which prevailed in India outside the area of immediate British administration. A screen of "native states," all in special treaty relationship to the British, was established; this screen shielded the western sea approaches to India and extended the range of British influence without increasing Britain's direct administrative responsibility. The nature of political relationships among the Gulf states was permanently altered, in that violence at sea among the principalities was outlawed and the political geography of the Gulf, traditionally in constant flux, was stabilized. In the future it would be most difficult for any Gulf city–state or littoral power to use violent means to dominate other parts of the region. The British themselves, little realizing the depth or immensity of the change in the traditional pattern of Gulf politics they had wrought, characterized their policy in the Gulf as one of "noninterference." True to the prevailing laissez-faire theories of the mid-nineteenth century, Britons claimed they were merely policemen preventing disorder which might threaten imperial communications. Despite such activities as their drive against the slave trade, one of the most lucrative activities of the Gulf's seamen, and an activity sanctioned by Islam, the British disclaimed any intention of interfering with the customs or daily lives of the local population. In reality, in the first half of the nineteenth century, there were a number of significant changes in the traditional pattern of Gulf life. These years stand as ones in which the process of modernizing the Persian Gulf's political practices were initiated. It is clear that decisions by British policymakers were fundamental in establishing this new era in Gulf history.

Since the initial results of the establishment of an active British supervisory regime in the Gulf were largely political in nature some explanation should be given of the machinery by which Britain exercised her political paramountcy. Since the seventeenth century the development of the British political position in the Gulf was the result of cooperation and compromise among the central British government in London, Anglo–Indian authorities in Calcutta and Bombay, and on-the-spot representatives of Britain in the Persian Gulf itself. At the top level of policy determination responsible Whitehall officials tended to think of the Persian Gulf in terms of empire-wide communications, power balances among the European great powers, and as a field in which Western "civilization" might be extended. Anglo–Indian authorities in Calcutta and Bombay viewed the Gulf mainly in the light of Indian frontier politics. The region was regarded as part of a screen of protectorates, buffer zones, and neutralized areas which surrounded India and shielded the subcontinent from attack. This screen stretched from Burma in the east, through the Himalayas, Afghanistan, Baluchistan, southern Persia, the Persian Gulf, and terminated in southern Arabia in the west. Finally, Britain's on-the-spot representatives in the Gulf concerned themselves mainly with day-to-day conditions, specific disorders or problems, treaty clauses, and individual personalities. Like most collaborations the actions of those three levels of imperial government produced compromises not entirely satisfactory to any single point of view.

In its design the political apparatus used by the British to secure their interests in the Gulf was introduced by Anglo–Indian personnel and was modeled on practices pioneered by the British in India. The key to the apparatus was the "residency system." Theoretically, a resident in Anglo–Indian practice was a kind of ambassador representing Britain, the paramount power, at the court of one or another of the local rulers allied to the British raj.[9] In reality, the resident represented and administered British power and predominance in the "allied" state. No local ruler who valued his position could refuse to heed the resident's advice. Before 1822 there had been a British resident at Bushire but his responsibilities revolved more around commercial than political concerns; his role was a relic of the days when the East India Company was a purely commercial enterprise. In 1822, as a consequence of Britain's newly assumed position in the region, the resident at Bushire became the "Resident in the Persian Gulf" and his responsibilities were recast so that his duties became primarily political. Moreover, he was placed in general charge of all British representatives in the Gulf area, including the agency that had operated at Masqat since 1798. It was he who was charged with directing the newly constructed supervisory system and Britain's newly asserted political predominance in the area. Until 1862 the role of the resident was primarily one of preventing or suppressing disorder. The residents during the early and mid-nineteenth century gave little thought to encouraging the Gulf's inhabitants to substitute modern civilization for their traditional one.

As in all segments of Anglo–Indian administration the residency performed its functions with the help of a minimum of officers. At his headquarters in Bushire the resident was assisted by a staff including an assistant resident, a surgeon, an accountant, a treasurer, and a clerk. In addition, Arab and Persian clerks, local labor, and a residency guard force were provided. Subsidiary "political agents," often Indians, were situated in al-Shariqah (Sharjah), Bahrain, Lingah, and Shiraz. Between 1800 and 1810 during the Napoleonic threat, and again in 1840, there was a European resident in Masqat, but during most years until 1861 a "native agent" represented Britain in Oman. The resident at Bushire worked closely with the "resident in Turkish Arabia" (Iraq) whose seat had been

[9] Today the British resident in the Persian Gulf officially ranks as an ambassador.

moved in 1798 from Basra to Baghdad, an arrangement made permanent in 1832. Between 1806 and 1873, although the resident was theoretically subordinate to the central Anglo–Indian government at Calcutta, his activities and his appointment were the responsibility of the governor of Bombay who supervised Anglo–Indian interests over the entire west Indian Ocean basin. Because of the need for familiarity with naval matters either the resident or his assistant normally was an Indian Navy man. Indeed, the Indian Navy came to consider the Gulf their particular preserve, and its officers set the tone of British administration there until 1862. Moreover, as the political officers in the Gulf acquired knowledge it became usual procedure for the Indian and Bombay governments to leave the bulk of policy decisions in the hands of officers on the the spot. The lack of quick communication between India and the Gulf prior to the opening of telegraphic links in 1864 encouraged this tendency.[10]

The second major element in the administration of British supervision in the Gulf after 1820 was patrol by ships of the Indian Navy; warships corresponded to the cavalry patrols guarding India's land frontiers. Seapower could be directed at any point along the Gulf's shore. But troublesome inland combinations, such as the Wahhabis, were relatively immune from direct British naval pressure.

The Anglo–Indian government did not maintain a large fleet on the Gulf. In the typical year, 1830, a five-ship squadron patrolled, whereas in 1834 only two patrol ships were in operation. Two ships were apparently insufficient for the task, since the squadron's strength was restored in 1835 following the outbreak of disorders on the Trucial Coast. A large part of the naval patrol's time was spent in the survey and navigational aid program that the Bombay Marine, the Indian Navy's predecessor, had initiated in the Gulf in 1772.[11]

[10] *Précis Gulf*, pp. 148-50, passim.
[11] *Précis Naval*, pp. 2-5.

Consolidation of British Paramountcy

From 1822 to 1862 the day-to-day tasks of dealing with the Gulf Arabs and of concluding treaties with them were left in the hands of the resident. The notable exception to this arrangement occurred in 1837–41 when Whitehall temporarily displayed more than normal interest in Persian Gulf affairs. Those years coincided with one of the periodic crises in the "Eastern Question," the diplomatic label for the politics of European rivalry in the lands embraced by the disintegrating Ottoman and Persian empires. The Persian Gulf was significant to the Eastern Question because it was a focal point where conflicting European designs and schemes converged. In 1840 British interests were well established in the Gulf area. On the other hand, Muhammad 'Ali of Egypt, an unofficial ally of France, had established his power in eastern Arabia, and Russian influence predominated in the Persian court. Thus potential French and Russian allies would have been free, if left unopposed, to squeeze the British out of the Gulf and re-create a situation in which British imperial communications would be faced with a possible threat based in the Persian Gulf. Complicating the crisis was the geographic significance of the triangle between the Mediterranean, Persian Gulf, and Red Sea as the potential site of a short route connecting Europe and the Indian Ocean. In an era of rapidly improving transport and free trade, control of this Levant triangle by one strong power would have given that power a stranglehold over the short routes connecting Europe and the expanding markets of Asia and east Africa. By skillful diplomacy Lord Palmerston scored a notable success in the Crisis of 1837–41. While British influence in the Middle East was preserved intact and even extended (Aden was occupied in 1839) both the French— and Russian—backed probes were repulsed. It was not until 1899–1902 that Britain's position in the Persian Gulf faced an equally dangerous situation. In the Gulf itself a legacy of the 1837–41 crisis was the tightening of the treaty net binding the Gulf principalities to Britain. By 1845, even Oman, hitherto less affected by the establishment of British surveillance than any other Gulf power, found its independence of action compromised by British treaty provisions.[12]

In 1856–57 a crisis of lesser magnitude than that of 1837–41 occurred. The Anglo–Indian authorities in Calcutta temporarily took over immediate direction of Britain's Gulf policy. This crisis ended after Persian moves against Herat, construed as a threat to India's northwest frontier, were abandoned after the dispatch of Indian troops to the Gulf and the occupation of Persian coastal points. This crisis illustrates the Anglo–Indian government's tendency to consider the Gulf in the perspective of Indian frontier politics.[13] Except in these two instances, however, the "old Gulf hands" generally were left to plot the way and preserve British interests. Thus the three levels that influenced Britain's Persian Gulf policy—imperial, Indian, local residency—all had their moments of dominance. But in the last analysis, the conduct of British affairs in the Gulf between 1822 and 1862 usually remained in the hands of Britain's on-the-spot representatives, with only sporadic flurries of outside interference. The residents normally exercised their authority lightly, discreetly supervising local affairs and the slave trade. This factor, coupled with the lack of well-developed modern economic interests in the Gulf before 1862 left the local Arabs with a substantial amount of independence and control over their internal affairs.

In 1862 a third stage in the development of Britain's role in the Persian Gulf began which lasted until 1903. It started in response to three developments: the reorganization of British rule in India and her dependencies as a result of the Great Indian Mutiny of 1857; the penetration of the Gulf by modern technology and communications after 1862; and the attempt by some Anglo–Indian officials to spread modern political, economic, and social practices in the region. It ended with the British turning back attempts by other modern imperial pow-

[12] Hoskins, *Routes to India*, chaps. 6-17; Aitchison—1933, XI, 289-302.
[13] Hurewitz, *Diplomacy*, I, 161-63; Low, *History of the Indian Navy*, Vol. II, chap. 2.

ers to create their own spheres of interest in the Gulf. Between 1862 and 1903 Britain's local representatives took the basic system, principles, and tools of British rule, fashioned in the early nineteenth century, and modified, refined, and applied them in such a way as to perfect the peculiar pattern of British dominion in the Persian Gulf. As a result of this process, by 1903 the British were exercising de facto if indirect supervision over many of the details of the internal as well as the external politics of the Gulf principalities. This was also a time when Britain's strategic interests and the dimensions of her imperial commitment in the Gulf were further defined and clarified. It will be this third development which will occupy our attention during the rest of this and the next chapter. Nevertheless, to present these events in perspective it would be well to mention the most recent two stages in the evolution of Britain's connection with the Persian Gulf.

Between 1903 and 1947 Britain's hold over the Gulf was at its strongest. The regional supremacy she declared unilaterally in 1903 was recognized by all her imperial rivals—France, Russia, Germany, and the Ottoman empire—during the course of diplomatic negotiations conducted in 1904-14. This supremacy was then ratified by the results of World War I, which ended with the British in occupation of Iraq and large parts of Iran. After the war one even could see Britons such as Sir Charles Belgrave in Bahrain or Bertram Thomas in Oman employed in the governments of local Arab rulers as advisors and administrators. Still, in some important ways the British grip began to relax in the 1920s. Iran reasserted her political independence and American diplomatic pressure aided United States oil interests in breaking the British monopoly of the region's rapidly developing petroleum resources. The period ended in 1947 when the British gave up their Indian empire. Since that time the British have been groping toward an accommodation with the new realities in the region. In their attempts to cooperate in evolving a more modern design for the Gulf the British have had to balance the demands of Arab and Iranian nationalists against their desire to live up to old political promises and to guarantee the continued flow of Gulf oil—oil which presently supplies a large percentage of the energy needs of Britain and Western Europe.

THE REORGANIZATION OF BRITISH INDIA AND ITS REPERCUSSIONS IN THE PERSIAN GULF

I have several times made statements in this work that major upheavals in India usually had their repercussions in the Persian Gulf. Another example of the validity of this idea is shown by the political changes that occurred in the Persian Gulf following the Mutiny of 1857. A major result of the Mutiny was the reorganization of the structure of British rule in India and her dependencies. In 1858 the old agency of British control, the East India Company, was discarded. The Government of India Act of 1858 placed supreme authority and policy direction, subordinate to crown and cabinet, in the hands of a "secretary of state for India" who sat in the London cabinet. The secretary was assisted by an appointed "Council for India" whose members were usually retired Anglo–Indian officials rich in honors and practical experience. Continuity of administrative procedure, despite elections and alternation of ministers, was insured by the India Office's hierarchy of permanent professional officials. The professionals ostensibly handled prosaic tasks such as assuring that correct constitutional procedures and proper forms were followed; actually they often made policy. During the senility of the East India Company its influence on high policy had virtually evaporated. When the India Office began to function in 1858 a new spirit was infused into the Anglo–Indian administration. London's desire to transform India into a more efficient and orderly state was infectious, and in a short time spread to the scattered segments of the Anglo–Indian government. The spirit of change was abroad by 1860 and was not long in appearing in the Persian Gulf.[14]

In India the governor-general remained the chief authority, but as the personal representative of the sovereign he received the title "viceroy." The viceroy was assisted by a council, but he was personally responsible for foreign relations. In these matters he was assisted by a personal "foreign secretary" and a "Foreign Department." This department watched over affairs among India's native states and in the areas (such as the Persian Gulf) included in India's buffer zone. Until 1873 responsibility for foreign relations over the huge area surrounding the western Indian Ocean basin was delegated to the governor of Bombay. This situation, a holdover from the days before rapid communication was possible, was changed in 1873 with the assumption by the central Anglo–Indian authority of supervision of all Indian Government representatives located outside directly administered British territory.

After 1873, then, Persian Gulf affairs were supervised in Calcutta in the office of the viceroy's foreign secretary. The Indian Foreign Department was concerned with two types of states. The department, through "residents," controlled relations with the native principalities within the Indian Empire and also handled foreign work proper—that is, administered India's relations with states outside the borders of the Indian Empire. These relations were supposed to be carried out in accordance with general imperial policy. Attached to the department in addition to the Calcutta staff were a considerable diplomatic or political service and several corps of troops for "residency duty." In practice officials usually became specialists either in relations with princes within the Indian empire proper or in relations with rulers in frontier and foreign areas such as the Persian Gulf.[15]

14 *Oxford History of India*, 3rd ed., p. 675; T. R. Metcalf, *The Aftermath of Revolt, India, 1857-1870* (Princeton, 1964).

15 P. Sykes, *Sir Mortimer Durand, a Biography* (London, 1926), pp. 55-56, 224-25; Mason, *Guardians*, p. 270; Lorimer, I, 265-66.

Despite the complexities of an imperial machinery which operated under superimposed levels of control, the system was depicted (after 1873) as one in which everyone was tied by a telegraph wire to the viceroy in Calcutta who in turn was tied by a telegraph cable to Whitehall.[16] Nevertheless, the viceroys found themselves caught up in the strong tide of system and precedent. Their actions were decided more by the force of the tide than by their own inclinations.[17] Whitehall, on the other hand, did not bother overmuch with the details of Indian affairs, let alone events of the Persian Gulf. Thus between 1862 and the 1890s there was great latitude for strong-minded, on-the-spot officials to make their wills felt. In the case of the Gulf, the structure and exercise of British power, if not always in essence, then at least in detail, was decided by Britain's local representatives.

The Jones Case, 1862-63—a new direction in the exercise of Britain's Gulf paramountcy. In 1862 Sir Bartle Frere assumed the governorship of Bombay and steamships began scheduled runs to Gulf ports. These two events signaled the start of a new era in Persian Gulf history. The old style laissez-faire administration of the Persian Gulf residency did not meet with the approval of Sir Bartle, a man, as noted earlier, very conscious of England's "civilizing mission" in the world. Frere had a clear idea of how he wanted events in the Gulf to develop and of what type man he wanted to guide Britain's interests there. Rather than being restricted to a policeman's activities, the resident, in Frere's mind, should enlarge the scope of this influence with the various princes he dealt with. In this way the resident could become an advisor not only in matters of external policy but also in domestic affairs. To Frere a good resident should not give the appearance of meddling in a prince's internal administration but should watch all that went on in a given principality. He should support the local chiefs as long as they maintained frank, friendly relations with

[16] C. E. Carrington, *The British Overseas* (Cambridge, 1950), p. 455.
[17] Mason, *Guardians*, p. 76.

179

the British. Finally the ideal resident should guide but not force the rulers to follow modern, "enlightened" practices. Frere believed the general principles under which a resident worked should be outlined by his superiors, but he felt the resident should be left to determine the details of policy execution.

Frere's views on what the role of the resident should be meshed with his plans for modifying Britain's Persian Gulf policy and also with his more general ideas on the mission of Britain's empire in the world. Instead of substituting a system of direct British administration he believed in an empire of pervading influence which would respect local cultures and operate through established rulers, while instilling new motive force into old machinery. At the same time there should be no uncertainty as to where final power lay. Local governments "must in essential conform to the civic standard of right and wrong" of the British. In addition, British supervision was to be a vehicle for spreading modern concepts of thought and technology. This type of colonial supervision was styled "indirect rule." In a sense, Frere thought modernization was the prerequisite to the ultimate conversion of the world to Christian ethics. Thus Frere's imperialism, paradoxically, was rooted in the tradition of English liberalism and to a lesser extent in evangelicalism. He believed empire to be a duty in that it spread both civilization and liberty.[18]

In Frere's eyes Britain had not measured up to its mission in the Persian Gulf. In particular, he did not approve of the resident, Captain Felix Jones, an Indian Navy officer with long experience in Iraq and the Gulf who had been officiating at Bushire for six years when Frere became Governor of Bombay in 1862. Under Jones the residency had continued to operate essentially as it had since 1822. In line with this policy a general atmosphere of live and let live prevailed. Jones himself

[18] Martineau, *Life of Frere*, I, 50-51, 69-70, 168-69, 495.

married into an Armenian–Persian family and integrated himself into the Gulf pattern of life. In 1840 the style of his residency probably would have earned praise but in 1862 Frere looked on Jones as incapable of serving as a model of English ideas, behavior, and civilization; it was not long before the governor began sending letters to his superiors saying that the job was too much for Jones.

Sir Bartle was able to act late in 1862 when Jones went on leave to England. He appointed as acting resident an energetic young cavalry officer, Lewis Pelly, who had distinguished himself in the Middle East and Zanzibar. Frere then proceeded to direct letter after letter to the Indian Office in London with the object of preventing Jones' resumption of his post as resident and of substituting Pelly. Each letter hammered at the theme that a new age had dawned in the Gulf and that although Jones might have been fit to head the old laissez-faire residency he was not the man to solve the problems of a region awakening to modern civilization.

Jones fought to keep his post, but to no avail, and Lewis Pelly became resident.[19] Jones represented the "old Gulf hands," many of them Indian Navy men, who regarded the Gulf as their exclusive preserve. Thinking that they knew more about the Gulf than anyone else, this group actually had a very circumscribed idea of the new situation and did not see the Gulf in its Indian, let alone imperial, perspective. With Pelly's appointment to the Persian Gulf residency a new period opened in Britain's connection with the region, a period marked by increasing British interference in the internal politics of the Gulf states. British policy decisions began to have more and more effect on the course of internal history there. By 1900 the independence of the Gulf states was so compromised that for all intents and purposes they had become part of the British empire.

[19] "Frere to Wood. 12 Feb. 1862," "27 Nov. 1862," "12 May 1864," India Mss.–1; Martineau, *Life of Frere*, I, 505.

Consolidation of British Paramountcy

LEWIS PELLY AND THE EXPANSION OF BRITAIN'S ROLE IN
THE PERSIAN GULF, 1862-72

The decade during which Lewis Pelly served as resident in the Persian Gulf was a time of rapidly expanding British influence in the region. It was a decade marked by the spread of modern economic enterprise and communications, and of an increase in British political involvement in the area. Significant as these events were in themselves, they seem far more dramatic when it is recalled that the 1860s were years of political caution and, in many cases, retrenchment in the Anglo–Indian empire. Of the buffer areas shielding India's frontiers, the Persian Gulf was almost unique, in that Britain's political responsibilities were greater in 1870 than they were in 1860. There are three reasons: the growth in Britain's economic stake in the Gulf resulting from the British India Steam Navigation Company's initiation of steamboat service there; the construction of the Indo–European telegraph through the Gulf and the consequent speed-up of communication within the region and between the Gulf and the outside world; and the fact that Britain's interests in the Gulf were being supervised by two energetic and dedicated men, Sir Bartle Frere, the Governor of Bombay, and his on-the-spot subordinate, Lewis Pelly, the resident in the Persian Gulf.

I have noted Sir Bartle Frere's convictions about British imperialism and Lewis Pelly's rather grandiose ideas concerning the economic development of the Gulf and his contention that the British residency should play an active part in modernizing the region. The question remains, however, how did Pelly administer his residency in order to translate his goals into accomplishments? Most of Pelly's actions had to be directed more toward political than economic concerns because he was convinced of the need to create the climate and the political prerequisites which would be conducive to widespread modernization. The resident thought modernization could be accomplished only if Britain actively supervised the process.

Hence, he worked to strengthen the empire's political influence in the Gulf. The assurance of a firm political order was to be prerequisite for creation of an environment favoring the continuing growth of "civilization" and trade. It is not surprising that he was willing to interfere in some institutions or practices characteristic of Persian Gulf civilization previously respected by the British. Pelly was an untiring if at times bombastic publicist concerning the economic potential of the region, and he called on his countrymen to take advantage of their dominance to push trade, warning that neglect could only stimulate challenges to Britain's position. He also held the opinion that British policy in the region could be most efficiently applied only if there was no question that he was Britain's chief representative in the Gulf and that all other British officials stationed there, both military and civilian, should be under his jurisdiction. It is difficult to determine just where Lewis Pelly differentiated between carrying out the duties of his office and furthering the modernization of the Gulf. He did not categorize his actions. He opposed any person or group that might bring disorder or threaten the realization of his schemes. All in all, Pelly displayed what was to become during the period of the "new imperialism" a typical British attitude concerning how best to stimulate modernization. It was an attitude that implied a large measure of tutelage by the West. It was not particularly sophisticated nor scientifically oriented; in practical terms it relied more on specific schemes tailored to particular localities than on universalistic theories of development.

It was the spirit of his administration—Pelly's desire that Britain should provide beacons to guide a modernizing Gulf —that was his most enduring legacy. An energetic, fearless, but somewhat arrogant man who could call upon both dash and perseverance to conquer adversity, Pelly's style of leadership betrayed the fact that he was a cavalryman by training who never lost his taste for adventure and headstrong action. He was given to dangerous, unprecedented treks. In 1860 he rode alone on horseback through wild tribal country from Iran through Afghanistan to India. In 1865, while resident, he undertook another brave march into the interior of Arabia when he went to Riyadh in an unsuccessful attempt to calm a serious crisis in British–Saudi relations. By training, temperament, and intellectual inclination Lewis Pelly was a stubborn guardian of what he considered to be Britain's interests during a time when the foundations of the Gulf's traditional life were being altered radically. After he retired from the Gulf residency in 1872 his career shifted to Afghanistan and India where he so distinguished himself as a diplomat that he was knighted in 1877. Honors continued to follow him until his death in 1892, by which time he had been appointed an honorary Lieutenant General and had made a name for himself as an imperialist spokesman in the House of Commons.

Pelly's qualities of energy, boldness, persuasive ability, and intelligence, although they were combined with the less admirable traits of vindictiveness and contentiousness, contributed mightily to the strengthening of Britain's position in the Gulf at a time when that position almost certainly would have deteriorated under a man with even slightly less ability or self-confidence. Pelly was fortunate because few offices were more susceptible to reflecting an occupant's strengths or weaknesses than that of a resident in the British Indian government. The effectiveness of the office, unlike that of viceroy, was not determined by the administrative structure which supported it. Rather, the post was an enlargement of the man who filled it. A resident could restrict himself "to keeping up a friendly intercourse with the reigning prince" or he could become an advisor to the local court not only in matters of foreign affairs but also in domestic politics and other matters. Pelly interpreted his role in the broadest sense. Indeed, he was something of a revolutionary. Even more than Frere, he looked upon himself as a spokesman for modernization, change, and a dawning new age. Pelly's career in the Gulf was punctuated with controversy and several failures, but because he was in the vanguard of a new, soon to conquer philosophy—the "new imperialism" of the "white man's burden" subvariety—his successes multiplied as his term as resident progressed.[20]

In administering his charge Pelly worked within the context of three primary problem complexes. First, he endured many policy disagreements with his superiors in Calcutta. Although his immediate superior, Sir Bartle Frere, generally shielded and supported Pelly, coping with Calcutta's retrenchment-minded policies was one of the resident's most frustrating experiences. Second, Pelly had difficulty in imposing his official authority over various British officers serving in the Gulf. Third, he was vexed with a perplexing situation of dealing with the various Gulf rulers, maintaining political order in the region during a time of profound economic, social, and political upheaval, and at the same time trying to create a political climate inside the various Gulf states conducive to their modernization.

Pelly, his superiors, and Persian Gulf policy. Lewis Pelly's difficulties with his superiors in Calcutta were caused by a clash in imperial philosophies. Pelly was in the vanguard of the "new imperialism." He believed Britain had to increase her involvement and commitment in places like the Persian Gulf where there was already in existence a structure of extraordinary treaty relationships. Those presiding over the central government of British India, especially Sir John Lawrence, viceroy of India from 1864 to 1869, and Charles Aitchison, secretary of the Foreign Department, 1868-78, were upholders of the nonaggressive policy of "noninvolvement," or, as Lawrence preferred to call it, "masterly inactivity." The adherents of this school held that Britain's Indian empire should be enclosed by a sharply defined border beyond which contacts

---

[20] For a sketch of Pelly's life see, *Dictionary of National Biography*, XLIV (1895), 275-77; also, Martineau, *Life of Frere*, I, 50-51, 503. Also see "Pelly to Anderson, 16 Feb. 1866," *Précis Int'l. Rivalry*, p. 29; "Pelly to Anderson, 12 May 1866," *Précis Commerce*, p. 30; "Hamilton to Curzon, 23 Oct. 1901," India Mss.–2, Vol. III.

should be restricted. In those regions beyond India's frontier where the maintenance of diplomatic relations and the assumption of some responsibility was required the "noninvolvement" school believed interference with the internal affairs and the customs of foreign principalities should be avoided or held to an absolute minimum. During the 1860s this laissez-faire-oriented approach to international and imperial relations was colored by two special circumstances. First, both the Calcutta and London foreign offices were anxious to reach an agreement with St. Petersburg over the respective spheres of British and Russian influence in Asia. It was Calcutta's view that both powers should cease their advances on the continent and agree to designate the territory separating their dominions as a neutral buffer zone. Corollary to preventing an Anglo–Russian clash in Asia was the Calcutta policy of trying to discourage any new undertakings in places such as Afghanistan or Iran that were envisioned as part of the proposed neutral zone. If powers such as Russia or France intervened in the transfrontier neutral area Calcutta hoped the interference could be halted by diplomacy exercised by London in the capital of the offending power.[21]

Another factor contributing to the Calcutta foreign policy in the 1860s was a desire to avoid friction and shun adventures of any type during a time when India was recovering from the Great Mutiny. Lord Canning during his viceroyalty had set this policy and John Lawrence followed it closely. Another dimension to the situation was the fact that the Indian government's budget was severely strained by the Mutiny and its aftermath. In 1863 the debt stood at £38,000,000 while the budget operated with a £7,000,000 deficit. Stringent economy and the reform of India's financial apparatus were considered far more vital by those in power in Calcutta than the initiation of what they view as dubious foreign programs and adven-

[21] Martineau, *Life of Frere*, I, 482; Sykes, *Sir Mortimer Durand*, p. 84. B. Prasad, *The Foundations of India's Foreign Policy* (Calcutta, 1955), pp. 26, 41.

tures that would only extend India's commitments and threaten financial recovery.[22]

Regarding the Persian Gulf, Calcutta believed Britain should continue its laissez-faire policeman's role and not initiate any new programs or radical departures in policy. Paradoxically, the central Anglo–Indian authorities supported both the construction of the Indo–European telegraph and the subsidization of the British India Steam Navigation Company's Persian Gulf service as defense measures. Yet the repercussions of the operations of these enterprises constituted a powerful stimulus to the very increase in British involvement in the Gulf that Calcutta was seeking to avoid. In general, Whitehall backed Calcutta's policy of masterly inactivity until the mid-1870s, when a more aggressive diplomacy came to the fore.

In opposition to noninvolvement during the 1860s was the youthful "new imperialism" which was not destined to reach full maturity until the 1880s and early 1890s. This concept held that the exercise of imperial sway was not a distasteful (if necessary) evil but a moral duty. The early "new imperialists" recoiled from doctrines which, like "masterly inactivity," would have cut off entire countries from modern influences— a "new imperialist" would have called them "civilized" influences. The British variety of new imperialism in its early stages of development, at least, was profoundly influenced by humanitarian and moral concerns. Its first saint was David Livingstone whose writings convinced many Britons that it was their Christian duty to spread British political influence in Afro–Asia as a first step in sowing the benefits of modern civilization. Imperial glory and international power were not the prizes sought by the early new imperialists. Rather, they felt themselves missionaries of a humane, enlightened way of life. Regrettably, as the new imperialism became more popular it began to take on a racist, jingoistic, strutting tone reflecting many of

[22] *Oxford History of India,* 3rd ed., p. 677; Anstey, *Economic Development of India,* p. 373; Martineau, *Life of Frere,* I, 289-99; Metcalf, *The Aftermath of Revolt,* passim.

the Social–Darwinist conceptions of the late nineteenth century.

In India Sir Bartle Frere was among the earliest converts to the new imperial philosophy. Because he was able to install another, younger disciple of the creed in the Bushire residency, the Persian Gulf was one of the first places in Afro–Asia to feel the new faith's influence. As governor of Bombay, Frere was charged with overseeing Anglo–Indian interests across a huge expanse of the western Indian Ocean littoral. Sir Bartle was not a man to ignore the possibilities of cultivating modernism and influencing the rulers within the western Indian Ocean basin—including those of the Persian Gulf—if the opportunity were presented.

Against the backdrop of the clash in opposing imperial philosophies Pelly carried out his duties as resident. Although he often found himself out of step with Calcutta policy and with many other Indian Foreign Department representatives in the field, he was supported and shielded by Frere when Calcutta's protests grew loud. Frere would claim that British policy in the Persian Gulf since 1820 had been one of active interference and that Calcutta's policy was unrealistic in view of Britain's past actions and the responsibilities she had assumed in the area.[23] Calcutta had to listen to Frere, the second most important man in India, even if it could have ignored a relatively junior official like Pelly. All through the 1860s the controversy wore on as Pelly and Frere continued to push for an enlargement of Britain's role in the Gulf, while Calcutta, supported by the harsh figures of financial crisis, opposed.

The friction between philosophies was especially apparent and the implications significant in the matter of policing the Persian Gulf. In his efforts to maintain order Pelly took a leaf from the book of General John Jacob, his old commander when the resident served in the cavalry on India's Sind frontier. Jacob's system of maintaining a border was based on the

[23] "Frere to Lawrence, 26 Apr. 1866," quoted in Martineau, *Life of Frere*, I, 509-10; see also p. 483.

use of a screen of cavalry patrols and on rendering the area immediately beyond the frontier peaceful through the personal influence of British officers resident in transfrontier principalities.[24] In other words the frontier was a rather indefinite concept, with British influence being exercised in a more and more shadowy fashion the deeper into a transfrontier region one traveled. Lawrence's frontier policy favored the drawing of a definite border and using force only if an enemy crossed over the line. Furthermore, he proclaimed that "under any circumstances, the principle of refraining from interference with the neighboring tribes and abstaining from any concern with their internal quarrels must be rigorously maintained."[25]

Pelly tried to adapt the Jacob system to the situation in the Gulf. He outlined his frontier policy, the source of it, and the difficulty of implementing it as follows: ". . . to keep the maritime peace along the strongholds of these littoral chieftainships, is no child's play. It is not by the sudden and occasional appearance of a man of war that this can be thoroughly done. What is required is uniform vigilance and pressure. The position of the Resident as arbiter of the Maritime truce may be aptly compared with that of an officer holding a civilized frontier against lawless borderers. . . . What is wanted is the constant pressure of watchful outposts ready at any moment to put down raids, and uphold the peaceful and well inclined. . . . Our light gun boats are such outposts and patrols for the Arab coast. . . ."[26]

Nevertheless, it was not the active opposition of Calcutta which caused Pelly most of his trouble in preserving the peace of the Gulf. It was Calcutta's lack of concern for transfrontier affairs in the 1860s and its consequent neglect of the Persian Gulf. The main prop of Pelly's or any Persian Gulf resident's

[24] *Oxford History of India*, 3rd ed., p. 698.

[25] "Muir to Gonne, 1866, no. 1,044: Calcutta," India Records-2, Vol. XLIII. At the time this letter was written Muir was the viceroy's foreign secretary in Calcutta while Gonne was secretary of the Government of Bombay.

[26] Pelly, "Trade Report, 1869," quoted in *Précis Commerce*, p. 33.

frontier policy had to be naval power. Until 1863 ships of the Indian Navy supplied the necessary naval units in the Gulf.[27] Between 1820 and 1862 a four or five-ship squadron nearly constantly patrolled there. As part of India's post-Mutiny reorganization the Indian Navy, however, was abolished in April 1863. At the time of abolition it was understood that the responsibility for patrolling the Gulf would be transferred to the Royal Navy. But it was not until 1871 that a practical system for utilizing Royal Navy vessels in the Gulf evolved. In the meantime the maritime peace and Britain's interests there suffered.[28] Ironically, Sir Bartle Frere precipitated these difficulties. In 1863 he argued the inefficiency of the Indian Navy and indicated his low opinion of its officers. Frere's objection was that the Indian Navy was not strong enough to mount the powerful naval display that he believed necessary to uphold British interests along Arabia's coasts.[29]

The substitution of the Royal Navy for the Indian Navy did not work for several reasons. The Royal Navy's East India station was so large, the climate so trying on crews and ships, and calls for vessels so numerous, that efficient supervision of the entire Indian Ocean area was impossible. There was always more work than ships in the 1860s. Royal Navy vessels would only stay in the Gulf in cool weather despite what the resident thought was the need for constant patrols.[30] Between 1863 and 1870 the Gulf was visited only three times by Royal Navy gunboats and responsibility for patrolling the Gulf was left to the little sail survey ships of the Bombay Marine. In 1864-65 and 1866-67 not a single British government armed vessel visited

[27] The Indian Navy's beginnings can be traced back to the early seventeenth century although it was not officially created until 1830. As part of the general reorganization of the Anglo-Indian administration following the Great Indian Mutiny, the force was abolished in 1863, but the maritime transport and survey arm of the Bombay government, the Bombay Marine, took over some of the functions of the defunct service. For details see Low, *History of the Indian Navy*.

[28] *Précis Naval*, p. 11; Lorimer, I, 247.

[29] "Frere to Wood, 12 Apr. 1862," "26 Aug. 1862," India Mss.–1.

[30] *Précis Naval*, p. 11; "Frere to Wood, 28 Apr., 1864," India Mss.–1.

the Gulf. But neither the viceroy nor Sir Charles Wood, the secretary of state for India in London, to whom the resident also appealed, heeded Pelly's call for ships.[31] Between 1861 and 1871 most survey and navigational aid work also ceased.[32]

The effects of this neglect on the British position in the Gulf were serious. There were numerous outbreaks of disorder in the Gulf in the 1860s, culminating in a revival of Arab naval wars around Bahrain in 1867-68. Frere was aghast at the serious situation his wrecking of the Indian Navy had caused, for it had been his understanding that the Gulf would be taken over by the Royal Navy, not abandoned. Conditions were so bad at times that Pelly, deprived of regular service, had to commandeer passing merchant vessels, even Arab dhows, to superintend his domain. Pelly complained repeatedly and bitterly of the impossibility of doing his job adequately without naval support.[33] Frere strongly supported Pelly and tried to convince his superiors to allow the resident permanent use of a fast cruiser.[34] In 1865-66 the question of Calcutta's neglect of the Gulf came to a head. For a time Lawrence considered placing Gulf affairs under a consul general residing in Isfahan high on the inland Persian plateau and permanently withdrawing the naval patrol, but, predictably, Pelly and Frere attacked this plan. Finally Lawrence told Frere that he did not want to concern himself with Gulf policy any more, that he was going to leave this to London.[35] The situation finally began to change in 1867 when Frere left India and assumed a seat on the Council for India in London. Here he was able to influence the secretary of state for India. Lawrence himself left India in 1869, an event which removed the "noninvolvement" school's chief

---

[31] *Précis Naval*, p. 11.   [32] Lorimer, I, 247.

[33] "Pelly to Gonne, 23 Apr. 1866," quoted in *Précis Trucial Chiefs*, pp. 33-34; "Frere to Lord Cranborne, 2 Oct. 1866," quoted in Martineau, *Life of Frere*, I, 465.

[34] "Frere to Wood, 28 Apr. 1864," "28 Oct. 1866," India Mss.–1.

[35] *Précis Int'l. Rivalry*, pp. 31-32; "Lawrence to Frere, 21 Apr. 1866," quoted in Martineau, *Life of Frere*, I, 509; also see pp. 445-46.

Consolidation of British Paramountcy

TABLE 6

British Warships in Persian Gulf Waters, 1863-72

	SHIP	REMARKS
1863-64	B.M.S. Clyde	Abolition of Indian Navy
	B.M.S. Hugh Rose	
1864-65	No ships	
1865-66	H.M.S. Highflyer	Anti-Saudi operations
	H.M.S. Berenice	
1866-67	No ships	
1867-68	B.M.S. Hugh Rose	
1868-69	H.M.S. Dryad	Operations: off Bahrayn;
	H.M.S. Vigilant	antislave trade patrol
	B.M.S. Hugh Rose	
	B.M.S. Sinde	
	B.M.S. Clyde	
1869-70	B.M.S. Clyde	Operations at Masqat
	B.M.S. Hugh Rose	
	B.M.S. Dalhousie	
1870-71	No ships	
1871-72	H.M.S. Bullfinch	Royal Navy starts rotation
	H.M.S. Magpie	patrol agreed upon in 1869
	H.M.S. Vulture	
	H.M.S. Lynx	
	H.M.S. Nimble	

Note: Compiled from *Précis Naval*, p. 6. Initials B.M.S. stand for Bombay Marine Ship.

spokesman and allowed India's foreign and imperial policy to begin a slow swing toward the "new imperialist" school.

Indicative of the changing situation was an agreement concluded between the Anglo–Indian government and the navy in 1869 and put into operation in 1871. This agreement provided that in return for a payment of £70,000 per year by the government of India to the Admiralty to cover operating costs, the Royal Navy would guarantee to provide India nine vessels a year. Of these, three ships were to be stationed off east Africa to suppress the slave trade. Three more were to be placed in constant patrol in and off the Persian Gulf to police the area and prevent slave trade operations. Also, navy vessels operating in the Gulf were to be placed once and for all under the control of the resident and no aggressive act was to be undertaken by these vessels without the approval of the resident.[36] The "navy episode" illustrates how a policy often considered the basis of British paramountcy in the Gulf—the maintenance of naval supervision—had to be reemphasized, fought for, and restated from time to time. The neglect of naval power in the Gulf is an excellent example of the attitudes Pelly had to contend with in implementing his program. Calcutta and London, in the 1860s both centers of noninvolvement thinking, were content if the machinery of British power in the Gulf rusted. Many officials would have preferred simply to ignore the Gulf. In their dispatches both Frere and Pelly issued constant warnings that London's and Calcutta's disinterest in Persian Gulf affairs could create dangers to India's frontiers and to imperial communications. Frere often painted gloomy pictures of a growing critical situation in the Gulf caused by Britain's "neglect of the warnings given . . . by local officers." He was also fond of conjuring up an image of Ottoman, Persian, and Gulf Arab restlessness being instigated from behind the scenes by sinister European agents. Raising the specter of European intervention and intrusion seemed to be one of the few ploys that could stimulate any concern in Calcutta or London about Gulf matters. Nevertheless, as long as John Lawrence was viceroy of India, the climate in both Calcutta and London favored withdrawal from exposed positions and noninvolvement in potentially entangling and expensive adventures in areas outside the zone of direct British administration. Any extension of British commitments was usually opposed on principle. For his part, Lawrence generally found fault with many of Pelly's actions, but the viceroy seemed unwilling to become embroiled in a heated controversy with Pelly's mentor, Frere, concerning

---

[36] "Instructions to the East India Squadron," quoted in *Précis Naval*, p. 17. Lorimer, I, 350. See Columb, *Slave Catching*, pp. 136-38, for the Royal Navy's views regarding the Persian Gulf patrol question.

the resident's ideas, or over what to Lawrence must have seemed such a trivial matter as Persian Gulf affairs.[37]

Pelly was fortunate that he could always count on the enthusiastic support of his immediate superior. In a letter to the secretary of state for India, Frere indicated his high opinion of Pelly as well as his Victorian sensibilities: "He has told us more of Northern Arabia . . . than any of our agents there for the past twenty years. . . . I think his views are generally sound. Nor do I know his equal in our service to travel, negotiate, and make friends with a barbarian or fanatical people without for a moment compromising his character as an English gentleman."[38]

The fact that British power in the Gulf did not evaporate during the cautious 1860s was due in no small measure to the dedication and drive of Pelly and the prestige and skill of Frere. Pelly broadcast his point of view concerning the present importance and the future potentiality of the Gulf region both in official dispatches and public writings. He fired barrages of letters and salvos of articles—which appeared in Indian and English journals—defending or propagandizing his opinions. Until Lawrence's departure in 1869 the outcome of the argument seemed uncertain, but, in fact, neglect of the Gulf was so common in both Calcutta and London that little time was spent in thinking about implementing a withdrawal from the area. In the last analysis, in the absence of any major crisis in the Gulf both Calcutta and London went along with the established "system." Normally Pelly was ignored in most official circles, just as the Gulf was ignored. Left to his own devices Pelly took the limited instruments that were his and attended to the birth of a new era in the Persian Gulf.

Pelly and his subordinates. Pelly's second major problem was assuring that the resident would be in command of all other British officers serving in the Gulf. Pelly had little trou-

[37] "Frere to Wood, 22 May 1863," India Mss.–1; Martineau, *Life of Frere,* I, 507-10, II, 107-108.
[38] "Frere to Wood, 22 Apr. 1865," India Mss.–1.

ble in controlling his residency staff, while in 1869 his supremacy over the naval personnel assigned to duty in the Gulf was finally clarified. The chief point of friction was the resident's relation to the British representative at Masqat. In 1861 the British reestablished their "political agency" at Masqat after the partition of the Omani empire into African and Asiatic halves necessitated appointment of a European officer to supervise relations with Oman. The Masqat Agency had been in existence unofficially since Imam Ahmad's reign (ca. 1749-ca. 1783) and officially since 1800. During most of its existence under the East India Company, the agency was administered by an untrained Indian official who performed necessary commercial and consular duties. No attempt was made to exercise political influence except when a European consul held the agency, as was the case in 1800-1809 and in 1840.

In May 1861 Lieutenant W. M. Pengelley of the Indian Navy became political agent at Masqat. Neither the scope of Pengelley's duties nor his place in the chain of command within the British establishment in the Gulf was defined clearly. These issues were not settled before Pengelley displeased the Anglo–Indian government with his fumbling actions during a revolt against the Masqati sultan. Pengelley was replaced by a Major Green who, in turn, was relieved as political agent by Lt. Col. Herbert Disbrowe in January of 1863, about the same time that Pelly took over as resident at Bushire.[39]

From the beginning Pelly and Disbrowe did not get along. Disbrowe had served in the Gulf since 1852, was a former assistant of the deposed Felix Jones, a representative of the previous laissez-faire era, and thought he knew considerably more about Gulf conditions than did Pelly. In a sense Disbrowe was the rear guard of a passing age.[40]

[39] Lorimer, I, 472-73.

[40] For an indication of Disbrowe's opinion of his own ability and knowledge as compared to Pelly's see, "Disbrowe to Gonne, 15 Sept. 1869, no. 514: Masqat," India Records–2, Vol. L.

Pelly, for his part, was hardly diplomatic and treated Disbrowe as a junior subordinate. In one of his first letters the resident ordered Disbrowe to send all his communications via the Bushire residency. Pelly's action was construed by Disbrowe as an attempt to turn him into Pelly's office boy at Masqat (which probably was the case). In 1865 Frere tried to halt the quarrel by instructing Disbrowe to correspond through Pelly or whoever else was resident. Frere's idea, and one enthusiastically agreed to by Pelly, was that the resident should be supreme in the Gulf.[41] Disbrowe was left with a loophole, however, in that he was allowed to correspond directly with Bombay in an emergency. For the rest of his term as agent at Masqat Disbrowe continued to write directly to Bombay, defending his actions by saying that "these have been no ordinary times."

In 1867 Disbrowe left Masqat for two years; in the interim the post was held by an intelligent young officer, Captain G. A. Atkinson, who, despite his junior rank carried on the struggle to keep the Masqat Political Agency free from complete subservience to Bushire. He earned Pelly's scorn by disagreeing with the resident and by reiterating Disbrowe's contention that the agent at Masqat would be powerless to act if he had to refer all matters to Bushire. In his relations with Atkinson Pelly again demonstrated his propensity to compound his troubles by embittering those with whom he disagreed. Disbrowe returned to his post at Masqat in 1869 and until he was forced to leave his position in January 1870 he continued to fight with the resident. After the agent's return to Masqat the issue was finally settled. On resuming his post Disbrowe once again started to bombard Bombay and Calcutta with letters attacking everything from "the ignorance of Colonel Pelly" compared to his own knowledge, to Pelly's plotting to lower his influence, and Pelly's lack of courtesy. Right or wrong, it became apparent to Disbrowe's superiors in India that his obsession against

[41] "Gonne to Disbrowe, 7 Nov. 1865, no. 2737: Bombay," India Records–2, Vol. L.

Pelly had reached a point by the autumn of 1869 that he could no longer effectively discharge British interests in Oman. Pelly, for once, remained fairly quiet and let Disbrowe destroy himself in a series of haranguing letters to Bombay. These showed Disbrowe to be a bitter man who had lost his sense of perspective and his value as a British representative in the Gulf.[42] In January 1870 Disbrowe's post was assumed by Major A. Cotton Way. Moreover, to prevent any future trouble Major Way was placed in strict subordination to the resident— Masqat was finally subjugated by Bushire.[43] This settlement effectively determined that the resident would be in complete command of the British administration in the Gulf and that thereafter he could more easily mobilize local British official-dom behind his policies.

Pelly and the growth of "indirect rule" in the Persian Gulf. The third major problem complex the resident had to contend with involved questions of strengthening relations with Gulf rulers, augmenting the residency's ability to uphold the peace, and encouraging modernization at a time when Gulf civiliza-tion was experiencing profound stress. Pelly used a variety of tactics to grapple with this situation, but his basic strategy remained constant: he sought to increase British political in-volvement to the point where a resident could exercise as decisive an influence in determining the political climate within the Gulf principalities as he could in controlling these states' foreign affairs. Encountering much trouble but ulti-mately achieving considerable success in realizing this policy, Pelly, when he stepped down as resident in 1872, had estab-lished a system whereby British interests were served not only by the special treaty network, the residency apparatus, and the Royal Navy, but also by the positive cooperation of many among the local Gulf rulers.

[42] "Pelly to Disbrowe, 21 Aug. 1869, no. 464: Residency," India Rec-ords–2, Vol. L. Defiant to the end, Disbrowe continued to report directly to Bombay and to attack Pelly. See India Records–2, Vol. xvi, passim.

[43] "Disbrowe to Gonne, 8 Jan. 1870, no. 17: Masqat," India Records–2, Vol. xvi; Lorimer, i, 488.

Pelly sought to create an identification of the interests of the maritime Arab rulers with those of Britain by using many devices. Most of these were based on a doctrine latent but not often or forcefully asserted in the pre-1862 special treaty system. By his public utterances and actions the resident publicized his resolve that the British would support the integrity of the various states stretching from Oman to Bahrain. In 1861, even before Pelly became resident, the Anglo–Indian government took the unprecedented step of giving the shaykh of Bahrain a specific guarantee that the security of his possessions would be safeguarded against foreign attack.[44] This declaration was issued to discourage a resurgent Saudi state from launching an attack that would upset the territorial status quo and threaten the maritime peace of the region. After he became resident Pelly was forced to underline the intent of this declaration by ordering gunboat bombardments in 1865 and 1866 against various coastal strong points held by the Saudis and their allies, to counter the continued menace to the territorial status quo in the Gulf posed by the Wahhabi state. Finally, in 1866 Pelly secured from the Saudi ruler, 'Abdallah ibn-Faysal, a declaration promising respect for the territorial integrity of those Gulf States enjoying a special treaty relationship with Britain.[45]

In binding the Arab rulers to Britain, however, Pelly went beyond protecting a state from outside invasion. He was also quite willing to aid cooperative rulers against internal enemies and rebellions. This was a new departure in Anglo–Indian practice in the Gulf, and one that was rather ineffectively resisted by the Foreign Department in Calcutta. Often Pelly would act and then present Calcutta with a fait accompli. Armed demonstrations by gunboats, public declarations of British support and recognition of certain rulers, as well as the manipulation of financial subsidies, were all techniques used by Pelly to prop up friendly rulers against internal

---

[44] Text in Aitchison—1892, x, 118. Also see Kelly, "British Position in the Persian Gulf," *St. Antony's Papers, Number IV*, p. 137.

[45] Hurewitz, *Diplomacy*, I, 172.

threats or to bring pressure against rulers who failed to gain favor.

The British involvement in the internal affairs of the Gulf states was also increased by new additions to the treaty structure which determined the politics of the area. New bilateral agreements, multilateral guarantees, and arbitration awards added to the superstructure of the treaty system. Moreover, there was a strong assertion under Pelly's aegis of extraterritorial privileges for British subjects—mainly Indian merchants —resident in the Gulf. The resident did not shrink from using diplomatic pressure, and even armed force in a few extreme instances, to protect Indian merchants or gain compensation for them after they were molested.

The different devices used to strengthen British preponderance were applied in various combinations within the region. The manner in which Britain's relations with Oman developed during the 1860s provides a good example of the rapid growth of British influence within a Gulf state.

In Oman, as in other parts of the region, many of the specific arrangements that increased British involvement in local domestic affairs were introduced to deal with new situations which appeared after the old basis of Gulf life began to change rapidly in the 1860s. In 1856 the British certainly had some capability of manipulating Oman's internal affairs, but their power was not really decisive. British–Omani relations were governed by the old alliance treaty of 1798, by a commercial agreement concluded in 1839, and by a number of antislave trade engagements, the latest of which dated from 1845.

This situation began to change in the aftermath of Sayyid Sa'id's death. Between 1856 and 1861 the Omani empire was vexed by heated contests among the late monarch's numerous sons, each seeking to succeed his father. To prevent a war of succession which could have spread anarchy over the breadth of the western Indian Ocean the British intervened and secured the promise of the contending princes to abide by Anglo–Indian arbitration. An investigation of rival claims was held and the viceroy, Lord Canning, announced his award in 1861. The typically British solution of partition was advanced: the once sprawling Omani empire was divided into two parts, a rich African domain centered at Zanzibar, and a poorly endowed Asiatic principality governed from Masqat. In order to adjust the inequality of the two inheritances Zanzibar was supposed to forward an annual subsidy of $MT 40,000 (£8,500) to Masqat. The award and subsidy were to extend to the respective successors of the contending rulers, who received the titles of "sultan" of Zanzibar and Masqat, respectively, and were to be final compensation to the sultan of Masqat for abandoning for all time all claims upon Zanzibar.[46] In 1862, unknown to Pelly, Frere, or Calcutta, London, and the French government jointly guaranteed the independence of both Oman and Zanzibar, thus ratifying the Canning Award.[47] This Anglo–French guarantee was destined to cause the British considerable difficulty later.

However loudly Calcutta might trumpet the slogan "non-involvement," Britain could not escape entanglement in Omani domestic politics after authoring the Canning Award. The numerous instances of British intervention in Omani affairs between 1862 and 1872 illustrate an increasing interaction of Anglo–Indian policy as applied by Pelly with internal events. Repeatedly in 1864-65 Pelly, in order to protect a country he considered an "outpost of civilization," intervened in Omani–Wahhabi troubles. In the course of this intervention he helped in the organization of anti-Saudi forces in Oman; bombarded Saudi forts at al-Qatif and al-Damman; destroyed the ships of the al-Janabah tribe, Wahhabi sympathizers in Oman; levied a fine of $MT 27,700 against al-Janabah for destroying the property of the Hindus of Sur who were British subjects; and finally in 1866, arranged a treaty by which the Saudi ruler agreed to leave in peace those Gulf states, includ-

[46] For text see Aitchison—1933, XI, 303.
[47] Text in Hurewitz, *Diplomacy*, I, 168-69.

ing Oman, which enjoyed a special relationship with the British.[48] Another legacy of the Canning Arbitration was the necessity for Britain to oversee and guarantee, if necessary, the payment of the Zanzibar subsidy. In the 1860s many rival princes came forward to claim the rule of Oman, and it became clear that the recognition of a leader and his designation as the recipient of the subsidy by the British augmented the revenue, prestige, and total power of even a locally unpopular contestant. The money from the Zanzibar subsidy assumed vital importance to the treasury of Oman's rulers after depression struck Oman's commerce in the 1860s and caused a consequent fall in customs collections, traditionally the main source of governmental revenue. Pelly described the effects that a British declaration of recognition of a ruler or the lack of it had on an Omani regime: "The Arabs understand that recognition does not mean support. But they and our own subjects understand that without recognition restoration of a confidence in a trade, which is largely in the hands of our Indians, is impossible . . . non-recognition implies to the Arab mind, a latent wish, on our part, for change in the government, and this impression begets a general doubt as to the future."[49] Between 1866 and 1868 British recognition and the support of the Zanzibar subsidy enabled the unpopular Salim ibn-Thuwayni to rule in Oman, while from 1868 until 1871 lack of recognition severely damaged 'Azzan ibn-Qays' fairly popular regime. No regime was successful in retaining control of Oman whenever recognition was withheld. One Omani leader went so far as to offer Oman to the British as a protectorate in return for support;

[48] For details of the Omani–Sa'udi troubles of the period and the British intervention into the situation, see *Précis Nejd*, pp. 7-30; Arabian American Oil Company, *Oman*, pp. 20-24, 255-57; Lorimer, I, 474-75; *Précis Trucial Chiefs*, pp. 11-25; Winder, "Su'ūdi State," pp. 211-15; Al-Salimi, II, 223-25; Ibn-Ruzayq, p. ciii; Saudi Arabia, *Memorial*, I, 226-40; Kelly, *Eastern Arabian Frontiers*, pp. 81-86.

[49] "Pelly to Duke of Argyll, 13 Feb. 1871, despatch no. 145-17: Residency," India Records-2, Vol. XVII.

he received a noncommittal answer.[50] In 1871, when Turki ibn-Sa'id, a son of Sayyid Sa'id, sought to oust Oman's ruler and establish his own rule in Masqat, he made sure to keep the British informed about his movements.[51] As soon as Turki captured Masqat he requested recognition, payment of the Zanzibar subsidy, and indicated that he would follow a pro-British policy.[52] Turki proved a willing tool of the British; it was during his rule (1871-88) that a system of British tutelage which amounted to indirect rule matured in Oman.

During the 1860s the question of extraterritorial jurisdiction over British subjects in Oman became very important, due to Oman's disturbed state and the consequent value of the protection of British citizenship. British subjects also enjoyed a number of other practical advantages including exemption from having their houses entered, exemption from direct interference by local authorities, exemption from all taxes levied on Omani nationals, the right of full discharge from creditors if bankrupt, aid in recovering debts, and the participation of the British consul in any trial resulting from crimes committed.

There was a great deal of uncertainty over who was due protection. Most who claimed British protection were Indians whose ancestors had lived in Oman for generations. Sometimes even Omani Arab seamen sailed to India, registered their ships there, secured naturalization papers, then claimed British protection in Masqat.[53] In 1870 one Omani in the employ of the British India Steam Navigation Company claimed exemption from Masqati taxation on the grounds he was a British protégé because he was the employee of a British company. Since

[50] "Pelly to Duke of Argyll, 19 Feb. 1871, despatch no. 156-19: Residency," India Records–2, Vol. xvii.

[51] "Turki ibn-Sa'id to Way, 1 Jan. 1871, enclosure in Way to Pelly, 16 Jan. 1871, no. 4-30: Masqat," India Records–2, Vol. xvii.

[52] "Turki ibn-Sa'id to Pelly, 13 Mar. 1871, enclosure in Pelly to Duke of Argyll, 14 Mar. 1871, despatch no. 314-37: Residency," "Turki ibn-Sa'id to Govt. of Bombay, 12 Feb. 1871, enclosure in Pelly to Duke of Argyll, 13 Feb. 1871, despatch no. 154-34: Residency," India Records–2, Vol. xvii.

[53] "Way to Pelly, 20 July 1870, no. 38: Masqat," India Records–2, Vol. xvi.

the company would have been greatly inconvenienced by loss of this particular Omani's services, the British gave him protection, although privately admitting that it was a doubtful case. It is pertinent that the Omani in question made his bid just as a heavy tax was levied in Masqat.[54] Any situation in which the economically dominant segment of a resident population claimed foreign status and freedom from taxation was bound to cause complications. The fact that there was a large British–Indian population was often a cause for British intervention in Oman's internal affairs in the late nineteenth century.

Until 1867 the local British agent, who also ranked as a consul, exercised jurisdiction over British subjects in Masqat by virtue of the Treaties of 1822 and 1839. He administered the law of British India, and his decisions could be appealed to the High Court of Bombay. In 1867 an order in council attempted to clarify the jurisdiction of Britain's consul in Masqat, but many loopholes remained. There was no accurate register of British subjects resident in Oman, commercial claims were not handled in the local consular court, the judicial powers of consular courts in Masqat as well as other places in the Gulf were severely limited, and no provision was made for consular jurisdiction over subjects of the native princely states of the Indian empire.[55] Not until after Pelly passed from the Gulf scene were all of these problems resolved. Meanwhile Pelly's vigorous attempts to increase and clarify British extraterritorial jurisdiction involved the British further in Omani domestic affairs.

Also during the Pelly period a British image of Oman was solidified. Until the 1820s Westerners generally respected Oriental culture, but between 1820 and 1870 this attitude changed under the pressure of evangelical and evolutionist thinking.

---

[54] "Way to Pelly, 24 Sept. 1870, no. 470: Masqat," India Records-2, Vol. XVI.

[55] Aitchison—1909, XII, clxix-clxxx; Aitchison—1892, XI, 78; *Précis Persian Coast*, p. 87.

The Omanis, although seen as more civilized than other Gulf Arabs, still were regarded as a people to be manipulated and "civilized."[56] It is only natural that British officers thought they were doing a positive good when they intervened and imposed Western-style mores and political procedures. From this belief it followed that a "good Arab ruler" was one who cooperated with the British and followed the resident's advice. If a ruler resisted British advice, he was pictured as falling away from "good" and reverting to "barbarism" and "evil." By 1871 the British, knowingly or not, had reached the point where they would support in Oman and other Gulf states only a ruler who would cooperate with them.

During the 1860s the British also determined their view toward the two wings of Oman Ibadism, the moderate and the conservative. This was to have major effect on internal politics in Oman during the late nineteenth century. The moderates had ruled in Masqat since Imam Ahmad's reign and had cooperated with the British. Before 1868 the conservatives were regarded as a group of fanatical malcontents whose chief desire was the destruction of a regime friendly to Britain. When the conservative 'Azzan ibn-Qays ruled in Masqat between 1868 and 1871 the situation, surprisingly enough to British officials, did not completely deteriorate. Yet there were a number of Omani–British incidents and a noticeable depression in commercial activities. Things remained touch and go as long as the conservatives remained in power at Masqat. When the moderate Turki ibn-Sa'id drove the conservatives out of Masqat in 1871 the British authorities in the Gulf were only too eager to welcome and recognize him. Thenceforth Britain always supported moderate rule in Oman, and on occasions opposed the conservatives with military force.

Finally, the British, ignoring Oman's rather turbulent history, began to imagine Oman as a state in the modern European sense where allegiance was owed to a recognized legiti-

[56] Lorimer, I, 1,391.

mate monarch whose capital was Masqat. Anyone who opposed this ruler was referred to as a "rebel," a "terrorist," a "brigand," a "pirate," or even a "murderer." In Oman, as has been indicated, large masses of the people thought the ruler at Masqat a despot who ruled without benefit of religious sanction. Conservatives felt it a religious duty to oppose any ruler who did not espouse their principles. But what the conservatives regarded as *jihad* (holy war) the British treated as "unrest" or, in extreme cases, as "rebellion." Obviously, Britain's image of Oman did not always correspond to local realities.

Pelly's career in the Gulf spanned a pivotal period there. He presided over an increase in British involvement in the region despite the opposition of important officials in Calcutta. He gained general recognition of the principle that all British civil and military authorities serving in the area were subordinate to the resident. He was unable to prevent some serious breaches of peace in the region during the 1862-68 period, but this failure was due mainly to the dearth of appearances in the Gulf by British warships. Moreover, by the early 1870s he had encouraged close ties between Britain and many of the maritime Arab princes and had used these ties as a strong prop for British predominance. But he was not able to maintain the impetus behind the economic development of the area, nor was he able to stimulate much sincere desire among the local population to lay down their traditions and values and embrace modernism.

Pelly interfered in the internal affairs of the Persian Gulf states as no Britisher before him had done. By the end of his term he had subtly but decisively altered the relationship of many of the local principalities with Britain. In 1862 it was still possible for a significant change in internal administration and policy to be effected within the Gulf principalities without much in the way of British interference or participation in the decision-making process. By 1872 such changes were practically impossible to accomplish, or at least to be secured permanently, without tacit British approval.

Consolidation of British Paramountcy

In December 1872, Lewis Pelly stepped down as resident in the Persian Gulf, to be succeeded by Edward Charles Ross, his subordinate at Gwadar and later at Masqat. The personalities and basic approaches of the two residents were dissimilar. While Ross was less flamboyant and imaginative than his predecessor, he was equally energetic and more tactful in his dealings with superiors, juniors, and Gulf rulers. If Pelly's underlying aim was to establish the preconditions necessary for the Persian Gulf's future modernization, the emphasis of Ross's work was more administrative and political in the narrow sense. While Pelly recognized and nurtured a new era in the Gulf's history, Ross consolidated and legalized Britain's new responsibilities in the region. Although Ross displayed the passion of a born antiquarian in undertaking his researches on the history of the Persian Gulf, he did not share Pelly's missionary zeal for propagandizing modern values and practices there. Ross skillfully took up Pelly's work of increasing British influence in the Gulf, but he was more interested in maintaining the region as a quiet political preserve serving Britain's imperial interests than he was in establishing the political prerequisites conducive to the spread of modern civilization.

In 1874 the Conservative Party came to power in London, and in 1876 Disraeli appointed the imperialist-minded Lord Lytton as viceroy of India. With these events the dominance of "noninvolvement" and "masterly inactivity" faded in Calcutta and London gave way to the age of late nineteenth century imperial expansion. Consequently, Ross was not faced with Pelly's problem of having to conduct the affairs of the residency in the face of Calcutta's and London's suspicion or neglect. However, during Ross's term at Bushire the Anglo–Indian government was absorbed with troubles in the buffer areas of Afghanistan, Iran, Burma, and Thailand. No major great power disturbed the Persian Gulf sector of India's trans-frontier screen, so Ross was left to regulate affairs there largely as he wished. The crown of his career was a series of treaties he arranged between Britain and the Gulf principalities in 1887-92 which reaffirmed and defined the terms of Britain's de facto protectorate over the Persian Gulf. Although other principalities joined the British treaty system in later years, it was not until Kuwait's independence was unequivocally recognized in 1961 that the legal basis of Britain's political position in the Gulf, modified as it was by Ross, was altered significantly.[57] No resident before or since wielded such power as did Sir Edward Ross. His superiors seldom countered his recommendations and Gulf rulers respected the might and security he represented. His encyclopedic knowledge of Persian Gulf lore, his efficient administration, his tact, and his sound judgment also contributed to his independence of decision-making.

The slave trade treaties of 1873. The only time an important British policy decision concerning Gulf affairs was implemented without prior consultation with Ross occurred in 1873 soon after he became resident.

At that time the London government forced the Omani and Zanzibari sultans to sign treaties explicitly outlawing the export and import of slaves. Slavery and the slave trade had been under heavy attack from evangelical and humanitarian groups in Britain since the early nineteenth century. In 1822, 1839, and 1845 Britain forced the reluctant ruler of the Omani Empire, Sayyid Sa'id, to sign treaties limiting the slave trade in his dominions.[58] Nevertheless, as late as 1870 the traffic was still considerable, few slaves had been freed, and the Gulf Arabs displayed little desire to give up an institution which was profitable and sanctioned by the Koran. As late as this century slavery had prestige as an entrenched institution in

---

[57] No Anglo–Indian treaties with Persian Gulf states were abrogated when India became independent in 1947. Instead the London Foreign Office assumed responsibility for applying them.

[58] Aitchison—1933, XL, 289-301.

Arabia; criticism of it only stimulated horrified protest or protective silence. Oman's religion allowed slavery and the social order condoned it.

In the 1860s the attack on the Indian Ocean slave trade was renewed, the impetus being the career, writing, and example of Dr. David Livingstone. In 1870 an investigative committee reported to a concerned Parliament on the matter.[59] And in September 1872 Sir Bartle Frere, a leading antislave trade agitator after his return to England, was sent by Parliament to negotiate treaties with the Zanzibar and Masqat sultans designed to halt the flow of slaves in their territories. Frere convinced Sultan Barghash of Zanzibar to abolish the trade only after a strong ultimatum, but Sultan Turki of Oman cooperated willingly. Turki signed a treaty with Frere agreeing to close his dominions to imports of slaves and spontaneously issued the following proclamation: "Let it be known that we have entirely forbidden all traffic in slaves either publicly or privately and that in event of our finding anyone engaged in the same in our dominions or dependencies he will forfeit his property as well as his personal safety."[60] By issuing this proclamation Sultan Turki gambled his popularity with his subjects in order to gain British good will and support. It seems the immediate reason for Turki's willing acceptance of the anti-slave trade treaty was his financial impoverishment. After he signed the treaty, Frere forwarded him $MT 40,000 immediately and $MT 20,000 three months later; the money shored up Turki's crumbling rule.[61]

In many respects the chief result of the Slave Trade Treaty

[59] Columb, *Slave Catching*; Great Britain, Foreign Office, "Report addressed to the Earl of Clarendon by the Committee on East African Slave Trade, c. 209," *House of Commons Sessional Papers, 1870*, Vol. LXI.

[60] "Proclamation of Turki ibn-Sa'id, enclosure in Ross to Duke of Argyll, 3 May 1873, despatch no. 572-30: Residency," India Records–2, Vol. XXIII; Aitchison—1892, XI, 77, for treaty text; Martineau, *Life of Frere*, II, 66-70.

[61] "Ross to Duke of Argyll, 3 May 1873, despatch no. 571-49: Residency," India Records–2, Vol. XXII.

of 1873 was the increased reliance of the Omani sultan on British support. In particular, it increased the sultan's financial dependence on Britain. Indeed, the entire question of the Zanzibar subsidy was intimately connected to the negotiations which preceded the signing of the various 1873 slave trade treaties. During preliminary talks the Zanzibar sultan complained that he could not be expected to surrender the lucrative customs revenues derived from the slave trade yet continue to pay $MT 40,000 per year to the Omani sultan, as called for in the 1861 Canning Arbitration. London agreed with this contention. The Anglo–Indian government, however, pointed out that if Oman did not receive the subsidy, faith in Britain's word would be shattered and the entire British treaty system with the Gulf states would be jeopardized. The financially hard pressed Indian government wanted the London treasury to pay the subsidy if Zanzibar was relieved of payment. This issue was still unsettled when Frere authorized the use of Indian funds to pay the subsidy to Turki in 1873 as a reward for his signing the slave trade treaty. Ultimately the subsidy became a permanent charge on the Indian treasury. Thus by 1873 the "Zanzibar subsidy," although retaining its label, became simply an annual gift by the British authorities to the Omani sultan. Since the subsidy was a vital part of the sultan's revenue it could serve as a lever by which the British could force the sultan to respect their "advice."[62]

Because the sultan lost face in his country by agreeing to sign the unpopular 1873 treaty British political and military support was more than ever a necessary prop to his regime.

[62] Eighth Duke of Argyll, *George Douglas, Eighth Duke of Argyll, Autobiography and Memoirs,* Duchess of Argyll, ed. (London, 1906), II, 277. "Ross to Duke of Argyll, 25 Jan. 1873, despatch no. 92-12: Residency," India Records–2, Vol. XXII; "Ross to Duke of Argyll, 3 June 1873, despatch no. 572-50: Residency," India Records–2, Vol. XXIII; "Minute Paper, India Office, 19 Apr. 1875," India Records–3, Vol. I; Martineau, *Life of Frere,* II, 66-70. Columb, *Slave Catching,* p. 386, estimated that the Sultan of Zanzibar pocketed some £10,500, a sum equal to approximately $MT 52,500, annually from slave trade duties before the 1873 treaties went into effect.

Finally, in the 1873 treaty the sultan agreed to let the British suppress the slave trade, dispose of captured slavers, slaves, and slaving vessels, and set up a naval patrol along the Omani coast.

Despite the 1873 treaties not until 1902 was the slave trade effectively throttled and even after that date an occasional cargo of slaves slipped into a Gulf port. The fact that the British took it upon themselves to interdict slave commerce earned them unpopularity in Oman.[63] The stationing of *H.M.S. London* off Zanzibar between 1874 and 1883 almost killed slaving, but traffic revived after 1883 when the *London* was removed from the Zanzibar station. In the 1890s a thriving commerce was shielded by the flying of French flags by Sur sailors, an action which prevented search of suspected slave ships by British warships and seriously disturbed Anglo–French relations before the issue was settled.[64]

The administration of the Persian Gulf residency under Ross. Under Ross the power of the Persian Gulf resident reached its apogee. The residency system was not overly complicated during the late nineteenth century. In 1873 the resident was removed from the intermediate control of the Government of Bombay and placed directly under the Calcutta Foreign Department. This meant little change in actual administration except that the resident's decisions no longer were submitted via Bombay but were cleared directly with Calcutta. Including the military and navy the personnel stationed in the Gulf under the resident's supervision might total several hundred at a given time. In the late 1890s the Indian government spent approximately £8,000 maintaining the residency administration, contributed about £1,200 to support Indian Army detachments in the Gulf, and budgeted over £30,000 to pay for the naval units there.[65]

[63] Lorimer, I, 2,500-14.

[64] *Admin. Rpt.: 1885-1886*, pp. 8-9; *Précis Slave*, pp. 49-55; *Précis Naval*, p. 24.

[65] See Hurewitz, *Diplomacy*, I, 227ff., for Lord Curzon's masterly analysis of the British position in Iran and the Persian Gulf in 1899.

The second most important British official in the Gulf was the political agent and consul at Masqat. Although a number of men occupied this post between 1872 and 1892, Lieutenant Colonel Samuel B. Miles, a man who shared Ross' interest in Persian Gulf history and scholarship, held it longest and most effectively. Miles began his Arabian service at Aden in 1867, took charge of the Masqat Agency for the first time in 1872, and remained there for various periods until 1887. As "political agent," Miles was an Indian government official, but as "consul" he was responsible to the London Foreign Office, too.

Although Pelly won the main battle over the place of sea power in the system of British rule in the Gulf, Ross fought two skirmishes over the issue. From 1871 to 1876 a small Bombay Marine steamer, *B.M.S. Hugh Rose,* was at the resident's personal disposal; when the *Hugh Rose* was withdrawn in 1876 it was not replaced. Ross argued that a dispatch ship was necessary if a resident was to adequately supervise his charge and avoid commandeering Royal Navy gunboats for routine tasks. The discussion continued until 1884 when *H.M.S. Sphinx,* a gunboat specially constructed for Gulf service, was sent out. But this was not the fast noncombatant vessel Ross wanted. The versatile Ross then submitted a plan which resulted in the building of *R.I.M.S. Lawrence,* a ship which proved to be a tremendous aid to the resident in facilitating his supervision over the Gulf. Using it, for instance, Ross could reach Masqat from Bushire in 40 hours instead of the 80 hours it took in one of the old gunboats.

The second discussion involving British sea power in the Gulf arose between 1884 and 1888 when the question of reducing the Royal Navy squadron was revived. Ross felt the squadron should be maintained at its post-1871 strength. Naval officers, however, were of the opinion that the necessary patrol work could be done by the *Lawrence* and the *Sphinx* alone. It was finally decided to keep one gunboat in the Persian Gulf proper and one in the Gulf of Oman. Two others would remain in repair, transit, or reserve in India. Despite this compromise, the Navy constantly complained about Gulf duty. They said regular service there was too hard on British crews, and again in 1888 the navy protested against their ships in the Gulf being under the resident's orders. Nevertheless, Ross's adroit arguments essentially preserved the naval arrangement won by Pelly. This was a key factor in the maintenance of Britain's position and the maritime peace in the Gulf.[66]

Ross's defense of Pax Britannica. Ross was adroit in strengthening British influence while at the same time avoiding resentment among the Gulf's potentates. Contributing to this was the fact that many rulers increasingly thought of Britain as a protector of their realms and titles against foreign and domestic threats. In the British view the chief enemy of the status quo in the Gulf during Pelly's time was the Saudi state. But the danger posed from this quarter dissolved during the late 1860s when the Wahhabi domains were convulsed by succession struggles and other internal disorders. The threat to regional peace and political stability presented by the Saudis was far less formidable and potentially dangerous than two new challenges which appeared in the 1870s. The new source of trouble were the revival of long quiescent Ottoman and Persian interests in the Gulf littoral.

It is true that both the Ottoman and Persian states were declining powers during the late nineteenth century. The decline, however, was relative rather than absolute. Compared to the growing power of the European nations the two Middle Eastern empires were falling behind. But the efforts being made by the Ottoman and the Qajar sovereigns to modernize their armies, administrations, and communications systems, efforts that could not keep pace with developments in the West, were successful enough to increase the ability of these rulers to control their own subjects and the inhabitants of weakly organized border areas. Both powers were able to mitigate to some extent their decline vis-à-vis the West by a coinci-

66 *Précis Naval*, pp. 25-34.

dent increase in control over districts inside their borders that had long enjoyed complete autonomy, or over frontier areas whose independence traditionally had been respected by both Constantinople and Teheran. The Persian Gulf qualified as a "weakly organized border area" of both empires and so became a focus of Ottoman and Persian political activity during the late nineteenth century.

In the case of the Ottomans a corollary of this situation, whereby the sultan found himself in a position to reassert the control of his dynasty over many autonomous parts of his empire, was the growth of Pan-Islam. This was a Muslim revivalist philosophy pioneered by Jamal al-Din al-Afghani and adopted by the Ottoman sultan Abdülhamid II (1876-1909), which called for the uniting of all Muslims under the banners of a revived universal caliphate so that the Islamic world could better resist Western imperialism. Naturally, Abdülhamid II pictured himself as the ideal organizer of this movement and actually styled himself as caliph on many occasions. One practical consequence of Abdülhamid's reliance on Pan-Islam was his use of the philosophy to explain his efforts to reestablish Ottoman control in areas once ruled by his predecessors. Although it was impossible to apply this policy in many countries once subject to Constantinople, the Arabian peninsula seemed an admirable arena in which to rebuild some of the prestige of the Ottoman state.

In Arabia Constantinople had controlled the holy cities of al-Hijaz for centuries. In 1871, five years before Abdülhamid II became sultan and many years before he began preaching Pan-Islam, the Ottomans had already begun expanding their holdings. A giant pincers movement began to move down Arabia's Red Sea and Persian Gulf coasts. This was accompanied by somewhat exaggerated claims that all Arabia, including Oman and the peninsula's southern coast, was historically and rightfully part of the Ottoman empire.[67] In 1873 Ottoman pressure

---

[67] *Précis Turkish Expansion*, pp. 1, 11-12.

in southwest Arabia grew so persistent that the government of India declared that the Turkish pretensions constituted a danger to Aden and to imperial communications and warned that they should be "peremptorily" halted.[68] The British representatives in Aden and other southern Arabian localities thereupon began to set their house in order. A series of treaties were negotiated with many of the Ottoman-threatened rulers of southern Arabia. These engagements formally gave the Anglo–Indian government protector status and exclusive control over the foreign relations of the petty principalities of the area. By 1878 nine southwestern Arabian states in close proximity to Aden were bound by protectorate and exclusive treaties, and by 1882 all of southern Arabia up to the borders of the Sultan of Masqat and Oman's territory in Dhofar were included in the British-protected sphere. These treaties were strengthened between 1887 and 1892 and, as later modified, became the legal antecedents of what today are the Aden Protectorate (officially, the Protectorate of South Arabia) and the South Arabian Federation.[69]

As happened in southern Arabia, Ottoman activity in the Persian Gulf was one of the factors that stimulated an extension and consolidation of the legal basis of British power in that region, too. It was Midhat Pasha, the capable Ottoman governor of Iraq and later apostle of Ottoman constitutionalism, as well as grand vizier of the empire, who directed Ottoman expansion into the Gulf. In 1871, taking advantage of the opportunity presented by the civil strife within the Saudi domain, an Ottoman army was landed on the coasts of al-Hasa by ships belonging to the Shaykh of Kuwait, who at that time considered himself a subject of the sultan in Constantinople. By the end of the year the star and crescent flag flew over the major towns of Arabia's east coast, including those of al-Hasa province, from Kuwait to Dawhah, the chief city of Qatar. Moreover, covetous glances were being cast toward Bah-

[68] Prasad, *India's Foreign Policy*, pp. 249-50.
[69] Aitchison—1933, Vol. x.

rain, the Trucial Coast, and even Oman. After some hesitation, the British decided not to contest the Ottoman conquest of al-Hasa, although this decision was made only after they informed the Porte that they could not recognize Ottoman claims to other parts of the Gulf littoral. It was at this point that Pelly first pointed out the legal weakness of Britain's position in the Gulf.[70]

Until the 1890s the British were more concerned with the possibility that the Ottoman expansion into eastern Arabia could trigger a revival of maritime disorder than with any fear that this expansion posed much of a threat to their dominance in the Gulf. Soon after the Ottoman occupation of al-Hasa the shaykhs of Bahrain and the Trucial Coast were warned not to involve themselves in the situation. This warning was accompanied by renewed assurances of British support. Since the Ottomans did not possess powerful naval forces on Gulf waters the British continued to patrol eastern Arabia's coastal waters and deal with any trouble at sea just as they had been doing since 1820.[71] After 1874 the Ottoman grip on al-Hasa relaxed and piratical attacks by ships cruising from nominally Ottoman ports began to disturb the upper Gulf. Exasperation over maritime disorder and Ottoman claims grew so acute in 1880 that Britain determined to "adopt all necessary measures for the preservation of the peace of the seas, without regard . . . to Turkish pretensions."[72] Indian troops were dispatched to Bahrain, whose shaykh was the first Gulf ruler to sign an "exclusive agreement" with Britain. The shaykh formally agreed to turn over the conduct of his foreign affairs to the British, as well as to refuse any power other than Britain the right to establish coaling stations on Bahrain. In essence, this treaty was similar to those being drawn up at the same time between

[70] "Pelly to Duke of Argyll, 8 Apr. 1871, despatch no. 388-45: Residency," India Records–2, Vol. XVII; *Précis Turkish Expansion*, pp. 15-16.

[71] Kelly, "British Position in the Persian Gulf," *St. Antony's Papers, Number IV*, pp. 132-33.

[72] *Précis Turkish Expansion*, pp. 15-16.

Britain and the southern Arabian rulers and would serve as a model for later treaties that would be concluded by Britain and her Gulf Arab associates between 1887 and 1892. The 1880 actions concerning Bahrain marked the initiation of a policy of severely restricting the areas of possible Ottoman expansion and was the first step in finally consolidating the legal basis for the British "protectorate" in the Persian Gulf.[73]

Despite obvious British irritation, during Ross's term as resident there were recurrent Ottoman claims and schemes put forth which asserted the Porte's intention of eventually extending its influence to include the Trucial Coast and even Oman. Twice Sultan Turki ibn-Sa'id of Oman informed the political agent at Masqat of attempts to transform him into an Ottoman vassal. It was common practice for Ottoman ships calling at Masqat to neglect or even to refuse to salute the Omani flag.[74] Some Pan-Islamic propaganda printed in Egyptian newspapers was sent to Gulf ports including Masqat. There were even some Ibadi books printed in Egypt that supported Pan-Islamic goals. Nevertheless, this propaganda was treated with indifference by most Gulf dwellers and had the effect of driving the dynasts on the Arab side of the Gulf deeper into the protective arms of Britain. Moreover, the British did not simply ignore the Ottoman claims. Between 1871 and 1893 there were ten major protests or warnings issued by British authorities concerning Ottoman actions or pretensions in the Gulf region.[75]

Ottoman ambitions in the Gulf were always more bluff than reality. Aside from the energy displayed by Midhat Pasha when their rule was initially asserted in the early 1870s, Ottoman government proved weak and a source of disorder in the upper

[73] Hurewitz, *Diplomacy*, I, 194; *Admin. Rpt.: 1887-1888*, pp. 6-7.

[74] "Miles to Ross, 25 Jan. 1876, no. 44-10: Masqat," India Records–3, Vol. II; "Ross to Lord Hartington, 13 Dec. 1880, despatch no. 25: Residency," India Records–3, Vol. IV; "Ross to Duke of Argyll, 27 Dec. 1873, despatch no. 1,750-170: Residency," India Records–2, Vol. XXIII.

[75] *Précis Turkish Expansion*, pp. 138-42. Between 1871 and 1893 there were 10 major British warnings against Ottoman actions in the Gulf.

Gulf. Finally, the revived Saudi power under ʿAbd al-ʿAziz ibn-Saʿud, the founder of modern Saudi Arabia, swept the Ottomans out of al-Hasa in 1913. Ten years later the Ottoman sultanate itself disappeared.

On the Iranian side of the Gulf the British had to adjust to an unspectacular but ultimately successful drive by the Qajar empire to reassert its sovereignty over Iran's Gulf coast. Between the fall of the Zand dynasty in the late eighteenth century and a revival of Teheran's interest in the mid-nineteenth no Iranian central government had concerned itself overmuch with the affairs of Iran's Gulf shore districts, although the Persian governors of Fars province displayed sporadic interest in Gulf affairs.[76] The Qajar shahs, preoccupied with Russian expansion into their Caspian provinces, for the most part restricted their activity to the Iranian plateau and neglected their southern and Persian Gulf dependencies. From 1800 to 1850 the tribes inhabiting Iran's Gulf coast were practically autonomous. Many of these tribes were Arab, offshoots of parent stock from Arabia. South and east of Bandar ʿAbbas Baluchi tribes predominated. Before the 1850s the coastal tribes and ports occasionally paid a small tribute to the Iranian provincial authorities in the interior, but otherwise were left alone.[77] But the British never established formal treaty relations with the Iranian coastal tribes as they had with those of the Arabian shore. Except for ad hoc arrangements concluded with some coastal shaykhs, Anglo–Iranian relations were carried on through normal diplomatic channels. Up to 1859 there was a certain amount of indecision on Britain's part as to whether London or Calcutta should administer British diplomatic interests in Iran. In 1859, as part of the post-Indian Mutiny administrative reorganization, the London Foreign Office finally was placed in charge of the British mission at Teheran and given the responsibility of supervising Anglo–Iranian relations. Nevertheless, the Anglo–Indian government

[76] Adamiyat, *Bahrein Islands*, chaps. 2-3.
[77] *Bombay Records—1856*, pp. 286-87.

continued to be intimately concerned with the conduct of British–Iranian relations, and in 1899 Calcutta contributed four times as much as London to defray the charges of maintaining British interests in Iran. Many British officials serving in Iran were, like the resident at Bushire, basically Anglo–Indian government appointees, although they also held London Foreign Office titles and performed British consular tasks.[78]

As early as 1853 the Iranian government exhibited a revival of interest in Persian Gulf affairs. In that year Persian troops expelled the Omani governor from Bandar 'Abbas, a city ruled by the Masqati authorities since 1798 when it, along with a 150-kilometer strip of coastline and the ports of Chahbar and Gwadar, were occupied by Sayyid Sultan ibn-Ahmad. Evidently, Sayyid Sultan agreed to pay Iranian authorities an annual rent of 6,000 tomans ($MT 15,000) for Bandar 'Abbas but this charge probably was left unpaid for many years.

It was not until 1856 that Sayyid Sa'id was able to restore Omani control over Bandar 'Abbas and then only after he recognized the city as Iranian territory and agreed to pay a 14,000 toman ($MT 35,000) yearly lease for use of the port.[79] This lease was renegotiated in 1868; the rent was raised to 30,000 tomans ($MT 75,000). However, the lease was revoked later in 1868 when 'Azzan ibn-Qays took control of Masqat's government and the Iranians invoked a clause allowing them to cancel the lease if a conqueror toppled the Omani sultanate. As soon as he gained the Omani sultanate in 1871 Turki ibn-Sa'id tried to renew the lease but the Iranians refused. Subsequent attempts by Turki to regain use of Bandar 'Abbas in 1872, 1878, and 1879 were also rebuffed.[80] After 1868, then, Omani dominance over Iran's southern coast was replaced by a revived Iranian control. Also signaling the revival of Iranian interest in the Gulf were the claims of sovereignty over Bahrain that the shah's government presented in the late 1860s. These

---

78 Hurewitz, *Diplomacy*, I, 240-41.
79 *Ibid.*, pp. 157-58; Wilson, *Persian Gulf*, p. 173.
80 *Précis Persian Coast*, pp. 31-32.

assertions were dodged by the noninvolvement-minded British foreign secretary, Lord Clarendon, in 1869 but not decisively countered.[81]

In the 1870s and 1880s the Iranians established a primitive but functioning political administration along their Gulf shore. Unfortunately, the new "Governorate of the Gulf Ports" which supervised the shah's interests in this part of his empire was less an apparatus of government than a machine for milking the region of tax revenues. After 1902 the trade of the once flourishing port of Lingah, a city whose population jumped up to 25,000 in the 1860s when it became a steamer port, was ruined by overtaxation.[82] In the mid-1880s the Iranian government's aggressive policy in the Gulf resulted in a determination to build a fleet on the Gulf and a renewal of the shah's authority over Iran's offshore islands. This was followed up in the late 1880s by attempts to interfere in the politics of the Trucial Coast. In the long run these overextended claims and ambitions resulted only in Ross's reemphasizing Britain's protectorate over the Trucial States and the construction of an Iranian navy consisting of two small gunboats of less than 600 tons, which were used mainly as dispatch ships.

Nevertheless, there was a real revival of the Iranian presence in the Gulf in the late nineteenth century. Although the reassertion of Iran's interests in the region was punctuated by some grandiose schemes and airy pronouncements, by 1900 some sort of Iranian political authority obviously had been reconstructed along much of the country's Gulf shore. By that time it was clear that in contrast to eastern Arabia, on the Iranian coast the British resident acted more in his capacity as a consul-general than as a pro-consul. The British were not able to simply dictate their wishes and have the Iranians comply with them. For instance, Ross unsuccessfully tried six times between 1878 and 1892 to have a British consul accredited to

[81] Hurewitz, *Diplomacy*, I, 172-73.
[82] Great Britain, Admiralty, *Iraq and the Persian Gulf*, p. 162.

Bandar 'Abbas; it was not until 1904 that the Iranians finally agreed to a subsequent, similar request.

Another challenge to the British position in the Gulf—more imaginary than real, it seems—resulted from the activity of certain individual Frenchmen on the Trucial Coast in the late 1880s. Ross was particularly upset by a certain M. Chapui whom he described as "half adventurer, half merchant, and wholly intriguer." Chapui, in reality a man obsessed with a number of get-rich-quick schemes, was painted as a probable French agent bent on substituting French for British supremacy in the Gulf. In any event, the Chapui matter was the final inducement required to stimulate the British to redefine their legal position in the Gulf. The resident pointed out that it was best to guard against any eventuality, so between 1887 and 1892 Ross concluded a series of treaties to fill the loopholes in the apparatus, which tied the eastern Arabian maritime principalities to Britain.[83]

The Exclusive Agreements of 1887-92 and the Omani Non-alienation Clause of 1891. We have noted that as a result of exasperation over the troubles produced by Ottoman and Iranian activity, as well as out of fear of European imperialist designs, Edward Ross in 1887 suggested that Britain should correct the weaknesses in her Persian Gulf treaty system.[84] At that time Britain's de facto protectorate in the Persian Gulf proper still depended basically on the 1820 "General Treaty" as modified by the 1853 "Perpetual Maritime Truce" giving the British power to mediate disputes among the Gulf powers. Between 1853 and 1880 it was usually assumed, but not explicitly stated, that Britain would conduct the foreign affairs of the Gulf states. In Oman the British legal position was even more loosely defined than in the upper Gulf principalities, and depended basically on the Treaty of 1839 which was mainly commercial in character. Until the 1880s there seemed to be

[83] *Précis Trucial Chiefs*, pp. 61-70.
[84] "Ross to Lansdowne, enclosure in Lord Lansdowne to Cross, 1 Sept. 1887, despatch no. 191: Viceroy," India Mss.–4, Vol. II.

little reason to make Britain's primacy in the region more explicit and formal. In 1880, however, as we have noted, Ottoman pretensions in the area prompted the British to conclude a treaty with the shaykh of Bahrain explicitly turning over to Britain the conduct of Bahrain's foreign relations.

Anticipating approval of his suggestion that Britain shore up its Gulf treaty structure, Ross in 1887 concluded unofficial agreements with a number of Gulf states, which, like the engagement concluded with Bahrain in 1880, gave Britain exclusive control over these states' foreign relations. These first "exclusive agreements" were never ratified because of the legal technicality that Ross had acted without plenipotentiary powers. Nevertheless, Calcutta and London, interested in Ross's ideas, were willing to recognize the 1887 documents as preliminary treaties and asked the resident to submit his proposals on the details of the agreements he wished to conclude. At the heart of each treaty was a "nonalienation" clause by which each signatory ruler promised never to cede territory to any power save Britain and a clause specifically giving Britain control of his foreign relations. In 1892 Ross's successor, Colonel Talbot presented the revised treaties to the rulers of Bahrain and the Trucial Coast for their signatures and the documents later were ratified by the viceroy.[85]

The problem of proclaiming what amounted to a British protectorate over Oman was far more difficult than in other Gulf states. In 1887 Ross suggested a new treaty to replace the 1839 agreement then in force. Despite official permission Ross could not pursue the project immediately because of the death of Sultan Turki in 1888. In 1890, however, the question of proclaiming a British protectorate over Oman was reopened. The viceroy, Lord Lansdowne, favored adding a secret clause to a new commercial treaty being prepared that would place Omani foreign affairs "distinctly" under British control. The

[85] "Lansdowne to Cross, 8 Sept. 1890, despatch no. 109: Viceroy," India Mss.–4, Vol. II; *Précis Trucial Chiefs*, pp. 69-70; see Aitchison—1933, XI, 238, 256-57, for treaty texts.

Indian Office said there were numerous proofs of a "virtual protectorate" over Oman including: (1) the guarantee of the 1861 Canning Arbitration, (2) the Zanzibar subsidy, (3) the importance of British recognition of any sultan's rule, (4) the numerous instances of British interventions in dynastic disputes and deportations to India of claimants to the throne, (5) the fact that the British resident handled the negotiations of the 1877 Dutch–Omani commercial treaty, and (6) the predominance of Anglo–Indian national and commercial interests in Oman.[86]

Lord Salisbury in the Foreign Office pointed out, however, that the 1862 Anglo–French Declaration jointly guaranteeing Omani independence, an engagement the Calcutta government only recently had learned of, would preclude Britain from assuming an exclusive protectorate over Masqat without first coming to an understanding with France.[87] Lord Lansdowne still had hopes that Britain could exercise what he termed "a virtual protectorate" in Oman with French blessings. But this dream was dashed by Salisbury who thought it "hardly practicable" to approach France on the subject at the time and preferred to wait for a better opportunity. Salisbury said that since the sultan in effect had no foreign relations it would be best to postpone any protectorate until it could be assumed openly and completely. The foreign minister concluded that a "quasi-protectorate" was as far as Britain could "safely go."[88]

In accordance with Salisbury's view, an Anglo–Omani commercial treaty extending British extraterritorial privileges was signed on March 19, 1891 by Sultan Faysal ibn-Turki (1888-1913) and Ross. Accompanying the treaty, however, was a secret bond in which the sultan promised "never to cede, to

[86] "Lansdowne to Cross, 10 Dec. 1890, no. 113: Viceroy," India Records–4, LXI; Lorimer, I, 534; Daud, "British Relations with the Persian Gulf, 1890-1902," p. 26off.

[87] "Lansdowne to Cross, 8 Sept. 1890, despatch no. 113: Viceroy," India Mss.–4, Vol. II.

[88] "Cross to Lansdowne, 23 Oct. 1890, no. 45: India Secty.," "7 Nov. 1890, no. 49: India Secty.," India Mss.–5, Vol. II.

sell, to mortgage or otherwise give for occupation save to the British government, the dominions of Muscat and Oman or any of their dependencies."[89] But no attempt was made to secure an exclusive control of Oman's foreign relations such as was gained in many of the other eastern Arabian principalities since the sultan already enjoyed treaty relations with other states. Thus, in the legal terminology of the day, Britain enjoyed in 1891 a "quasi-protectorate in Oman where her influence was 'paramount' but not 'exclusive.' " The fact that Britain's influence was not "exclusive" meant that Oman provided a loophole in the British protectorate system in the Gulf because Oman was legally free to conduct her own foreign affairs.

The maturing of indirect rule in Oman, 1872-92. The treaties of 1887-92 were the crown of Ross's term as resident. They were concerned chiefly with legalizing the hold Britain had attained over the foreign relations of Gulf states. However, they said little about Britain's methods of supervising and guiding the internal affairs of the Gulf principalities, techniques which constituted an "indirect rule." These techniques were first established in the Gulf in the 1820s, were modified and developed by Pelly in the 1860s and were perfected by Ross in the 1870s and 1880s. Indirect rule in its unique Persian Gulf manifestation allowed Britain a great deal of influence in determining the course of internal affairs within the region's principalities, yet it saved the trouble and expense of establishing and running a direct administration. In the Gulf, indirect rule was based on a conglomeration of treaties, documents, unwritten practices, and personal relationships. Like Britain's unwritten constitution indirect rule was a system that developed over a long period of time. It reflected the ideals and prejudices of the various Britons who directed it and those of the various Arabs who lived under it.[90]

[89] Aitchison—1933, XI, 317-18.
[90] In view of some of the ultralegalistic statements by certain writers, to the effect that the Gulf states are not British protectorates and that

Oman is a good example of the indirect rule developed in the Gulf under Edward Ross. In Oman between 1871 and 1891 the growth of British influence was largely the product of the sultan's need for British support if he was to remain Oman's ruler. In return for this support the sultan gave Britain his loyal cooperation.

This process was especially apparent under Sultan Turki ibn-Sa'id (1871-88). One reason the British aided Sultan Turki was that despite his faults Britain could trust the prince to live up to agreements and to back British policies. Support of Turki ibn-Sa'id's government afforded a cheap, convenient way "to prevent disturbance and revolution" in a country where Britain wanted peace maintained for strategic reasons, as well as for the protection of the trade of resident Anglo–Indian merchants.[91] Sultan Turki's willingness to risk his popularity among his subjects to insure British support was best illustrated by the sultan's acceptance of the Slave Trade Treaty of 1873. All through his reign Sultan Turki was beset by internal enemies. Masqat itself was attacked in 1874, 1877, and 1883; by conservative Ibadi armies. In each of these instances British gunboats backed the faltering sultan while other attacks were prevented by timely letters of warning sent to potential insurgents by the British. The British did not wish to exchange a loyal tool for an unknown quantity. Without British diplomatic, financial, and armed support it is reasonably certain that Turki ibn-Sa'id's regime would have crumbled.[92] Sultan Turki's Omani enemies realized that British aid was decisive in keeping him on his throne. Usually the sultan's conservative

---

the British have no control over the domestic policy of the various princes in the region, it is interesting that all of the viceroys of the 1890s asserted that the Gulf principalities—including that ruled by the sultan at Masqat—were, in fact, if not according to strict treaty stipulations, British protectorates.

[91] "Minute Paper, India Office, 17 Dec. 1874," India Records-2, Vol. xxv; "Ross to Kimberley, 9 Nov. 1885, despatch no. 36-9: Residency," India Records-3, Vol. vi.

[92] Admin. Rpt.: 1879-1880, p. 133.

enemies attempted to gain British neutrality before delivering an attack. Conservative elements never clearly understood why the British supported Turki ibn-Sa'id; they looked on this British aid to the sultan as undue interference in Omani domestic affairs. After British gunboats blunted a conservative attack in 1877, the acting political agent in Masqat received a letter from Ibrahim ibn-Qays, the late imam's brother and a prominent conservative leader, which complained: "You have interfered in the war of the Arabs between the ruler and his subjects and you have begun war without reason and this is contrary to all custom. This was not to be expected of you and if your arm is long and your sovereign mighty and your nation powerful yet God is the stronger and the mightier and it is He on whom we depend. . . . We desire your friendship and that you should not dislike us without reason."[93]

For their part the British had little conception why the conservatives were opposed to Sultan Turki despite the fact that conservative leaders informed the British that they opposed the sultan because of his irreligiousness and lack of morals (i.e., his adherence to moderate rather than conservative Ibadism).[94]

To the British religiously motivated disorder or war in Oman was pictured as the action of "rebels in arms" against their sultan or else as "chronic disorder" due to the "unruly temperament" of the Arab.[95]

British aid to Turki ibn-Sa'id was not restricted to military support. After 1873 the Zanzibar subsidy paid directly from the Indian treasury propped up Turki's regime. The subsidy was paid to Turki for the duration of his reign without interruption and often in advance.[96] Its proceeds were liberally bestowed by Sultan Turki to various influential Omanis in the form of bribes, tribal subsidies, and salaries. It filtered down

---

93 "Ibrahim ibn-Qays to Robertson, 18 June 1877," India Records–3, Vol. III.

94 "Hamad ibn-Ahmad to Miles, 6 June, 1874," India Records–2, Vol. XXIV; Lorimer, I, 505-506.

95 *Admin. Rpts., 1874-1904*, passim.

96 Lorimer, I, 512-19.

to many individuals and often influenced their conduct during one crisis or another. If money was not in itself enough to rule in Oman it was a necessary element in rule.

The British also aided Turki ibn-Sa'id in ridding him of family rivals whose attempts to secure the throne contributed to disorder. In 1874 ex-Sultan Salim was granted a pension in return for giving up his claim to rule in Oman and accepting exile in India. After a subsequent unsuccessful attempt to leave India and return to Oman, Salim was placed under arrest by the British, confined to a house inside a fort, and guarded by sentries. This treatment, it seems, was earned not so much for causing Sultan Turki trouble as for defying the Anglo–Indian government. Salim ibn-Thuwayni ended his days in 1876; an unhappy exile in India. In another instance the political agent at Masqat, Samuel B. Miles, nipped a potential rebellion in the bud by warning two young princes, Hamid ibn-Thuwayni and Muhammad ibn-Thuwayni, Sultan Turki's nephews, that if they caused trouble for the sultan they would merit Britain's displeasure. The boys then made peace with the ruler.[97] Turki's most serious family rival was 'Abd al-'Aziz ibn-Sa'id, the sultan's half-brother. Numerous British attempts to bring the two men together succeeded only temporarily. It was not until after Sultan Turki's death in 1888 that 'Abd al-'Aziz finally accepted a British pension and exile in India, a move which removed a serious potential threat to the rule of Turki's successor and son, Faysal ibn-Turki.

The British authorities often intervened in disputes between the sultan and Omani tribal shaykhs. Usually this intervention took the form of mediating disagreements. But because British influence in the Gulf ultimately rested on seapower, there was a limit beyond which the Pax Britannica could not be upheld directly. This limit was well expressed in 1874 when the Government of India instructed Ross: "You have full power to help Turki actively so far as guns of vessels of war will reach.

[97] "Ross to Salisbury, 3 Sept. 1874, despatch no. 1,019-1100: Residency," India Records–2, Vol. xxv.

... Undertake no operations on shore."[98] These instructions were issued after the failure of peaceful attempts to persuade the Al Sa'd tribe of al-Batinah to settle their differences with the sultan. British gunboats eventually restored the sultan's sway over the Al Sa'd and al-Batinah coast. This incident, plus others similar to it, proved that no Omani coastal tribe could hope to carry out a successful rebellion against the sultan if the British became embroiled in the affair.

Oman's interior tribes, however, were far less susceptible to direct British influence, threats, or pressure than those on the coast. But Britain and the sultan could and did employ various indirect techniques to bring pressure on the interior tribes. Punitive taxes could be levied on the foreign exports—or occasionally even the imports—of interior tribes who defied the sultan or his British allies. Another source of indirect pressure was provided by judicious use of the moneys of the Zanzibar subsidy, some of which could be directed into the coffers of interior shaykhs.

The close ties between Sultan Turki and the British were formalized in 1886 by the announcement of an Anglo–Indian guarantee that Britain would "uphold Sayyid Turki in repelling unprovoked aggression during his lifetime. . . ."[99] This support was to be contingent upon the sultan's continuing to conduct his administration in a manner "not unsatisfactory to the government of India." The issuing of this guarantee originally had been suggested by Ross in 1885. He felt the frequent attacks on Masqat would stop if enemies of the sultan understood that even if they took Masqat they would be driven out. Initially, Sir M. Durand, the Indian foreign secretary, echoing Calcutta's traditional reserve in Arabian affairs, thought that such a guarantee would be "a great new responsibility" toward a ruler who was having difficulty holding his throne. Ross

[98] "Govt. of India to Ross, 20 Jan. 1874, telegram no. 208-p," India Records–5 Vol. III.

[99] "Dufferin to Ross, 9 Feb. 1886, enclosure no. 1 in Dufferin to Cross, 20 Aug. 1886, no. 144: Viceroy," India Records–4, Vol. XLVII.

countered this argument by claiming that the guarantee would not entail much more responsibility than the British had actually assumed already toward supporting Sultan Turki, yet it might encourage stability. Ross added that Turki ibn-Sa'id "always supported the British from the first," that his cooperation in the slave trade matter had hurt his popularity in Oman and was an aid to his enemies, and that "his fall would be a blow to the British." Colonel Miles concurred with Ross, saying that one British gunboat could secure Masqat for the sultan and added that the guarantee was "owed" to Sultan Turki for his cooperation. Ross's control over Gulf policy is well illustrated by this incident because, despite misgivings in both Calcutta and London, his suggestion was ultimately approved.[100] Nevertheless, the Government of India insisted on restating the fiction that "noninterference in dynastic struggles and internal administration" was still Britain's official policy toward Oman and that the Guarantee of 1886 was an exception granted to Sultan Turki in recognition of services rendered. On July 13, 1886 Turki ibn-Sa'id was informed of the guarantee at a durbar at which he also received the insignia of a Knight Grand Commander of the Star of India. Britain's hold over Oman's ruler appeared complete.[101]

In return for aid and protection Turki ibn-Sa'id cooperated with the British in effecting their policies in Oman. Basically, the British wanted Oman neutralized and free of any potential threat against India or imperial communications. The slave-trade cooperation of Sultan Turki has been mentioned. The sultan also had to promise Ross that he would not absent himself from Masqat for any length of time, for the British felt need of the sultan's presence if order was to be kept. Sultan

[100] "Ross to Durand, 12 Aug. 1885, enclosure no. 3; Durand to Ross, 16 Sept. 1885, enclosure no. 4; Ross to Durand, 7 Oct. 1885, enclosure no. 5; Durand to Ross, 9 Feb. 1886, enclosure no. 6; in Dufferin to Kimberly, 16 Feb. 1886, no. 36: Viceroy," India Records–4, Vol. xlvi.

[101] "Dufferin to Cross, 20 Aug. 1886, no. 144: Viceroy," India Records– 4, Vol. xlvii.

Turki was prone to underestimate his value to the British; he suffered from periodic fits of depression and on more than one occasion was dissuaded by Ross or Miles from abdicating.[102] In the detailed conduct of his government Sultan Turki was generally left alone by the British as long as he kept peace on the coast.

Sultan Turki was extremely courteous toward the British, which was reciprocated. One Christmas day the sultan went so far as to fire a 21-gun salute. The salute earned him the thanks of resident Britons but did not enhance his popularity with conservative Ibadis. He allowed the political agent access to any spot in his domain, and Miles traveled into interior Oman in 1875, 1876, 1884, 1885, and 1886.

Most vexing for the sultan were those tasks connected with providing protection for the British Indian traders in Oman. In instances where the sultan was unable to provide protection and the Indians suffered property loss or bodily harm Sultan Turki himself usually paid compensation if he could not find the guilty parties. In several instances, however, the sultan protested that he could not provide the Indians protection if they traded in certain outlying districts, and he tried to restrict them to areas along the coast under his control. Nevertheless, the Indians persisted in going into dangerous areas. If they were attacked or robbed, their claims were invariably backed by British representatives. In extreme instances when the sultan could not act, the British took matters into their own hands, sent gunboats, and collected fines.[103] It was admitted that Indian merchants often abused the political agent's protection by exaggerating complaints, inflating loss claims, and expecting backing even in reckless commercial dealings.[104]

The entire question of British extraterritorial jurisdiction

[102] "Grant to Turki ibn-Sa'id, 8 Jan. 1883," India Records-3, Vol. VI.
[103] Lorimer, I, 513-19.
[104] "Pelly to Way, 23 Apr. 1870, no. 11-43: Residency," India Records-2, Vol. XVI.

in Oman came to a head during Sultan Turki's reign. Turki ibn-Sa'id maintained that many merchants who claimed British protection—and thus escaped Omani taxes—were not entitled to it. In particular, he held that the entire Khojah community were his subjects and only grudgingly in 1873 and 1876 admitted a claim that they, like the Hindus, were due British protection. In 1876 citizens of India's British-protected Indian princely states were placed under the agent's protection. As early as 1870 the Masqat political agency had started to compile a register of all British-protected subjects in Oman, but the list was not free of discrepancies until at least 20 years later. Most disputes coming before the consul were between Indians and Omanis. Before 1878 the resident exercised full consular jurisdiction on the Persian Gulf, but without the strict legal right to do so according to British law. Not until 1878 did the resident get full consular powers and not until 1890 did the Foreign Jurisdiction Act pass Parliament and clarify the legal power of the resident. In the Gulf the law of British India was made binding upon British subjects and the region was placed under the general supervision of the High Court of Bombay. Judicial appeals of consular decision could be made to that body. In actuality the High Court had long exercised de facto judicial jurisdiction in the Gulf.[105]

Britain's role in the Persian Gulf and Oman in 1892. When Sir Edward Ross departed in 1892 he left behind a smoothly functioning machine of British supervision and indirect rule. It was an efficient system and one that was much cheaper to operate than a direct British administration.[106] In part, the British Empire at its pre-World War I peak, at least in Africa and Asia, was built on rulers like the Sultan of Masqat and Oman. In many areas the British wanted orderly rule in peaceful communities for strategic and commercial reasons. Such was obtainable with the least effort and expense oftentimes

[105] *Ibid.*; "Ross to Salisbury, 6 Feb. 1875, despatch no. 153-10: Residency," India Records-3, Vol. I; *Précis Persian Coast*, p. 87.

[106] "Hamilton to Elgin, 4 Dec. 1896, no. 50: India Secty." India Mss.-6.

by supporting the rule of existing local chiefs and binding these rulers tightly to Britain through military aid, monetary subsidies, and other support. Sometimes, when such a chief did not in fact exist, the British manufactured one. The British often assumed that everyone under their charge or vision was, or should be, organized into states.[107] Thus the fact that large areas of Oman and sizeable tribal groups in the country had never been included in the actively controlled domain of the sultan at Masqat was overlooked by the British. To them those who defied the sultan were "rebels" or "malcontents."

British interference, usually veiled, was overt only in instances such as the slave-trade issue where local mores clashed too violently with British humanitarian ideals, or else when protection of British imperial security interests required that the sword be unsheathed. Most Britons did not realize their very presence indicated that the traditional cultures they were "protecting" were being subjected to a barrage of modern ideas, institutions, and technology. In fact, the British often claimed theirs was a rule of noninterference and nonintervention in local ways. Only a person such as Pelly, very perceptive of the effects of modernization and indeed an advocate of modernization, was aware of the revolutionary changes which could occur behind the smokescreen of "noninterference."

In the Gulf and in Oman indirect rule was largely based on Indian precedents and succeeded in quieting an area that had previously been marked by constant violent political upheaval. Such seemed the best course to safeguard larger British imperial interests.

The principles of indirect rule in the Gulf included "paramountcy," the idea that ultimate power belonged to the British. This was not specifically claimed by treaty but was tacitly recognized by all concerned. There were also degrees of subordination to the paramount power. Oman was less restricted by

107 J. A. Barnes, "Indigenous Politics and Colonial Administration with Special Reference to Australia," *Comparative Studies in Society and History*, Vol. II (1960), no. 2, pp. 133-48.

treaty than was Bahrain, Bahrain less restricted than an Indian principality. Control over external relations by Britain was always implied and exercised even when, as in the case of Oman, circumstances prevented the British from proclaiming this power by treaty. If Britain's official policy was one of "non-interference" in the internal affairs of the Gulf principalities, actual circumstances modified the official policy to the point where British actions exercised a decisive effect on local events. Arab princes who cooperated with indirect rule were secure from invasion, revolution, indeed most risks save assassination. Yet the British often complained of weak rule on the part of the dependent chiefs. Overlooked was the fact that the rulers' weaknesses were due in part to their loss of face caused by overreliance on British power or by acceptance of locally unpopular policies favored by Britain. The local ruler was in an uncomfortable position of having to satisfy the British on one hand and his subjects on the other. It was nearly always an impossible task. The difficulties of the local ruler often were increased by economic embarrassment. Local pressures on his patronage unbalanced the local budgets, and loans only made things worse. In time, many dependent rulers, because of a lack of incentive to strong rule (indeed the British would not have tolerated too strong a course), reverted to regimes of apathy or irresponsibility.

Thus the exact place of Great Britain in the Persian Gulf and in Oman was not defined clearly—especially so in regard to the specific relationships between the paramount power and the individual local princes. It is important to remember, however, that by 1892 the British position was not based solely on formal engagements. It was founded also upon a constantly changing body of practices and procedures not sanctioned officially by treaty but nevertheless accepted as binding by the local rulers. Much of this body of unofficial usage, such as the practices whereby the residents interfered in succession disputes within the various Gulf states or in contests among the several Gulf potentates, virtually had the status of legally recognized understandings. Moreover, the post-1862 changes in the Persian Gulf's economic and social environment that accompanied the spread of modernization also tended to lessen the independence of the locals and increase their dependence upon the British. The coming of the steamships, the area's lack of independent financial strength, and the domination of the region's commerce by British and Indian firms were all factors that strengthened, if indirectly, Britain's grip. By 1892 the Gulf princes had been forced into a situation whereby they had to operate within a context of ever-changing and ever-tightening rules, guidelines, and limits on their freedom of action. A major and constant task for the British residents and agents was to ensure that the local rulers, their subjects and enemies all understood the continually evolving content of the rules and guidelines that were being applied in the Gulf at a given time. The rulers themselves were principal links in the process of transmitting this information to their people.

Between 1892 and the 1920s the peculiar Persian Gulf version of the British system of indirect rule reached its maturity. After that time it began to weaken, although important vestiges of the system still operate today. There was a gradual increase in permissiveness toward the locals and a decrease in controls as a result of, first, the fading of Britain's monopoly over modern enterprise in the Gulf, second, the increasing impatience of the locals with the old unofficial restrictions—a situation which led to a consequent relaxing of many restraints, and, finally, the post-World War II changes in the British empire, coupled with a rapid rise in the wealth of several Gulf states which allowed many regional rulers to press for modification or abrogation of obligations officially sanctioned by treaty. In the twentieth century indirect rule increasingly proved to be a limited method of administration, suitable mainly for preserving a status quo. It came to stand neither for continuity nor for change and more and more often was buffeted by partisans of both positions. But in 1892 Sir Edward Ross had brought indirect rule in the Persian Gulf to its zenith.

CHAPTER 6

The Defense of British Predominance, 1892-1903

WHEN Sir Edward Ross stepped down as resident in the Persian Gulf in 1892 it appeared the British position there was unassailable. Britain's predominance seemed solidly based on her virtually complete control over the foreign relations of the maritime Arab principalities, a strong voice in shaping the internal political climate within these principalities, an overwhelming economic role as well as near monopoly over the modern communications operating in the region, and her armed forces and administrators deployed in the area.

There was one uncertainty, however, which derived from the fact that during the nineteenth century, except for sporadic flurries, major policymakers in Calcutta and particularly in Whitehall had not developed much sustained interest and informed involvement in Persian Gulf affairs. To many, dominance in the Gulf seemed convenient but not absolutely vital. Given the reality, it was always possible that the strong structure built by the various residents before 1892 would be allowed to erode in the future if officials less able to cope with the normal disinterest of Calcutta and London began to be assigned to the Gulf. Moreover, it was also possible that in the event of a change in the climate of great power relations, or if a major threat to India appeared at some point along the subcontinent's frontier buffer, the Anglo–Indian and/or British home governments might compromise Britain's preponderance in the Persian Gulf in order to settle some other, more immediate difficulty.

During the 1890s both possible threats to the British position in the Gulf did in fact begin to develop. A "new breed" of British officials, less able and less well prepared, appeared while coincidentally the Persian Gulf became the object of

French, Russian, and German imperial ambitions. For a time the continuation of Britain's supremacy in the region seemed in doubt. But by 1903 the will to use the apparatus bequeathed by Ross and to assert decisively British preponderance in the Gulf was articulated first in Calcutta and finally in London. By 1903 policymakers were concerning themselves with Gulf affairs, and Whitehall clearly had signaled its intent that in the future it was going to take charge of deciding and supervising British interests there.

THE WEAK RESIDENTS: 1892-99

Although the machinery used by Ross to influence Gulf affairs was quite efficient, those who operated this apparatus had to be skilled if good results were to be produced. In 1862-92 residents and subsidiary officers of talent and energy served well British interests in the Persian Gulf. After Ross's retirement from Bushire in 1892, however, the quality of British personnel in the region dropped to a humdrum level. If the 1890s had been ordinary times ordinary men might have sufficed, but they were years of unusual crisis in the Persian Gulf, a decade holding the most serious threat to Britain's regional hegemony that she had had to face up to that time. The crisis proved too much for the abilities of Britain's Gulf representatives, and in 1899 Calcutta, and then London, became involved in the minute details of Gulf happenings. The chief move associated with Britain's residents which increased the empire's hold in the Gulf during the 1890s was the extension of loans to various rulers, particularly the Sultan of Masqat. But never after 1892 did any resident wield the influence of a Pelly or a Ross. Contributing to the deterioration of the resident's position during the 1890s was the fact that the Persian Gulf became an arena of great-power imperial rivalries which in turn instigated numerous local disorders. No local official could have successfully met this double-barreled threat alone and unsupported. Nevertheless, until 1899 Calcutta and London left a succession of post-Ross residents to flounder almost unassisted. The challenges faced by the Gulf residency were regarded as undemanding or unimportant, and Calcutta selected mediocre officials to supervise the area. By 1899 British prestige in the Gulf had begun to fall.

Lt. Col. A. C. Talbot succeeded Ross as resident in 1892, but left the post in 1893 to become deputy foreign secretary at Calcutta. Three men held the office in 1894. Col. F. A. Wilson took over in Bushire from 1894 to 1897 and was followed by Lt. Col. M. J. Meade, who remained until 1900. This alternation of residents contrasts with Ross's 20 years and Pelly's 10. The situation at the Masqat political agency was little better. Five different men held the post of political agent between 1892 and 1899, only one of whom, Major J. Hayes-Sadler, occupied the post for more than two years. On three separate occasions, which together totaled over a year's time, the agency surgeon, Dr. A. S. G. Jayaker, substituted for various vacationing agents.

The rapid turnover of British personnel in the 1890s proved injurious to the efficient manipulation of the existing machinery of British supervision in the Gulf. Personal influence and knowledge of the area built up over the course of years were among the most valuable assets of previous British officials in the Gulf. Prior to the 1890s most personnel destined for important Gulf billets were given long periods of on-the-job training in the region as junior officials. A man's language talents and knowledge of local conditions were highly developed before he was given a responsible post. Edward Ross served a nine-year apprenticeship in lesser jobs in the Gulf before taking over as resident.[1]

In the 1890s the new breed of officials arrived. They were described as "men whose diplomatic experiences have been limited to India, to the jovial round of club and army life and

[1] "Lansdowne to Kimberley, 27 Sept. 1893," India Mss.–5, Vol. v; Lansdowne decried the bad effect that the rapid turnover of officers in the Indian Foreign Department had on relations with local princes; *India Office List, 1896*, p. 491.

the no less jovial tail twisting of native princes."[2] Gulf posts and Masqat especially, because of its almost unendurable climate, were among the least coveted posts in the Indian government.[3] During this period the Anglo–Indian government in general lacked sufficient numbers of officials who were trained in Oriental languages and who possessed intimate knowledge of the peoples whom they ruled; it was not until this century that the importance of such training was admitted.[4]

The newer officials had a vastly different attitude toward the Gulf, their jobs, and the Arabs they guided than did the men of Ross's time. Ross and Miles had carefully cultivated the respect and friendship of the locals. They enjoyed their work and, as their published works indicate, even grew to love the harsh Gulf. They treated Arab rulers with friendship and respect, and they carefully observed local customs of courtesy. In the 1890s, however, too many British officials displayed little of the tact or enthusiasm of their predecessors. Evidently, most of the "new breed" would have agreed with the opinion of the disenchanted Major Hayes-Sadler, the agent at Masqat from 1892 to 1896, that "one Arab [was] about as untrustworthy as another."[5] The dispatches of the decade indicate lack of rapport between British and Arab and testify to an eclipse in the spirit of mutual trust of the Ross period. This was particularly true in Masqat, where relations between the British and Sultan Faysal ibn-Turki grew progressively worse until 1898-99 when the sultan attempted to substitute French for British "protection."

It is obvious that the quality of British representatives in the Gulf deteriorated as the 1890s progressed. Between 1892 and 1896 most British representatives, despite their generally sour

[2] Excerpt from a letter by Dr. Cantine of the Dutch Reformed Church Mission in Masqat, quoted in P. Graves, *The Life of Sir Percy Cox* (London, 1941), p. 55.

[3] J. T. Bent, "Muscat," *The Contemporary Review*, LXVIII (1895), 875.

[4] J. D. Rees, "Russia, India, and the Persian Gulf or the Western Frontiers of India," *Asiatic Review*, XXXIV (1903), 247.

[5] "Elgin to Hamilton, 30 Sept. 1896, no. 39: Viceroy," India Mss.–6.

attitudes, could use Arabic and knew something of local conditions. Between 1896 and 1899 the personnel situation in the Gulf reached the depths. The resident, Lt. Col. M. J. Meade, was well meaning but clumsy. Meanwhile, the agent at Masqat, Major C. G. F. Fagan, whose experience was mainly military campaigning in India, guided Anglo–Omani relations to their all-time low. Fagan did not know Arabic and could not communicate directly with the sultan. For an interpreter he depended on a local clerk who was prone to discuss state secrets in the bazaar. Fagan's relations with Sultan Faysal broke down completely by 1899. Fagan's usual technique of dealing with the sultan was to issue arrogant and thinly veiled ultimatums, and if these went unheeded to threaten gunboat action.[6] By 1899 even Calcutta and London were seriously concerned with the drift of events. Fagan was recognized as "lacking in the first rudiments of diplomacy" and was described by the secretary of state for India as "a real duffer."[7] In 1899, after five years of French assaults had began to crack Britain's position in the Persian Gulf region, it was decided that better personnel had to be recruited despite the area's unattractiveness.[8] It was recognized that bad management was at the root of many of Britain's troubles and that British influence, in order to be reasserted, required capable men. With everyone, including himself, gasping with relief Major Fagan left Masqat in September 1899. Colonel Meade surrendered the residency to his successor in April 1900.

Fagan's successor was Major Percy Cox who later won fame as the organizer of the mandate kingdom of Iraq. Cox remained in Masqat until 1904 when he took over as resident.

[6] "Hamilton to Curzon, 6 Feb. 1899," "15 May 1899," "18 May 1899," India Mss.–2, Vol. I; Lord Salisbury, the prime minister, was especially critical of Colonel Meade; *Précis Maskat*, pp. 60-61.

[7] "Hamilton to Curzon, 5 Jan. 1900," India Mss.–2, Vol. II. As early as 1896 Lord George Hamilton, the secretary of state for India, began complaining about Britain's Persian Gulf representatives. See "Hamilton to Elgin, 9 Sept. 1896, no. 38: India Secty.," India Mss.–6.

[8] "Hamilton to Curzon, 16 Feb. 1899," India Mss.–2, Vol. I.

His career at Masqat was a conspicuous success. In his very first interview with the sultan he cleared the way for a resumption of friendly Anglo–Omani relations, and by the end of his term Oman was more firmly in the British sphere than ever before.[9] Cox, although he never enjoyed the independence of either Pelly or Ross, nonetheless ranks with these men among Britain's great Persian Gulf representatives. Colonel Meade's immediate successor as resident was Lt. Col. C. A. Kembell who served from 1900 until 1904. Kembell did his job competently but was given little chance to shine because between 1899 and 1905 India's viceroy, Lord Curzon, supervised many of the details of administering Gulf policy himself.

The interested—indeed, some might call it meddlesome—attitude of Curzon toward Gulf affairs was a notable contrast to that of his predecessors. Between 1892 and 1899, despite a growing challenge to British hegemony in the Gulf, neither Whitehall nor the Government of India gave serious attention to Gulf matters. Writing in 1892, Lord Curzon complained that the importance of British control over the Gulf for Indian defense was little recognized in either England or India.[10] At that time British opinion regarded the Afghanistan passes as the only vulnerable spot in the shield protecting the Indian empire.[11]

In the years 1894 and 1895 it is impossible to find a reference to the Persian Gulf in the viceroy's personal correspondence with the secretary of state for India; only in 1896 did the worsening situation stimulate even general comment concerning the region from the two men most responsible for formulating Indian policy. The habit of leaving the Gulf in the capable hands of Ross had grown so strong before 1892 that even after the great resident's departure Calcutta did not worry itself about Gulf affairs. In the early 1890s both London and

[9] "Hamilton to Curzon, 5 Jan. 1900," India Mss.–2, Vol. II; *Précis Maskat*, p. 81; Cox's career is fully treated in Graves, *Life of Cox.*
[10] G. Curzon, *Persia and the Persian Question* (London, 1892), II, 397-98.
[11] V. Chirol, *The Middle Eastern Question, or some Political Problems of Indian Defense* (New York, 1903), p. 291.

Calcutta agreed that India and her approaches were secure. In 1894 the British were so confident everything was under control that they planned to reduce Indian military expenditure.[12]

Still, Persian Gulf matters occasionally caught the viceroy's attention. Lord Elgin in 1896 complained he often had Masqat papers before him, that they comprised "one of the biggest files I know."[13] Nevertheless, he went on to exclaim how difficult it was to do anything about Gulf problems and proceeded to ignore the area's difficulties. In fairness to Elgin one must remember that he was occupied with a more immediate problem in the unruly North-West Frontier which diverted Calcutta's attention from any shadowy "threats" in the Persian Gulf. Late in 1897, however, it was suspected that munitions imported into the Persian Gulf might be the source of arms for the Indian–Afghan frontier tribes. By 1898 conclusive evidence of the fact was uncovered so the Omani sultan and other Gulf rulers were induced to agree to restrict the arms traffic through their territories.[14] Persian Gulf affairs finally had attracted the attention of the major Calcutta authorities and the drift in the Gulf began to be brought under control.

LORD CURZON, THE PERSIAN GULF, AND THE CHALLENGE OF IMPERIALISM, 1899-1903

The 1890s were the climax of "the age of imperialism." Between 1870 and 1885 most Western powers and Russia annexed vast areas of the non-Western world. Despite occasional disputes the expansion of the domains of the modern powers was relatively simple until 1885, but the "Panjdeh crisis" that year signaled the beginning of the end for the "colonial frontier." The world over, great powers began to rub against each other uneasily as there was no room left to expand without stepping on some other imperialist power's toes. Rival claims and pretensions collided as the unclaimed buffer areas that

---

12 "Kimberley to Elgin, 9 Feb. 1894, no. 2: India Secty.," India Mss.–6.
13 "Elgin to Hamilton, 30 Sept. 1896, no. 39: Viceroy," India Mss.–6.
14 Lorimer, I, 2,574-75; Aitchison—1909, XII, 241-42.

once separated the respective spheres of the modern powers evaporated.

The collision zones were legion—the Far East; southeast Asia; central Asia; north, east, and south Africa; and the Caribbean. The various Asiatic zones in aggregate formed a single twisting snake of territory winding from Arabia through Persia, central Asia and Afghanistan, on to west and north China; there the band turned southward toward Korea and China's Pacific coast; it terminated in southeast Asia in the region of Indo–China and Siam. By the 1890s the Persian Gulf was included among the contested territories in this strip; it is well to remember that the imperial clashes which occurred on the Gulf's shores were part of a larger pattern of confrontations.

In the Gulf the claims and schemes of four powers came into conflict. Britain's claim in the Gulf, established in the early nineteenth century, had gone uncontested but unrecognized by the other great powers. Agents of the Anglo–Indian empire had presided over the gradual absorption of the Gulf into the amorphous fabric of the British empire, yet in the 1890s most Britons would have been hard put to describe the essence, the structure, or even the reason for Britain's Gulf primacy. Only a few Britons remembered that the Gulf principalities protected Indian communications and saw that they had become vital segments in the chain of "protected states" and "spheres of influence" which shielded India. In retrospect the lack of concern over the Gulf may appear strange since Indian defense in the late nineteenth century was, next to defense of the home islands, the major concern of British imperial policy. Defense of the subcontinent depended on maintaining Britain's worldwide naval supremacy, sustaining a small but efficient Indian Army, protecting the communications between Britain and India, and finally on supporting a ring of buffer states to protect India's flanks. Thus the implications and problems of Indian defense involved Britain in Morocco, Cyprus, Oman, and Egypt as much as in Afghanistan. Not even Gladstone, anything but an ardent imperialist, could ignore the implications of Indian defense; hence his involvement in 1882 in Egypt and in the Panjdeh crisis in 1885.

Probably the most potentially dangerous of the various imperial thrusts against the British position in the Gulf was that presented by Russia's assertion of her interests there in the 1890s. By consolidating her hold over the central Asian khanates in the 1870s Russia was established adjacent to northeastern Iran (Khurasan) and Afghanistan. Whitehall and Calcutta since the 1830s had been wary of Russian expansion toward India, and between 1876 and 1894 the British, through the use of alliances, missions, subsidies, war, and border commissions, secured the Afghanistan frontier and turned that country into a buffer separating the Anglo–Indian and Russian empires. The crisis period of this settlement was during the Panjdeh dispute of 1885. But after 1885 the scene of this confrontation moved west to Iran. The Qajar empire consequently became the focus of Anglo–Russian rivalry until 1914 despite the 1907 Convention defining British and Russian spheres of influence. In the 1890s Russian influence expanded considerably in northern Iran. Some British began to fear that Russia still aimed its expansion toward India and that, if the Muscovites were barred from using Afghanistan, they would try to expand through Persia, establish themselves on the Persian Gulf, and thus be in a position to mount either a land or sea attack on India from the west. But if Russia's position in Iran appeared more menacing than ever before, in actuality until 1904 her main imperial effort was directed toward the Far East and not the Middle East. Nonetheless, during the years 1899-1903, when Britain was occupied with the great imperial and international crisis caused by the Boer War, the Russian drive toward the Persian Gulf picked up momentum.

The third power involved in the Persian Gulf imperial rivalry was France. France had been interested in the Gulf off and on since the seventeenth century. Until 1810 this interest was connected with the French desire to dominate India, after that time with commercial objectives, or with a vaguely defined desire to strengthen France's imperial interests in the Indian Ocean basin. Next to Britain, France was the European power most involved in the Indian Ocean area. She possessed small colonies in India and several island colonies. Between 1885 and 1894 she annexed the large island of Madagascar, established a colony at the mouth of the Red Sea (French Somaliland), and enjoyed considerable influence in Ethiopia. On the other side of the Indian Ocean she pushed her influence into Indochina and Siam. Meanwhile, by virtue of an 1862 joint declaration she was co-guarantor, with Britain, of the independence of Zanzibar and Oman, while numbers of Arab dhows sailing the waters of the Gulf and the Indian Ocean flew the French flag thanks to the liberal registration laws of the Third Republic and the desire of the Arabs to engage in slaving and other illicit trade under the tricolor's protection. Finally, in 1894 France established a vice consulate at Masqat, an event which signaled French plans to expand their influence and involvement in the Persian Gulf and which commenced a long period of Anglo-French wrangling there.

France's aggressive policy in the Gulf derived from a number of factors. Most important was the adoption in 1894 of an anti-British imperial policy identified with M. Hanotaux. Until Hanotaux was replaced by Delcassé in 1898 as foreign minister, France allowed her rivalry with Germany to remain relatively quiescent while becoming involved with Britain in colonial disputes the world over.[15] The Fashoda crisis of 1898 demonstrated the dangers of Hanotaux's policy, but vestiges of it remained operative, in the Gulf at least, for several more years. 1894 also marked the conclusion of the Franco–Russian alliance. Certain groups in France favored an aggressive policy in the Gulf area to prove to the Russians how valuable French aid could be in influencing the outcome of Russian–British rivalry in Asia. Finally, the French interest in the Gulf is cer-

[15] W. Langer, *The Diplomacy of Imperialism, 1890-1902* (New York, 1956), p. 796.

tainly consistent with other, simultaneous French advances (notably in Madagascar and Siam) aimed at increasing France's imperial stature in the Indian Ocean.

The fourth power showing interest in Gulf affairs during the 1890s was Germany, although the heyday of this interest was between 1903 and 1914. In the 1890s strong German economic probes were directed toward the Ottoman empire, and these were extended to Iran in the following decade. Marshall von Bieberstein (German ambassador in Istanbul, 1897-1912), an architect of Germany's Near Eastern policy, popularized a plan to transform part of the Middle East into a German "economic colony." According to this scheme the Middle East was to be opened up as a market and exploited as a source of raw materials for German industry, although local industry would not be encouraged. Also, the Ottoman and Iranian governments were to be supported against encroachments by other European powers. In return for this political aid the Germans expected to gain special economic privileges. Markets, not territory, was the aim. The key to success in this plan was the extension of a land communications network to penetrate into many previously inaccessible parts of the Middle East's interior. The primary element in this network was to be the Berlin–Baghdad railway; from this trunkline feeder routes were to place the entire Near East within the reach of German industry.[16] It was envisioned that the eastern terminus of the railroad would be a Persian Gulf port—probably Kuwait. So these plans injected Germany into the Persian Gulf picture. In actuality no German railway terminus on the Gulf appeared and the chief German interest in the Gulf before 1914 was limited to an increasingly strong economic challenge to British markets posed by the activities of German steamship interests.

In the Gulf in the 1890s there were three areas where the four great powers interested in the region clashed. The first

[16] For details see *ibid.*, chap. 19; B. Martin, *German–Persian Diplomatic Relations* (The Hague, 1959); E. M. Earle, *Turkey, the Great Powers and the Baghdad Railroad* (New York, 1923).

focus of conflict was in the southern part of the Persian Gulf and Oman; there France sought to gain influence at the expense of Great Britain. The second zone of contention was the Ottoman-dominated upper Gulf coast which included al-Hasa, Kuwait, and Iraq. Initially it appeared that this would be a place of British–Russian rivalry when in 1898 a scheme of Count Kapnist to build a Russian-financed railroad from the Mediterranean to Kuwait was revealed. However, nothing developed from the Kapnist plan. After 1900 this area became the object of British–German rivalry focusing on the Baghdad railway project. The third sphere of rivalry was Persia's Gulf and Arabian Sea coasts; there Russian–British rivalry was particularly acute between 1899 and 1903.

Within these three collision zones of the Gulf there operated in microcosm the same factors and forces which determined the worldwide pattern of imperial age diplomacy. Britain was the predominant power; when the other contestants sought to expand their influence it was Britain's naval strength that blocked the way. The main British fear was that a combination of her rivals might throw her down. Many of the imperial clashes occurred behind a legalistic facade with both the British and their adversaries declaring they were acting in the interests of one or another of the countries which lined the Gulf's shores. The Shah of Persia, the Ottoman sultan, or the Sultan of Masqat and Oman were often used as dummies by various great power ventriloquists.

Oman and the French in the 1890s. Oman was the scene of the first major imperial contest of the decade in the Gulf, when in 1894 the French challenged Britain. In the nineteenth century a sporadic French interest in Oman had been displayed during the Napoleonic period, in the 1860s in connection with the Suez Canal enthusiasm, and finally in the 1890s.

French involvement in Omani affairs in the last decade of the nineteenth century was not the product of sudden inspiration. Between 1883 and 1885, when Jules Ferry was directing French colonial affairs, a subsidized steamer service between

France and the Gulf was attempted. That this indication of interest was followed by the activities of the Frenchman Chapui on the Trucial Coast was one of the factors that stimulated Britain to conclude the series of exclusive agreements of 1892 with various Gulf rulers. Even before 1894 French consuls at Aden, Obock, and Zanzibar on numerous occasions had given French flags and registration papers to natives of Sur and other Omani ports.[17] In November 1892 M. Deloncle, an ardent imperialist, speaking in the Chamber of Deputies, declared that French honor demanded that a consular agent be appointed to Masqat "to keep a register of French protected subjects." Deloncle added that France would be in a position to cooperate with Russia and demonstrate her potential as an ally if she were established in the Gulf. In the budget debate of 1893 Deloncle again called for an active French policy in the Gulf and proposed a supplementary credit of 7,000 francs for establishing a vice consulate at Masqat. The foreign minister, M. Denville, promised during the debate that the post would be created.[18] It was possible for the French to do this because Oman, unlike the Trucial States to the north, was not bound by treaty to conduct its foreign relations through a British intermediary.

On November 8, 1894 M. Ottavi, an Arabic-speaking diplomat with extensive experiences in Zanzibar and other Indian Ocean posts, arrived in Masqat to take up his duties as vice consul. Ottavi, like many of France's representatives in the Orient, was a Corsican, and proved to be an industrious, intelligent, and smooth-talking diplomat who was more than a match for the succession of uninspired agents who guided Britain's interests in Oman in the 1890s.[19] The Omani sultan, Faysal ibn-Turki, initially was disturbed over Ottavi's arrival for he feared that France would try to assert a protectorate

17 Daud, "British Relations with the Persian Gulf, 1890-1902," pp. 213-14.

18 *Précis Maskat*, p. 45; Lorimer, I, 546-47.

19 *Annuaire Diplomatique et Consulaire de France—1899* (Paris, 1899), p. 240.

over those Omanis who had been given the right to fly the French flag on their ships, and perhaps the French might attempt to detach Sur from his realm. Within five months of Ottavi's arrival, however, Sultan Faysal's attitude changed after the British did not afford him the military aid which he expected during the course of a conservative Ibadi attack on Masqat in February–March 1895. The British added to the sultan's ire when they followed up their lack of aid with a demand that the sultan pay $MT 77,895 damages to the Indian merchants who suffered losses during the attack. In contrast, Ottavi offered to help the sultan ward off Masqat's attackers and had the gunboat *Troude* sent to the city. *Troude* arrived too late to actively support the sultan but the incident indicated France's good will, as well as the power at her disposal and ushered in a four-year period of French ascendancy in the court of Sultan Faysal.[20]

By 1896 the British were beginning to show concern over the cooling relations between themselves and the sultan. Unsuccessfully they tried to counter growing French influence and get back into the sultan's favor by offering arms, naval assistance, and loans. Next, talk of a protectorate was renewed among the British but again dropped.[21] Ottavi, in his interviews with the sultan, constantly amplified the fact that the sultan was free to run his own foreign affairs and that he alone was legally responsible for his government.[22] He encouraged the sultan to assert his independence from British tutelage. Ottavi's success in driving a wedge between the Omani ruler and the British was essentially due to British mistakes and to the personal influence Ottavi won among the sultan's confi-

[20] *Précis Maskat*, pp. 22, 53; Daud, "British Relations with the Persian Gulf, 1890-1902," p. 215; Lorimer, I, 547-53; "Hamilton to Curzon, 14 Apr. 1899," India Mss.–2, Vol. I; "Hanotaux to Cogordon, 24 Feb. 1895, no. 379: Paris," *Documents Diplomatiques Français*, 1st series, Vol. XI.

[21] Wilson, *Persian Gulf*, p. 239; *Précis Maskat*, pp. 16-22; Lorimer, I, 550-52.

[22] "Ottavi to Hanotaux, 23 Feb. 1897, no. 4: Masqat," French Records.

dants and with Sultan Faysal himself.[23] The British became particularly disturbed over the fact that 'Abd al-Aziz, Ottavi's dragoman, also occupied a key position as the sultan's confidential secretary, while other anti-British Omanis also were welcomed at court. Sultan Faysal, for his part, encouraged French interests in Oman in the hope that they could balance British interests and thus allow Oman to enjoy some real measure of independence.[24]

Ottavi's greatest success in Oman occurred in March 1898 during a visit by the French gunboat *Gabes* to Masqat. Faysal ibn-Turki agreed to give the French a concession for a coaling station at Bandar Jissah, a small defensible harbor five miles from Masqat.[25] The concession was followed up by a two-week visit to Masqat in October 1898 by the French gunboat *Scorpion*. At that time valuable presents were exchanged, including a gift of a field gun to the sultan. Several secret conferences also were held, the pro-British *wazir* (prime minister) was dismissed, and Bandar Jissah was reconnoitred by Ottavi and a party from the *Scorpion*.[26] France appeared on the verge of detaching Oman from its century-old alliance with Britain and establishing a fortified beachhead in an area up to then considered Britain's exclusive preserve.

In June 1898, however, Hanotaux was replaced by Delcassé at the Quai d'Orsay, while in September 1898 Curzon was appointed Viceroy of India (taking office in January 1899). These moves anticipated changes in the existing French and British policies in Asia and the Gulf. In the early 1890s, as the Franco–Russian alliance was consummated, the ultra-imperialist school had moved to the fore, and this group, headed by Hanotaux, was dominant between 1894 and 1898. Hanotaux, a follower of Jules Ferry, believed that France absolutely

[23] "Hamilton to Curzon, 6 July 1899," India Mss.–2, Vol. I.
[24] *Précis Maskat*, p. 77; Lorimer, I, 556; Daud, "British Relations with the Persian Gulf, 1890-1902," p. 211.
[25] Text in "Curzon to Hamilton, 25 Feb. 1899, telegram no. 315," *Précis Maskat*, p. 75.
[26] *Ibid.*, pp. 62-65; Lorimer, I, 556.

required an overseas empire if she was to remain a great power. He was even willing to ease Franco–German tension in Europe in order to direct France toward imperial expansion in Afro–Asia. Such a program was bound to bring trouble with Britain. Moreover, the ultra-imperialists were quite willing to use the new Russian connection, when convenient, as France began to challenge Britain at various points all over the world.[27] Siam in 1893-96, Oman in 1894-98, the Sudan in 1896-98, west Africa in 1897-98, all became scenes of bitter Anglo–French disputes as Hanotaux and his agents "attacked" in those areas where it appeared British influence was not too secure. Ottavi's work at Masqat is an excellent specific example of this general trend; the spring of 1898, the time when France gained her coaling station concession in Oman, marked the culmination of this forward policy. However, by that time the British appeared ready to make a stand and fight over Sudan (the Fashoda crisis) and over Nigeria. Also, at that critical hour France was convulsed and weakened internally by the Dreyfus affair. In this precarious situation the French finally backed away from their extreme foreign policy and between 1898 and 1904 proceeded to compromise their imperial difficulties with Great Britain.

The ending of the danger of a British–French imperial war was largely the work of Theophile Delcassé (foreign minister, June 1898–June 1905). Delcassé was not an ardent imperialist; rather he thought France should concern herself mainly with assuring her continental safety by countering growing German power. He wished to promote British–French friendship as a keystone of his foreign policy; indeed it seems he preferred an English connection to the one already existing with Russia. As soon as he took office he set about to calm the Anglo–French imperial problem bequeathed by Hanotaux.[28]

But on November 20, 1898 news of the concession of Bandar Jissah was published in Paris, an announcement that precipi-

---

[27] Langer, *Diplomacy of Imperialism*, pp. 796-97. [28] *Ibid.*

tated what came to be known as the "Masqat crisis."[29] On learning of the concession Monson, the British ambassador in Paris, inquired about the matter from Delcassé who denied that he possessed any knowledge concerning the statement. Delcassé was obviously embarrassed by the prospect of having one more of Hanotaux' anti-British projects to deal with.[30] Lord Salisbury (prime minister, June 1895–July 1902) took a soft line regarding the problem raised by the announcement, for he wanted to give Delcassé a chance to escape from an embarrassing situation. Salisbury, like Delcassé, was trying to mediate French–British difficulties. In 1897 he had proposed to the French that an arbitration treaty be signed to "regulate all our little mutual difficulties."[31] Although the idea was rejected because of Hanotaux' hostility and because French public opinion was not then in favor of the idea, it is clear Salisbury wanted to avoid trouble with France and reach a general colonial agreement with her. Consequently, between September 1898 and March 1899 Salisbury and Delcassé proceeded to work out an agreement which settled the most pressing of the imperial problems clouding Anglo–French relations, despite the occurrence of numerous incidents that threatened to wreck the negotiations in midstream.[32]

Not the least of these threats was provided by Curzon, the new viceroy of India, who assumed office in January 1899. Since 1892 Curzon had been urging Britain to strengthen her Indian defenses. The Persian Gulf and Iran he regarded as especially vulnerable parts of India's buffer zone, believing imperialist encroachments by Britain's great power rivals into those regions should be resisted.[33] Within days of his arrival in

[29] *Journal des Débats* (Paris, Nov. 20, 1898).

[30] "Monson to Salisbury, 2 Dec. 1898, no. 663: Paris," Public Record Office Mss., F.O. 27/3489.

[31] Daud, "British Relations with the Persian Gulf, 1890-1902," pp. 220-21; "Courcel to Hanotaux, 26 Mar. 1897," *Documents Diplomatiques Français*, 1st series, Vol. xiv.

[32] This agreement was signed on March 21, 1899.

[33] Curzon, *Persia and the Persian Question*, ii, 465; Hurewitz, *Diplomacy*, i, 219ff.

Calcutta Curzon began combatting what he regarded as the three main existing anti-British imperialist probes into Iran and the Gulf region. In Iran itself he attempted (but never fully succeeded) to halt Russian penetration into the eastern and southern parts of the country. When he learned of the French concession in Oman he determined to void the document—by force if necessary. Finally, he undertook to block the use of Kuwait as a terminus for any non-British-controlled railway. He envisioned such a railway as being Russian-controlled, although it developed that the Germans were to be the most likely power to gain such a concession.[34]

In the absence of any directions from Whitehall Curzon instructed the Gulf resident, Col. Meade, to settle both the Kuwait and Oman matters. Meade's action in Kuwait did not provide an immediate crisis. There Shaykh Mubarak, who was looking for allies to bolster his position vis-à-vis internal rivals and his nominal Ottoman overlords, agreed not to cede any of his territory nor receive the representatives of any power without the previous consent of the British government.[35] But in Oman Curzon set in motion events which immediately developed into a crisis and seriously disturbed Salisbury's and Delcassé's negotiations.

On January 17, 1899 Fagan, under orders from Curzon, interviewed Faysal ibn-Turki who admitted giving France the grant for a coaling station. Fagan protested, saying such a grant was an infringement of the Anglo–Omani Non-Alienation Treaty of 1891. Sultan Faysal bravely but rashly replied that his promise had been given to the French and that if Britain objected she should settle matters directly with the French.[36] Curzon, when he learned of the sultan's defiance, issued instructions that a British flag be hoisted at Bandar Jissah if a French warship should appear in the harbor.[37] Next,

---

[34] Langer, *Diplomacy of Imperialism*, pp. 642-43; Earl of Ronaldshay, *The Life of Lord Curzon* (London, 1928), chaps. 2, 23.

[35] Aitchison—1933, XI, 262.   [36] *Précis Maskat*, p. 69.

[37] "Hamilton to Curzon, 20 Jan. 1899, telegram," *Précis Maskat*, p. 70.

Curzon withheld the Zanzibar subsidy from Sultan Faysal and sent Colonel Meade to Masqat with an ultimatum the resident delivered to the sultan on February 9, 1899. The document contained references to several problems which had vexed Anglo–Omani relations since 1895, but its heart was a demand, made without Whitehall's knowledge, that the sultan cancel the concession of Bandar Jissah to the French. The sultan was given 48 hours to reply. Curzon clearly paced the action by first presenting demands to the sultan and then submitting a fait accompli to London for approval. The culmination of this process occurred between February 11th and 15th. On February 13th Faysal bowed to the inevitable and indicated he would revoke the concession, while at the same time he applied for British protection against France in case his action instigated armed French intervention. This surrender was not enough for Meade and Curzon. On February 14 Admiral Douglas, the commander of the India station, arrived off Masqat with a small fleet. Meade demanded that the sultan publicly cancel the lease. This action, of course, meant that Curzon was determined to openly humiliate both the sultan and the French government. On February 16, when the sultan did not answer, Admiral Douglas ordered Faysal ibn-Turki to meet him aboard his flagship. Meanwhile, the British ships moved into position to open fire on the palace and forts of Masqat and a warning was given to the town that bombardment was imminent. The sultan capitulated. He came out to the flagship and agreed to all demands. Ironically, when Sultan Faysal rowed away Admiral Douglas fired the 21-gun salute reserved for an independent sovereign in the ruler's honor.[38]

As far as the British were concerned, relations with the sultan took an immediate turn for the better. Sultan Faysal went so far as to visit Major Fagan—whom he cordially disliked—at the agency in March. Still, it was not until Percy Cox

[38] *Ibid.*, pp. 70-76.

replaced Fagan as agent in October 1899 that Anglo–Omani relations regained their traditional warmth.[39] Regarding Britain's place in Oman, the "Masqat crisis" illustrated that Curzon was willing in an emergency to dispense with the sham that Faysal ibn-Turki enjoyed full independence. In February 1899 Sultan Faysal realized, legal niceties and 21-gun salutes notwithstanding, that his position depended on British good will and that if he defied Britain again it would probably cost him his throne. Indeed, British government lawyers, when asked their opinion, declared the sultan could be removed from his throne if he broke engagements made with Great Britain. This ruling was issued on the grounds that the 1862 guarantee of Oman's independence insured only the independence of Oman's territory and not the office of the individual ruler.[40]

When Paris heard of the proceedings at Masqat they were horrified. On February 22, 1899 the French protested Admiral Douglas's action.[41] Delcassé had already indicated his belief that many in England wanted war with France and would try to provoke hostilities.[42] Curzon's action seemed to prove that Delcassé's fears were well founded—especially so when English public opinion enthusiastically applauded the viceroy's exploits. Adding to the publicity was a Parliamentary debate on the Masqat situation; by late March, however, public interest had waned and Parliamentary questioning had ceased.[43] The

---

[39] *Ibid.*, pp. 77-81; "Hamilton to Curzon, 5 Jan. 1900," India Mss.–2, Vol. II.

[40] *Précis Maskat*, pp. 74, 77; "Hamilton to Curzon, 10 Mar. 1899," India Mss.–2, Vol. I.

[41] "Cambon to Foreign Office, 22 Feb. 1899," Public Record Office Mss., F.O. 27/3530. See Public Record Office Mss., F.O. 54 and F.O. 27 series for British–French–Omani relations during this period.

[42] "Monson to Salisbury, 13 Jan. 1899," Public Record Office Mss., F.O. 27/3455.

[43] *The Times*, London, Feb. 22, 1899. *The Times* strongly supported Curzon's action; Great Britain, *Parliamentary Debates, House of Commons*, 4th series, LXVII, 293-95; "Hamilton to Curzon, 28 Mar. 1899," India Mss.–2, Vol. I.

incident was also well publicized in France, but the chagrined Delcassé leaned over backward to quiet the storm and save his negotiations with Salisbury.[44]

For his part, Salisbury was shocked at the manner in which the situation had been handled by the Indian authorities and thought the action a "serious mistake." Like Delcassé, he was particularly disturbed by what he termed "the unnecessary publicity of the whole proceeding."[45] Salisbury feared that a flare-up concerning a "petty prince" would jeopardize his negotiations with Delcassé, which aimed at reaching a general African settlement. As far as the Masqat issue itself was concerned, Salisbury was quite willing to protest any actual cession of territory, but on the other hand said the French were justified in having coal storage facilities such as the British enjoyed in Masqat. In short, Salisbury wanted to settle the Masqat affair with as little fuss as possible.[46] Curzon for his part, thinking Salisbury was being soft on the French, tried to defend the harsh line he had taken by claiming that France still wanted a port in Oman and that such a port would threaten Indian security.[47] Finally, early in March 1899 Salisbury took the fire out of the controversy by proposing that France share with Britain the use of the existing coaling sheds inside Masqat harbor. From that point until their conclusion in April 1900 the negotiations dragged on, but without the previous air of crisis. The French continued their efforts to get a separate coaling station outside Masqat harbor while the British kept insisting these facilities should be within Masqat harbor where they could not possibly become the nucleus of

[44] *Journal Officiel, Débats de la Chambre des Députés,* 7 Mar. 1899, p. 677; "Hamilton to Curzon, 3 Mar. 1899," "28 Mar. 1899," India Mss.–2, Vol. I.

[45] "Salisbury to Monson, 22 Feb. 1899," quoted in G. Gooch and H. Temperley, *British Documents on the Origin of the War* (London, 1926-38), I, 209-10.

[46] Ronaldshay, *Life of Curzon,* II, 47-50.

[47] *Ibid.* "Curzon to Hamilton, 5 Sept. 1900," India Mss.–3, Vol. II.

a naval base. Finally, the French accepted the British proposal to share the existing facilities.[48] Ottavi, his attempt to subvert the sultan a failure after 1899, turned to a new tactic in pushing French influence. Since the 1860s the French had given flags and registration papers to various Omani ship captains, most of whom called Sur home port. Ottavi claimed the various Omani seamen who held French flags should be treated as French protégés and were due the protection of the Third Republic.[49] The British supported Sultan Faysal in his contention that the grant of the tricolor was an illegal attempt to detach Omani subjects from their rightful allegiance. The British, of course, feared the presence of a large body of French protégés in Oman would give the French numerous chances to intervene in Omani affairs or even to detach Sur or some other part of the sultanate. The "French flags affair" was a touchy one involving the "sovereign honor" of several states and was not settled until it was submitted to the Hague Tribunal. Although the tribunal decision handed down in 1905 essentially supported the British against the French, the French–British rivalry in Oman was reduced to relative unimportance after the rapprochement that heralded the Anglo–French Entente in 1904.[50]

The main result of French activity in Oman between 1894 and 1904 was to force the sultan even more into the arms of the British. If Faysal ibn-Turki encouraged the French in order to play them off against the British, then his strategy backfired. In the Masqat crisis of 1899 the sultan was made pain-

---

[48] *Précis Maskat*, pp. 74-82; Gooch and Temperley, *British Documents on the Origin of the War*, I, 214.

[49] The question of Omani and other Arab ships flying the French flag is treated in *Précis Maskat*, pp. 46-55, 86-101; Lorimer, I, 549-69; Wilson, *Persian Gulf*, pp. 239-43; France, Ministry of Foreign Affairs, *Boutres Mascataises Françaises* (Paris, 1905); Great Britain, Foreign Office, *Muscat Dhows Arbitration* (London, 1905).

[50] Hague Permanent *Court of Arbitration, Recueil des Actes et Protocoles Concernant la Difference entre la France et Grande Bretagne. . . . Boutres de Mascate* (Hague, 1905); Carnegie Endowment for International Peace, *The Hague Court Reports*, J. B. Scott, ed. (New York, 1916), pp. 98-109.

fully aware of the realities of British paramountcy. On the other hand, the French saved the sultan from falling to the same level of dependence as other Gulf rulers found themselves vis-à-vis Britain. It is quite possible that if no crisis had developed Curzon might have quietly asserted a protectorate over Masqat "in name as well as in fact."[51] The French challenge dramatized to Britain the threat to her Persian Gulf hegemony that had risen in the 1890s. British authorities in both London and Calcutta were forced to recognize their government's vital interests in the region and to determine how to best protect those interests. In world affairs the Anglo–French wrangles over Oman were not too important in themselves. Nevertheless, given the chaotic state of European relations in the early 1900s, such conflicts endangered negotiations on more important matters by infuriating public opinion and giving grist to antirapprochement opposition leaders. Although important policy-makers in both Paris and London, after 1898, were interested in fostering good mutual relations, it took time for this conciliatory spirit to filter down to the local level. British and French representatives in Oman continued their verbal dueling, especially about the arms trade, until 1914. Ultimately the Anglo–French quarrel over the Masqati munitions trade and the squabbles of their Oman representatives over local affairs had to be settled by involved high-level negotiations.[52]

Whitehall's assumption of active responsibility for the conduct of Britain's Persian Gulf policy. In 1820 effective power in the Persian Gulf began to be taken away from indigenous rulers and transferred to the British resident and his assistants. Also, we have seen that between 1820 and 1892 normally the resident's place in forming Gulf policy was dominant although officially Calcutta or even London authorities set policy. Contributing to the dominance of on-the-spot decision making was the relative absence of major challenges to British interests

[51] "Elgin to Hamilton, 30 Sept. 1896, no. 39: Viceroy," India Mss.–6.
[52] "Cambon to Lansdowne, 2 Jan. 1902, memo," Public Record Office Mss., F.O. 27/3611.

in the Gulf, and the consequent lack of any necessity that Gulf matters require a great deal of attention in either London or Calcutta. In the 1890s the situation changed as the men of limited talent who supervised the Gulf were tested by the challenge of rival imperialisms and other problems too strong for them to control. Nevertheless, until 1899 neither Calcutta nor London roused itself to halt the course of drift toward disaster. Finally in 1899 Curzon arrived in India with a definite Gulf policy and energetically applied it. Thus effective control over the formation of Gulf policy and the efficient supervision of British interests there, abdicated by the weak residents of the 1890s, passed into the hands of the viceroy in Calcutta. But Calcutta's de facto supremacy over the Gulf was brief. Despite the presence of the masterful Curzon in India until 1905, Whitehall seized effective control over the decision-making machinery involved in producing and overseeing British Gulf policy even before the great viceroy's departure. The basic cause for this happening, like the decline in the independent power of the residents, was an outgrowth of world imperial conflicts. In a time of worldwide great power rivalry it became obvious that the British empire could not afford the luxury of separate and sometimes divergent Indian and London foreign policies.

The trend toward London's supremacy had been discernible since the 1870s, when Whitehall began to watch Asiatic events more closely. Still, during the last decades of the nineteenth century India retained a good deal of independence over its foreign affairs, especially during the viceroyalty of Lord Lytton (1876-80) and during the first years of Curzon's administration. During that period the London cabinet, when dealing with Asiatic problems—problems which usually contained some dimension of Russian involvement—always kept in mind the situation in Europe and the Balkans as well as southwest and central Asia. Calcutta, however, seldom looked beyond Asia when considering a situation.[53]

[53] *Oxford History of India*, 3rd ed., pp. 694, 752-53.

The Indian government was not unaware of this blind spot, however. The question was debated in the 1890s whether to add some European specialists to the Indian Foreign Department. But Lord Elgin (viceroy 1894-99) said such a move was unnecessary, because whenever a European power was involved in a question of Indian foreign policy he did not move a step without the consent of the London Foreign Office.[54] Adding to the seriousness of the problem was the fact that in the 1890s it was recognized that the Indian Foreign Department's administrative apparatus was "inefficient, inadequate, and out of date" at a time when the department's work was mounting rapidly.[55] Even the India Office in Whitehall lacked the capability to evaluate foreign events and coordinate Indian and Whitehall foreign policy, the machinery there being described as "clumsy and dilatory in its operations and quite unsuited for dealing with questions which require . . . sharp decisions."[56] Thus, as Indian foreign affairs increasingly became enmeshed in questions involving European states and great power rivalries, the London Foreign Office was required to take an ever more active role in the formulation of Indian foreign policy decisions.

The question of reorganization had not been resolved before Curzon arrived in Calcutta in 1899 and quickly brought to a head the matter of who was going to control Indian foreign policy. Lord Salisbury since the early 1890s had shown his displeasure with the Anglo–Indian government's autonomy in formulating foreign policy. He had sent a number of sharply worded notes to the India Office in the early nineties charging India with following too parochial and provocative a policy in Asia.[57]

Within two months of Curzon's arrival there was the Masqat crisis. Salisbury was, of course, seriously disturbed over the

---

[54] "Elgin to Hamilton, 20 Oct. 1895, no. 43: Viceroy," India Mss.–6.

[55] "Curzon to Hamilton, 4 June 1899," India Mss.–3, Vol. I.

[56] "Hamilton to Curzon, 13 Feb. 1903," India Mss.–2, Vol. v.

[57] "Lansdowne to Cross, 3 Feb. 1892, no. 6: Viceroy," India Mss.–5, Vol. IV; "Fowler to Elgin, 12 Oct. 1894, no. 30: India Secty.," India Mss.–6.

manner in which the matter was handled by Curzon and his subordinates in the Gulf. Salisbury thereupon proceeded to take over the Masqat negotiations. Concerning Oman, Salisbury set aside Curzon's no compromise policy, which he considered too harsh, and opened the way for negotiations.[58] Curzon was disturbed by Salisbury's attitude, but he could do nothing but capitulate to his chief.[59] Never again, after February 1899, was Curzon able to pursue his own course in the Gulf without first convincing Whitehall he was right. By 1903 Curzon complained that the Indian Foreign Department was becoming the Asiatic branch of the London Foreign Office.[60] This does not mean the voice of the Anglo–Indian government was not raised concerning Gulf affairs; it did mean Calcutta lost its dominant power over Gulf affairs almost as soon as Curzon stopped the policy drift there. After 1899 the opinion of Calcutta was one among many that were sifted in London before policy decisions concerning the Gulf were determined. At times, even with Curzon still in India, London settled a Gulf matter without consulting Calcutta. Curzon was incensed that he was not informed before the Omani French flags case was referred to the Hague Tribunal.[61] After Curzon left India, Whitehall's supremacy in formulating Indian (hence Gulf) policy was obvious to all. In fact, Lord Hardinge of the Foreign Office, writing of the Anglo–Russian Convention in 1907, said, "Recently we have left the government of India entirely out of our account."[62]

The Great Debate over Britain's Gulf supremacy. The question of Calcutta vs. London was still sputtering when it was absorbed in an even more basic debate. As the conflicts of im-

---

[58] Ronaldshay, *Life of Curzon,* II, 48; "Hamilton to Curzon, 10 Feb. 1899," "3 Mar. 1899," "10 Mar. 1899," "15 Mar. 1899," India Mss.–2, Vol. I.

[59] "Curzon to Hamilton, 5 Sept. 1900," India Mss.–3, Vol. II.

[60] "Budget speech of Lord Curzon, 25 Mar. 1903," quoted in Chirol, *The Middle Eastern Question,* p. 3.

[61] "Curzon to Hamilton, 28 May 1904," India Mss.–3, Vol. VI.

[62] *Oxford History of India,* 3rd ed., p. 694.

perialism reached their crescendo Britain was forced to determine if the continued maintenance of her Gulf supremacy was absolutely necessary for her vital interests.

The Boer War began in October 1899. Many Englishmen, fearful that France, Russia, and Germany would combine to seek advantage from Britain's plight, advanced schemes to prevent such an alliance. In actuality, no serious threat of an anti-British continental alliance ever appeared. France, diverted by a domestic political crisis, and guided by Delcassé in foreign matters, was not willing to revive the anti-British policy of Hanotaux. Germany, regardless of her desires, realized she did not have sufficient naval power to challenge Britain in a colonial war. Only Russia seriously tried to take advantage of Britain's preoccupation with South Africa.

Between 1900 and 1903 the Russians sought to expand their sphere in Iran in the direction of the Persian Gulf. There is no doubt that many Russian leaders, from the Tsar down, wished to advance in the Persian area. The following quotation from a letter of Nicholas II to his sister, written on the outbreak of the Boer War, is most informative: "I do like knowing that it lies solely with me in the last resort to change the course of the war in Africa. The means is very simple—telegraph an order for the whole Turkestan army to mobilize and march to the frontier. That is all. The strongest fleets in the world can't prevent us from settling our scores with England precisely at her most vulnerable point. But the time for this has not yet come; we are not sufficiently prepared for serious action, principally because Turkestan is not yet linked up with the interior of Russia by a through railway line."[63]

Nicholas's desire to "settle" with England was shared by some of his principal ministers. On the other hand, the influential Count Witte attacked such adventures as wasteful folly and favored a patient strategy of economic penetration coordi-

[63] *Krasnyi Archiv*, LXIII (1934), 125-26, quoted in, B. H. Sumner, *Tsardom and Imperialism in the Far and Middle East, 1880-1914* (London, 1942), pp. 7-8.

nated with the growth of the internal Russian economy. Until 1903, when the adventurers won out, Russian foreign policy continued in dispute.[64] Given the realities of the situation, any dramatic moves such as the occupation of Herat or a Persian Gulf port were vetoed by St. Petersburg. Tyrtov, the navy minister, declared that a Russian port on the Gulf could not be defended.[65] Nevertheless, between 1900 and 1903 the Russians did seek to expand their influence in Iran and the Gulf by using several devices open to them: (1) through loans, financial manipulation, and restrictive trade practices an attempt was made to take over the economy of northern Iran; (2) consulates were opened in Bushire, Bandar 'Abbas, Seistan, Muhammarah, and Baghdad; (3) Russian-led Persian cossacks were stationed in Isfahan; (4) "scientific expeditions" surveyed transport routes; (5) a quarantine service of Russian doctors, backed by cossacks, obstructed overland trade between India and Iran; (6) Russian warships began to visit Gulf ports regularly; (7) a subsidized shipping line was set up between Odessa and Gulf ports (the Russians later admitted that this line was run at a loss and was instituted for political reasons); (8) an unsuccessful attempt was made to open a consulate at Masqat. It should be emphasized that some of these moves were made on the authority of subsidiary officers without approval by St. Petersburg.[66]

These actions stimulated argument both public and private in Britain over what reaction should be made to them. The first phase of the debate lasted from late 1899 until mid-1902. During this phase three main viewpoints emerged within government circles—those of Lord Salisbury, Lord George Hamilton, the secretary of state for India, and Lord Curzon.

[64] M. Florinsky, *Russia: a History and an Interpretation* (New York, 1953), II, 1,268-69.

[65] *Krasnyi Archiv*, IV (1926), 29, quoted in Sumner, *Tsardom and Imperialism*, pp. 8, 22.

[66] *Ibid.*, passim; Florinsky, *Russia*, II, 1,268-70; *Précis Naval*, pp. 20-21, 37-38; Daud, "British Relations with the Persian Gulf," pp. 171-209.

Lord Salisbury's basic response to Russia's probes into the Gulf was to try to ignore them. This is not surprising when one recalls that one of Salisbury's primary concerns during the time he guided Britain's foreign affairs (1894-1902) was to reach an agreement with Russia. Salisbury felt that Russia was the one great power relatively immune from attack by British naval power and that a successful Russian overland attack on India could reduce Britain to the status of a second rank nation.[67] He thought it misleading to picture the Gulf as a shield for India and believed the only successful defense against a Russian attack would be to concentrate British forces in Baluchistan where they could be backed up by rail-carried supplies. Any attempt to defend Iran, in Salisbury's view, depended on the extension of the Indian railroads into that country.[68] Suspicious of the policy and efficiency of the Anglo–Indian government in an age of imperialism, he also believed Calcutta's warnings over the possible consequences of the penetration of other European powers into the Gulf were overdrawn.[69] Once the Boer War began he followed a quiet policy in the Gulf. He thought energetic moves to counter Russian and other European soundings might bring retaliation in the area, with the British unable to answer because of being "terribly tied up in South Africa."[70] Curzon and the India Office tried to convince Salisbury that he should clarify Britain's Gulf policy, but the prime minister refused to move. Lord George Hamilton described Salisbury's course as one of "drift," albeit calculated drift.[71] Believing Britain's Gulf problems were petty compared

[67] Langer, *Diplomacy of Imperialism*, pp. 788-89.

[68] "Salisbury to Lansdowne, 21 Oct. 1891, no. 115; Prime Min.," India Mss.-5, Vol. III.

[69] "Salisbury to Curzon, 21 Apr. 1899," quoted in Ronaldshay, *Life of Curzon*, II, 48; "Hamilton to Curzon, 10 Mar. 1899," India Mss.-2, Vol. I; "Hamilton to Curzon, 27 Feb. 1903," India Mss.-2, Vol. V.

[70] "Hamilton to Curzon, 21 June 1901," India Mss.-2, Vol. III.

[71] "Hamilton to Curzon, 23 Mar. 1900," "29 Mar. 1900," "10 Apr. 1900," "10 May 1900," India Mss.-2, Vol. II.

to the others he faced, Salisbury refused to be much bothered by them.[72]

A second response to the Boer War crisis was that of the secretary of state for India, Lord George Hamilton. Unlike Salisbury, he was very concerned over Russian moves in Iran and the Gulf. On several occasions he tried to get Salisbury to agree to some definite propositions regarding British policy in Iran and the Gulf.[73] He advocated that Britain abandon its policy of upholding the independence of Persia but claim as a sphere of influence that part of eastern Iran and the Gulf coast (Seistan and the eastern Gulf ports) which it considered absolutely essential for India's protection. On the other hand, he warned against claiming more than Britain could defend adequately.[74] He was against what he called the "extreme forward" policy of trying to maintain predominance over the entire Gulf, and would have excluded the northern Gulf, including Kuwait, from the British sphere. He was sure Russia eventually would establish herself on the Gulf, take over Turkey, Persia, and Afghanistan, and that in the long run this might be best for civilization. Hamilton believed the Russian desire for a warm water outlet would be satisfied by a port in the upper Gulf and that possession of such a harbor would act as a safety valve, not a danger.[75] He feared Russian power, saying that Britain could not hope to fight it successfully on land except in the India frontier region.[76] When the Boer War broke out Hamilton advocated keeping quiet and not stirring up trouble. He said, "We have a magnificent empire in Asia,

[72] Ronaldshay, *Life of Curzon,* ii, 48; "Hamilton to Curzon, 18 May 1899," "16 June 1899," India Mss.–2, Vol. i; "Hamilton to Curzon, 18 Jan. 1901," India Mss.–2, Vol. iii.

[73] "Hamilton to Curzon, 29 Mar. 1900," "27 Apr. 1900," India Mss.–2, Vol. ii.

[74] "Hamilton to Curzon, 23 Mar. 1900," "6 June 1900," India Mss.–2, Vol. ii; "Hamilton to Curzon, 13 June 1901," India Mss.–2, Vol. iii.

[75] "Hamilton to Curzon, 11 Jan. 1900," "1 Feb. 1900," India Mss.–2, Vol. ii; "Hamilton to Curzon, 8 Apr. 1903," India Mss.–2, Vol. iv.

[76] "Hamilton to Curzon, 2 Nov. 1899," India Mss.–2, Vol. i.

let's not endanger it by taking on too much."[77] He thought Britain might have to face a combination of European powers in a war, and in such an eventuality India could not expect reinforcements, would have to defend itself with its own resources, and would probably have to retreat from any advanced outposts. For this reason he wished to prevent dissipation of India's resources by limiting her commitments.[78]

Curzon's policy in the Gulf is well known. Generally, Curzon had public opinion behind him and was supported by such influential writers as Valentine Chirol of *The Times*. In essence he believed Britain should retain exclusive sway over the entire Gulf and its littoral. He believed the retention of Britain's monopoly in the region was absolutely necessary for the safeguarding of India's security.[79] He claimed that Salisbury, and to a lesser extent, Hamilton, followed an "ostrich policy" in Persia and that the only way to meet the Russian challenge was to "fight Russia all along the line," even to the point of dispatching Indian troops to the Gulf.[80] There is a question as to how much of the Russian and the continental European powers' challenge existed only in Curzon's imagination, but, be that as it may, his outspoken defense of his views was a major reason why the Boer War was weathered with Britain's position in the Gulf strengthened.

The second phase of the debate over possible British Gulf policy was carried on through the last half of 1902 and first half of 1903. In July 1902 Salisbury retired, to be succeeded by Balfour as prime minister. It was not until 1903 that the new government began to assert itself, but once it did, it displayed considerable interest in Asiatic affairs and even set up committees to study the area. Balfour himself, although resentful of

[77] "Hamilton to Curzon, 9 Nov. 1899," India Mss.–2, Vol. I.

[78] "Hamilton to Curzon, 3 Jan. 1901," "13 June 1901," India Mss.–2, Vol. III.

[79] See Hurewitz, *Diplomacy*, I, 219-49, for Curzon's classic analysis of Britain's position in Iran and the Persian Gulf.

[80] "Curzon to Hamilton, 22 Apr. 1901," India Mss.–3, Vol. III.

Curzon in many ways, shared the viceroy's distrust of Russia.[81] Lord Lansdowne, who stayed on as foreign minister, came into his own under Balfour, even though as Salisbury's subordinate he had displayed a harder attitude toward both Germany and Russia than did his old chief.[82] Curzon had written regularly to Lansdowne, a former Indian viceroy, since 1901 to propagandize his views. In April 1901, for instance, Curzon complained in a letter meant exclusively for Lansdowne that the situation in Persia and the Gulf was grave. He begged Lansdowne to get the Foreign Office to act because India had done all that it could.[83] Lansdowne was certainly impressed by Curzon's arguments and set in motion a loan to Persia and a visit of the shah to London.[84] He also answered Curzon, saying that, although Britain could not stop other countries' commercial steamers from plying there, he "would not allow Russia to acquire a footing for naval or military purposes in the Gulf."[85] Obviously Curzon's April 1901 letter and those that followed it influenced Lansdowne to formulate an opinion concerning British policies in the Gulf that essentially followed that of Curzon, although he was not in a position to act independently until 1902. As the war in South Africa drew to a close Britain adopted a stiffer policy. As early as January 1902, the Persian government was warned privately that Great Britain would not consent to a Russian base on the Gulf.[86]

By 1903 the Boer War was over and Britain had abandoned

81 "Hamilton to Curzon, 27 Feb. 1903," India Mss.–2, Vol. v; B. Dugdale, *Arthur James Balfour* (London, 1936), I, 392.

82 "Hamilton to Curzon, 8 Aug. 1901," India Mss.–2, Vol. III; "Hamilton to Curzon, 27 Feb. 1903," India Mss.–2, Vol. v.

83 "Curzon to Hamilton, 14 May 1903," India Mss.–3, Vol. v, contains several references to letters sent by Curzon to Lansdowne. See too "Curzon to Lansdowne, 5 Apr. 1901," quoted in Gooch and Temperley, *British Documents on the Origin of the War*, IV, 356-63.

84 Lord Newton, *Lord Lansdowne, a Biography* (London, 1929), pp. 232-38.

85 "Lansdowne to Curzon, 5 May 1901," Foreign Office Library, Lansdowne Papers, Vol. XXIX, no. 277.

86 *Précis Int'l. Rivalry*, p. 46.

her late nineteenth century diplomatic stance of "splendid isolation" by concluding an alliance with Japan. This strength plus the attitude of the new leadership allowed Britain to adopt publicly a harder line than previously displayed. The new hard line was unveiled early in 1903 after news was received that the Russians were planning an expedition aimed at Tibet.[87] This caused a flurry of anxiety in India and drove Lansdowne to clarify the central Asian and Persian questions. After conferring with his diplomats and sounding Russian official opinion he decided to resist all further Russian advances in southwest Asia. On May 5, 1903 Lansdowne publicly announced in the House of Lords: "We should regard the establishment of a naval base or a fortified port in the Persian Gulf by any other power as a very grave menace to British interests and we should certainly resist it with all the means at our disposal."[88] The Russian reaction to this statement was unexpectedly mild, due to the fact that they were heavily committed in the Far East. Indeed, Ambassador Benckendorff exclaimed that Russia "had no idea of establishing a naval base in the Gulf."[89] Lord George Hamilton, however, thought the declaration a mistake and resigned within five months.[90] Curzon, of course, was elated by the declaration. One could even say he wallowed in the triumph of his views: "I cannot help feeling some personal sense of congratulation"—"this is what I contended for, in language which has since become famous. . . ."[91]

In the fall of 1903 Curzon traveled to the Persian Gulf "to testify to the paramount political and commercial ascendancy" of Great Britain in that region and to inspect possible naval base sites there. He believed his visit "the logical corollary" of

---

[87] *Oxford History of India*, 3rd ed., pp. 753-54; actually it seems the Dalai Lama invited Russian aid to counter growing Chinese pressure on Tibet.

[88] Great Britain, *Parliamentary Debates, House of Lords: 1903*, 5 May 1903.

[89] *Précis Int'l. Rivalry*, p. 48.

[90] "Hamilton to Curzon, 5 June 1903," India Mss.–2, Vol. v.

[91] "Curzon to Hamilton, 14 May 1903," India Mss.–3, Vol. v.

Lansdowne's declaration which the viceroy characterized as "establishing a British Monroe Doctrine over the Gulf."[92] The visit itself was a procession of pomp from one Gulf port to another. At Masqat Curzon invested Sultan Faysal with the Grand Cross of the Order of the Indian Empire and declared that the sultan could count on British aid in any rebellion. He described Sultan Faysal's demeanor as that of "a loyal feudatory of the British Crown rather than that of an independent sovereign." Curzon further declared that the sultan manifested his desire to range himself alongside the Indian princes in his relations to the British Crown.[93] To the world Curzon's voyage to the Gulf was a clear gesture signifying that Britain meant to stay in the Gulf; it ended much of the political maneuvering concerning the area which animated the decade 1893-1903. Moreover, Britain's determination to retain control of the region was reinforced in 1907 when, during the negotiations preceding the conclusion of the Anglo–Russian Convention on Iran, the Russians recognized British supremacy over the Gulf. Also, between 1911 and 1914 the British were able to convince both the Germans and the Ottomans to sign agreements which essentially accepted Britain's ascendancy in the area.

By 1903 the British definitely decided they would retain their paramount position in the Persian Gulf. After that time the destinies of the Gulf states obviously and inseparably were bound to Britain. The fact that Salisbury had asserted Whitehall's supremacy in formulating Gulf policy meant that questions affecting those destinies would be decided many thousands of miles from the Gulf. The machinery of British paramountcy by 1903 was an amalgam containing the ideas of Salisbury and Curzon as well as Frere, Pelly, Ross, and earlier officials involved in shaping Britain's Gulf policies. The forceful assertion of British power meant that modernizing influences operating in the Gulf region would continue to reflect

[92] "Hamilton to Curzon, 21 June 1903," India Mss.–2, Vol. v; *Précis Int'l. Rivalry*, p. 50.
[93] Lorimer, I, 2,634-36.

primarily British and Indian influences. Thus, we can say that by 1903 political prerequisites were established which have colored the subsequent history of the region and which influenced the quality and direction of the rapid modernization which certain parts of the Persian Gulf have undergone since the coming of the oil industry.

PART IV

Oman's Political Accommodation

to a New Age

CHAPTER 7

Collapse of the Moderate Regime, 1856-71

THE death of Sayyid Sa'id ibn-Sultan in 1856 destroyed the aura of stability which until that time obscured the underlying weaknesses of the Omani empire. The sprawling maritime domain whose influence extended from the central African lakes in the west to the approaches to the Indian subcontinent in the east was revealed as essentially an extension of Sayyid Sa'id's intelligence, energy, and personality. Although the African half of Sa'id's realm was able to revivify itself, in Oman the 15 years following the great monarch's death saw the whole structure that supported the moderate Al Bu Sa'id regime topple down. It is doubtful, however, if even a ruler of Sayyid Sa'id's caliber could have prevented all of the misfortunes that struck Oman between 1856 and 1871. No Omani monarch could have deflected the thrust of modern communications and modern economic activities into the western Indian Ocean and the Persian Gulf during the 1860s. No Omani monarch could have negated the fact that the country's maritime establishment had been rendered obsolete once modern steamships began sailing the Arabian seas. Yet this spread of modern technology was the main cause of the eclipse of Oman's commercial and maritime vitality and of the undermining of the economic foundations that supported the political apparatus of the moderate Ibadi regime which ruled Oman's coast and which claimed overlordship over Oman's interior.

Still, it is possible that a strong and perceptive ruler in Masqat could have acted to cushion the effects of the economic revolution of the 1860s and, at least, could have prevented the political collapse of the moderate Al Bu Sa'id government that took place in 1868. Be that as it may, Omani politics during the reigns of Sayyid Sa'id's two moderate successors, his son, Thuwayni ibn-Sa'id (1856-66), and grandson, Salim ibn-Thuwayni (1866-68), were marked by an increasingly inefficient

271

domestic political administration, very disturbed foreign relations with the Sa'udi and Iranian authorities, a large increase in British involvement in Omani domestic affairs, and finally the rise of an energetic, conservative Ibadi opposition that eventually drove the moderates out of Masqat and reestablished in 1868 a conservative imamate as Oman's government.

The conservative government headed by Imam 'Azzan ibn-Qays (1868-71), a scion of a cadet branch of the Al Bu Sa'id family, initially appeared to be popular and strong. Soon, however, the uncompromising, ultra-conservative bias of the new regime, plus its inability to solve its grave financial problems, began to undermine the imamate. By 1871 it too was replaced, this time by a restored but shaky moderate government reestablished in Masqat under another of Sayyid Sa'id's sons, Turki ibn-Sa'id. Nevertheless, in 1871 Turki's authority was hardly secure; it seemed probable that Oman would split into a number of petty, quarrelsome principalities and soon lose all semblance of political unity. The remainder of this chapter will focus on the temporary collapse of the moderate Al Bu Sa'id monarchy in Oman between 1856 and 1871.

THE SUCCESSION CRISIS IN THE OMANI EMPIRE, 1856-68

The partition of the Omani empire. None of Sayyid Sa'id's sons possessed the talent or political support necessary to hold the Omani empire together. In fact, as soon as Sa'id died the empire, in effect, split in two. One reason was a consequence of the fact that during his lifetime Sayyid Sa'id had set up two of his sons as viceroys to supervise the Asiatic and the African parts of his empire during the inevitable absences from one part of the realm or another. Thus since 1833 Thuwayni ibn-Sa'id had ruled at Masqat during Sayyid Sa'id's long absences from that city, while Majid ibn-Sa'id had deputized since 1854 when his father was not in Zanzibar. Both princes built up a base of power in their respective viceroyalties, but neither had reached the point where he commanded enough strength to dominate the other. Also, it does not appear that Sayyid

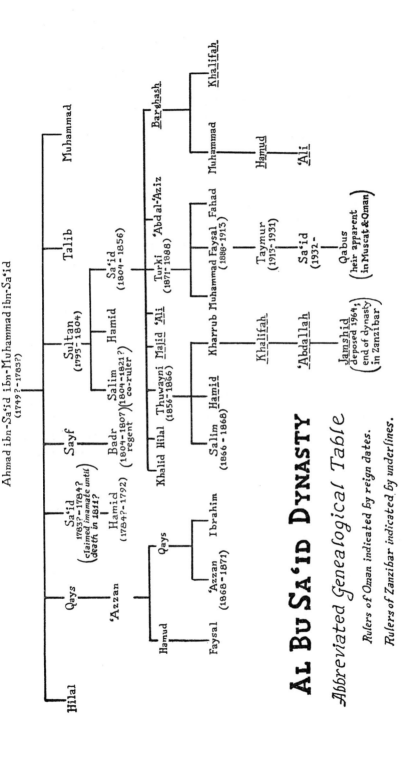

Ahmad ibn-Sa'id ibn-Muhammad ibn-Sa'id
(1749?-1783?)

Hilal   Qays   Sayf   Sultan   Talib   Muhammad
                        (1795-1804)

Sa'id   Badr   Salim   Sa'id
(1783?-1784?   (1804-1807)(1804-1821?)(1804-1856)
claimed imamate until   regent)   co-ruler)
death in 1811?)

Hamid   Hamid
(1784?-1792)

'Azzan

Qays   Ibrahim

Hamud

Faysal   'Azzan
         (1868-1871)

Khalid Hilal Thuwayni Majid 'Ali
                        (1856-1866)

Salim   Hamid
(1866-1868)

Turki   'Abd al-'Aziz
(1871-1888)

Barghash

Muhammad   Khalifah

Hamud

'Ali

Kharrub Muhammad Faysal Fahad
                  (1888-1915)

Khalifah

'Abdallah

Taymur
(1913-1931)

Sa'id
(1932-)

Jamshid
(deposed 1964;
end of dynasty
in Zanzibar)

Qabus
(heir apparent
in Muscat & Oman)

AL BU SA'ID DYNASTY

Abbreviated Genealogical Table

Rulers of Oman indicated by reign dates.

Rulers of Zanzibar indicated by underlines.

Sa'id left clear instructions concerning who his successor should be.

The news of Sayyid Sa'id's death stimulated Majid ibn-Sa'id and Thuwayni ibn-Sa'id to start negotiations designed to solve the political dilemma that confronted the Omani state and the ruling family. Thuwayni started the process by dispatching his (and Majid's) cousin, Muhammad ibn-Salim, to Zanzibar as an envoy. The result of these initial talks was a promise by Majid that in view of the fact that the African part of the Omani state was richer than the Asiatic half, he would send $MT 40,000 annually to Thuwayni if the latter agreed not to assert a claim to Zanzibar. Thus, it appeared an amicable partition of the empire would be the solution to the succession problem.[1]

Majid, however, possibly because of a drop in Zanzibar's customs receipts, did not deliver the promised sum to his brother. Consequently, in 1858 Thuwayni replied to his brother's negligence by proclaiming that he was the rightful and sole heir and ruler of all the territory once governed by Sayyid Sa'id. To underline this assertion Thuwayni set about instigating rebellions among Majid's subjects and began to organize an expedition of 10 ships carrying 2,500 troops to attack Zanzibar and dispossess his rival. It was only after Thuwayni's fleet had quit Masqat harbor for the high seas and when the threat of war in the western Indian Ocean was about to be translated into actuality that the British intervened, turned back Thuwayni's seaborne fleet, and forced a truce on the quarreling brothers.[2]

For two years the uneasy truce threatened to break down, a circumstance that damaged the trade of both Masqat and Zanzibar. Finally in May of 1860, Sayyid Thuwayni, faced with rising unrest in Oman, which was being fed by the unstable political climate, agreed to accept the suggestion of Lord Can-

[1] Al-Salimi, II, 219; Lorimer, I, 469.

[2] Rigby, "Report on Zanzibar," *Records of the Bombay Government*, no. LIX (1861), p. 23; Lorimer, I, 470.

ning, the viceroy of India, that the Government of India arbitrate the dispute. Sayyid Majid previously had agreed to this same course.

Accordingly, a "commission of enquiry" was appointed and its findings and recommendations were announced in April 1861 by Lord Canning in the form of an arbitration award. The main feature of the award was to recognize the fact that the once united Omani empire had split into two independent states. Therefore, Oman's and Zanzibar's independence from one another was recognized and the ruler of each state received the official title of "sultan." Also, Majid ibn-Sa'id and his successors were obligated to pay to Thuwayni ibn-Sa'id and his successors a sum of $MT 40,000 a year in perpetuity. This sum was the same amount as Majid already had agreed to pay his brother as a result of their initial negotiations. It was stated that this payment did not constitute tribute but was an adjustment of two unequal inheritances and a compensation for the Omani ruler's abandonment of his claims on Zanzibar. Majid was also instructed to forward to Thuwayni an arrears payment of $MT 80,000.[3]

A year later, in 1862, France, heavily involved in east African affairs at that time, agreed to honor the award by reciprocally engaging with Britain to respect the independence of both the Masqati and Zanzibari sultans. These negotiations, however, were undertaken by the British ambassador in Paris, acting for the London Foreign Office. It was not until 1890, when the question of declaring a British protectorate over Oman was being aired, that the Anglo–Indian government and British representatives in the Persian Gulf became aware of the joint Anglo–French guarantee. It was this co-guarantee, then, that prevented the British from declaring the much-discussed protectorate over Oman in 1891, that gave France a

[3] Aitchison—1933, XI, 269-86, 303; F. Kajare, *Le Sultanate d'Oman: la Question de Mascate* (Paris, 1914), pp. 83-185; Coupland, *East Africa and its Invaders*, chaps. 5, 16. The commission of enquiry included Brigadier W. Coghlan, resident at Aden, the Reverend G. P. Badger, an Arabic scholar, and H. Rassam, the temporary agent of the Bombay government at Masqat.

lever to intervene in Omani affairs in the 1890s, and which also preserved for the sultan of Masqat and Oman a greater degree of legal independence than that enjoyed by the other rulers of maritime Arab states in the Gulf.[4]

The dismemberment of the Omani empire was very damaging to Oman and particularly to its coastal provinces. Most of Sayyid Sa'id's warships and merchant vessels were anchored at Zanzibar when he died; these valuable capital investments were taken over by Majid. Neglect and lack of money to pay for the upkeep of that small part of the fleet that was anchored at Masqat in 1856 led Thuwayni to sell off all but two or three of the Omani government's remaining ships by 1863. Also, Oman's traditional trade with Zanzibar began to decline even before Mackinnon's steamers appeared in the Persian Gulf in 1862. In the early 1860s, due to the political tension between Masqat's and Zanzibar's rulers, Omani shipping began to confine itself to an Asiatic carrying trade with Bandar 'Abbas as its center.[5] Prior to 1861 Omani capital was often invested in booming Zanzibar land development, trade, or shipping, and the proceeds from such investments had helped to support the country's economy. After 1861 the dearth of economic opportunity in Oman prompted many Arabs and Indian merchants to migrate from Arabia to Zanzibar. Also disquieting was the fact that Zanzibar became a haven for dissident Omani political leaders. More than once in the future Zanzibari gold was to play an important role in determining the outcome of Omani political disputes. In 1861 the Canning Commission estimated that the Masqat government's revenues were less than half as large as those collected by the Zanzibar authorities, and no longer did an Oman regime have ready access to these financial resources as in the years before 1856.[6] It is possi-

---

[4] For text of the guarantee see Hurewitz, *Diplomacy*, I, 168-69.

[5] W. Palgrave, *Narrative of a Year's Journey through Central and Eastern Arabia* (London, 1866), II, 336; A. F. M. Rouire, *La Rivalité Anglo–Russe au xix*e *siècle en Asie* (Paris, 1908), p. 39. "Pelly to Anderson, 16 Feb. 1863," *Précis Int'l. Rivalry*, p. 27.

[6] *Admin. Rpt.: 1877-1878*, pp. 127-29; Ibn-Ruzayq, p. ci; Columb, *Slave*

ble the relaxation of political tension between the two Al Bu Sa'id kingdoms following the announcement of the Canning Award in 1861 would have brought a restoration of the old close economic relationship between Zanzibar and Oman. Unfortunately, the results of the initiation of British India Steam Navigation Company steamer service to the Persian Gulf in 1862 meant Oman's politically inspired economic troubles of 1856-62 were transformed into a cataclysmic economic collapse.

Economic disaster contributed to political disaster. The decline in customs revenue and other taxable income derived from maritime activity accelerated during the 1860s. No Omani government of the time knew how to cope with the difficulties that accompanied shrinking revenue resources. Indeed, all Omani rulers during the late nineteenth century faced serious revenue situations which severely limited their political capabilities. Nevertheless, the post-1871 rulers worked out a variety of adjustments to their plight which were beyond the grasp of the leaders of the 1860s. Because the effects of the economic disaster of the 1860s were felt most severely on Oman's coast and because the Masqati authorities were deprived of what up to that time had been normal revenue collections, there was a consequent upheaval in Omani politics during the 1860s. The coast, and the moderate Al Bu Sa'id regime, deprived of their traditional economic supports, lost the means to maintain their superiority over the interior and the conservative Ibadi groups concentrated there. So there was a dramatic shift in the relative political strength of coastal-based moderates and interior-based conservatives. The political fortunes of Oman's interior and of conservative Ibadism improved in the 1860s, culminating in 1868 in the establishment of a regime which united all Oman for a short time under a conservative imam.

Catching, pp. 384-86; states that in 1867 Zanzibar's trade was worth £700,000 a year and was still expanding while the sultan of Zanzibar's revenue amounted to some $MT 345,000, or £72,000 annually, exclusive of slave trade income.

Oman's Accommodation to a New Age

The reign of Thuwayni ibn-Sa'id, 1856-66. The man most occupied with the bewildering array of misfortunes that engulfed Oman in the decade after Sayyid Sa'id's death was the great monarch's son and successor in Masqat, Thuwayni ibn-Sa'id. Thuwayni was an administrator of ordinary talents who had the misfortune to be called to rule at a time which clearly called for a leader of the most extraordinary abilities. He was probably a little over 40 at the time. The son of an Abyssinian mother, Thuwayni had a bushy black beard, was about six feet tall, tended to be a little stout, and resembled his father. He was not a man with a winning personality nor was he a person who inspired personal loyalty (he was murdered by his own son!). He had the reputation of being rather arrogant and conceited. Neither was he a particularly consistent ruler. His reign was characterized by periods of bold action interspersed with a lack of decisiveness and energy.[7] In retrospect it appears Thuwayni ibn-Sa'id was a man who depended on the political organization and techniques created by his father; he was an unimaginative ruler whose effectiveness was based on the "system" he had inherited. He was never able to surmount the difficult situation in which he found himself, a situation of rapid flux which called for a man who could do more than manipulate an established apparatus. Still, Thuwayni ibn-Sa'id at least held the moderate regime together in Oman as long as he lived, no mean accomplishment, given the times. In fact, he probably was one of the few who could have saved the moderate government, and it is instructive to note that this government simply disintegrated within two years of his death.

Thuwayni ibn-Sa'id's political administration was forced to deal with problems caused by the ever-decreasing trade revenues that flowed into his treasury, by intra-family rivalries which necessitated his employment of numerous Al Bu Sa'id

[7] References to Thuwayni ibn-Sa'id's personal characteristics are scattered. See especially Osgood, *Notes*, pp. 78, 105; Columb, *Slave Catching*, p. 115; Lorimer, I, 476.

princelings in his government lest they join the opposition, and by the foreign difficulties posed by the Zanzibaris, the Sa'udis, and the Persians. Internally, his prestige was bolstered primarily by his possession of Masqat and by his control of other coastal strong points, as well as by his titular headship of the Omani state, a dignity expressed after 1861 in his title of "sultan." His military forces consisted of a handful of armed vessels, a number of strong forts, a mobile mercenary infantry force of 600 troops—nearly half of whom were Najdi Wahhabis—small cavalry and artillery corps, and any tribal levies he could muster in times of emergency. This force was powerful by Omani standards; it was equipped with firearms at a time when most Omani warriors were armed with spears. Later sultans lost this weapons advantage.[8]

When he became the ruler at Masqat Thuwayni ibn-Sa'id found his relations with Zanzibar, troubled though they were, were not the most immediate of his problems. The new ruler faced a bewildering domestic political situation and many serious threats closer to home. Besides the establishment controlled by the sultan, there were numerous other nearly autonomous loci of political power in Oman. Unless Sultan Thuwayni found a way to manipulate and dominate the congeries of political forces present in the country he could not hope to rule effectively or for long. Serious rivals to his continued leadership existed among the various Al Bu Sa'id princes in Oman. They included Thuwayni's younger brother, Turki ibn-Sa'id, who since the early 1850s had been entrenched with his retainers in the al-Batinah stronghold of Suhar, and even Thuwayni's ambitious and twisted son, Salim ibn-Thuwayni. Similarly, the conservative leader of the Qays branch of the royal house, 'Azzan ibn-Qays, was at best an uncertain element in the political mix. Second, the great tribal forces of the country, particularly the restless Hinawi combination headed by Shaykh Salih ibn-'Ali of the al-Hirth tribe of al-Sharqiyah and the volatile Ghafiri groups of Ja'lan and Wadi Sama'il had to

8 Palgrave, *Central and Eastern Arabia*, II, 356-75.

be won over by the new ruler. Also, the conservative Ibadi ulema were beginning to search once more for a political vehicle to carry their fundamentalist programs to fruition. Moreover, the country's old tormentors, the Wahhabis, were again active along Oman's Rub' al-Khali border and were spreading their political influence there from their outpost at al-Buraymi. Even the British, now that they had taken over the responsibilities implicit in the Canning Award, including the supervision of the Zanzibar subsidy, figured as an important factor in Omani domestic politics. The sultan, because of his long period as Sayyid Sa'id's viceroy at Masqat, was practiced in dealing with most of these elements in Oman's political mosaic, but on the other hand, any Omani ruler had to expect a certain amount of succession upheaval and in the country's uncertain post-1856 political and economic climate unrest would necessarily be difficult to control.

Thuwayni ibn-Sa'id spent his entire reign trying to assert his supremacy in Oman, a goal he never fully accomplished. During the first six years of his reign he put down a number of local challenges in various parts of Oman. Immediately upon his formal accession Thuwayni learned that several Ghafiri tribes in the Wadi Sama'il revolted. An expedition was dispatched and restored Masqat's authority without undue difficulty in that strategic pass area.[9] The most serious challenge to Thuwayni ibn-Sa'id's rule was issued by his younger brother, Turki ibn-Sa'id, who had been involved with the government of Suhar during the reign of Sayyid Sa'id, had been confirmed in this position by the new sultan, but who nevertheless wished to assert his total independence. Because he was left alone, Turki's animosity toward his older brother remained fairly quiescent while the sultan was occupied with the Zanzibar dispute—that is, until the announcement of the Canning Award in 1861, which recognized Thuwayni ibn-Sa'id as Oman's sole monarch. After the award was publicized, Turki ibn-Sa'id determined to break free from his brother's rule.

9 Al-Salimi, II, 221.

Therefore, he prepared to oppose the sultan. Disregarding British advice, he declared the independence of the district he governed around Suhar. At this point British intervention took a more active form; Lieutenant Pengelley, the newly appointed British agent in Masqat, arranged a truce between the two disputing brothers as well as a peace conference at al-Sib. The conference was a disaster for Turki. Despite the fact that Pengelley assured all participants that the talks at al-Sib were to be conducted under his personal safe conduct, when Turki ibn-Sa'id balked at the sultan's terms and prepared to return to his base at Suhar, the British agent withdrew his safe conduct and Thuwayni ibn-Sa'id thereupon promptly seized and imprisoned his younger brother. For his part in this treachery Lieutenant Pengelley was quickly sacked by the Anglo–Indian government, but the way was now open for the sultan to extend his sway northward along the coast to include all of al-Batinah. Soon Suhar was occupied and the sultan's son, Salim ibn-Thuwayni, appointed its governor. One ominous aspect of this episode was that before his dispute with Turki was settled, Thuwayni ibn-Sa'id had called upon the Wahhabi authorities in al-Buraymi to aid him. Apparently no help arrived at any strength before the struggle was resolved but the sultan's panicky move reintroduced an extremely dangerous element into Omani politics.[10]

Al-Batinah continued to trouble the sultan even after the occupation of Suhar. In September 1861, the Al Sa'd, al-Batinah's largest tribe, revolted after Thuwayni ibn-Sa'id revoked a tax exemption that had been granted to the tribe in Sayyid Sa'id's time. Obviously, the sultan's dwindling revenues forced him into taking this unpopular course at such an unlikely time. The most famous incident in this revolt occurred after Hilal ibn-Muhammad, a member of the royal house and the long-time governor of Suwayq, was murdered in the midst of an effort to explain why a reintroduction of taxa-

[10] *Ibid.,* p. 225; Lorimer, I, 472-73; Ibn-Ruzayq, pp. ci-cii; H. St. J. Philby, *Arabia* (London, 1930), pp. 122-23.

tion was necessary. Suwayq became the focus of fighting and an unusual situation appeared when the dead governor's sister, Jukhah bint-Muhammad, renowned for an earlier role in a revolt against Sayyid Saʻid in 1829, inspired a brave resistance by the government garrison at Suwayq. Ultimately, the Al Saʻd overwhelmed Suwayq's fort—just before Thuwayni arrived at the head of a relief column. Both sides, exhausted, eagerly negotiated a settlement which resulted in the sultan's reoccupation of Suwayq's fort and in his issuing a new tax exemption to the Al Saʻd. Basically this restored the prerevolt situation.[11]

Thuwayni ibn-Saʻid was well advised to pacify al-Batinah, for clearly a more fundamental danger to his leadership was abroad. This was the revival of antiregime activity by the powerful Qays branch of the royal Al Bu Saʻid dynasty. On a number of occasions since the early nineteenth century descendants of two of Imam Ahmad ibn-Saʻid's sons, Sultan ibn-Ahmad and Qays ibn-Ahmad, had fought for the leadership of the Al Bu Saʻid and of Oman. Sultan ibn-Ahmad's descendants had won all of the contests up to the 1860s, a situation which hardly calmed the ambitions of the disgruntled Qays branch of the ruling family. Thuwayni's father, Sayyid Saʻid, had faced a number of challenges by the Qays branch and their allies among the ranks of conservative Ibadis. It was only to be expected that Thuwayni ibn-Saʻid would have to dispute with them, too.

By 1861 the stronghold of the Qays family was in the grim old fortress of al-Rustaq, a place perched on a Hajar mountain peak which overlooked al-Batinah and which was once the capital of the conservative imams of Oman. Descending from his aerie into al-Batinah in 1861, Qays ibn-ʻAzzan, the longtime leader of the family, was one of the prime instigators of the Al Saʻd revolt. He met his death during one of the first battles that marked that contest. Qays ibn-ʻAzzan's place as

11 Al-Salimi, II, 221-25; Ibn-Ruzayq, pp. ci-cii; "Disbrowe to Gonne, 14 May 1869, no. 289: Masqat," India Records–2, Vol. L; Lorimer, I, 472-73.

leader of the family was taken by 'Azzan ibn-Qays, an able leader who quickly filled the void left by his father's death. Indeed, it was 'Azzan ibn-Qays who was destined to bring the fortunes of the Qays branch to their zenith as well as to lead conservative Ibadis to temporary supremacy in Oman.

Thuwayni ibn-Sa'id, however, did not fare badly against 'Azzan ibn-Qays in their struggles. Once the Al Sa'd uprising had been settled, troops of the sultan and of 'Azzan fought a series of inconclusive, small battles in al-Batinah over a period of more than two years. However, in 1864 Thuwayni ibn-Sa'id finally amassed enough resources to attack the Qays' stronghold of al-Rustaq. But at this point the threat of Wahhabi intervention into Oman's uncertain political climate, a possibility that had been hovering over the country since 1861, became a reality. 'Azzan ibn-Qays, fearing that he could not withstand the sultan's onslaught, called on the Sa'udi commander at al-Buraymi, Turki ibn-Ahmad al-Sudayri, to send troops to aid him. The Sa'udi imam, Faysal ibn-Turki, an extremely able ruler who had presided over a mid-nineteenth century revival of Wahhabi power in Arabia, determined that he could use 'Azzan ibn-Qays' plea for his own benefit in one way or another. First, Faysal ibn-Turki addressed a demand to Sultan Thuwayni, that an increased amount of tribute be sent to Riyadh, it having been customary in most years since the first decade of the century for the Masqati authorities to send an annual bribe to the Sa'udis to forestall Wahhabi-backed incursions into Oman. When the Sa'udi bid to Thuwayni met an indefinite response the Riyadh authorities determined to apply direct pressure. Already, al-Sudayri, the Sa'udi commander at al-Buraymi, had sent a force under 'Abd al-'Aziz ibn-Mutlaq to relieve the seriously pressed 'Azzan ibn-Qays at al-Rustaq. When the strength of 'Azzan's new allies forced Sultan Thuwayni to abandon the attack on al-Rustaq, ibn-Mutlaq next turned southeast, crossed the Hajar mountains, and sweeping down the western side of that range, entered Ja'lan. In Ja'lan ibn-Mutlaq first interfered in the affairs of the Al Wahibah tribe and then joined forces with the Bani-Bu-'Ali, a Ghafiri tribe of Wahhabi persuasion settled in that province.[12]

The British, meanwhile, ever wary of Sa'udi moves near the Omani coast, tried to mediate the trouble. Lewis Pelly went so far as to undertake an unprecedented trek to Riyadh in March 1865 in an attempt to settle the Omani and other Persian Gulf difficulties that were being complicated by the aggressive, expansionist policies then being pushed by the Sa'udis.[13] But the mediation attempt failed, and in August 1865 the Sa'udi adventure in Oman moved to its climax. At that time, elements of the al-Janabah tribe in the port of Sur, seeking to rid themselves of any vestige of control by the Masqat government, invited Wahhabi aid. Taking up this invitation, ibn-Mutlaq's troops and their allies and coreligionists, the Bani-Bu-'Ali, joined the disaffected townsmen of Sur, attacked the city, looted it of approximately $MT 30,000, and killed an Indian merchant during the course of the raid. The raid on Sur, however, added a new element to the situation—the British took it as a direct challenge to their position in the Gulf. The enraged Pelly, who had only recently received assurances in Riyadh that the Sa'udis would, as he described it, "turn over a new leaf," asked that a naval squadron be dispatched to the Persian Gulf at once. The Anglo–Indian authorities were impressed by Pelly's arguments that the maritime peace in the Gulf was threatened by Sa'udi actions in Oman and on the waters off Bahrain, and two gunboats were sent to the region. One of these, *H.M.S. Highflyer*, actually bombarded the Sa'udi ports of al-Qatif and al-Dammam on the al-Hasa coast in February 1866 after Riyadh failed to respond to a Pelly ultimatum. Sur, too, was visited by British warships at the same time, but Sultan Thuwayni had already secured the Wahhabis's withdrawal

12 Al-Salimi, II, 222-24; Ibn-Ruzayq, pp. cii-ciii; Winder, "Sa'ūdi State," p. 212; Saudi Arabia, *Memorial*, I, 226-36.

13 L. Pelly, "A Visit to the Wahabee Capital, Central Arabia," *Journal of the Royal Geographical Society*, XXXV (1865), 169-91; Arabian American Oil Company, "Pelly's Visit to Riyadh," *Oman*, pp. 255-57.

from that port by bribing them with $MT 10,000 and 6,000 rupees.[14]

The British show of force in the Gulf produced a change in the political climate in Oman. The sultan finally accepted Pelly's urgings that he adopt a more active defense against the Sa'udi interlopers and began to organize an offensive to attack al-Buraymi, the seat of Wahhabi power in southeastern Arabia. It is now clear that one reason that Thuwayni ibn-Sa'id did not move against his tormentors with more vigor before the winter of 1865-66 was lack of money. The sultan's revenue problems were complicated due to the revival of Sultan Majid of Zanzibar's bad habit of neglecting to send the Zanzibar subsidy. Early in 1866 the British solved this difficulty by forcing Majid to pay his arrears, so Thuwayni finally had enough money to organize his forces. Thuwayni previously had tried with indifferent success to raise money by seizing the properties Majid owned in Oman. The British also aided Thuwayni by supplying him with two field guns and ammunition.[15]

Besides the British, Salih ibn-'Ali, the tamimah of the powerful al-Hirth tribe of al-Sharqiyah and prominent Hinawi and conservative Ibadi leader, had been urging the sultan to adopt a more aggressive attitude against Sa'udi pretensions. Salih ibn-'Ali went so far as to organize a formidable Hinawi tribal alliance which he placed at the disposal of Thuwayni ibn-Sa'id. The coalition of anti-Sa'udi forces was also strengthened by the reconciliation of the sultan with his lately rebellious younger brother, Turki ibn-Sa'id. Consequently, when the sultan shifted his headquarters to Suhar early in 1866 to make the final arrangements to launch an attack on al-Buraymi he stood at the pinnacle of his power in Oman as the ruler of a country more or less united against the Sa'udi threat.[16]

14 Al-Salimi, II, 225; Lorimer, I, 473-74; Arabian American Oil Company, "Pelly's Visit to Riyadh," *Oman*, p. 257.

15 "Playfair to Wood, despatch no. 3-24: Zanzibar," India Records–2, Vol. XLII; Lorimer, I, 474-75.

16 Al-Salimi, II, 224-25.

It was at this apparently propitious moment, however, that disaster struck. One night in February 1866, as Thuwayni ibn-Sa'id was asleep in his chambers in the great fortress at Suhar, his son, Salim ibn-Thuwayni, aided by a Wahhabi accomplice and perhaps instigated by the Wahhabis, slipped into the monarch's bedroom and shot his father in the head with a double-barreled pistol. The anti-Wahhabi offensive was never launched, Oman's newfound unity dissolved, and the moderate regime itself began to disintegrate. But at least the Sa'udis were not able to take advantage of Oman's confused state. Thuwayni ibn-Sa'id's death was nearly coincident with that of the great Sa'udi ruler, Faysal ibn-Turki, and the successors of both fallen monarchs abandoned the Sa'udi-Omani war to consolidate their personal hold on their new realms. Moreover, in April 1866 Pelly stabilized the situation by eliciting a written assurance from the new Sa'udi imam, 'Abdallah ibn-Faysal, to the effect that the Sa'udis would "not injure or attack the territories of the Arab tribes in alliance with the British Government, especially . . . the Kingdom of Muscat. . . ."[17]

Thuwayni ibn-Sa'id was succeeded by his patricidal son, Salim ibn-Thuwayni, who seized the apparatus of state and subsequently received British recognition as Oman's sultan. As for Thuwayni ibn-Sa'id, he must stand as a rather tragic figure in his country's history. He ruled amidst disorder and was cut down just as it appeared that Oman was to enjoy a period of inner unity. He was not a popular monarch. The British records describe him as a man of weakness and duplicity. For their part, conservative Ibadis did not approve of Thuwayni's moderate Ibadism, but they admitted that he held "dominion over Oman" and many of them supported him against the Wahhabis.[18] Sultan Thuwayni certainly had no

[17] *Ibid.*, pp. 225-26; Lorimer, I, 476; Hurewitz, *Diplomacy*, I, p. 172; Aitchison—1933, XI, 206.

[18] Al-Salimi, II, 219-25. Al-Salimi, although a conservative Ibadi spokesman well versed in the history of Oman and a founder of the 1913-55 imamate, does not assert that Oman is historically divided into two countries—a coastal "Muscat" and an interior "Oman"—as do certain modern

comprehension of most of the underlying causes of the troubles that vexed his reign. But even if he had viewed his problems with more perspective he did not possess in any case the means to solve these problems. Compared to other rulers who ruled in similar circumstances Thuwayni ibn-Sa'id appears better than sometimes painted.

The reign of Salim ibn-Thuwayni, 1866-68. Thuwayni ibn-Sa'id's son and successor, Salim ibn-Thuwayni, inherited his father's problems. Although he had some success in coping with the puzzles of Oman's foreign relations, Salim ibn-Thuwayni proved to be completely inept in his handling of domestic political questions. A person of consuming ambition and suspicious nature, Salim made constant errors in judgment, particularly in his decisions concerning his closest advisors and his allies. In the space of two years these errors combined to unseat him.

At the time he became sultan Salim was reputed to have conservative Ibadi or even Wahhabi religious leanings; when the Masqat merchant community heard that he was the new ruler, the city, particularly its Indian community, panicked as bazaars closed and trade stopped. The panic even spread across the Gulf of Oman to Gwadar, which did not return to normal until May 1866 after Salim had demonstrated that he was actually a moderate.

The first of Salim's problems was to gain British recognition. Frere and Pelly decided on a policy of nonrecognition after learning the circumstances of Salim's coup. But Salim decided to press his claim and in April 1866 two of his envoys arrived in Bombay, requested British recognition, and protested Pelly's hostility. The envoys did their job well; they went on to Calcutta and impressed the Anglo–Indian officials there. Finally the viceroy, Sir John Lawrence, thinking Salim ibn-Thuwayni would soon consolidate his power, and wishing to prevent him

---

works such as Hazard, *Eastern Arabia*, or Arabian American Oil Company, *Oman*. To al-Salimi, the imamate was an ideal for all Oman, not just its interior provinces.

from falling under French or other foreign influence, overruled his subordinates in Bombay and Bushire and decided to grant de facto recognition to Salim. Neither Frere nor Pelly agreed with Lawrence's move, but in September 1866 Pelly visited Masqat and formally recognized Salim as sultan of Masqat and Oman. In January 1867 Captain Atkinson officially reopened the agency in Masqat.[19]

Salim's gaining British recognition did not mean he immediately received the Zanzibar subsidy, because Majid, in Zanzibar, refused to pay the money when he learned of his brother Thuwayni's death. Majid contended the 1861 award applied only to him and to Thuwayni personally and that in any case he would not subsidize a patricide. The British, although they would not allow Majid to escape his obligation, did agree to receive the payment and transmit it to Salim so Majid would not have to deal with his nephew. Majid was also warned not to send arms or otherwise interfere in Omani internal politics. Majid finally forwarded the subsidy in the spring of 1868.[20] Meanwhile, Salim suffered an acute revenue shortage, a situation that continued throughout his reign. Nothing seemed to work. For instance, in 1867 the Government of India delivered $MT 40,000 to Salim as security against the Majid's withheld subsidy, but the sultan had to use most of it immediately upon receipt to pay off overdue obligations. Salim also sent several letters requesting cash to the British and finally had to rely on the loan services of two Masqat Indian merchants to support his government. Meanwhile, receipts from customs continually fell during Salim's regime because of a rapid decline in trade.[21]

Contributing to Salim's succession troubles were unsatisfactory relations with Persia. Since the partition of Sayyid

[19] Al-Salimi, II, 226-27; Lorimer, I, 477-78.
[20] "Pelly to Atkinson, 1 Mar. 1868, No. 33: Residency," India Records-2, Vol. L.
[21] *Ibid.*; "Atkinson to Gonne, 17 Sept. 1868, no. 412: Masqat," "4 Mar. 1869, no. 139: Masqat," India Records-2, Vol. L; Lorimer, I, 479-81.

Sa'id's empire, control of Bandar 'Abbas, the Makran coast, and the trade of these places was relatively more important to Oman than it was before the partition of 1861. But the trend toward resumption of active Persian administration in that area, first apparent in 1853, continued. Even before Thuwayni's death in 1864 Persia raised claims to the port of Chahbar and even to Gwadar, moves which signaled the course of future events, although they did not immediately extend Persian administration into Makran and end Oman's nominal sway over that coast.[22] In 1866 the Persians asserted that Salim's usurpation of sovereignty in Oman voided the 1856 agreement by which Iran leased Bandar 'Abbas and the islands of Qishm and Hormuz to the Masqati government.[23] At this juncture, Salim took energetic steps to prevent Bandar 'Abbas's loss, threatening a naval attack if the Persians did not continue the 1856 arrangement. Since the Persians had no navy they requested British mediation. Colonel Pelly and Salim's *wazir*, Hajji Ahmad, visited Shiraz and in August 1868 signed a new engagement allowing Salim to continue to lease Bandar 'Abbas, but for an increased yearly rent of 30,000 tomans ($MT 75,000). According to article twelve of the new lease the agreement applied to Salim and his dependents only; if a conqueror took Oman then Bandar 'Abbas would revert to Persia.[24] Nevertheless, by the summer of 1868 Salim had put his foreign relations in order and in fact had displayed a certain flair for diplomacy.

Salim was far less fortunate in his domestic relations. His *wazirs* were uniformly unfortunate choices. The first, Thuwayni ibn-Muhammad, was a prince of the royal house who had served Sultan Thuwayni as *wazir*. Prince or not, he became involved in fraud and was dismissed by Salim.[25]

22 Lorimer, I, 476.

23 Hurewitz, *Diplomacy*, I, 157-58.

24 Aitchison—1909, Vol. XII, Apt. xlv, cxlii-cxliii; *Précis Persian Coast*, pp. 25-30; Lorimer, I, 480.

25 "Atkinson to Gonne, 31 Oct. 1868, no. 486: Masqat," India Records-2, Vol. L.

Thuwayni ibn-Muhammad's replacement, the above-mentioned Hajji Ahmad, was also a dishonest intriguer but managed to avoid detection. On one occasion, unknown to the sultan, he received the Zanzibar subsidy in his capacity as the sultan's agent, then appropriated the money for his own uses.[26]

Salim ibn-Thuwayni had no lack of advisors. He maintained good relations with the Wahhabis who had some influence on his policies, some of them being attached to his personal service. The best known conservative Ibadi in Oman, Sa'id ibn-Khalfan al-Khalili, was long a friend, an advisor, and a supporter of Sultan Salim. Apparently al-Khalili sought to influence the sultan to adopt conservative Ibadism, but in time the two became estranged because of Salim's continued adherence to moderate Ibadi practices. Sultan Salim until late 1867 also had the support of the powerful conservative Salih ibn-'Ali, shaykh of the al-Hirth tribe, a man who previously had championed Sultan Thuwayni.[27]

It is apparent that Sultan Salim's hold on Oman was never more than precarious. He unsuccessfully tried to explain away the murder of his father, and never dispelled his unsavory reputation. After taking power Salim ibn-Thuwayni had imprisoned his uncle Turki ibn-Sa'id, who had been assisting Sultan Thuwayni when the latter was killed. But the British soon forced Salim to set Turki free. The prince quickly fled to the interior, first to al-Zahirah and then to al-Sharqiyah, where he traveled among the tribes seeking support for a move to depose the sultan. He was unsuccessful in enlisting allies on the Trucial Coast (due to Pelly's intervention) and in al-Zahirah but successful in al-Sharqiyah and Ja'lan. He convinced some elements of al-Hirth and the bulk of Bani-Bu-Hasan and al-Hajariyin, all Hinawi tribes, to support him. However, Salih ibn-

[26] "Atkinson to Gonne, 4 Mar. 1869, no. 139: Masqat," India Records–2, Vol. L.

[27] Al-Salimi, II, 230; Aitchison—1933, XI, 274; Ibn-Ruzayq, pp. cxix-cxx; "Atkinson to Gonne, 17 Sept. 1868, no. 412: Masqat," India Records–2, Vol. L.

'Ali, the chief Hinawi leader in that region, remained aloof from the combination, along with the bulk of al-Hirth. Nevertheless, in the summer of 1867 Turki and his allies marched to the coast, occupied Matrah, and prepared to attack Salim in Masqat. Just as it appeared that Turki's move would succeed Pelly arrived and intervened to keep the peace. The British in 1866 had saved Turki ibn-Sa'id when he was in Sultan Salim's hands, so he was indebted to them. When Pelly insisted that Turki call off the attack, accept a pension from Salim, and exile himself to India, Turki had no choice but to accept. Thus the British temporarily saved Salim's government.[28]

Following this episode Salim committed a prime blunder, that of assuming he was strong enough to rule even if he provoked conservative displeasure. The support of Salih ibn-'Ali had been invaluable to Salim during Turki's rising. Yet the sultan, perhaps thinking that Salih ibn-'Ali was secretly in league with Turki, decided to seize the shaykh when he came to Masqat for a visit late in 1867. Salih barely escaped the sultan's trap and first fled to al-Batinah, then to al-Rustaq, and finally back to his home province, al-Sharqiyah.[29] But this incident decreed that the alliance of Salim and the conservatives was at an end. Of Salim's one-time allies, only a small group of Ghafiri tribes in Ja'lan and in Wadi Sama'il remained loyal to him by the summer of 1868. Salim's tendency to drive his adherents to desert him prompted the British agent, Captain Atkinson, to write that the sultan's rule was "not so much endangered by the strength of his enemies as by want of support."[30] Already, in 1867, Salim ibn-Thuwayni's governor in al-Masna'ah, his cousin Hamad ibn-Salim, had revolted.[31] Now, in the summer of 1868, Salih ibn-'Ali upon his return to al-Sharqiyah set about to forge a league against the sultan. First,

---

28 Al-Salimi, II, 226-29; Ibn-Ruzayq, p. cviii; Lorimer, I, 480-81.

29 Al-Salimi, II, 229.

30 "Atkinson to Gonne, 22 Sept. 1868, no. 420: Masqat," India Records–2, Vol. L.

31 Al-Salimi, II, 229; Lorimer, I, 479-80.

the shaykh contacted his old teacher, the above-mentioned conservative religious figure, Sa'id ibn-Khalfan al-Khalili, who saw that his dream of reviving the medieval Ibadi imamate, a desire which he had actively pushed in the 1840s, might be realized, given the weak state of the sultan's rule. Al-Khalili took over from Salih ibn-'Ali the work of organizing a coalition and began corresponding and meeting with other conservative leaders and shaykhs, including 'Azzan ibn-Qays. By the late summer of 1868 a conservative coalition had been organized to rise against Salim ibn-Thuwayni, expel him from Masqat, and revive conservative Ibadism as the ruling political and religious norm for all Oman.[32]

In September 1868 the conservatives set their plan in motion. A two-pronged attack was delivered against Masqat by their forces. 'Azzan ibn-Qays struck out from al-Rustaq and took Barka on the al-Batinah coast before turning south toward Masqat. Outside the capital 'Azzan's force was joined by another group under Salih ibn-'Ali and the shaykh of the Bani-Ruwahah. Before the attack of the combined armies was launched the traditional Khawarij invitation to repent was extended to Sultan Salim, a proposal that demanded that the sultan change his tyrannical government, eschew all public deviations from the right path, "return to the ways of the faithful" (i.e., the conservatives), and follow the advice of the conservative religious leaders. In other words, al-Khalili was willing to let Salim ibn-Thuwayni continue to reign if the actual power passed to the conservative leadership. Sultan Salim, counting on British and Ghafiri aid, refused the proposal. But his defenses were weak and on September 29, 1868 Matrah fell; on October 1 Masqat itself was stormed. The conservative warriors were well disciplined and only the sultan's palace was sacked during the attack. As a precaution, however, all British subjects were embarked on British ships lying in the harbor. Pelly arrived, ready to intervene to save Sultan Salim's throne,

[32] Al-Salimi, ii, 229-30.

but on October 7 instructions arrived from India forbidding any such interference. The abandoned sultan, who had held out in the Masqat harbor forts after the city's fall in the expectation of a British rescue, had no choice but to flee. So, on October 12 he left for Bandar 'Abbas on one of his own ships and the conservatives hoisted their white banner over the city. Salim ibn-Thuwayni at his fall had no more than 500 men at his side. His Ghafiri allies, the Bani-Bu-'Ali and Janabah, gave him no aid since they were fighting each other. Meanwhile, Salim's other major tribal ally, the Bani-Jabir, who dominated the Wadi Sama'il passes, had been alienated by Salim's recent bad treatment of their shaykhs so they allowed the invaders to descend out of the mountains unmolested on their way to Masqat.[33]

Thus between 1856 and 1868 the moderate Ibadi Al Bu Sa'id monarchy at Masqat collapsed. Reading the chronicles of the period leaves one with the feeling that the rulers had no perception of why they were floundering. Events out of the control of any Omani ruler, such as British intervention or the maritime and economic changes in the Indian Ocean area, were perhaps basic to the collapse. The compelling conclusion is that intelligent use of the political and economic resources remaining to the sultans, particularly by Salim, could have at least prevented the conservative success in 1868. At a time when the moderate wing of the ruling dynasty required the cooperation of all its members the various sayyids proved too short-sighted and too egotistic to combine. At the end of his reign Sultan Thuwayni appeared, with British help, about to restore a semblance of political order. Salim's bullet ended this chance. Men like Hajji Ahmad, who had everything to lose if moderate rule ended, thought only of lining their pockets. The failure of the coastal moderate rulers to cope with spreading economic and political crisis resulted in growing disorder,

[33] *Ibid.*, pp. 231-35; "Insurrection chiefs to Sultan Salim, 29 Sept. 1868, enclosure in Atkinson to Gonne, no. 429: Masqat," "15 Oct. 1868, no. 448: Masqat," "Atkinson to Pelly, 21 Sept. 1868, no. 419: Masqat," India Records –2, Vol. L; Lorimer, I, 481-82.

growing exasperation with the government, and finally in the conservative triumph of 1868.

THE CONSERVATIVE INTERLUDE—THE IMAMATE OF
'AZZAN IBN-QAYS, 1868-71

The nature of the conservative uprising. The events of 1868 were more than a simple substitution of one ruler for another. They were the product of a fundamentalist revolution that aimed to alter basically the trend of Omani history as it had operated since the sixteenth century, when the Ya'aribah dynasty initiated the secularization of the central Omani government. The conservative Ibadi revolution of 1868 displayed characteristics generally shared by major revolutions in other premodern Muslim societies: The ideology of the revolutionaries was expressed and summarized in theological terms, consequently social aims and even political aims were conceived as religious goals. The ideology of the revolution was presented as a fundamentalist attempt to restore the Islamic community to its pristine state. The revolution struck against the prevailing form of religion and accused it of containing innovations and impurities. The revolutionaries were puritanical in social attitudes and classified all who did not join in their movement as nonbelievers. The revolt was organized in a remote province far from the center of existing power. The revolution hinged on an attempt to take over the apparatus of state so that reforms might be effected to assure the maintenance of a proper Islamic environment. The revolt was organized primarily by a provincial religious and political elite representing a distinct geographic or ethnic grouping. Class differences were not an important factor contributing to the outbreak of the revolt but the wealthy supporters of the displaced regime suffered considerable loss, often by confiscation, after the revolutionaries assumed power. The revolt took place in a time of economic change and caused further economic repercussions. The state revolted against was inefficient and corrupt.[34]

[34] These generalizations are an amalgam of some remarks expressed by Professor Bernard Lewis during a session of his seminar on Islamic history

The revolt of 1868 had its antecedents in the unsuccessful conservative attempt of the 1840s to substitute a medieval-style imamate for the moderate government of Sayyid Saʻid.[35] A fundamental weakness of the 1840s movement was the fact that it was largely dominated by conservative ulema who failed to enlist sufficient military force to realize their movement's political needs. Nevertheless, the abortive undertaking of the 1840s enhanced the reputations of two forces that contributed to the successful 1868 upheaval. These were the conservative religious groups dominated by Saʻid ibn-Khalfan al-Khalili, the spiritual and organizational genius behind both uprisings, and the Qays branch of Al Bu Saʻid. Hamud ibn-ʻAzzan of the Qays branch was al-Khalili's nominee for the imamate in the 1840s, while Hamud's nephew, ʻAzzan ibn-Qays, actually became imam in the 1860s. When Salih ibn-ʻAli joined the conservative league in 1868 he carried with him potent Hinawi tribal support that had earlier contributed to the strength of the moderate sultans. Salih's shift was very important because it tipped the scales in favor of the fundamentalists.[36] The conservatives' victory in 1868, then, was due to the attractiveness of their program to many in Oman, dedicated leadership from the conservative religious class, the presence in the conservative camp of respectable "legitimate" leaders from the Qays branch of the royal house, the adherence of Hinawi tribal leaders to the conservative cause after 1867, and finally the growing weakness and inefficiency in the camp of the moderate sultans. The immediate cause of the revolt was Sultan Salim's blundering alienation of supporters, notably Salih ibn-ʻAli.

The consolidation of the conservative government. After

at London University in 1958, combined with a number of my own thoughts on the subject.

35 Al-Salimi, I, 60-64, II, 209-30, treats the program and growth of the conservative Ibadi movement between the early 1840s and 1868.

36 "Atkinson to Gonne, 29 Oct. 1868, no. 479: Masqat," India Records–2, Vol. L; al-Hirth, Hajariyin, and Bani-Bu-Hasan, previously supporters of Salim ibn-Thuwayni, all deserted him for the conservative camp early in 1868.

Salim's flight from Masqat in October 1868 the conservative leaders called a general conclave in the capital to organize what they hoped would be an ideal Muslim state according to Ibadi principles. The first item of business was the election of an imam. The election was conducted according to the ancient Ibadi pattern whereby a group of tribal and religious leaders decided on their nominee and presented him to the people for final ratification. The committee of leaders, dominated by al-Khalili, Muhammad ibn-Sulayyim al-Gharibi, a religious dignitary of the Al Sa'd tribe of al-Batinah, and Salih ibn-'Ali, voted that 'Azzan ibn-Qays should be their candidate for imam, a position held by 'Azzan's great great grandfather, Ahmad ibn-Sa'id, the first Al Bu Sa'id ruler of Oman, in the eighteenth century. The leaders' decision was ratified by the rank and file by public acclamation and 'Azzan next received the oath of allegiance from the people. This consisted of the people's promise to obey 'Azzan if he agreed to rule according to certain conditions. This pledge, then, was one traditionally designed for "weak" imams, whose independence was limited by the necessity that they receive prior approval from the religious leaders before certain actions could be taken.[37]

The apparatus of government set up by the conservatives in Masqat was modeled on the pattern of the medieval imamate. Although the imam was the nominal and executive head of government, in actuality, the decision-makers consisted of an oligarchy of leading conservative figures that included the imam. The influence of the oligarchy leaders varied. Even more important than Imam 'Azzan was Shaykh Sa'id ibn-Khalfan al-Khalili, for it was al-Khalili who determined the new regime's overall policy, guided its administration of laws, and set its general tone. Most of the measures undertaken by the conservative government between 1868 and its fall in 1871 found their source in al-Khalili's fertile mind. Never was the title of "power behind the throne" more accu-

[37] Al-Salimi, II, 236-37.

rately used than in describing al-Khalili's place in the imamate of 'Azzan ibn-Qays.

Al-Khalili had been a conservative leader since his attempt to revive the imamate in 1843-46. Apparently he spent the 1850s teaching and preaching in Oman's interior. His tribal ancestry is unclear, although he considered himself one of the Hinawi Bani-Ruwahah of Wadi Sama'il. Al-Khalili's influence and power were based on his intellectual authority as an interpreter and propagandist of conservative dogma.[38] His followers believed he possessed magical powers. Some said he could raise the dead and that the Angel Gabriel talked to him. Al-Khalili was puriticanical in outlook, frowning on the use of tobacco, strong drink, music, rich dress, and even the wearing of long mustaches. Al-Khalili's official positions in the regime were those of governor of Masqat and chief *qadi* (judge) of the realm; unofficially he was the chief religious, financial, and political advisor. All questions of even the slightest importance were referred to him.[39]

He was fanatically supported by a group called the *mutawwi's* (compellers of obedience), who were the spearhead of militant conservative Ibadism and who were comparable to the *ghazis* (warriors who spread Islam) of other traditional Islamic powers. The mutawwi's used a white turban as their badge. The institution was well established among the Ibadis, going back at least to the eighteenth century, but in the 1860s their unity was largely provided by their common loyalty to al-Khalili. Apparently there were two types of mutawwi's: those learned in religion whose function was much like the intellectual *qurra'* of the Khawarij of old, and those warriors and "enforcers" who carried out the programs laid down by the religious leaders. With his intelligence, his reputation for wisdom and piety, and the active support of the mutawwi's, whose ranks included most of the qadis in Oman, al-Khalili was in a posi-

---

[38] *Ibid.*, pp. 209, 229; Arabian American Oil Company, *Oman*, p. 108.

[39] "Disbrowe to Gonne, 9 June 1869, no. 324: Masqat," India Records–2, Vol. L; Lorimer, I, 482.

tion to control the civil apparatus of the conservative government.[40]

The nominal head of government, the Imam 'Azzan ibn-Qays, was not particularly friendly with al-Khalili, but he was dominated by his chief qadi during most of his reign. 'Azzan ibn-Qays was chosen imam because of his upright character and his royal Al Bu Sa'id descent, not because he was the strongest personality available, for doubtless al-Khalili did not want too strong an imam. The fact that al-Khalili arranged a marriage between his daughter and the imam added to the chief qadi's influence. Imam 'Azzan's primary role was that of commander of the imamate's armies, in which he was fairly successful but not brilliant. 'Azzan's personality was austere but polite, qualities which gave him general respect in tribal Oman although the conservative bias of the imamate made him unpopular in coastal ports. As Iman 'Azzan developed skill in mediating between the rival elements in his government he gained experience and reputation, while al-Khalili's fell.[41]

The third member of the ruling oligarchy was Salih ibn-'Ali, shaykh of the al-Hirth tribe. Salih's importance derived from his leadership over the Hinawis of al-Sharqiyah. Originally he held an official position in the new government analogous to a secular prime minister. But al-Khalili increasingly usurped the functions of a prime minister so Shaykh Salih's relations with his associates cooled as time went on. Although he was active in its creation, Salih ibn-'Ali was not very involved in the central administration of the imamate by the time of its fall in 1871. Nevertheless, he retained his military importance as a bulwark of the conservatives.[42]

---

[40] Ibn-Ruzayq, pp. 203, 247-48, 385-98; Major Grey, "The Mutawwa' sect of Ibadhis," Lorimer, I, 2,375ff.; "Disbrowe to Gonne, 27 Oct. 1869, no. 616: Masqat," India Records–2, Vol. L.

[41] Al-Salimi, II, 237; "Disbrowe to Gonne, 6 Aug. 1869, no. 424: Masqat," India Records–2, Vol. L; Lorimer, I, 491.

[42] Al-Salimi, II, 231-37; "Atkinson to Gonne, 31 Oct. 1868, no. 486: Masqat," "Atkinson to Pelly, 18 Feb. 1869, no. 69: Masqat," "Disbrowe to Gonne, 11 Aug. 1869, no. 437: Masqat," India Records–2, Vol. L; "Way to Pelly, 11 Apr. 1870, no. 223: Masqat," India Records–2, Vol. XVI.

Another of the imamate's founding oligarchy, Muhammad ibn-Sulayyim al-Gharibi, a religious leader of the Al Sa'd tribe, also grew disenchanted with his associates as time went on. Al-Gharibi, although a conservative Ibadi, was not a fanatic, and being a native of coastal al-Batinah, he felt that many of al-Khalili's extremist policies were unrealistic. By 1870 al-Gharibi left Masqat and returned to al-Batinah, embittered by his lack of real influence.[43]

A personage who grew in importance as the imamate matured was Imam 'Azzan's brother, Ibrahim ibn-Qays. Ibrahim, who became an outspoken critic of al-Khalili, served as a military commander and troubleshooter for his brother. He inherited the position as leader of the Qays branch of Al Bu Sa'id after Imam 'Azzan's death and the destruction of the imamate in 1871. Another prominent military leader and troubleshooter was Faysal ibn-Hamud, Imam 'Azzan's cousin.[44]

Once the conservative regime was organized it set to work to consolidate its hold over Oman and the country's overseas dependencies. The regime was very successful during its first year in extending its political control, to the extent that by the fall of 1869 it dominated all of Oman and even had eliminated the Sa'udis as an immediate threat to the Rub' al-Khali border provinces. On the other hand, the overseas dependencies on the Makran coast did not fall under the imam's sway, and by 1870 financial difficulties and growing disenchantment with some of the government's political policies began to undermine the popularity and strength of the conservative authorities.

The major accomplishment of the imamate was the rapid subjugation of virtually all of Oman by the imam's government. Few other Omani potentates had ever attempted, much

[43] Al-Salimi, II, 230, 235, 246-47; "Atkinson to Gonne, 18 Nov. 1868, no. 520: Masqat," "Disbrowe to Gonne, 7 Aug. 1869, no. 430: Masqat," "21 Aug. 1869, no. 465: Masqat," India Records–2, Vol. L.

[44] Al-Salimi, II, 245-46, 251-53; "Atkinson to Gonne, 18 Nov. 1868, no. 520: Masqat," "Disbrowe to Gonne, 7 Aug. 1869, no. 430: Masqat," "21 Aug. 1869, no. 465: Masqat," India Records–2, Vol. L.

less carried out, such an ambitious plan of domination as that accomplished by Imam 'Azzan ibn-Qays in 1868-69. When the imamate was formed in October 1868 most of the Hinawi tribes pledged allegiance and support to the new imam. On the other hand, few Ghafiri tribes were involved in the uprising that created the imamate; although a few Ghafiri tribes recognized the supremacy of the new government most of them did not wish to submit to the imam. Thus one of the first moves of the imamate was a decision to move against any Ghafiri tribes which did not display enthusiastic adherence to the new regime.

The most strategically placed concentration of Ghafiri tribes was in the Wadi Sama'il area. It was natural that 'Azzan ibn-Qays directed his first large pacification expedition toward that district. However, even before Imam 'Azzan's forces marched inland, the ruler received the good news that al-Batinah, already dominated by the Al Sa'd tribe and other conservative forces, had fallen completely under his authority when Hamad ibn-Salim, ex-Sultan Salim's governor at al-Masna'ah, had surrendered.[45] In January 1869 the vanguard of the imam's army marched into Wadi Sama'il and undertook a month-long series of operations which ended only after the Ghafiri tribes of the region had submitted. Fighting unusual in its ferocity even in terms of the normal intensity of Arabian tribal warfare accompanied the subjugation of al-Siyabiyin. When this group refused the imam's initial invitation to recognize his authority he attacked them with an army of 3,000 recruited in al-Batinah and supported by two field cannon. At the same time Salih ibn-'Ali attacked from the west with 1,500 warriors of al-Hirth. The result of this twin assault was the near annihilation of al-Siyabiyin's fighting capability and the subsequent quick capitulation of the other nearby Ghafiri tribes. Each of the major Ghafiri tribes of the district, the Bani-Jabir, al-Nidabiyin some lesser tribes, and of course al-Siyabiyin, were required to hand over hostages to the imam as a guarantee for their future

[45] Al-Salimi, II, 229-41.

good conduct. It should be noted that Bani-Jabir had aided the conservatives during their revolution but even they had to hand over 20 hostages.[46]

The only large Ghafiri tribe of the central Hajar which continued to defy Imam 'Azzan after February 1869 was the Bani-Riyam. This tribe, settled as it was on the forbidding slopes of the highest mountain in the Hajar chain, the peaks of al-Jabal al-Akhdar, and led by its doughty shaykh, Sayf ibn-Sulayman, remained aloof even after 'Azzan ibn-Qays sent them a gift of 200 fetters as a not too subtle warning of what their insolence could bring. Since Imam 'Azzan's threats were not carried out they only caused Sayf ibn-Sulayman and some lesser Ghafiri shaykhs who had escaped the imam's sweep to join a plot to restore ex-Sultan Salim to power.[47]

Salim ibn-Thuwayni's activities posed a minor threat to the imam during the spring of 1869. After his flight from Masqat in October 1868 the ex-sultan took refuge at Bandar 'Abbas and began to plan ways of regaining his throne. Finally, early in the spring of 1869 Salim, after being warned by the British not to disturb the maritime peace, quietly crossed over to Dubayy on the Trucial Coast. There he was repectfully received and began negotiations to form alliances with various Trucial Coast shaykhs, with some Omani tribes that had not yielded to 'Azzan ibn-Qays, and with his old ally, Turki al-Sudayri, the Wahhabi commander at al-Buraymi. Initially Salim seemed to pick up considerable support and received promises of aid from al-Sudayri, the Bani-Riyam, and the Bani-Jabir who were mortified by 'Azzan's insulting treatment of them during his Wadi Sama'il campaign. But in April 1869 Salim's cause suffered a blow from which it never recovered. Al-Sudayri was killed in a scuffle while visiting at the Trucial Coast port of al-Shariqah. Despite this setback Salim ibn-Thuwayni struck out on a tour of inland Oman to rally the

[46] *Ibid.*, pp. 242-44; "Atkinson to Pelly, 15 Feb. 1869, no. 69: Masqat," India Records–2, Vol. L.
[47] Al-Salimi, II, 244.

tribes of al-Zahirah, 'Uman province, and Ja'lan to his side. Courteously greeted everywhere, Salim nevertheless received concrete assurances of help nowhere. Without al-Sudayri's backing Omani tribes were no longer willing to support him. Finally Imam 'Azzan sent patrols out to capture Salim who, realizing his cause was hopeless at that time, returned to Dubayy and in May 1869 sailed once again into exile. He settled at Qishm Island in the Straits of Hormuz where he would be close enough to Oman to move quickly if an opportunity for his restoration ever developed.[48]

Meanwhile, while 'Azzan ibn-Qays was conducting his Wadi Sama'il campaign and occupying himself with countering the machinations of the Bani-Riyam and ex-Sultan Salim, the imam's cousin, Faysal ibn-Hamud, was traveling through southeastern Oman receiving pledges of loyalty from the tribes of that quarter. Starting from Masqat and receiving a warm welcome in Sur, Faysal ibn-Hamud's party marched through Ja'lan until it halted for a time at Bilad Bani-Bu-Hasan. While Faysal was there, the Ghafiri Bani-Bu-'Ali shaykh pledged his loyalty to 'Azzan ibn-Qays. Faysal ibn-Hamud concluded his tour with a visit to al-Sharqiyah and the al-Hirth tribe and returned to Masqat satisfied that the imam's grip over southern Oman was firm.[49]

By the summer of 1869 only the inland provinces of 'Uman and al-Zahirah—with the exception of the domains of some mountain tribes such as the Bani-Riyam—contained large areas still free of the imamate's control. A major problem facing any Omani ruler who wanted to move into al-Zahirah, however, was that this was a province which since the early nineteenth century had been included in the sphere of influence radiating from the Sa'udi stronghold at al-Buraymi. But the violent death of Turki al-Sudayri in April 1869 inevitably

---

[48] *Ibid.*, p. 251; "Salim ibn-Thuwayni to Disbrowe, 6 June 1869, enclosure in Disbrowe to Gonne, 27 June 1869, no. 358: Masqat," India Records–2, Vol. L; Lorimer, I, 483-86.
[49] Al-Salimi, II, 245-46.

meant that a new element of uncertainty was injected into the picture. It was largely because of this new atmosphere of uncertainty that the Ghafiri Nu'aym tribe, which inhabited al-Buraymi and the surrounding district, decided to throw off Sa'udi control. Nu'aym timed their movement well, for not only was Turki al-Sudayri succeeded by his inexperienced brother, 'Abd al-Rahman al-Sudayri, as commander of the Wahhabi garrison at al-Buraymi, but the central apparatus of the Sa'udi state itself was being shaken apart by a ruinous civil war which pitted the late Sa'udi ruler's two sons, Sa'ud ibn-Faysal and 'Abdallah ibn-Faysal, the new titular imam of the Wahhabis, against each other.

'Azzan ibn-Qays became involved in Nu'aym's struggle against the Sa'udis for a number of reasons. First, the imam was angered by the aid Turki al-Sudayri had promised to ex-Sultan Salim. Also, Imam 'Azzan had stopped paying the customary annual bribe of $MT 20,000 to the Sa'udis, so he was expecting trouble with them. Finally, Nu'aym's shaykh, Muhammad ibn-'Ali, seeking backing for his defiance of the Sa'udis, had gone to al-Batinah and convinced Muhammad ibn-Sulayyim al-Gharibi, a leading oligarch in the imam's government, that Omani forces should occupy the al-Buraymi forts in order to neutralize the Sa'udi threat.[50] After this preliminary agreement the two men then approached 'Azzan ibn-Qays with their plan which the imam agreed to support.[51]

The Ibadi army gathered at Suhar during early June 1869, crossed the Hajar mountains via Wadi al-Jizi, and combined with Nu'aym and allied Bani-Ka'b tribesmen. At this time 'Azzan ibn-Qays also concluded an alliance with the ambitious Zayid ibn-Khalifah, the ruler of Abu Dhabi and a man destined to be a prominent figure on the Trucial Coast until his death in 1909. Imam 'Azzan's troops and those of his allies reached al-Buraymi in mid-June and immediately opened their

[50] *Ibid.*, p. 248.

[51] Lorimer, I, 484-85; "Atkinson to Gonne, 29 Oct. 1868, no. 479: Masqat," "Disbrowe to Gonne, 9 June 1869, no. 324: Masqat," India Records–2, Vol. L.

attack on the Sa'udi-held forts that dominated the oasis.[52] On June 18, 1869 the main Sa'udi stronghold was reduced after a battle 'Azzan ibn-Qays described as follows: "We looked upon the place and saw a most formidable fort which forbade us entry. The fort is a most lofty one and famous for its strength. In it, too, were soldiers united and powerful. . . . Preparations for battle were made on either side. . . . Then commenced firing, the giving and taking of blows, horse and foot, dagger and spear, and men fell from their horses—Oh, how they fell! Enemies of each other bit the dust. The battle continued for three days and three nights. On the fourth the ardor of the Muslims [the Ibadis] reached its height and they showed their determination . . . to storm the fort. . . . When the news spread . . . the enemy took to supplication, tendered submission and asked for quarter. Now in accordance with Arab custom and Arab generosity when anyone asks for quarter . . . quarter is given. . . . The enemy departed and there remains of them only their names not their presence. . . ."[53]

In his description Imam 'Azzan failed to credit the Nu'aym for their invaluable help in infiltrating the fortress and neglected to mention that it was Salih ibn-'Ali's timely arrival with reinforcements that broke the spirit of al-Buraymi's defenders and prompted them to ask for terms. 'Azzan ibn-Qays left a garrison of 200 men in the main fort, Qasr al-Khandaq, and established a provincial administration headed by a Ghafiri shaykh, Burayk ibn-Salimin, to govern al-Zahirah province.[54] Evidently the Nu'aym were not too pleased with the turn of events which saw them exchange a Sa'udi overlord for an Ibadi governor for within a year they were preparing

[52] Arabian American Oil Company, *Oman*, p. 29; Saudi Arabia, *Memorial*, I, 244-46; Kelly, *Eastern Arabian Frontiers*, pp. 87-88; "Pelly to Duke of Argyll, 7 May 1870, despatch no. 147-2: Residency," India Records–2, Vol. XVI.

[53] " 'Azzan ibn-Qays to Disbrowe, 4 July 1869, enclosure in Disbrowe to Gonne, 9 July 1869, no. 377: Masqat," India Records–2, Vol. L.

[54] Al-Salimi, II, 249-50.

to challenge Iman 'Azzan's authority.[55] The conquest of al-Buraymi naturally contributed to the prestige of the imamate. Even Masqat, sullenly enduring the trials of conservative rule, celebrated the event.[56] But enthusiasm soon gave way to fear of Sa'udi retaliation, a subject that will be discussed below.

After his conquest of al-Buraymi, the imam returned to Masqat where he spent the summer preparing for an offensive drive into 'Uman province, the last district of any importance in Oman that remained outside his grasp. The expedition set forth in September and completed its work by the end of October 1869. The objectives included the humbling of some large Ghafiri tribes in the western Hajar mountains and in 'Uman province, as well as the reduction of a number of fortress towns in 'Uman. 'Azzan ibn-Qays, utilizing his ancestral seat at al-Rustaq as a jumping-off point, thrust southwest across the Hajar until he hit the Bani-Shukayl tribe in 'Uman and took the great fortress of Bahla in the process. Using the same tactics that had been so devastatingly successful against al-Siyabiyin nine months earlier, Salih ibn-'Ali, meanwhile, struck the Bani-Shukayl from another direction and forced the surrender of the fortress at Manah. Still another column, this commanded by the imam's brother, Ibrahim ibn-Qays, wrested Izki and its protecting fortress from the hands of a prominent Ghafiri shaykh, 'Ali ibn-Jabr. This success was followed up by Ibrahim's occupation of the great circular fortress and the town of Nazwa. Before the attack on Nazwa it appeared that Hamad ibn-Sayf al-Bu-Sa'idi, the governor of the town and apparently a holdover from the previous moderate regime, would resist. Consequently, Ibrahim ibn-Qays sought help from the Bani-Riyam shaykh, Sayf ibn-Sulayman, who was seeking a way to end his dispute with the imam and whose tribe held part of Nazwa. In any event, Nazwa fell and Salim ibn-'Udaym of the Hinawi Bani-Ruwahah was appointed its new governor.

[55] Kelly, *Eastern Arabian Frontiers*, p. 88.
[56] "Disbrowe to Gonne, 9 July 1869, no. 377: Masqat," India Records–2, Vol. L.

Unfortunately for Sayf ibn-Sulayman his attempt to gain the imam's good graces ended disastrously. Shortly after Nazwa's conquest 'Azzan ibn-Qays requested that Shaykh Sayf visit him under a pledge of safe conduct. In reality, 'Azzan had not forgiven the shaykh for his defiance at the beginning of the year, or for the aid he had promised ex-Sultan Salim during the deposed ruler's abortive search for allies in Oman six months earlier. So, despite his promise of safe conduct, 'Azzan ibn-Qays seized Sayf ibn-Sulayman as soon as the shaykh arrived for his visit. The Bani-Riyam chief died a prisoner in Masqat a short time later.[57]

The final episodes in the consolidation of the imam's dominion over Oman took place in November 1869. First, 'Azzan ibn-Qays suppressed an uprising by the Ghafiri—indeed many in the tribe were Wahhabis—Bani-Bu-'Ali in Ja'lan, but the lenient terms offered the vanquished tribesmen by Imam 'Azzan merited al-Khalili's scorn. Doubtless the chief qadi was more pleased with the outcome of the last campaign in the pacification of Oman. This was the successful siege of al-Hazm, a fortress belonging to the old royal tribe of Ya'aribah which threatened the approaches to al-Rustaq. The Ya'aribah were virtually wiped out by the imam's troops during the fighting for their stronghold.[58]

The height and extent of the imamate's power over Oman reached its peak in the late autumn of 1869. This rule was one of the strongest ever attempted in Omani history. Few rulers in Omani history could boast, as 'Azzan ibn-Qays could, that their realms included the coastal provinces as well as the main inland tribal areas, forts, and towns.[59] Yet the strong centralizing policy of the imamate's leaders, seemingly so successful in 1869, carried with it seeds of dissension and weakness. Imam

[57] Al-Salimi, II, 251-54; Lorimer, I, 484-86; "Disbrowe to Gonne, 10 Nov. 1869, no. 657: Masqat," India Records–2, Vol. L.

[58] Al-Salimi, II, 254-57, 263-66; Lorimer, I, 484-86.

[59] The present ruler of Muscat and Oman, Sa'id ibn-Taymur, since 1955 has controlled a domain equal in size to that ruled by 'Azzan ibn-Qays a century ago. But in addition, Sultan Sa'id also administers Dhofar.

'Azzan's initial success was due, in large part, to the fact that virtually all of the powerful Hinawi tribes united behind him. The Ghafiri tribes, on the other hand, were not enthusiastic supporters of the imamate, but neither were they united against it. Unfortunately, when 'Azzan ibn-Qays began subjugating the Ghafiri tribes one by one he also treated the few Ghafiri groups that did rally behind him—tribes such as Bani-Jabir—to a humiliation very little different from that which he visited upon the tribes that took up arms against him. Their common humiliation prompted many Ghafiri elements to accept the chance to combine against the imam when the opportunity came in 1870-71. Traditionally, no imamate in Oman has long endured except when it represents a fusion of some powerful adherents of both the Ghafiri and Hinawi factions. The imamate of 1868-71 increasingly appeared to be a vehicle to assure the supremacy of certain powerful Hinawi tribes rather than as a focus of Omani unity; thus this situation almost automatically produced its nemesis. Moreover, by 1870 the enthusiasm of even Hinawi tribes for the imamate cooled when they saw that the imam's tax collectors did not discriminate between a Hinawi and a Ghafiri. Thus the disease which had so weakened the government of Sultan Salim ibn-Thuwayni—the alienation of allies—began to sap the strength of Imam 'Azzan ibn-Qays as well.

One of the reasons that the imam's government believed it had to maintain a relatively tight control over Oman despite the risk of disaffection was that the regime needed all the revenue it could collect. The most immediate, yet the most persistent, administrative problem that taxed the ingenuity of the conservative leaders during their period of supremacy in Oman was the question of how to raise money. It was unfortunate for the regime's sake that it resorted to money-raising methods which ultimately brought it a great deal of opposition. Financial and economic affairs were generally the responsibility of the chief qadi, Sa'id ibn-Khalfan al-Khalili, a man of great religious and political learning, strong ethical convictions, but practically no business or financial training or experience.

The new regime did not have the capacity to solve Oman's —particularly coastal Oman's—economic woes, and many of its measures only further damaged the economic health of the country. The day the red flag of the sultanate was hauled down to make room for the white banner of the imamate was a particularly sad one for the city of Masqat. The new government was dominated by inland tribal and intellectual personalities who had little sympathy for the mores of an international port. Al-Khalili and his mutawwi' supporters clamped down on the easygoing Masqatis to the point where proclamations were circulated throughout the town forbidding dancing, the use of liquor or drugs, and playing music or drums. Only two of the 11 coffee houses which operated in Masqat prior to the revolution remained open by mid-1869. The ultra-strict application of the conservative Ibadi version of Koranic law in the port outlawed many commercial practices long sanctioned by the business community, ruined the confidence of Masqat's merchant classes, and thus aggravated the already serious economic depression that had gripped the city since her entrepôt function was destroyed in the early 1860s. In 1869 the decree was promulgated that all Muslims must attend mosque services, while non-Muslims had to conform at least outwardly to the prevailing puritanism. The mutawwi's who acted as censors and guardians of the city's morals were often ignorant or over bearing tribesmen who formed flying squadrons of "enforcers" who were quick to administer beatings or close down shops if they witnessed some action they did not like or understand. Many non-Omani sailors began to adopt the practice of staying aboard ship when anchored at Masqat. Other captains avoided the port altogether in order to escape harassment by mutawwi's or other fanatics roaming the port. Late in 1869 trade had fallen to the level where rice imports from India were but one quarter of their usual volume at Masqat. Many of Masqat's inhabitants doubtless would have echoed the lament of one unhappy professional soldier who complained: "I am a poor man trying to earn a few dollars for my family. I am nobody —I think of the happy times of Sayyid Sa'id and Sayyid Thuwayni and I live in hopes of seeing some of their sons coming to save us."[60]

The fundamentalist piety of the conservatives served neither the social nor the economic climate of Masqat, a city where traditionally all kinds of religions were practiced openly but where the "golden calf," in the words of the traveler Palgrave, counted "more sincere worshippers . . . than any other divinity soever."[61] The major Arab merchants still active in the port in 1868 were almost all driven out of business during the period of the imamate. The British-protected Indian merchants fared little better. Hindu traders were in a particularly delicate position. Imam 'Azzan claimed he did not want to interfere with their religion, yet he objected to the use of drums, bells, and cymbals in Hindu religious ceremonies.[62] There were countless beatings, plunderings, and even murders of Hindus. Their houses were invaded on occasion by mutawwi's checking to see that bans on tobacco were being observed. One Hindu was imprisoned for a time for shaving his beard. It was worse outside Masqat. In al-Khaburah the entire Hindu quarter was burned. As a result of this unhappy situation many of those Indian merchants who could, emigrated to Zanzibar or other Indian Ocean emporiums, taking their goods and treasure. Most of the Indian community, however, lacked the mobility —unless they were willing to suffer a crippling financial loss. Many of them possessed landed properties, claims, or other immovable assets.[63] Also, the Indians were unable to sue

---

[60] "Disbrowe to Gonne, 6 Aug. 1869, no. 424: Masqat," "Disbrowe to Pelly, 9 Dec. 1869, no. 704: Masqat," India Records–2, Vol. L; Lorimer, I, pp. 482-83; *Précis Commerce*, p. 29.

[61] Palgrave, *Central and Eastern Arabia*, II, 366.

[62] " 'Azzan ibn-Qays to Disbrowe, 11 Aug. 1869, enclosure in Disbrowe to Gonne, 19 Aug. 1869, no. 461: Masqat," India Records–2, Vol. L.

[63] Lorimer, I, 536; "Disbrowe to Gonne, 26 Apr. 1869, no. 250: Masqat," "12 May 1869, no. 278: Masqat," "26 June 1869, no. 353: Masqat," India Records–2, Vol. L.

Omani subjects for debts owed because most local businessmen were in no position to pay such demands due to actual or threatened confiscations of their wealth. By 1870 some of the mutawwi'-inspired harassment of business activity abated, but the situation was still bad enough that the port was hit by a labor strike caused by general dissatisfaction over the levying of a heavy tax disguised as a "loan."[64] The continuing decline of trade that marked the imamate's rule in Masqat also saw a consequent drop in customs revenues. Not until the very eve of its fall did the imamate's commercial policy begin to accommodate the needs of the coastal economy.[65]

Al-Khalili's original appointee as customs director was Sa'id ibn-'Amr, a tribal figure from the inland Hajariyin tribe. One of his first moves was to cut the customs duties drastically, but instead of stimulating trade this action, taken at a time when trade was evaporating, cost the government half its usual customs receipts. Sa'id ibn-'Amr's ignorance of port practices and his general inefficiency ultimately induced al-Khalili early in 1869 to try to secure the services of the Masqat Hindu firm of Gopaldass–Mowjee to administer the customs, a move the British agent, Lt. Col. Disbrowe, prevented. Finally, al-Khalili tricked a Khoja, Sulayman ibn-Jum'ah, to bid $MT 35,000 for the concession to manage the customs, with the understanding that a sizeable refund would be forthcoming. After ibn-Jum'ah concluded this bargain al-Khalili denied he had contracted to pay the promised "kickback" and threatened ibn-Jum'ah with a fine and imprisonment if he tried to get out of the deal.[66]

An infamous, unpopular, and ultimately injurious device used by al-Khalili to shore up the government's financial strength was the large-scale confiscation of the property of

[64] "Pelly to Duke of Argyll, 8 Oct. 1870, despatch no. 433-33: Residency," India Records–2, Vol. xvi.

[65] *Précis Commerce*, p. 29; "Pelly to Duke of Argyll, 19 June, 1869, despatch no. 147-2: Residency," India Records–2, Vol. xvi. "Disbrowe to Gonne, 9 June 1869, no. 324: Masqat," "21 Aug. 1869, no. 464: Masqat," "25 Nov. 1869, no. 683: Masqat," India Records–2, Vol. l.

[66] "Disbrowe to Gonne, 13 Nov. 1869, no. 666: Masqat," India Records–2, Vol. l.

members and close supporters of the old, moderate regime. The use of confiscations was not popular even with several of the conservative ruling oligarchy, including both Salih ibn-'Ali and Muhammad ibn-Sulayyim al-Gharibi. Nevertheless, although these men considered confiscations a dangerous and radical policy they could not prevent their use, so entrenched were al-Khalili and his clique as the pacesetters of the imamate.[67] Al-Khalili found that the mere threat of confiscation might produce as much revenue in some instances as actually invoking the penalty. Many were hit by the policy. One man's date garden was confiscated because he had been a clerk for Sayyid Sa'id; another was fined $MT 3,000 on grounds that he had purchased his land from Sayyid Sa'id; and various other estates were taken over on the pretense they were "state property." By the summer of 1869 confiscations were so numerous there were not enough buyers for the property although one man who grew rich buying confiscated property at reduced prices was Hilal ibn-Sa'id, an Al Bu Sa'id supporter of al-Khalili.[68] In time, al-Khalili went so far as to extend his confiscations to include the property of supporters of the regime. In 1869 Shaykh 'Ali of the Bani-Jabir, originally a government supporter, was forced to give up an estate and $MT 4,000 for "state expenses." This action completely alienated the already disgruntled 'Ali and encouraged the rise of a Ghafiri coalition which later contributed to the downfall of the imamate.[69]

Despite al-Khalili's drastic and unpopular measures the treasury was depleted by 1870. As an emergency measure al-Khalili then authorized 'Azzan ibn-Qays to raise a "loan" among citizens of the realm, using force if necessary to collect the money. Once they were collected the proceeds of the "loan" were then treated as contributions not subject to repayment.

[67] Al-Salimi, I, 66, II, 246-48. Al-Salimi himself condemned the policy of confiscations.

[68] "Disbrowe to Gonne, 7 Aug. 1869, no. 430: Masqat," "9 Sept. 1869, no. 499: Masqat," India Records-2, Vol. L.

[69] "Atkinson to Pelly, 1 Feb. 1869, no. 50: Masqat," India Records-2, Vol. L.

The Al Sa'd tribe, however, refused to pay what was demanded of them and drove off tax collectors.[70]

In order to save money al-Khalili cut expenditures to the bone. One budget-cutting move of the most serious implication was his refusal to allow 'Azzan to pay the customary $MT 20,000 per year tribute to the Wahhabis. Al-Khalili said it was unlawful for an imam to pay any tribute.[71] Naturally, this action contributed to the revival of the Omani–Wahhabi feud discussed above. On another occasion he refused to pay the powerful Nu'aym tribe of al-Zahirah a $MT 3,000 grant he had promised in return for the tribe's military aid, an action which alienated Nu'aym.[72] As imam, 'Azzan ibn-Qays was allowed only $MT 200 per month, and payments to the army were always in arrears.[73] Salih ibn-'Ali himself once refused to campaign, complaining that he had not been rewarded or even paid expenses for past expeditions; he added that "he did all the work and al-Khalili got all the pay."[74] Various leaders in addition to Salih also protested prevailing revenue policies but seemingly without effect.

Imam 'Azzan's government never received British recognition, hence it never drew the Zanzibar subsidy. Sultan Majid of Zanzibar, of course, had no wish to pay if he could help it. Requests were sent by 'Azzan ibn-Qays for recognition and the subsidy, but his government fell before the matter of recognition was settled or before any money was received.[75]

The revenue difficulty was one the conservatives never

[70] Al-Salimi, ii, 257-70; "Disbrowe to Gonne, 21 Aug. 1869, no. 465: Masqat," "9 Sept. 1869, no. 499: Masqat," India Records–2, Vol. L.

[71] "Atkinson to Gonne, 29 Oct. 1868, no. 479: Masqat," India Records–2, Vol. L.

[72] "Disbrowe to Gonne, 7 Aug. 1869, no. 430: Masqat," India Records–2, Vol. L.

[73] "Disbrowe to Gonne, 9 June 1869, no. 324: Masqat," India Records–2, Vol. L.

[74] "Way to Pelly, 11 Apr. 1870, no. 223: Masqat," India Records–2, Vol. XVI.

[75] "Pelly to Duke of Argyll, 24 July 1870, despatch no. 299-17: Residency," India Records–2, Vol. XVI; Lorimer, I, 490-91.

solved. Their inability to do so increasingly hampered governmental operations. Al-Khalili and his associates, most of whom were inland-born intellectuals, had even less understanding of Oman's economic and fiscal situation than did the moderate sultans of 1856-68. In any event, the conservative government's policy depressed business, drove capital into exile or hiding, generally aggravated the revenue crisis, and cost the regime much support, particularly on the coast. The problems of wealth and trade, it seems, were not ones that particularly inspired conservative intellectuals or warriors. If Oman's ancient prosperity was dying under the sultans of 1856-68 then the conservatives issued the *coup de grace*.

Conservative foreign relations. The imamate had little success in conducting its foreign relations, which—especially its failure to gain British recognition—contributed to its eventual fall. A question which might be considered an aspect of domestic politics but which became essentially one of foreign politics involved the conservative regime's relations with Oman's dependencies on the Makran coast between Bandar 'Abbas and Gwadar. Since the 1850s this region had been the focus of increasing Persian interest. When 'Azzan ibn-Qays took Masqat in 1868 the Iranian government invoked a clause in the lease agreement they had concluded earlier in the same year with Salim ibn-Thuwayni and revoked the Omani contract to rent the port because a "conquerer" had obtained possession of Masqat. However, the Iranian authorities appointed Hajji Ahmad, the deposed sultan's wazir, as Persian governor of the port and allowed Salim ibn-Thuwayni to settle there after his exile. Since the British would not allow Imam 'Azzan to dispatch warships against Bandar 'Abbas he was unable to regain the port for Oman. In October 1869 the imam did succeed in smuggling a raiding force into the city, but although the place was sacked, the conservatives were unable to hold it. Bandar 'Abbas has remained in Iran's hands down to the present but the first years of direct Iranian administration continued to display a strong Omani flavor due to the presence of Arab governing officials like Hajji Ahmad.[76]

In Gwadar 'Azzan ibn-Qays was able to install a governor, but one who could not gain the loyalty of the locals. Thus the stage was set for an anti-imamate coup in April 1869. At that time Sayyid Nasir ibn-Thuwayni, a son of the late sultan and of a Baluchi concubine who came from the vicinity of Gwadar, secretly slipped out of Masqat and reached Gwadar. Because of his family connection with the locality, he had little trouble in recruiting a force in the neighborhood and taking Gwadar. Imam 'Azzan's governor appealed to the British to intervene, which they would not do because Nasir ibn-Thuwayni did not use an armed ship to gain the city and did not threaten the maritime peace. In fact, a British gunboat prevented 'Azzan ibn-Qays from sending an armed ship to counterattack.[77] Thus British intervention in this instance took the form of extending the maritime truce principles current in the upper Gulf into the Gulf of Oman and so shielding Imam 'Azzan's foes from attack and preserving bases from which the moderates could mount or organize counterattacks against Oman itself.

The initial British opinion of the conservatives and their policies was very unfavorable, and grew worse before it improved. Very early in his reign Imam 'Azzan sent a delegation to India in an attempt to gain recognition, but the move failed.[78] The chief block to the establishment of cordial relations was the appearance of what the British believed was fanaticism among some in 'Azzan's regime and among his supporters in Masqat. This impression was heightened by the steady drop in trade and the intolerant treatment being received by the Hindus. Colonel Disbrowe and 'Azzan ibn-

[76] "Hajji Ahmad ibn-Muhammad to Pelly, enclosure no. 1 in Pelly to Disbrowe, 9 Oct. 1869, no. 528: Masqat," India Records–2, Vol. L.

[77] Lorimer, I, 484; "Disbrowe to Pelly, 12 Apr. 1869, no. 189: Masqat," "12 Apr. 1869, no. 190: Masqat," India Records–2, Vol. L.

[78] " 'Azzan ibn-Qays to Atkinson, enclosure in Atkinson to Gonne, 30 Sept. 1868, no. 429: Masqat," "10 Dec. 1868, no. 558: Masqat," India Records–2, Vol. L.

Qays had a complete falling-out in the summer of 1869 after a British gunboat was hit by small arms fire while it lay off one of the Masqat forts. Disbrowe vehemently fought any idea of recognizing the conservative government. After he left Masqat early in 1870 Anglo–Omani relations improved, and late in 1870 Pelly changed his mind about the conservative regime and advocated recognition. It was decided after much deliberation to recognize 'Azzan ibn-Qays, but his government fell early in 1871 before the British relayed notice of their decision to Masqat.[79]

The first phase of the imam's stormy relations with the Sa'udis has been discussed. 'Azzan's refusal to pay tribute in 1868 was the first event in a series which led to the conquest of al-Buraymi in 1869. This action in turn caused the Sa'udi imam to send the following short letter to Imam 'Azzan: From 'Abdallah ibn-Faysal "Imam of the Muslims" to Sayyid 'Azzan ibn-Qays, "Imam of the Robbers. We have heard what you have done. We intend to pay you a visit with 20,000 men. We hope you will receive us suitably."[80] The winter of 1869-70 was one of dread in Oman as the country prepared for an expected Wahhabi counterattack and Imam 'Azzan and Ibrahim ibn-Qays, along with their armies, went to al-Buraymi to await the blow. The expected attack was never delivered, mainly because of the civil war between the brothers 'Abdallah ibn-Faysal and Sa'ud ibn-Faysal for control of the Sa'udi domain and also because of Sa'udi fears of Britain's reaction. Nevertheless, preparations for the defense of Oman against the expected attack aggravated the internal pressures within the imamate because of the extreme measures taken to raise revenue quickly.[81]

---

[79] Prasad, *India's Foreign Policy*, pp. 237-41; Lorimer, I, 487-90; a perusal of India Records–2, Vols. XVI, L, will indicate the opposition of Colonel Disbrowe to recognizing the conservative regime.

[80] " 'Abdallah ibn-Faysal to 'Azzan ibn-Qays, enclosure in Disbrowe to Gonne, 21 Aug. 1869, no. 465: Masqat," India Records–2, Vol. L.

[81] Al-Salimi, II, 257-63; *Précis Nejd*, pp. 32-37; Kelly, *Eastern Arabian Frontiers*, p. 88. Saudi Arabia, *Memorial*, I, 245.

Oman's Accommodation to a New Age

Imam 'Azzan's relations with Zanzibar grew progressively worse. Sultan Majid of Zanzibar lived in fear of an attempt by conservative Ibadi groups to attack or instigate revolution in Zanzibar in order to take over the island in 'Azzan's name. Majid, for his part, wished to see his branch of the Al Bu Sa'id family restored at Masqat. Therefore, late in 1869 Majid contacted his brother Turki ibn-Sa'id, a voluntary exile in India since 1867, to promote a counterattack on 'Azzan ibn-Qays which Turki would lead and Majid finance. In time Sultan Majid's scheme was destined to succeed; one reason the imamate was overthrown was the availability and the liberal use of Zanzibar gold in behalf of the moderate cause.[82]

The collapse of the conservative imamate. The internal situation in the imamate grew progressively worse in 1870. During the winter the country lived in fear of a Wahhabi attack. In the summer unrest among the bedouin tribes on the edge of al-Rub' al-Khali and among the Ghafiri tribes of Rus al-Jibal, al-Zahirah, and 'Uman grew to such proportions that the imam and Salih ibn-'Ali were forced to undertake military operations to end the disorder.[83] In September 1870 Masqat was hit by a strike protesting the imposition of a compulsory and heavy "war loan" on the citizenry. Meanwhile, unrest among the Hinawi tribes of Ja'lan and al-Sharqiyah, previously strong supporters of the imamate, grew dangerously.

But 'Azzan ibn-Qays doubtless could have solved his difficulties had not a strong rival, supported by foreign interests, appeared to contest his rule. Encouraged by Imam 'Azzan's troubles with the Sa'udis, and by promises of Zanzibari financing, Sayyid Turki ibn-Sa'id, son of Sayyid Sa'id and a popular figure in Oman, set forth to restore the moderate sultanate. Early in 1869, a time when the British still regarded Imam 'Azzan's regime very unfavorably, the limits on Turki's move-

[82] "Pelly to Duke of Argyll, 23 May 1870, despatch no. 166-4: Residency," "27 Aug. 1870, despatch no. 343-26: Residency," India Records–2, Vol. xvi.
[83] Al-Salimi, ii, 267; "Pelly to Duke of Argyll, 24 Sept. 1870, despatch no. 391-31: Residency," "8 Oct. 1870, despatch no. 433-33: Residency," India Records–2, Vol. xvi.

ments outside India were removed. But not until March 1870 did the Omani prince leave India for Bandar 'Abbas, when he took passage as a private passenger aboard a British steamship. There was a flutter of worry when Masqat learned of Turki's moves because 'Azzan's government thought that they might be approved by the British. After being received by Salim ibn-Thuwayni's old wazir, Hajji Ahmad, now the Persian governor of Bandar 'Abbas, Turki ibn-Sa'id sailed on to Dubayy on the Trucial Coast to organize his movement. He convinced the Trucial Coast shaykhs that he had British backing and that he expected some Sa'udi help as well. Nevertheless, although most Trucial Coast shaykhs were friendly to his cause Turki ibn-Sa'id could not gain the support of Zayid ibn-Khalifah of Abu-Dhabi, an ally of 'Azzan, nor of Shaykh Muhammad of the Nu'aym tribe. In actuality Turki ibn-Sa'id did not have British backing either. Indeed, Britain had warned the sayyid not to violate the maritime truce or attack Masqat unless the prince wished to be regarded as her enemy. In early June Turki, disheartened by his failure to find enthusiastic allies on the Trucial Coast, gave up the attempt to raise a coalition and returned to Bandar 'Abbas.[84]

In Bandar 'Abbas Turki ibn-Sa'id's failing spirit was revived when promises of massive financial support arrived from his brother, Sultan Majid ibn-Sa'id of Zanzibar. Turki ibn-Sa'id then organized a comprehensive program of bribing various strategically situated Omani shaykhs to defect from the imam and to transfer their support to him. Altogether, Turki received from Sultan Majid $MT 20,000 for immediate use, plus promises of $MT 30,000 as soon as one Omani port was taken and $MT 10,000 if the Sa'udi Amir Sa'ud could be convinced to provide further aid.[85] Turki's largesse could not be matched by the financially weak imam, and when in September 1870

[84] Al-Salimi, II, 266-67; Lorimer, I, 486; "Pelly to Duke of Argyll, 7 May 1870, despatch no. 147-2: Residency," India Records-2, Vol. XVI, Saudi Arabia, *Memorial*, I, 245-46.

[85] "Pelly to Duke of Argyll, 27 Aug. 1870, despatch no. 343-26: Residency," India Records-2, Vol. XVI.

Turki ibn-Sa'id landed on Rus al-Jibal he was joined by the shaykhs of the Trucial Coast states of Dubayy, 'Ajman, Ra's al-Khaymah, as well as by the chiefs of the Nu'aym and Bani-Qitab tribes. Gradually, Turki bought or convinced other tribes, particularly those of Ghafiri persuasion, to aid him. These included al-Janabah, al-Duru', al-Hubus and Al Wahi-bah.[86] 'Azzan ibn-Qays tried to concentrate a counterforce at Nazwa, but with the exception of Salih ibn-'Ali and a few other loyal shayks, most of 'Azzan's nominal supporters refused to advance into al-Zahirah to meet Turki's advance. In late October disaster struck the conservatives when Turki, after some indecisive sparring with Zayid ibn-Khalifah at al-Buraymi, moved southward. 'Azzan was forced to block this move or face the loss of Oman's inland provinces, so he began a march north despite dissension among his men and the desertion of some of his army. Just outside the town of Dank, Imam 'Azzan's column of 4,000 men and two guns entered a narrow defile only to be ambushed by Turki's waiting army. The imam suffered a loss of 400 men and fell back in some disorder to Masqat leaving Salih ibn-'Ali to defend al-Sharqiyah as best he could.[87] More tribes joined Turki ibn-Sa'id after his victory, and al-Zahirah and 'Uman were overrun by him. Turki ibn-Sa'id continued to advance until he reached Ja'lan where the Bani-Bu-'Ali and Bani-Bu-Hasan joined him and the augmented coalition forces marched on to Sur.[88]

By November 1870 Turki had spent almost $MT 80,000 on subsidies. But Majid ibn-Sa'id of Zanzibar died in November and it appeared that Turki's supply of money, the cement that held together his coalition, was exhausted. 'Azzan ibn-Qays, meanwhile, was regrouping his forces. For their part, the British issued another warning to Turki ibn-Sa'id about observing the maritime truce. So by December it appeared Turki had

[86] Al-Salimi, II, 267-69; Lorimer, I, 486.

[87] Al-Salimi, II, 267-69; "Pelly to Duke of Argyll, 5 Nov. 1870, despatch no. 520-45: Residency," India Records-2, Vol. XVI; Kelly, *Eastern Arabian Frontiers*, pp. 88-89.

[88] Al-Salimi, II, 269-70.

bogged down; even Pelly thought that there would be no attack on Masqat.[89]

But Pelly was wrong. Realizing he had to strike immediately or risk his army's dissolution, Turki divided his force. He led the main body from Sur back to Samad in al-Sharqiyah where Salih ibn-'Ali was entrenched. At the same time, he sent the Bani-Bu-'Ali and Bani-Bu-Hasan, normally blood enemies, straight up the coast to surprise Masqat. This force was led by Sayf ibn-Sulayman al-Bu-Sa'idi, ex-governor of Matrah under the previous moderate regime and Turki's chief assistant. Late in January 1871 Sayf ibn-Sulayman's column struck Matrah at night. 'Azzan ibn-Qays himself joined the hand-to-hand fighting on Matrah's walls and in the melee was shot and killed. Sayf ibn-Sulayman was also killed. But victory was with Turki ibn-Sa'id—Matrah and Masqat surrendered when news of the imam's death spread. When Turki, still engaged against Salih ibn-'Ali in al-Sharqiyah, heard of Masqat's fall he rushed to the capital city escorted by 500 camelmen to claim his prize.[90]

Al-Khalili did his best to preserve the disintegrating conservative regime. He barricaded himself in one of the Masqat harbor forts and tried to get Ibrahim ibn-Qays to take 'Azzan's place as imam. Al-Khalili even asked the British to guarantee Ibrahim ibn-Qays' rule in return for a yearly tribute of one-fourth of Masqat's revenues. Pelly gave a noncommittal answer and waited to see what would happen. Ibrahim, for his part, felt the situation was hopeless and escaped to Suhar. Finally, early in February 1871, Pelly intervened to lessen the chance of damage to trade and property and convinced al-Khalili to surrender when Turki agreed to the following conditions: (1) that al-Khalili would not be held responsible for the actions of Imam 'Azzan's regime, including the policy of prop-

[89] "Pelly to Duke of Argyll, 3 Dec. 1870, despatch no. 605-52: Residency," 30 Dec. 1870, despatch no. 665-65: Residency," India Records-2, Vol. XVI.

[90] Al-Salimi, II, 270-71; "Pelly to Duke of Argyll, 13 Feb. 1871, despatch no. 145-17: Residency," India Records-2, Vol. XVII.

erty confiscation; (2) that al-Khalili could reside where he wished under Turki's protection and that he should be escorted to his new home; (3) that all property remain in the hands of present owners; (4) that all claims and demands be regarded as settled; (5) that Turki ibn-Sa'id pay Imam 'Azzan's soldiers their wages; (6) that these provisions extend to all members of the conservative government and their dependents; and (7) that Pelly guarantee the agreement.[91] Despite this guarantee the agreement was not kept: al-Khalili died—followed by his son 48 hours later—in March 1871 amid circumstances that strongly suggested foul play, and the property confiscated by the imamate was returned to its original owners.[92]

The conservative imamate lasted just two and a quarter years. It failed, just as the sultanate between 1856 and 1868 failed, to accommodate Oman to a new age. One underlying reason for the conservative failure was their basic belief that they could in the nineteenth century govern a society according to the model of seventh century Mecca. Such a goal, while possible at the time in the remote interior of Oman, could not be achieved on Oman's coast. The desire of the imamate leaders to include all Oman—coast and interior—in their state doomed the conservative plan. More immediate causes for the failure of the imamate were its faulty administration of finance, the coastal economy, and foreign affairs; the serious policy disagreements that divided the ruling oligarchy; its failure to include significant Ghafiri elements as full participants in the state; and finally the gradual alienation of Hinawi tribes by the government's attempt to impose strong rule on Oman. Just like Salim's sultanate when it fell, the imamate in its last agony was practically deserted even by those who theoretically supported its aims.

[91] *Ibid.*; "Pelly to Duke of Argyll, 19 Feb. 1871, despatch no. 156:19: Residency," India Records–2, Vol. XVII.

[92] Al-Salimi, II, 272; Lorimer, I, 492; "Way to Pelly, 27 Mar. 1871, no. 170: Masqat," India Records–2, Vol. XVII; "Ross to Salisbury, 1 Sept. 1875, despatch no. 937-81: Residency," India Records–3, Vol. I.

CHAPTER 8

Reconstruction of the Moderate Regime, 1871-1903

THE upheaval and uncertainty that had characterized the course of Oman's history after 1856 did not end with Turki ibn-Sa'id's recovery of Masqat and the restoration of the sultanate in February 1871. Not until 1876 did the reestablished moderate regime display much real solidity and even after that year the sultan had to face serious threats to his rule. Nevertheless, the reign of Turki ibn-Sa'id was a significant one in Oman's history because it witnessed the rebuilding of the moderate government at Masqat upon a new foundation. However reluctantly it was done, the pillars that upheld Sayyid Sa'id's state were abandoned as the ultimate supports of the sultanate. In their place was substituted reliance on the Anglo–Indian government. The price of this dependence on foreign power was the acceptance by Oman's rulers of de facto if not de jure British paramountcy. However, this arrangement was tested severely by Turki ibn-Sa'id's son and successor, Faysal ibn-Turki, who assumed the dignity of sultan in 1888 with an unrealistically exalted belief in his own strength and his ability to sail a course independent of British tutelage. It was not until the first years of this century that Faysal ibn-Turki learned the facts of political survival in Oman. By 1903 he too had become convinced of the wisdom of his father's policy. Consequently, much of the essential design and many techniques of government which evolved in the time of Turki ibn-Sa'id have remained valid until our own day. Now, with the decline of British power in the Indian Ocean, with the rise of a new spirit of independence among the Arabs—including those of the Persian Gulf—and with the probability that oil revenue will overflow the coffers of the Masqati government, doubtless we will see significant changes made in the political apparatus of Oman within a very few years.

When he became Sultan of Masqat and Oman in 1871 Turki ibn-Sa'id was about thirty. The offspring of a union between the great Sayyid Sa'id and an Ethiopian mother, he was of dark complexion and an athletic build. He had a mild and liberal disposition, was courteous, diplomatic, and quite religious—all qualities that gave him considerable popularity before he had grown very old. While still in his teens he was established as the lord of Suhar under his father's suzerainty, a place he retained until he was captured and dispossessed by Sultan Thuwayni in 1861. Mention has already been made of his subsequent reconciliation with his brother, Thuwayni ibn-Sa'id, his near overthrow of Sultan Salim in 1867, his voluntary exile in India in 1867-70, and his ultimate triumph in his war with Imam 'Azzan ibn-Qays. All through these adventures Turki ibn-Sa'id's popularity, his pragmatic sense of political reality (especially his appreciation of the great power of the British) and his energy were apparent. After becoming sultan he was presented with the difficult problem of consolidating his regime, but just as it appeared he was on the verge of success he was hit in 1873 by a near fatal sickness whose symptoms suggest he suffered either a heart attack or a stroke. This sickness marks a watershed in Turki ibn-Sa'id's life; after it the bold, energetic actions that characterized the early phase of his career gave way to a less decisive, more introspective and passive style. After 1873 recurrent illnesses sapped the sultan's vitality. He began to suffer from chyluria, a disease which forced him to hobble about on crutches and which depressed his once high spirits. On more than one occasion during periods of sickness Turki was on the verge of abdication. During his final illness his mind failed altogether but even before this his sicknesses, plus his belief in sorcery—a superstition he shared with most of his contemporaries—led him into flights of fancy.

Nevertheless, despite his physical weakness it was the post-1873 phase of Turki ibn-Sa'id's life which was the most significant, for it was then that he began to cooperate with Sir Edward Ross and Colonel Miles, the British agent at Masqat throughout most of his reign, in reconstructing the bases of moderate rule in Oman. Perhaps Turki saw Oman's weakness as akin to his own personal weakness, but at any rate after 1873 he knew that he had to depend on others if he was to continue to rule and to hold his state together. Compromises were made with the British, some of which, particularly his bow to British wishes in the slave trade issue, cost the sultan much local popularity. But these compromises meant that in several crucial instances when the sultan's throne seemed ominously weak British power was available to shore it up. It seems certain that on occasion Turki ibn-Sa'id had grave doubts whether he was following the correct course but since he was unable to secure high quality loyal aids and advisors among the Omani elite and since he had seen British power in India with his own eyes, in the end his reliance on that power was without serious reservation. For their part, the British liked Turki; to them he was a trustworthy although rather weak ruler. It appears unlikely that the administration Turki constructed in Oman was the product of a well-reasoned plan; the sultan was not an intellectual, and after 1873 his prime joy apparently was spending his time in inactive leisure. Rather, the new machinery was built up over a long period as a pragmatic blend combining the application of traditional political procedures, an intensive employment of conciliatory techniques, and a dependence on British aid. It was manipulated by Turki ibn-Sa'id to head off trouble before it started, to create a climate where he would not have to expend a great deal of effort in punitive expeditions, and to preserve rather than extend the sultan's role in Oman. In a way, the manner in which the sultan used his government after 1873 reflected the relatively passive personal life that he was forced to live after his illness, in contrast to the activity which was the hallmark of his early career.[1]

The initial instability of Turki ibn-Sa'id's regime, 1871-76. The apparent strength of Turki ibn-Sa'id's government at the time of his triumph over the imamate in February 1871 was largely illusory. It is true that the new sultan had gained a sovereign's title and direct control of Masqat and Matrah while his tribal allies controlled many of Oman's interior strong points and held the port of Sur. But these allies had been attracted to the sultan's banner by the lavish subsidies which had bought their services as well as by a desire to rid themselves of the constant interference that characterized the government of Imam 'Azzan ibn-Qays. After February 1871 the coalition that brought Turki ibn-Sa'id to power began to disintegrate because both the coalition members' common enemy and the new sultan's money had disappeared. Because no more funds were forthcoming from Zanzibar's rulers—the source that had financed the drive to unseat the imam—and because the sultan was not a practiced financial manager in the early part of his reign, Turki ibn-Sa'id was unable to follow up his initial success.

The new regime faced plenty of enemies. The conservatives, although they were scattered and seriously weakened, had not been destroyed. They regarded the new sultan as a revolutionary usurper who had destroyed a religiously sanctioned and just government. Ibrahim ibn-Qays, the late imam's brother, still held Suhar and most of al-Batinah, a province that had been the fount of his family's strength since the late eighteenth century. Another of 'Azzan ibn-Qays' lieutenants, Faysal ibn-Hamud, was ensconced in the fortress of al-Rustaq which

---

[1] The sources on the life and character of Turki ibn-Sa'id are varied and scattered. See especially Lorimer, I, 501, 517-22; *Admin. Rpt.: 1888-1889*, p. 23; *Bombay Records—1886*, p. 287; "Ross to Salisbury, 6 June 1875, despatch no. 606-52: Residency," India Records–3, Vol. I; "Ross to Hartington, 4 Feb. 1882, despatch no. 8: Residency," "Miles to Ross, 7 July 1884, no. 192: Masqat," India Records–3, Vol. VI.

overlooks al-Batinah, while Salih ibn-'Ali still maintained his grip over al-Sharqiyah. Many Hinawi tribes had not been seduced by Turki's gold and could be expected to cause trouble. Also, Turki ibn-Sa'id had to contend with the disruptive ambitions of some of his close relatives who began plotting to gain power themselves rather than rallying to the side of the new champion of the moderate Ibadis. Chief among these family rivals was ex-Sultan Salim who, operating from exile on Qishm Island, schemed to regain supremacy. Also, 'Abd al-'Aziz ibn-Sa'id, Turki's younger brother, jealously eyed the throne. Fortunately for Turki ibn-Sa'id, some of the Ghafiri tribes continued to afford the new sultan enough support to maintain his new position in Masqat.[2]

Obviously, the most immediate danger to Turki ibn-Sa'id was posed by the concentration of conservative strength in al-Batinah under the leadership of Ibrahim ibn-Qays. Indeed, one of Turki's first moves after taking Masqat was to marshal his remaining resources in an attempt to clear al-Batinah and take Suhar. This drive was launched in June 1871 but was unsuccessful, and its failure depleted what little money was left in the sultan's treasury.[3] This was the beginning of three frustrating years for Turki as his repeated efforts to clear al-Batinah failed. Success finally came in 1874 only after British gunboats came to his assistance.

After the collapse of his June 1871 offensive the sultan resorted to less direct methods to strike at Ibrahim ibn-Qays. Realizing he had to break up the combination of forces that supported Ibrahim in al-Batinah if the conservative leader was to be dispossessed of the province, Turki ibn-Sa'id resorted to trickery and diplomacy. First, he agreed to partition Oman so that Ibrahim ibn-Qays would be left in control of Suhar and the rest of al-Batinah down to al-Khaburah. This agreement actually cost Turki ibn-Sa'id nothing in the way of territory

[2] Al-Salimi, II, 277; Lorimer, I, 491-93.

[3] Al-Salimi, II, 277-78; "Pelly to Duke of Argyll, 17 July 1871, despatch no. 783: Residency," India Records–2, Vol. XVIII.

since it merely recognized the existing state of affairs. By concluding the pact, however, the sultan may have hoped that he would shatter Ibrahim ibn-Qays' alliance system and infuriate those ultra-conservatives who thought that any compromise with the moderate regime was akin to apostasy.[4] Also, Turki ibn-Sa'id wrote a letter in June 1871 to the British resident in the Persian Gulf, Lewis Pelly, in which he brought up the subject of Ibrahim ibn-Qays' alliance with the able and powerful Zayid ibn-Khalifah, the shaykh of the strongest state on the Trucial Coast, Abu Dhabi. By late summer Turki's protest had moved Pelly to influence Zayid ibn-Khalifah to renounce his connection with Ibrahim ibn-Qays. A year later Turki ibn-Sa'id and Zayid ibn-Khalifah went so far as to conclude an alliance themselves. These developments were important because during the late nineteenth century Zayid ibn-Khalifah dominated the northern and inland approaches to al-Batinah, and anyone wishing to hold the province with a minimum of trouble required good relations with him. Significantly, the relations between Masqat and Abu Dhabi generally have continued to be friendly since 1872.[5]

These several stratagems resorted to by Turki ibn-Sa'id in an effort to deprive Ibrahim ibn-Qays of allies seemed so successful that in October 1871 the sultan felt himself able to resume the offensive in al-Batinah. At first the drive went well for the government because Ibrahim ibn-Qays' hold over Suhar was weakening steadily as his popularity in the region was declining. Ibrahim's resources were so low by the fall of 1871 that he began extorting revenue from Hindu merchants

[4] "Turki ibn-Sa'id to Way, 9 Aug. 1871, enclosure in Pelly to Duke of Argyll, 28 Aug. 1871, despatch no. 987-107: Residency," India Records–2, Vol. XVIII.

[5] "Turki ibn-Sa'id to Pelly, 17 June 1871, enclosure in Pelly to Duke of Argyll, 3 July 1871, despatch no. 703-87: Residency," India Records–2, Vol. XVII. "Turki ibn-Sa'id to Pelly, 20 Sept. 1872," India Records–2, Vol. XVI; see Kelly, *Eastern Arabian Frontiers*, chap. 3, for an account of Zayid ibn-Khalifah's ascendancy over the Trucial Coast during the late nineteenth century.

resident in Suhar. Finally, in December 1871 Ibrahim ibn-Qays sent a plea for aid to Salih ibn-'Ali in al-Sharqiyah.[6] This move produced some results, because Salih ibn-'Ali set up a very effective diversion which worried the sultan into holding back his advance into al-Batinah for most of 1872. To Turki ibn-Sa'id the most disturbing aspect of Salih ibn-'Ali's harrying tactics was the shaykh's sponsorship of a new move to put ex-Sultan Salim back on the Masqati throne. Probably Salih ibn-'Ali thought a restored Salim would be so dependent on him and on other conservative leaders that the ex-sultan could be nothing more than a pliable puppet. However, Salih ibn-'Ali, like the other major conservative leaders, lacked the money to transform his idea into a potent movement and the offensive that he finally launched was broken up by Turki-Sa'id's Ghafiri tribal allies before it achieved any momentum. The frustrated ex-Sultan Salim then left Oman in December 1872 never to return and Sultan Turki again was able to turn his attention to Ibrahim ibn-Qays and Suhar.[7]

The sultan's continued lack of money prevented him from mounting an energetic attack against Suhar until the situation changed radically in April 1873.[8] Turki ibn-Sa'id's money worries were due in no small way to the fact that since the day of his accession he had received no revenue from the Zanzibar subsidy because of a Whitehall–Calcutta disagreement over who should pay the charge. In April 1873 Sir Bartle Frere settled this difficulty when he decided to reward the sultan for signing the Anglo–Omani Slave Trade Treaty of 1873 by authorizing the Masqat government to draw $MT 40,000

---

[6] "Ibrahim ibn-Qays to Salih ibn-'Ali, 5 Dec. 1871, enclosure in Pelly to Duke of Argyll, 13 Jan. 1872, despatch no. 58-2: Residency," India Records –2, Vol. xx.

[7] Al-Salimi, II, 279; Lorimer, I, 493-95, 503; "Pelly to Duke of Argyll, 25 Mar. 1872, despatch no. 566-36: Residency," "6 Sept. 1872, despatch no. 1479-145: Residency," India Records–2, Vol. xx. Salim ibn-Thuwayni died in exile in India in 1876.

[8] "Miles to Ross, 8 Feb. 1873, no. 54-22: Masqat," India Records–2, Vol. xx.

immediately and $MT 20,000 three months later from the British Masqat Agency treasury, money which ultimately was charged against the Anglo–Indian government.[9] The flow of money into the sultan's starved exchequer revitalized his thitherto bankrupt regime. Soon troops were moving into position before Suhar where they linked up with levies supplied from the Nu'aym tribe, the shaykhs of Dubayy and Umm al-Qaywayn, and some locally recruited men. Badr ibn-Sayf, the sultan's commander on the Suhar front, advanced in July 1873; a short siege and a bombardment induced Ibrahim ibn-Qays to surrender the town in return for a compensation of $MT 5,000 plus a monthly subsidy of $MT 100. After his victory Badr ibn-Sayf was appointed wali of Suhar and various Al Bu Sa'id princes were given other posts in al-Batinah. The cost of the pacification of the province, including payments to the sultan's tribal and Trucial Coast allies, amounted to $MT 3,000.[10]

So it appeared in August 1873 that many of Turki ibn-Sa'id's troubles were solved. Salih ibn-'Ali and ex-Sultan Salim had been thwarted, al-Batinah had been occupied, Ibrahim ibn-Qays had become a pensioner of the sultan, newly revitalized alliances with tribal groups—especially those of Ghafiri persuasion—had calmed the interior, and the renewal of the Zanzibar subsidy had eased the government's revenue problem. It was just at this time, however, that Turki ibn-Sa'id was struck down by serious illness. Near death for several months and with his left arm paralyzed, Turki ibn-Sa'id never regained his old physical vigor.[11]

The sultan's old adversaries did not let the unexpected opportunity presented by Turki ibn-Sa'id's incapacity pass by. Ibrahim ibn-Qays, without a base after his expulsion from

9 "Frere to Miles, 15 Apr. 1873, enclosure in Ross to Duke of Argyll, 3 May 1873, despatch no. 571-49: Residency," India Records–2, Vol. xx.

10 Al-Salimi, II, 278-79; "Ross to Duke of Argyll, 28 July 1873, despatch no. 889-83: Residency," India Records–2, Vol. xxII.

11 *Ibid.*; Lorimer, I, 295.

Suhar but with his finances restored by the compensation he had received for surrendering the city, went to his uncle Faysal ibn-Hamud, the lord of al-Rustaq, and reached an agreement which stipulated that he could have al-Rustaq and the neighboring fortress of al-Hazm in return for a payment of $MT 2,200 and certain date groves. Faysal ibn-Hamud, thereupon, retired from public life, but Ibrahim ibn-Qays was once more, after the autumn of 1873, the possessor of a strong base from which to carry on his operations.[12] The situation became even more threatening in January 1874 when rumors spread that the sultan had died. Salih ibn-'Ali sought to take advantage of the confused situation by sponsoring a drive to set up the late imam's son, Hamud ibn-'Azzan, as ruler of a revived conservative regime. Accordingly, he requested that Ibrahim ibn-Qays launch a number of diversionary raids into al-Batinah while he, a force of 300 men from various Hinawi tribes, and young Hamud ibn-'Azzan moved down upon Matrah and Masqat. After avoiding the Ghafiri tribes blocking the way through Wadi Sama'il, Salih ibn-'Ali surprised and defeated a garrison of Wahhabi mercenaries under Badr ibn-Sayf, took Matrah, and plundered the port's bazaars. Sultan Turki, unable to leave his sickbed, was able to save Masqat and his throne only by bribing Salih ibn-'Ali with a sum of $MT 6,000 and 100 bags of rice. The sultan also had to promise that property confiscated by the late Imam 'Azzan and subsequently purchased by certain al-Sharqiyah Hinawi tribesmen—particularly those from Shaykh Salih's own tribe of al-Hirth—should be left in the hands of the purchasers, as well as that the property of the chief minister of the imamate, the late Sa'id ibn-Khalfan al-Khalili, should be returned to his family. A final insult was added when Salih ibn-'Ali stipulated that the sultan should publicly pardon him for any transgressions that he might have committed against the government. As a result of this attack and humiliating settlement, Sultan Turki's pres-

---

12 "Ross to Duke of Argyll, 4 Oct. 1873, despatch no. 1309-135: Residency," India Records–2, Vol. XXIII.

tige and treasury suffered severely. He was forced to request an advance in the Zanzibar subsidy in order to restore some semblance of strength to his exchequer but repairing his image was necessarily a more difficult maneuver.[13]

Meanwhile, Ibrahim ibn-Qays rather belatedly carried out the promise of aid he had made to Salih ibn-'Ali and moved into al-Batinah. After instigating an uprising by the conservative dominated Al Sa'd tribe in the coastal province, Ibrahim ibn-Qays himself captured the ports of Suwayq and al-Masna'ah in March 1874. Although the sultan's position looked particularly desperate at that point Ibrahim's move into the al-Batinah ports was to be a decisive turning point in the seesaw efforts of the moderate regime to consolidate its hold over Oman. That this was the case was the result of the fact that a Hindu merchant—a British subject—was killed during the plundering of al-Masna'ah's bazaars when Ibrahim ibn-Qays' men marched into the town. It had become customary under Lewis Pelly for the Anglo–Indian authorities in the Gulf to respond very energetically whenever the interests or lives of British subjects were threatened, a practice continued by Edward Ross. Accordingly, British gunboats arrived off the al-Batinah coast. On the orders of Colonel Miles, the British agent at Masqat, al-Masna'ah was bombarded on March 23, 1874. Miles also issued an ultimatum that Ibrahim ibn-Qays desist from all further attacks on the sultan and that his allies among the Al Sa'd tribe pay what at first seemed to be a staggering compensation of $MT 15,000 to pay for the damage their uprising had caused. Ibrahim ibn-Qays bitterly protested the British intervention, but since he was a practical man he made a nominal submission to the sultan in return for a restoration of his $MT 100 per month subsidy, then returned to al-Rustaq.[14]

---

[13] Al-Salimi, II, 280; Lorimer, I, 495-96; "Ross to Duke of Argyll, 31 Jan. 1874, despatch no. 134-12: Residency," "Turki ibn-Sa'id to Ross, 5 Feb. 1874," India Records–2, Vol. XXIV.

[14] Al-Salimi, I, 280-81; "Ibrahim ibn-Qays to Ross, 25 Mar. 1874, enclosure

The Al Sa'd, for their part, did not submit right away, and the British resident, Edward Ross, who had already received permission to take punitive action against Sultan Turki's tormentors, determined to act against the tribe. Ross reasoned that the Al Sa'd's property was particularly vulnerable to naval attack since it consisted largely of a four-mile deep line of thickly settled date groves and villages extending for more than twenty-five miles along al-Batinah's coast. In July 1874 two British gunboats arrived off the Al Sa'd territory fully prepared to carry out Ross's instructions to support the sultan "as far as guns of vessels of war will reach."[15] At the same time the regrouped army of Sultan Turki moved northward into the Al Sa'd populated district. Faced with this overwhelming power the tribe capitulated and, surprisingly, as early as January 1875 had paid all but $MT 400 of the reparations they owed.[16] Al-Batinah never again was to be a major source of conservative strength; it became, in fact, one of the Omani provinces most closely attached to the sultanate. Certainly the British armed interference of 1874 in the sultan's behalf was decisive in creating this shift in al-Batinah's alignment. This intervention might well have saved the sultanate itself.[17] Its lesson was lost neither on Turki ibn-Sa'ids enemies nor his friends: the sultan's cooperation with Britain was being repaid in very concrete fashion.

Meanwhile, the British also had played a role in Sultan Turki's efforts to solve another of his chronic troubles. From the beginning of his reign, but especially after the onset of his serious illness in August 1873, the sultan's effectiveness had

in Ross to Salisbury, 17 Apr. 1874, despatch no. 529-48: Residency," India Records–2, Vol. xxiv.

[15] "Government of India to Ross, 20 Jan. 1874, telegram no. 208-p," India Records–3, Vol. iii.

[16] "Ross to Salisbury, 30 July 1874, despatch no. 896-87: Residency," India Records–2, Vol. xxv; "Turki ibn-Sa'id to Miles, 16 Jan. 1875," India Records–3, Vol. i.

[17] "Ross to Salisbury, 20 May 1874, despatch no. 641-55: Residency," India Records–2, Vol. xxiv.

suffered because he lacked trustworthy, efficient advisors and lieutenants. In the spring of 1874 an effort was made to correct this weakness when Sultan Turki, with British approval, wrote his half-brother, 'Abd al-'Aziz ibn-Sa'id, requesting him to take over some of the burdens of government.[18] 'Abd al-'Aziz ibn-Sa'id accepted and became chief minister, or *wazir*. The new wazir was a young, vigorous, intelligent, but over-ambitious, prince. In some ways he reminds one of Sultan Turki in his own younger days. He had assisted the sultan for a time in 1871, but the two brothers argued constantly; ultimately 'Abd al-'Aziz ibn-Sa'id quit Masqat to establish himself in Gwadar in virtual independence. In 1873 he began plotting with the sultan's conservative enemies with a view toward securing the supremacy of Oman for himself. This foray into Oman's tangled politics ended ignominiously for the prince when British warships intercepted him on the high seas and deported him to Karachi where he was kept in "honorable detention," enjoying a pension of $MT 300 per month but unable to cause Sultan Turki more trouble. 'Abd al-'Aziz ibn-Sa'id was still in honorable detention in India when the invitation to become Sultan Turki's chief minister arrived.[19]

The two half-brothers got along well for the balance of 1874. But disagreements broke out anew in 1875 because of the ill sultan's partiality for certain ignorant, unscrupulous companions who began usurping 'Abd al-'Aziz's role of advisor and also because of the wazir's conviction that the government should base itself primarily on Hinawi rather than Ghafiri support. In August 1875 'Abd al-'Aziz forced the issue by submitting his resignation. Sultan Turki, still in very poor health and unable to rule alone, thereupon decided to leave the government in 'Abd al-'Aziz ibn-Sa'id's hands and take an extended vacation in Gwadar. So from August to December 1875 'Abd al-'Aziz ruled Oman as Sultan Turki's regent.[20]

[18] "Turki ibn-Sa'id to 'Abd al-'Aziz ibn-Sa'id, 1 May 1874," India Records–2, Vol. xxiv.

[19] Lorimer, I, 493-95, 498.   [20] *Admin. Rpt.: 1875-1876*, p. 75.

One of the main reasons Sultan Turki left Masqat for Gwadar in August 1875 was his discouragement over the collapse of his tribal policy. His troubles had begun a year and a half before when many of his Ghafiri allies were alienated by the settlement of January 1874, which Salih ibn-'Ali had forced from the invalided ruler and which, among other things, recognized the legality of many of his confiscations carried out in the time of 'Azzan ibn-Qays. These had transferred a large amount of Ghafiri property into the hands of conservative Hinawi owners. Also, an attempt of the sultan's in the summer of 1874 to mediate some disputes among the Ghafiri tribes of Wadi Sama'il backfired when the ruler's decisions pleased nobody and angered all. Tribal unrest became chronic after the summer of 1874 and grew steadily worse in 1875. By 1875 large-scale Hinawi–Ghafiri tribal warfare, fed by disagreement over who controlled the "confiscated estates," broke out and extensive damage was done to date groves and other property. Meanwhile, the sultan's government, under the immediate administration of 'Abd al-'Aziz ibn-Sa'id, fell more and more under Hinawi influence. This developed to the point in the early summer of 1875 that Sultan Turki was induced to dismiss his guard of Wahhabi mercenaries and substitute a guard recruited from Hinawi tribal elements. The sultan, therefore, was no longer able to maintain any sort of neutrality since his Hinawi praetorians were in a position to force decisions upon him. Turki ibn-Sa'id became so discouraged by August 1875 that Colonel Miles was hard put to prevent him from abdicating instead of merely appointing a temporary regent.[21]

The character of 'Abd al'Aziz ibn-Sa'id's regency was conservative. The regent relied on Hinawi support, and naturally Ghafiri groups opposed him. Even more controversial, however, was 'Abd al-'Aziz ibn-Sa'ids's open flirtation with the conservative forces that had caused so much trouble for his half-brother, the sultan. Salih ibn-'Ali himself became a major advisor to the regent and mutawwi's began flocking into

[21] Lorimer, I, 497.

Masqat as they had in the days of Imam 'Azzan. Even the anti-pleasure laws of the imamate were reintroduced. The British took a very dim view of what was developing and continued to pay the Zanzibar subsidy to the sultan in his Gwadar retreat. This meant that Turki ibn-Sa'id still controlled enough financial resources to reestablish himself in Oman if and when his health permitted.

The long vacation at Gwadar worked wonders on Sultan Turki's physical health and restored his spirits as well, so he was ready to return to his capital late in 1875. Certain that 'Abd al-'Aziz ibn-Sa'id would oppose his resumption of power, the sultan quietly slipped back to Masqat and took up his task in December 1875 during a time when the regent was absent from the city. The sultan's suspicions of his half-brother's loyalty proved correct because 'Abd al-'Aziz, when he learned of Turki ibn-Sa'id's return, immediately raised a force to drive the returned monarch out of the country. The timely arrival of Ghafiri aid in Masqat ended this threat and so 'Abd al-'Aziz ibn-Sa'id fled into the interior, rallied some support, and entrenched himself in Wadi Sama'il. The defiance ended when Sultan Turki marched up into the Wadi Sama'il in February 1876 at the head of an army and bombarded his half-brother into exile. 'Abd al-'Aziz ibn-Sa'id continued to wander from place to place in interior Oman for another 14 years in a vain attempt to organize a successful drive to topple the sultanate. Turki ibn-Sa'id, in any event, could not have picked a better time to return to Masqat. The long months of upheaval and civil conflict had so exhausted Oman's tribes that the sultan was able to establish peace fairly easily throughout the country and, in the process, reestablish good relations with his old Ghafiri allies.[22]

Turki's resumption of rule and pacification of Oman during the winter of 1875-76 marked the finish of the initial, chronically unstable, period of his rule. He moved with

[22] *Ibid.*, pp. 502-504; Al-Salimi, II, 281; *Admin. Rpt.: 1875-1876*, pp. 75-76.

remarkable vigor in the first months of 1876, and by the end of the year had restyled his government so as to show that he had profited from his earlier uncertainty and mistakes in administration.

The defense of the moderate regime, 1876-88. With his resumption of rule late in 1875 Turki ibn-Sa'id's fortunes improved. One factor contributing to the relative success of the later years of his reign was that Oman's commerce recovered somewhat from the depression of the 1860s due to an increase in date exports to India and the United States. Political unrest within Oman was by no means stilled between 1876 and 1888, but the situation never deteriorated to the point of virtual anarchy as it had several times during the first five years of the sultan's reign. Conservative Ibadi groups in interior Oman remained as a danger to the sultanate and in 1877 and 1883 conservative armies were able to launch determined attacks against the sultan, but in both instances British gunboats arrived to aid the sultan.

Also contributing to the post-1876 strength of the sultanate was an increasing disarray in the conservative ranks. Lacking an outstanding religious–intellectual leader of the caliber of the late Sa'id ibn-Khalfan al-Khalili, the conservative cause was unable to sustain the support it had once commanded nor could it attract many new adherents of real importance and strength. Muhammad ibn-Sulayyim al-Gharibi, of al-Batinah, was the most learned figure in the conservative camp during the early years of Turki ibn-Sa'id's rule, but this onetime pillar of Imam 'Azzan's government made his peace with the sultan in 1876.[23] Salih ibn-'Ali was the most prominent tribal leader, while Ibrahim ibn-Qays and Faysal ibn-Hamud were also influential among the conservatives; but cooperation among these men was so minimal that by 1876 the fundamentalist wing of Ibadism was split into numerous factions. Salih ibn-'Ali always seemed suspicious of any movement or enterprise

[23] "Muhammad ibn-Sulayyim al-Gharibi to Turki ibn-Sa'id, 4 Oct. 1876," India Records–3, Vol. II.

he did not direct while Ibrahim ibn-Qays in his later years enjoyed the subsidy he received from the sultan too much to give more than halfhearted support to projected coalitions.[24] Even if they had been able to combine, the conservative factions—particularly after the loss of al-Batinah in 1874—could not have equaled the sultan's British-guaranteed financial resources and his consequent ability to subsidize tribal supporters. Nor could they call on powerful allies in the way that Sultan Turki could request British aid in emergencies. In order to finance an attack on Masqat in 1883 Salih ibn-'Ali had to mortgage his personal property to the amount of $MT 9,000.[25]

Still, although their appeal was more limited than in the 1860s, conservative aims held the loyalty of many Omanis. The conservative program retained the same theoretical basis that supported 'Azzan ibn-Qays' successful revolution and his imamate. For instance, prior to attacking Masqat in 1877 conservative propagandists revived the same accusations of "irreligiousness and laxity of morals" among the sultan's followers that were part of their propaganda stock in 1868.[26] During Sultan Turki's reign the ultimate goal of the established conservative leaders that had been associated with 'Azzan ibn-Qays, men like Salih ibn-'Ali, remained the restoration of an 1868-style imamate that would include Masqat and Oman's coast, as well as its interior. After 1876, however, certain younger men were rising among the conservatives who in time were to embrace the idea that the imamate should restrict itself to the interior and not include Masqat and the coast.[27] When the imamate was in fact revived under Salim ibn-Rashid al-Kharusi

[24] "Miles to Ross, 12 Dec. 1874, no. 557-216: Masqat," India Records–2, Vol. xxv; Lorimer, I, 516.

[25] "Mockler to Ross, 22 July 1883, no. 182: Masqat," India Records–3, Vol. vi.

[26] "Prideaux to Salisbury, 4 May 1877, despatch no. 10: Residency," India Records–3, Vol. iii.

[27] "Muslim ibn-'Ubayd to Turki ibn-Sa'id, 2 Mar. 1879," India Records–3, Vol. iv, contains an early expression of this view.

in 1913 it limited itself to the interior after Anglo–Indian troops turned back a drive against the coast. This bit of expediency enabled the imamate to survive in Oman until 1955. But from 1876 to 1913 the general insistence of most fundamentalist leaders that Masqat be included in any revived imamate was a basic cause for the frustration of conservative political goals, because the British opposed their rule on any part of the Omani shore to the point where they would intervene with armed force to crush those conservative combinations which held designs upon Masqat and the coast.

During the last 12 years of Turki ibn-Saʿid's reign, in addition to the usual tribal uprisings, he had to contend with two major conservative efforts to unseat him. Both drives displayed a similar pattern. The first was an attack on the Masqat–Matrah district delivered by 1500 men under the leadership of Salih ibn-ʿAli in June 1877. Achieving surprise, the attackers were able to occupy Matrah and plunder its bazaars, but Masqat itself was defended successfully by its 200-man garrison until the arrival of *H.M.S. Teazer*. The British gunboat shelled Salih's men until they abandoned their assault. Before leaving the Masqat area Salih ibn-ʿAli tried to frighten the sultan into giving him $MT 20,000 in return for his withdrawal, but Turki ibn-Saʿid knew the enemy was beaten and refused, an action which sent the sultan's prestige soaring throughout Oman.[28]

The conservative advance in 1883 was precipitated by a failure on Sultan Turki's part to prevent disorders from breaking out among his allies, the Ghafiri tribes of Wadi Samaʾil. These were charged with blocking the passes through which almost any attack on Masqat that originated in Oman's interior had to come. The al-Rahbiyin and al-Nidabiyin, disgruntled over Sultan Turki's admission of another local Ghafiri tribe, the Bani-Jabir, into the pass defense system, temporarily defected to Salih ibn-ʿAli. The sultan desperately tried to

28 Al-Salimi, II, 281; "Prideaux to Salisbury, 5 July 1877, despatch no. 15: Residency," India Records–3, Vol. IV.

soothe the trouble but was unsuccessful. In October 1883 Salih ibn-'Ali, together with the sultan's half-brother, 'Abd al-'Aziz ibn-Sa'id, led contingents from the Hinawi tribes of al-Hirth, al-Hubus, and Hajariyin through the undefended pass and descended on Masqat. The most spectacular feature of this attack was a charge against Masqat's walls in the dead of night by black-robed assault teams. Turki ibn-Sa'id himself helped to man the walls of his capital that night and contributed to the repulse of the attackers who left 70 dead behind them. Meanwhile, because an attack seemed imminent after the failure of the sultan to close the passes, the British already had sent *H.M.S. Philomel* to Masqat to aid in the city's defense. When the crisis came its firepower contributed to the defeat of the conservatives.[29] This particular episode ended when 3000 Ghafiri reinforcements arrived at Masqat to scatter the remaining attackers and Prince Faysal ibn-Turki, the sultan's son and heir, led 1700 men into Wadi Sama'il to punish the tribes that allowed Salih ibn-'Ali's force to pass through their territory unmolested.[30] As a result of this victory Sultan Turki's prestige was so enhanced that he never had to contend with any attacks on Masqat for the rest of his reign. It is well to point out, however, that the British declaration of 1886, which promised to uphold the existing ruler in all eventualities, certainly contributed to the climate of peace and political stability which marked the sultan's last years of rule. Besides these two attacks led by Salih ibn-'Ali the only other conservative thrusts of any consequence were two diffident ventures by Ibrahim ibn-Qays who ventured out of al-Rustaq and into al-Batinah in 1881 and 1883; each time Ibrahim ibn-Qays abandoned his adventure when the sultan threatened to cut off his pension.[31]

[29] Al-Salimi, ii, 281-82; Lorimer, i, 508-12; "Ross to Kimberley, 9 Nov. 1883, despatch no. 36: Residency," India Records–3, Vol. vi.

[30] Lorimer, i, 508-12; "Faysal ibn-Turki to Turki ibn-Sa'id, 12 Nov. 1883, enclosure in Jayakar to Ross, 26 Nov. 1883, no. 313a: Masqat," India Records–3, Vol. vi.

[31] Lorimer, i, 516; *Admin. Rpt.: 1881-1882*, pp. 13-15.

By the time of his death in 1888, Turki ibn-Sa'id claimed at least the tacit allegiance of most Omanis. His rule was not particularly a strong one but his walis did govern in all the major coastal cities and such interior towns as Nazwa and Izki in 'Uman, as well as in Nakhl and Sama'il in the Wadi Sama'il district. Even al-Rustaq and some of the al-Sharqiyah towns occasionally pledged their submission although this happened usually at a time when the local political leaders were low on funds and were seeking a subsidy from the sultan. Most tribal areas remained at least nominally friendly to the Masqat government, although elements from the Hinawi tribes of al-Hirth, Hajariyin, and al-Hubus joined all the combinations which menaced the sultan during his reign.[32] The fact that Turki ibn-Sa'id was succeeded by his son Faysal ibn-Turki peacefully and without a succession struggle indicates the quality of the order established between 1876 and 1888. For the first time since the eighteenth century violence did not accompany a change of ruler at Masqat.

The structure and operation of the moderate government, 1876-88. The relative efficiency of the government of Turki ibn-Sa'id after 1876 is a testimony to the appropriateness of the political policies and administrative practices adopted by the sultan when he reorganized his government. Evidence of this is also provided by the fact that the arrangement worked out during Sultan Turki's reign has survived in its essentials down to the present. As was stated earlier the system was a blend which combined the application of well-tested indigenous political procedures, an intensive employment of conciliatory and arbitration techniques, and the use of British aid. It took time for the capabilities of this machinery to be developed and constant tinkering and modification of it continued throughout Sultan Turki's reign.

The major innovation added by Turki ibn-Sa'id to the inventory of administrative processes customarily used by ear-

[32] Lorimer, I, 510; *Admin. Rpt: 1878-1879*, p. 116.

339

lier moderate rulers was his open use of and dependence on British support. Reliance on the Anglo–Indian government's aid was substituted for the strength that formerly came from trade and shipping revenues in the days of Sayyid Saʿid. During Sultan Turki's time the growth of Britain's imperial interests in the Persian Gulf region coincided with the Masqat government's need to find a new prop to replace the vanished economic prosperity that had energized the pre-1856 regime. Thus it was in the interests of both the British and the moderate sultanate to tighten their mutual bonds and deepen channels of mutual assistance. From 1874 on, British aid to Turki ibn-Saʿid provided a combination of military help in emergencies, a regular financial subsidy, the detention in India of would-be rivals of the sultan, ready advice on solving governmental problems, diplomatic services, and in 1886 went so far as to specifically guarantee the stability of the sultan's rule on Oman's coast by publicly declaring that no change in government there would be tolerated. The price for this support was the sultan's acceptance of various British-sponsored policies or programs even if these might be locally unpopular, such as the Anglo–Omani Slave Trade Treaty of 1873.

Turki ibn-Saʿid, unlike Sultans Thuwayni, Salim, and Imam ʿAzzan ibn-Qays, saw the problems vexing Oman since 1856 in their essential perspective. He realized his situation was not the same as the one found by Sayyid Saʿid and that policies that had worked 20 years earlier were no longer applicable to the Oman of the later nineteenth century. In particular, he saw that the intrinsic strength of the sultanate had evaporated to the point where he could no longer maintain the moderate government in Oman solely by relying upon his independent resources. Turki ibn-Saʿid, always a realist, recognized that if he had British power backing him he need fear no coalition of hostile Omani forces. In the final analysis, he was willing to cooperate with the British in any way if in return he could assure their support for his regime. Maintaining close ties with Britain was the keystone of his policy.[33] But the sultan also had to govern as best he could in Oman with the means he found available. One reason the British were willing to help Sultan Turki was that they judged him to be the best hope for providing stability and peace in the country.[34] Since the prime aim of Turki ibn-Sa'id was to preserve order and the rule of his moderate government most of the day-to-day tasks of administration that required his attention involved tribal matters. To cope with these and other political problems Sultan Turki had to depend on a traditional administrative apparatus, albeit one strengthened by British aid. In a large sense the entire structure of moderate government was merely an extension of the person of the sultan. As is true in most personal monarchies if the ruler, or his designated chief minister, is able and energetic then the machinery of government moves; if he neglects his duties the system falters. If there were no statutory limits to the sultan's absolutism, his actual power was severely restricted because of the limitations imposed by Oman's geography, political and social structure, religious–intellectual ideology, and economy. It is well to recall also that the sultan's government was one which reflected forms that had evolved in the traditional Persian Gulf city-state monarchies of secular and commercial orientation. Unlike an imam whose power derived from ancient Islamic religious and moral considerations, a sultan's power rested more on the rule's skill in wielding purely political resources and on his personal prestige and ability.

Until Sultan Turki reorganized his regime in the mid-1870s, government in Oman was largely a shared responsibility of the members of the senior branch of the Al Bu Sa'id tribe.

---

[33] Lorimer, I, 522; "Turki ibn-Sa'id to Governor of Bombay, 12 Feb. 1871, enclosure in Pelly to Duke of Argyll, 13 Feb. 1871, despatch no. 154-34: Residency," India Records–2, Vol. xvii; Prasad, *India's Foreign Policy*, p. 240.

[34] Lorimer, I, 517-22; "Minute Paper, India Office, 17 Dec. 1874," India Records–2, Vol. xxv; "Ross to Kimberley, 9 Nov. 1885, despatch no. 36-9: Residency," India Records–3, Vol. vi.

The sultan himself was at one and the same time the ruler of the country and the head of the royal house. His aids were drawn mainly from the ranks of the Al Bu Sa'id, although aristocrats from other tribes and some leading Masqat businessmen of both local and Indian extraction also served; few men of humble origin reached high positions. Turki retained this system to a large degree after 1876, although he was less dependent than his moderate predecessors had been on the help of his close kinsmen, and he began the practice of regularly seeking the counsel and professional administrative advice of the resident British agent. Colonel Miles, who filled this post for most of Turki ibn-Sa'id's reign, as well as Colonel Ross, Miles's immediate superior in the Gulf, both enjoyed a very close relationship with the sultan, who kept them well informed about the course of Omani events. One reason the local representatives of the Anglo–Indian government gained such influence within the Masqati government, in addition to their skillful handling of the sultan, was that throughout his reign Sultan Turki suffered from a lack of effective, dedicated Omani advisors.

Although he sought—and largely was successful in maintaining—friendly relations with most of his close Al Bu Sa'id relatives we have noted the sultan's troubles with his half-brother, 'Abd al-'Aziz ibn-Sa'id, and with ex-Sultan Salim ibn-Thuwayni. In 1876 he was forced to deport to Qishm his nephews Muhammad, Hamud, and Hamdam, all sons of Thuwayni ibn-Sa'id, because they joined 'Abd al-'Aziz ibn-Sa'id's intrigues. Sultan Turki's own sons Muhammad, Faysal, and Fahd were each associated with their father's government as walis of districts or of cities. Muhammad ibn-Turki, the oldest son, was wali of Suhar between 1878 and 1884, but he proved to be so incompetent as an administrator that the sultan decided to recognize his young second son, Faysal ibn-Turki, as heir apparent. In summary, Turki ibn-Sa'id was unable to rely on his immediate family for strong support.[35]

[35] Lorimer, I, 511-12.

Theoretically, a wazir, or chief minister, served as the sultan's senior assistant and advisor, but with the exception of 'Abd al-'Aziz ibn-Sa'id's term in this post, the office was never held by a powerful, able personality during Sultan Turki's tenure. Indeed, Turki ibn-Sa'id's first wazir was Thuwayni ibn-Muhammad, the Al Bu Sa'id prince who similarly had served Sultans Thuwayni and Salim but who was dismissed during the latter's reign for engaging in dishonest and corrupt practices. Thuwayni ibn-Muhammad was no better a wazir for Sultan Turki, and before 1871 was over the sultan wished to be rid of him. It was this wazir, a very jealous man, who first instigated the unfortunate rift that grew up between Turki ibn-Sa'id and 'Abd al-'Aziz ibn-Sa'id. But Thuwayni ibn-Muhammad hung on as Sultan Turki's wazir until early in 1873 when he was finally dismissed for his complicity in the murder of Nasr ibn-'Ali, the wali of Masqat. He died a short time after his fall when he was shot down in the capital's streets by vengeful supporters of the murdered wali.[36] Sultan Turki did not appoint a new wazir and he was acting as his own prime minister in August 1873 when he was struck down by illness. Without an active sultan or a wazir the moderate government drifted aimlessly until 'Abd al-'Aziz ibn-Sa'id became chief minister in the spring of 1874. But 'Abd al-'Aziz's self-serving conduct as wazir and as regent until December 1875 must have contributed to the sultan's growing exasperation with his Al Bu Sa'id assistants.

Ultimately, Sultan Turki found his man—Sa'id ibn-Muhammad, another Al Bu Sa'idi, the brother of the late wazir Thuwayni ibn-Muhammad, and long an official in Turki's government. An intimate of the sultan since the early days of his reign, Sa'id ibn-Muhammad was appointed wazir immediately after Turki ibn-Sa'id resumed direction of the Masqati government in December 1875. Sa'id ibn-Muhammad was a compe-

[36] *Ibid.*, p. 489; "Pelly to Duke of Argyll, 1 Nov. 1871, despatch no. 1,234-140: Residency," India Records–2, Vol. XIX; "Miles to Ross, 8 Feb. 1873, no. 54-22: Masqat," India Records–2, Vol. XX.

tent if not brilliant official whose entire public career was spent in the service of the sultanate. He was not a particularly original person who could be counted on to supply new ideas —evidently this role was filled by the Anglo–Indian officials accredited to Masqat—rather, he was a loyal functionary who carried out orders. Sa'id ibn-Muhammad's career was typical of those who served in high posts in the administration of the sultanate. His first commission was under Sultan Thuwayni ibn-Sa'id, for whom he supervised food and transport matters. He served Turki ibn-Sa'id as a wali in Masqat prior to becoming wazir. He was popular with the British because he favored close ties with them. Also, he was an advocate of conciliating the Ghafiri tribes and was much disliked by conservatives. As wazir one factor that limited his influence was his bitter rivalry with another of Sultan Turki's assistants, Badr ibn-Sayf, who was the monarch's friend and chief military aid. During Turki ibn-Sa'id's final illness in 1888 Sa'id ibn-Muhammad was dismissed and exiled to Qishm because the sultan suspected his wazir of practicing "sorcery," but the wazir resumed his high post under Sultan Faysal in 1896.[37]

Sultan Turki's charge that his wazir was a sorcerer is an example of the superstition that periodically clouded his judgment, especially during periods of illness. For instance, from 1872 to 1875—and particularly after his health failed in 1873 —he placed much trust in a former sugar cane merchant named Numaysh, an unscrupulous, Rasputin-type of individual who evidently claimed magical powers. Numaysh was paid a salary $MT 15 a month yet before he lost influence he had amassed a fortune of some $MT 40,000 through graft and influence peddling. Even after 'Abd al-'Aziz ibn-Sa'id became wazir in 1874, Numaysh retained the sultan's confidence, and it was

[37] *Admin. Rpt.: 1875-1876*, pp. 75-76; *Admin. Rpt.: 1901-1902*, pp. 10-11; "Pelly to Duke of Argyll, 5 June 1871, despatch no. 563-72: Residency," India Records–2, Vol. xvii; "Miles to Ross, 12 June 1878, no. 16: Masqat," India Records–3, Vol. iii; "Euan-Smith to Ross, 17 Oct. 1879, no. 410: Masqat," India Records–3, Vol. iv; Lorimer, i, 511.

not until the wazir became regent in August 1875 that the ex-dealer in sugar cane retired from politics. After Sultan Turki's return to Masqat in December 1875 his British advisors used to warn him on occasion against trusting people such as Numaysh who sought to take advantage of the sovereign's loneliness, gullibility, or dark moods.[38] Besides the wazir, the sultan was also assisted by certain general troubleshooters and special advisors. Such was Badr ibn-Sayf who variously served as commander of Sultan Turki's armies, factfinder, and wali at Suhar between 1873 and 1878 and at Matrah after 1879. Another such figure was Sulayman ibn-Suwaylim who was an African slave of the sultan but whose abilities allowed him to become his master's private secretary and then a wali in a number of trouble-prone places such as the port of Sur or the newly annexed South Arabian district of Dhofar.[39] A forceful and energetic man, Sulayman ibn-Suwaylim's career illustrates how high a slave of ability could rise in Oman.

The lesser officials attached to the sultan's government worked as members of the sultan's personal entourage, as assistants to the wazir, or as aides to one of the ruler's special advisors. The central apparatus of government included a fluctuating number of loosely organized bureaus. Apparently, each of these was under the active supervision of a secretary, or *katib*.[40] Too much should not be made of the formal organization of the government, since many and various kinds of tasks were assigned on an ad hoc basis to different individuals who happened to be convenient to the ruler at a given time. The problem of finding and recruiting men able to discharge administrative tasks effectively must have been considerable.

---

[38] "Miles to Ross, 16 July 1873, no. 327-121: Masqat," India Records-2, Vol. xxiii; "Ross to Salisbury, 11 June 1875, despatch no. 606-52: Residency," "Ross to Salisbury, 6 Aug. 1875, despatch no. 825-69: Residency," India Records-3, Vol. i.

[39] Lorimer, i, 511; *Admin. Rpt.: 1875-1876*, pp. 75-76; al-Salimi, ii, 221.

[40] *Admin. Rpt.: 1901-1902*, pp. 10-11; "Prideaux to Salisbury, 4 May 1877, despatch no. 10: Residency," India Records-3, Vol. iii.

Certainly, family connections played a key role in determining job qualifications. Most officeholders of any consequence were members of an elite consisting of close relatives of the sovereign or of families that habitually had supported the moderate Al Bu Sa'id government. They in turn were usually assisted by their personal retainers. Since education in Oman went little beyond providing a grounding in religious fundamentals, most administrative or military training was of the on-the-job variety. Moreover, so varied were the functions of an officer of the sultan that his exact duties were not well defined. That this system of administration by a governing elite without much professional administrative training had its limitations is well attested by the sultan's reliance on the Indian business community of Masqat to minister to his financial requirements. Also, the sultan had to steer a zigzag course among the personal rivalries, tribal feuds, and family ambitions that were too often the primary concern of his assistants. Sultan Turki, like Omani rulers before and after him, had his problems in harnessing an unruly governing elite to his administrative machine. Men like Sa'id ibn-Muhammad or Badr ibn-Sayf, loyal as they were to Turki ibn-Sa'id, were—with all their limitations—virtually the best kind of official available to the sultanate. It is small wonder that Turki ibn-Sa'id turned occasionally to favorites such as Numaysh or, on the other hand, decided his survival in an uncertain age depended on consulting really strong, capable, and trustworthy allies such as his British "advisors" proved to be.

The provincial administration directly responsible to the Masqati government was even more unsophisticated than the central apparatus. Most of the chief towns of Oman were governed by walis who, according to their means, inclinations, and abilities, carried out the sultan's orders. Many Al Bu Sa'id "sayyids" held posts as walis, often considering the areas they governed virtual hereditary fiefs. Nominally at least, the wali acted in the sultan's name as the chief military-police, judicial, and financial officer within his jurisdiction. The wali of Masqat's post was the most prestigious among the local governorships, but the holder of this office, because of the sultan's proximity, actually had less independence than some of the other walis. Next to the walis of Masqat, those of Matrah and Suhar were considered the most important; those of Sama'il and Dhofar were also posts of consequence. The organization supervised by the wali of Suhar was the most complex of the Omani governorships. Suhar's governor was served by deputy walis at Sahm, Liwa, and Shinas, as well as by officers commanding military outposts overlooking passes leading out of the Hajar Mountains into al-Batinah. For the most part, a wali's real power did not extend far beyond the limits of the town which served as his seat. In country districts the walis' influence was insignificant compared to that of the shaykhs of the local tribes. In the interior it was not unusual for the sultan to recognize a tribe's de facto control of an area or to honor an important tribal ally by investing the tribal shaykh as wali of the chief town of the district.[41]

The administrative tasks performed by the sultan's government inside Oman were concerned mainly with maintaining order, assuring justice, and raising and spending money. The sultan's capability for direct administration was limited almost exclusively to Masqat and Matrah, a few other coastal towns, and some outlying points such as Sama'il, Gwadar in Baluchistan, and Salalah in Dhofar. In rural, tribal-controlled areas —that is, in most of Oman—the sultan's influence was indirect at best and was filtered through the shaykhs and the elders of the many tribes. The ruler's role in most places was to attempt to act as a peacemaking balance leaving actual administration to local chiefs.

In the towns and suburban districts under the sultan's control, order was maintained by the garrisons of the walis, while civil and criminal justice was dispensed by the sultan's officials. The sultan himself was a court of final appeal, and it was normal that cases of murder and extreme personal abuse

41 Lorimer, II, 1,418-25.

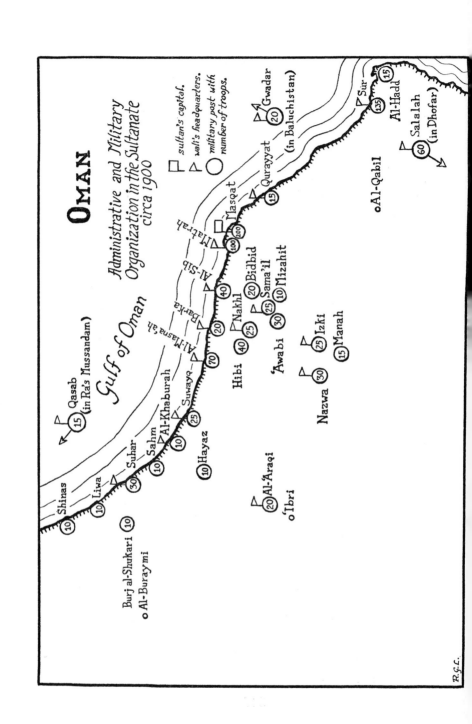

OMAN

Administrative and Military
Organization in the Sultanate
circa 1900

□ sultan's capital.
△ wali's headquarters.
◯ military post with
  number of troops.

Gulf of Oman

be tried by the sultan personally if it were possible to do so. In Oman, murder was the only crime punishable by death; murderers were often executed according to the same method they had used to kill their victims. In practice, certain political crimes, such as treason, also might earn the death of the guilty party, but such political murders were not condoned by law. Lesser offenses were tried occasionally by walis, usually by judges or qadis, and rarely by panels of qadis. The decisions of these courts normally were reported to the sultan. Besides the Koran no written legal code existed, although many commentaries on Ibadi law were available and were used by those qadis who boasted some religious-legal training. Depending on the particular judge who was hearing a case, a matter might be decided either by conservative or moderate Ibadi interpretations, and in the latter situation the literal requirements of the Koran might be modified. It was common practice to try to influence judgments by offering bribes. In tribal areas the local shaykhs, often together with the tribal elders, administered the tribe's customary law and the sultan seldom was involved in decisions. However, in complicated cases or in disputes among members of different tribes a respected local qadi might be consulted and in intertribal disputes the sultan, or one of his walis, was often asked to mediate. Usually misdemeanors were punished with a few blows of a stick, while reparation to the injured party—often in the form of a monetary fine—was a penalty favored over imprisoning a guilty party. There were no regular prisons—dungeons in forts were the usual jails. Prisoners had to purchase their own food, but except for major political prisoners, generally it seems prison life was not as harsh as it was in many other parts of the Middle East. For example, rather than being left to die in prison Omani inmates were usually released after they had been in jail for a year. By 1870 the British consular court was handling many commercial and even civil cases since the dominant element in Oman's commercial community were Indian British subjects who enjoyed extraterritorial immunity from local justice.[42]

Since the power of the sultan and his ability to influence chiefs to accept his decisions were directly affected by the amount of revenue at his disposal, financial administration was an exceedingly vital concern of the government. The sultan was assisted in financial management by his walis, by other officers of the government, and by special appointees drawn from the commercial groups. The government's main source of revenue in the late nineteenth century was—just as it had been in earlier years—the *'ushr,* or customs duties levied on imports. Although the word 'ushr means "tenth," in reality the duty amounted to only five percent ad valorem on imports, the maximum charge permitted according to the commercial treaties that the Masqati authorities had concluded with the Western powers in the mid-nineteenth century. In the days of Sayyid Sa'id the Masqat–Matrah customs used to yield fairly large revenues for government use; in 1840 the proceeds were estimated to amount to $MT 240,000.[43] In 1876, however, the customs afforded only $MT 110,000, and the figure remained at that level for the rest of Sultan Turki's reign despite a steady decline in the value of the Maria Theresa dollar.[44] The job of operating the customs house and collecting 'ushr duties was awarded on an annual basis to a private contractor in return for a set fee paid into the sultan's treasury. Almost without exception the customs farmer, officially at least, was one of the eminent Hindu merchants but in fact the responsibilities and even the profits of the enterprise often were shared by the several major Hindu business houses. During much of the late nineteenth century the large firm of Ratansee Purshatam held

[42] *Ibid.*; Ibn-Ruzayq, p. 384; Rigby, "Report on Zanzibar," *Records of the Bombay Government,* no. LIX (1861), pp. 6-7; *Admin. Rpt.: 1875-1876,* p. 74; "Miles to Ross, 18 Aug. 1884, no. 233: Masqat," India Records–3, Vol. IV.

[43] *Bombay Records—1856,* p. 631.

[44] *Admin. Rpt.: 1875-1876,* p. 77; *Admin. Rpt.: 1887-1888,* p. 56.

the customs franchise.[45] The sultan collected large customs receipts only at Masqat–Matrah. On one occasion he tried to establish a customs house at the thriving port of Sur in hopes it could earn $MT 50,000 a year. Unfortunately, the sultan's political power was not strong enough in Sur to effectively enforce the 'ushr. On the other hand, the sultan derived anywhere from $MT 30,000 to $MT 20,000 in Gwadar after local expenses were deducted.[46]

An implied obligation of any customs farmer was that he should be willing to extend loans to the sultan. The Hindu community in general was the source of most credit and both the government and private individuals borrowed from there. The sultan of Zanzibar was also a source of loan funds. In 1884 the Masqati government borrowed 32,000 rupees from Zanzibar's ruler to cover a temporary deficit in its treasury. Because of Turki ibn-Sa'id's continuing financial embarrassment during his reign, borrowing became an increasingly important source of revenue and a significant aspect of the financial system of the sultanate.[47]

Another, less bountiful, source of revenue was *zakah*, which supposedly, in Oman at least, was a tax on agricultural produce. But since the sultan could not collect the zakah in most tribal domains, the term actually referred to an export tax which was collected on all produce from the interior tribal areas which passed through Masqat bound for export. Sultan Turki tried mightily to increase his take from this levy and in 1881 he went so far as to increase the rate of the zakah from two to five percent, an action that caused considerable grumbling among some tribesmen. Evidently the tax was rather haphazardly applied, for in 1900 the total amount of zakah collected, both real and so-called, approximated only

[45] *Précis Slave*, p. 18; *Admin. Rpts.: 1887-1888 to 1897-1898*, passim.

[46] Lorimer, II, 1,422-25; "Miles to Ross, 3 July 1878, no. 25: Masqat," India Records–3, Vol. III.

[47] Lorimer, I, 520, II, 1,422-25; "Turki ibn-Sa'id to Robertson, 25 June 1877," India Records–3, Vol. III.

$MT 62,000, of which amount only about one-fourth was passed on to the central treasury.[48]

A subsidiary income came from *bayt al-mal* funds. Normally in traditional Muslim states, the term "bayt al-mal" meant the central treasury itself or the total amount of revenue from all sources. In Oman, however, the term referred to proceeds from the rent of state-owned land, property, or buildings. In Sultan Turki's time these rents amounted to a mere $MT 1,250 in a normal year.[49] The treasury also profited from the existence of other charges and fines, many of which were originated by Turki ibn-Sa'id in an effort to ease an ever-tightening revenue supply. In 1872 a requirement was introduced that called for each vessel entering or leaving Masqat harbor to carry an official manifest which could be secured upon payment of two Maria Theresa dollars. In 1873 the payment of wharfage fees started, while in 1877 a charge began to be applied on all dates weighed at the official scales preparatory to shipment abroad. Occasionally, punitive taxes were levied on exports or imports belonging to tribes defying the sultan.[50]

Of all the income available to the sultan the most dependable was the "Zanzibar subsidy," a charge shared by Calcutta and London after 1873 but which subsequent to 1883 was paid entirely out of the Anglo–Indian government's treasury. The fact that this subsidy was delivered to the sultan in Indian rupees benefited the Masqat government because the rupee, although its worth declined after 1873, did not drop in value as precipitously as did the Maria Theresa dollar during the late nineteenth century. In 1873 the subsidy's official valuation of $MT 40,000 was put at 86,400 rupees. This was the sum credited to the sultan's account each year thereafter. Because it was paid in rupees the Zanzibar subsidy, supposedly equal to £8,500, was actually worth about £7,900 in 1875. By 1900 the real value of the subsidy had dropped to about £5,660 because of the decline in the exchange value of the currency in

---

[48] Lorimer, I, 523-24, II, 1,420-22.
[49] *Ibid.*, II, 1,423-24.   [50] *Ibid.*, I, 523-24.

which it was paid; the fall in the subsidy's real value would have been far greater if it had been disbursed in Maria Theresa dollars.

The steady decline in the value of the Maria Theresa dollar from 1875 to 1900 was certainly of great political importance in Oman during the period. It was Sultan Turki's son, Sultan Faysal, who had to cope with the worst problems caused by this decline, but even Turki ibn-Sa'id was faced with the necessity from time to time, especially late in his reign, of borrowing to meet normal governmental operating costs. In 1900 the total income, including that from personally owned estates, reaching the sultan's treasury may have approximated $MT 300,000 annually, a figure then equal to about £24,000.[51] In good years Sultan Turki's total revenues in dollars amounted to somewhat less than the 1900 dollar totals because he received less from the customs. But since the Maria Theresa dollar was worth more than twice as much in terms of pound sterling exchange during Sultan Turki's reign than in 1900, it is estimated that the revenue of the Masqati state approximated £45,000 in the late 1870s in terms of international purchasing power. These figures also illustrate the growing and vital importance of the Zanzibar subsidy to the Masqati government. In the early 1880s the subsidy contributed about one-sixth of the sultan's real income; by 1900 the proportion was up to one-fifth. Clearly, the necessity of maintaining close ties with the British was more than a matter of choice if the sultanate was to retain any financial stability at all.

The sultan's financial strength was, of course, a fundamental element in his overall political strength. The fact that Oman's currency was declining in value after the early 1870s complicated the political situation tremendously because it decreased his capability to undertake certain activities. The annual expenditure of the sultan was distributed among state expenses such as military outlays, salaries, pensions, bribes, and tribal

[51] *Ibid.*, II, 1,420-22; "Ottavi, Commercial Report, 1901," French Records, Vol. II.

subsidies as well as among the sovereign's personal expenses such as the upkeep of the royal court and the maintenance of the many members of the immediate royal family. The money was spent according to the wishes of the sultan; there was apparently no distinction between state and personal spending, and very often expenses exceeded income, a circumstance met by resorting to loans and other devices of deficit financing such as postponing the payment of bills.[52]

The government's major expenses were those involving military and police activities, especially the ones which were undertaken to assure tranquility among Oman's many tribes. The sultan himself was the commander of his armed forces and was often called on to lead armies in the field. He was aided in the task of preserving order by most of his major assistants, his walis, and indeed by virtually all of the personnel attached to his administration, since there was little distinction between the military and civil functions of government.[53]

The permanent army numbered over 1,000 men but most of them were dispersed in small detachments garrisoning several forts scattered strategically around the country. Though costly to maintain these forts were important as strong points which dominated certain districts and the routes linking various parts of the country. They were also visible symbols of the sultan's power and as such contributed to his prestige. Even if there were ways a hostile force could avoid one of these strong points it was dangerous to leave a garrison in one's rear. Moreover, the sultan's effective intelligence network operated out of these bastions. Some of the most important strongholds were occupied by the sultan's own soldiers, while others were held by his tribal allies who received payments in

---

[52] Lorimer, II, 1,422-24.

[53] Information concerning the military and police functions of the Masqati government during the late nineteenth century is scattered. See especially *ibid.*, pp. 1,418-25; "Ottavi, Commercial Report, 1901," French Records, Vol. II; "Ross to Salisbury, 15 Jan. 1875, despatch no. 57-5: Residency," India Records–3, Vol. I; "Ross to Hartington, 13 Dec. 1881, despatch no. 51: Residency," India Records–3, Vol. v.

return for performing guard functions. The largest garrison was the one at Masqat–Matrah which normally numbered about 300 men; most posts were manned by an average of 30 men.

A majority of the sultan's permanent troops, or *'askaris,* were foreign mercenaries without Omani tribal connections. During Sultan Turki's reign almost 400 'askaris were Wahhabis from Najd and al-Hasa; approximately 250 were South Arabians from the Hadramaut; 100 were Baluchis from the Makran district across the Gulf of Oman; some were Negroes from east Africa; and only about 250 were native Omanis. The private 'askari was paid anywhere from three to five Maria Theresa dollars per month. In large units the soldiers were grouped into sections of about 20 men, each of which was led by an *'aqid,* or sergeant. Each regular garrison was in charge of an officer called a *jama'dar* who was paid $MT 20 to $MT 30 a month and whose rank was roughly equivalent to that of a captain. On campaigns during Sultan Turki's time the troops were generally led by the ruler himself, one of his sons, or by a general such as Badr ibn-Sayf. All in all, the sultan's mercenaries were rather listless campaigners whose training was rudimentary at best.

The royal troops were not elaborately equipped. In Sultan Thuwayni's time some soldiers evidently wore a semi-European uniform to the extent of being outfitted with a red tunic patterned after those issued to Indian sepoys, but evidently the issuing of uniforms was not common in Turki ibn-Sa'id's army. The fact that the sultan's men were equipped with modern rifles gave them some advantage in dealing with hostile tribesmen. But this advantage was erased in the 1890s when Masqat became an importing center for European rifles which were reexported to many areas of southern Asia, a traffic which gave the Omani tribes easy access to modern weapons. Sultan Turki possessed a number of old muzzle-loading cannon, some of which may have dated back to the Portuguese period. The artillery still usable was served by a small corps of Persian gunners; although most of the guns were situated in stationary mounts in various fortresses, two of the cannon were mobile field pieces. These field guns used by Sultan Turki's troops may well have been the same ones the British had given to Sultan Thuwayni in 1864. The sultan also possessed a rudimentary supply service which endeavored to supply a campaign with food and ammunition by camel. Unlike the tribal forces, the government's soldiers were discouraged from living off the land insofar as possible during campaigns.

In Sayyid Sa'id's day the navy was quite large, but with the partition of the Omani empire in 1856 it declined rapidly. Sultan Turki did little to restore Oman's navy to its ancient glory. In 1872 he possessed two old sailing warships, relics of Sayyid Sa'id's armada, the *Multan* and the *Rahmani,* but by 1875 they were disposed of. In the late 1870s he tried to purchase a steam vessel from the British but was refused. Finally, in the early 1880s Turki ibn-Sa'id's brother, the sultan of Zanzibar, presented the old steam yacht *Dar al-Salam* to the Masqati authorities. This ship, plus another turned over by Zanzibar in 1886, the steamship *Sultani,* considerably strengthened the government's command along the Omani coast.[54]

Warfare in a country as poor in resources as Oman could be very destructive. During the Hinawi–Ghafiri strife of 1875, over $MT 50,000 worth of difficult to replace date palm trees were cut down by the belligerents.[55] In the expedition led by "crown prince" Faysal ibn-Turki into Wadi Sama'il in 1883 much property was destroyed, entire groves of date palm trees were hacked down, and a stiff indemnity of $MT 20,000 was levied against the offending tribes as well.[56] Raids on town marketplaces could be equally costly. There are many instances in Omani history when town fathers or religious leaders tried

54 Lorimer, I, 511, 520; "Ross to Pelly, 23 Mar. 1872, no. 155: Masqat," India Records–2, Vol. xx.

55 "Ross to Salisbury, 20 Feb. 1875, despatch no. 218-219: Residency," India Records–3, Vol. I.

56 "Faysal ibn-Turki to Turki ibn-Sa'id, 12 Nov. 1883, enclosure in Jayakar to Ross, 26 Nov. 1883, no. 313a: Masqat," India Records–3, Vol. vii.

to mediate disputes threatening both town and countryside in order to avoid ruinous destruction.[57] The favorite campaign time was the period just after the ripening of the date harvest.[58] It is obvious from the account of the sultan's military resources that he was far from able to overawe Oman. Practically speaking, the basis of his influence in the country was determined by his ability to gain the active or even the tacit support of a decisive number of strong tribes—especially those located in strategic districts, such as Wadi Sama'il, and by his willingness to serve as an arbitrator, as well as his skill in settling local disturbances. Since the primary aim of the ruler was the preservation of his regime and law and order he found that most of the day-to-day tasks of governing his realm involved his relationship with one or more tribes. As a perusal of this work amply illustrates, no Omani ruler could retain his throne if he lost his tribal allies. The tribes were intensely jealous of their autonomy and were wary of any and all attempts by sultans or imams to abandon their balancing role or attempt to impose too strong or direct a rule over them. Thus the usual tactic of any sage Omani ruler was to attempt to gain only enough respect and prestige among the tribes to convince them to come to his aid in emergencies, to recognize him as titular overlord, and to accept his arbitration if their intertribal disputes threatened to develop into civil war. In tribal areas, then, the sultan was satisfied to rule, to influence, and to umpire, but not to administer.[59] One should not make the mistake of assuming that modern Western concepts of the functions of a central government were those that Omanis expected their rulers—be they sultans or imams—to perform.

Since the sultan did not possess the military resources to force his will upon any large combination of tribes his political

---

[57] "Ross to Hartington, 13 Dec. 1887, despatch no. 51: Residency," India Records-3, Vol. v.

[58] *Admin. Rpt.: 1900-1901*, p. 14.

[59] For a concise description of the relationship between an Arabian king and his tribal "subjects" see Thesiger, *Arabian Sands*, p. 32.

efforts were successful insofar as he was able to gain his ends without using force. The sultan had more subtle weapons in his arsenal than bullets. To preserve order and to retain the nominal loyalty of the tribes he made himself available to arbitrate tribal disputes; he judiciously bestowed subsidies and tax exemptions on certain tribes to cement existing alliances or to ease the resolving of disagreements; and he just as carefully imposed punitive taxes and trade controls designed to convince stubborn shaykhs that compromise was better than conflict. Only as a last resort would the sultan use his limited military power, and before bringing force into any situation he was careful to shore up his alliances with friendly tribes so as to gain additional support. It was rare that the sultan took the offensive against even a small tribe alone, without the active cooperation of some tribal allies. The sultan's financial resources, considerable by Omani standards, were a mainstay supporting his overall political influence. While other Omani leaders might on occasion form combinations equal to the military strength commanded by the sultan, and whereas some other leaders might surpass the ruler in diplomatic skill, none could match his monetary resources. Persuasion and arms could not always bring results, but money usually brought at least a temporary settlement of problems. Gifts and other payments could often gain or retain the nominal, sometimes even active, loyalty of most tribal shaykhs. Apparently, many shaykhs periodically received a gift of money from the sultan which almost amounted to a retainer paid to the individual tribal leader to reward him for remaining a friend of the ruler.

A successful tribal policy also depended on the sultan's maintaining his overall prestige. Prestige, an elusive but necessary ingredient of a ruler's strength, was earned in a number of ways, not the least of which were through the personality traits of the sovereign. A strong personality was important in a country where government was largely a matter of dealing in an individual way with numbers of individual semi-autonomous leaders. Prestige was also gained by display: the token garrisons stationed in certain forts, the token subsidies and gifts bestowed on some individuals, even the token arbitration procedures used to end formally a dispute already settled in actuality, were symbols used to create an impression of strength rather than being actual manifestations of royal power.[60]

But lest the impression be given the politics in Oman was some sort of game played according to highly stylized rules, mention should be made of some of the concrete actions undertaken by Sultan Turki to realize his general policies. In a few key areas, for instance, the sultan's power and control had to be more than token or his regime would crumble. Masqat itself, of course, was the key position to be held. Outside the capital, Wadi Sama'il was probably the most vital district, for this valley and the passes branching out from it formed the main passageway linking the Masqat district with Oman's interior provinces. Hence necessity required that one of the sultan's main political efforts be directed toward guaranteeing that peace prevailed among the several tribes of Wadi Sama'il and toward assuring that the tribes of the region remain loyal enough to block any hostile thrusts coming through the pass toward the capital.[61] The sultan subsidized several of the Ghafiri tribes of the district, maintained a garrison with one of his best walis at Sama'il and at other strong points in the pass area, and operated an elaborate spy and warning network to alert him to any potential dangers. If this system failed for any reason the way was open for interior tribes to descend on the coast to raid and pillage.[62]

[60] "Miles to Ross, 15 Sept. 1884, no. 225: Masqat," "10 May 1885, no. 139: Masqat," India Records–3, Vol. VI. These letters describe some of Sultan Turki's attempts to set up token waliships and garrisons.

[61] *Admin. Rpt.: 1883-1884*, p. 17; "Ross to Duke of Argyll, 4 Sept. 1873, despatch no. 1,140-118: Residency," India Records–2, Vol. XXIII: "Mockler to Ross, 22 July 1883, no. 182: Masqat," "Miles to Ross, 15 Oct. 1883, no. 279: Masqat," India Records–3, Vol. VI. The last two letters cited describe a diplomatic failure of the sultan in the Wadi Sama'il area which was a prelude to an attack on Masqat.

[62] "Government of India to Kimberley, 16 Feb. 1886, no. 36: Calcutta,"

Sultan Turki grew more adroit in his handling of the tribes as his reign progressed. In his first years he squandered a considerable amount of money on payments to tribal leaders without receiving much back in political benefits.[63] By 1875 Turki ibn-Sa'id learned his lesson and developed in outline the tribal policy he was to use during the remainder of his rule. With most interior tribes he asked only for a token submission in return for a small subsidy. With a few inland groups, however, he concluded active alliances: the 'Ibriyin in al-Zahirah, al-Janabah, and Bani-Bu-'Ali in Ja'lan; and Bani-Jabir, al-Nidabiyin, al-Rahbiyin, Bani-Ruwahah, and al-Siyabiyin in Wadi Sama'il. The Bani-Ruwahah also supplied men to garrison the fort at al-Masna'ah in al-Batinah. Conversely, the sultan expended some money to aid local opponents of his principal enemies, particularly those who could cause trouble for Salih ibn-'Ali.[64] Generally—except for the time 'Abd al-'Aziz ibn-Sa'id was wazir and regent—Sultan Turki was closer to the Ghafiri than the Hinawi tribes, many of which tended to be conservative in their leanings. The ruler did not often use the device of concluding marriage alliances with his principal tribal adherents because the Al Bu Sa'id generally restricted their marriages to others within the royal tribe, a practice which at least tended to unify its various branches. For instance, in 1873 Sultan Turki helped his prestige in al-Batinah by marrying the daughter of his cousin Hamad ibn-Salim, a popular governor in the province.[65]

India Records–4, Vol. xlvi; enclosures in this document contain several examples of intelligence reporting to the sultan by his agents in the pass area.

[63] Lorimer, I, 499; "Miles to Ross, 16 Oct. 1874, no. 449-181: Masqat," India Records–2, Vol. xxv. One source estimates Turki ibn-Sa'id wasted as much as $MT 100,000 on badly used subsidies during the first four years of his reign.

[64] "Ross to Salisbury, 19 Aug. 1874, despatch no. 944-92: Residency," India Records–2, Vol. xvii; "Miles to Ross, 16 Jan. 1879, no. 26: Masqat," India Records–3, Vol. iv.

[65] *Admin. Rpt.: 1885-1886*, p. 22; Lorimer, I, 495.

Reconstruction, 1871-1903

The importance of the sultan's judicious use of financial resources for the preservation of his political position has been emphasized. Alliances with tribes were cemented by subsidies and tax exemptions. The shaykhs of al-Nidabiyin and al-Rahbiyin each received $MT 30 a month, plus occasional presents to hold two small passes linking al-Sharqiyah, Salih ibn-'Ali's home province, with Wadi Sama'il.[66] In 1881 Turki ibn-Sa'id, forestalled an outbreak of disorder in the pass area by sending $MT 500 to some of the notables in the district.[67] The sultan also experimented with payoffs to his individual rivals to transform them into peaceful subjects: after 1883 he agreed to supply Salih ibn-'Ali with $MT 50 each month while 'Abd al-'Aziz ibn-Sa'id was to receive $MT 200 monthly as long as they kept the peace. Also, the sultan's payments were instrumental in keeping Ibrahim ibn-Qays relatively quiet in al-Rustaq after 1875.[68] Certainly many Omani leaders took advantage of the sultan's largesse. Some tribal shaykhs had the habit of manufacturing and then broadcasting rumors of an impending disturbance in the hope that the sultan would be worried into sending a large and extraordinary present.[69] In their letters to the sultan the shaykhs seldom failed to ask for money. If the sultan ignored these requests it was a reflection on his prestige and personal honor because no shaykh really believed the sultan's protests that the royal coffers were not bottomless. Their attitude is well summarized by a statement one shaykh directed to the sultan: "With you the question of money is nothing."[70]

Sultan Turki also developed arbitration procedures to a considerable degree because he realized that settling a dispute before it was necessary to dispatch soldiers was the cheapest

[66] "Mockler to Ross, 29 May 1883, no. 126: Masqat," India Records-3, Vol. VI.

[67] *Admin. Rpt.: 1881-1882*, pp. 13-15.

[68] *Admin. Rpt.: 1877-1878*, p. 127; *Admin. Rpt.: 1882-1883*, pp. 13-15.

[69] *Admin. Rpt.: 1877-1878*, p. 127.

[70] "Muhammad ibn-Nasir al-Ruwahi to Turki ibn-Sa'id, 9 Oct. 1883," India Records-3, Vol. VI.

way to maintain peace and the effectiveness of his government. It was the responsibility of a wali to try to keep the peace among the tribes of his district, although these officers had little in the way of soldiery or money to back up their influence. Serious disputes between tribes usually came before the sultan himself, who devised a fairly elaborate procedure to settle tribal arguments. A delegation was sent to the disputants, which was charged with the task of settling the disagreement, or failing that, with arranging a truce. The sultan used the truce period to discover the facts of the situation, often sending a second factfinding delegation to do this. Next, the sultan would request each party to meet with him at Masqat or some mutually agreeable place—often the scene of the trouble—and using the facts at his disposal, would personally try to arrange a compromise settlement. At this stage it was common to consult with various learned qadis concerning the legal aspects at issue in a case. Failing all efforts to find a solution the sultan normally left the quarreling tribes to fight, although after this had gone on for a time the ruler would try again to solve the problem. Occasionally, though, when the sultan himself was party to a dispute the British would step in as mediators.[71]

Sultan Turki was also fond of charging fines or levying punitive taxes on the commerce of recalcitrant tribes to force settlements of intertribal quarrels or to restore his nominal sovereignty in an area. In 1874 the Al Sa'd paid out some $MT 15,000 for their part in an uprising while the Hinawi tribes which plundered Matrah in 1877 were subjected to a stiff punitive tax and export controls, devices perfected by Sultan Faysal during his reign.[72]

By using all these various techniques, Turki ibn-Sa'id established his nominal control over most of the large towns and fortresses of Oman by 1885. Admittedly his rule was not strong

71 "Ross to Salisbury, 20 Mar. 1875, despatch no. 350-35: Residency," India Records–3, Vol. I; "Miles to Ross, 15 Apr. 1884, no. 107: Masqat," India Records–3, Vol. VI.

72 "Robertson to Prideaux, 18 July 1877, no. 284: Masqat," India Records –3, Vol. III.

in the interior and his influence was felt in tribal areas only if the various shaykhs cooperated.

Corollary to these many practices used by Turki ibn-Saʻid to assert his authority in Oman was an effort to strengthen, or extend, his rule in the overseas territories of Gwadar and Dhofar. Gwadar, situated on the coast of Baluchistan, had been an Omani possession since 1794, which it was destined to remain until it was sold to Pakistan in 1958. The sultan's main worry in this quarter was the possibility that the port might be attacked by local tribesmen, but this became almost impossible after the British annexed most of Baluchistan in 1886.[73] Dhofar, on the other hand, was annexed by Turki ibn-Saʻid in 1879 when he sent Sulayman ibn-Suwaylim to Salalah. In 1829 Sayyid Saʻid temporarily had occupied the district, so the Masqat government believed that they had a legitimate claim to it. Nevertheless, both the neighboring South Arabian state of the Qaitis and, more seriously, the Ottomans, coveted the province. Ottoman-instigated disorders broke out in Dhofar in 1880, 1883, and 1885, while in 1886 the British were forced to intervene to prevent an outright Ottoman occupation. By 1887 it appeared the Al Bu Saʻid annexation of Dhofar was complete, but revolts periodically erupted there until Omani domination was solidified early in this century. Sultan Turki's adventure in Dhofar originally was a drain on his resources, but the province was destined to be a source of strength rather than of weakness for subsequent Al Bu Saʻid monarchs, most of whom kept Dhofar's administration quite separate from that of their Omani dominions.[74]

In foreign affairs Sultan Turki's main concern, of course, was to maintain and, if possible, strengthen his ties with Britain. In this regard, as in other aspects of his reign, his success increased as the years passed. Most Anglo–Indian officials with

[73] Lorimer, I, 602-22; Gwadar remained a possession of Muscat and Oman until 1958 when the enclave was purchased by Pakistan for £3,000,000.

[74] *Ibid.*, pp. 595-602; an example of Dhofar's special regime is seen in the fact that at the present time the sultan of Muscat and Oman issues a separate coinage for use in that province only.

any firsthand experience with Persian Gulf affairs respected Turki ibn-Sa'id. Nevertheless, although he gained official British recognition as Oman's ruler in August 1871 it was not until April 1873 that he received any of the proceeds from the Zanzibar subsidy which subsequently became such an indispensable part of his financial resources. Only during 1874-75 did some officials in the Anglo–Indian government display real reluctance in supporting him. But even at this time, and especially after 1875, in the final analysis the sultan's cooperative attitude netted him decisive British naval and political support. This trend was crowned in 1886 with the Anglo–Indian government's declaration which guaranteed his throne. Calcutta and London showed a certain official hesitancy from time to time concerning Turki ibn-Sa'id and the limits to which British power should be committed in his behalf. But Colonels Ross and Miles were always able in any serious emergencies to influence their superiors to give the sultan all necessary support. For his part, Sultan Turki was content to leave his foreign relations—except for his contacts with Zanzibar—in the hands of the British. They intervened in his interests with both the Ottoman and Qajar governments and conducted negotiations in Sultan Turki's name with Western powers, such as the Dutch who concluded a commercial treaty with Oman in 1877.[75]

Because of the extent of foreign support and the fact that this was a main prop holding up the state, Sultan Turki's reign marks a new departure in Omani politics. It is true that previous Omani rulers, including the great Sayyid Sa'id, maintained close relations with Britain but their main reliance was on their own resources. Turki ibn-Sa'id, however, determined that his survival depended on British aid, so consequently he was willing to accept a place in the system of indirect rule through which Britain asserted her interests within the Persian Gulf principalities. The situation was summarized neatly in 1886 when on the occasion the Anglo–Indian government

[75] See chap. v; also, Lorimer, I, 520.

officially announced it was guaranteeing Sultan Turki's throne, he was invested with the insignia of a knight commander in the Order of the Star of India. The grand master of this order was the viceroy of India. Turki ibn-Sa'id's honorable but still subordinate place in the order was a reflection of the honorable but subordinate position he occupied vis-à-vis the Anglo–Indian government. At any rate, when he died in 1888, Turki ibn-Sa'id bequeathed a fairly orderly realm to his son.

THE TESTING OF THE RECONSTRUCTED MODERATE REGIME, 1888-1903

Faysal ibn-Turki was the first among the Al Bu Sa'id rulers in Oman to mount his throne peacefully. The new ruler, about 24 when he became titular master of Oman, still had to prove himself to be a man who could govern. Much of Sultan Turki's political effectiveness in his last years was the product of the close personal relationships he had established with many Omani leaders during the course of his reign. This network of personal confidences would have to be restored by the new sultan if he was to continue to rule effectively.

But Sultan Faysal did not wish to preside over a regime bent on merely continuing his father's policies and restoring the old system of personal relationships which animated these policies. Faysal ibn-Turki nurtured a more romantic dream. He wished to be the monarch of a united Oman truly independent of foreign tutelage. The new sultan seemed particularly sensitive to the fact that the British exercised a large influence in determining the actions of the Masqat government, but he did not really comprehend why this was the case. From the beginning of his reign, Faysal ibn-Turki indicated his impatience with the pervasiveness of the British presence in his domain, as well as with those Omanis who championed the continuation of Sultan Turki's subservient posture vis-à-vis the Anglo–Indian government. One of Faysal ibn-Turki's first acts was to refuse to accept the services of his father's longtime wazir, the pro-British Sa'id ibn-Muhammad. Indeed, the young sultan drove the ex-wazir out of Masqat and would have confiscated his property but for British protests.

As was the case with his father, Faysal ibn-Turki's reign as sultan divides into two periods. During the first, Sultan Faysal tried to assert his independence of the restraints on his father and strike out on a new but somewhat romantically reactionary course. He wanted to become a ruler around whom all Omanis could rally. In various ways Faysal courted favor with the conservatives, especially Salih ibn-'Ali, and went so far as to use, on occasion, the title of "imam" as well as that of sultan. Unfortunately, these youthful pretensions, plus his early attempts to establish a strong rule in some interior districts, only convinced most conservative and tribal leaders of the new ruler's weakness or lack of political maturity. Even more damaging to the realization of Sultan Faysal's dream during this high water mark of the age of Western imperialism was the anti-British tone of his early administration.

By 1899 Faysal's political adolescence had ended, with his complete humiliation by the British and his influence among Omanis at its nadir. Between 1899 and 1903 he painfully faced up to the reality of his weakness and restored, as much as he could, his father's policies and techniques of government. The last 10 years of his life were spent in meek but successful efforts to retain his throne. His dependence on the British during his final years was as apparent as were his efforts to be free of them during his early years. In 1911 one traveler pictured the sultan as a weak but kindly and dignified man whose main pleasures came from inspecting visiting British warships and pursuing his hobby of photography.[76]

Indeed, this picture of Faysal—often without mention of the qualities of kindness and dignity—is fairly universal among descriptions of the monarch. The traveler Theodore Bent interviewed Sultan Faysal in 1889 soon after his accession and drew a colorful illustration of the shy, beardless, nervous

[76] L. Fraser, *India under Curzon and After* (London, 1912), pp. 90-91.

young man who was boyishly full of questions but who, although he was "not much like a king," was "an autocrat." Bent took considerable pains to describe Faysal's practice of holding prisoners in a low cage situated in his palace courtyard where they had a good view of an adjacent pen in which the sultan kept his pet lion, an animal sometimes given the duty of executing the worst criminals.[77]

Matching the sultan's actions against his surface timidity, one can reach the conclusion that in his early days Faysal ibn-Turki possessed a certain inner resolve—and some energy. His problems arose from the fact that he used these resources in an undisciplined, unsophisticated fashion. He gained some governmental experience during his father's administration, but his contacts did not expose him to much outside the limited Al Bu Sa'id family society. He was born of an Ethiopian mother, was married to his first cousin Aliyah, a daughter of Sultan Thuwayni, and reputedly could neither read nor write although he could sign his own name. Unlike his father, he had gained little knowledge, let alone a firsthand acquaintance, of any countries save his own before coming to the throne.[78]

The fate of Faysal ibn-Turki's "independence" policy, 1888-99. It has been noted that immediately after he came to power Faysal ibn-Turki signaled that he intended to change the tone of the Masqat government's policies when he neglected to appoint Sa'id ibn-Muhammad to a high government post. The ex-wazir was not only pro-British but also was cordially disliked by conservatives. Since the sultan intended to make overtures to the conservatives in an effort to bring them over to his side, Sa'id ibn-Muhammad could only have been an embarrassment to Sultan Faysal if he were given an office. It was not until the sultan's flirtation with the conservatives ended that Sa'id ibn-Muhammad returned to power. The sultan's closest advisor was actually his younger brother, Fahd ibn-Turki; but

---

[77] Bent, *Southern Arabia*, pp. 56-58.
[78] Lorimer, I, 525; Graves, *Life of Cox*, p. 56.

Fahd suffered from mental illness and ultimately committed suicide in 1894 to escape an unhappy marriage. The sultan's elder brother, Muhammad ibn-Turki, even if he was of little help to the new government, at least was quite content to enjoy his large monthly subsidy of $MT 600 without trying to become a focus of anti-regime intrigues. Not until May 1889 did Sultan Faysal select a wazir—Muhammad ibn-'Azzan, a veteran official of Al Bu Sa'id lineage who served as chief minister until 1896 and for a short four-month long term in 1898-99, but who never seemed to seriously influence the course of events. The two strongest men in the sultan's entourage were two old confidents of Sultan Turki, Badr ibn-Sayf, the military member of the sultan's council, and Sulayman ibn-Suwaylim, a general assistant who served in many posts, including that of wali in Dhofar, and who eventually became wazir in 1902. Apparently none of Sultan Faysal's advisors had a really decisive influence in the early part of his reign because of the young monarch's firm, albeit unannounced, determination to engineer his own program.[79]

This penchant of the sultan was noticeable particularly in his relationship with the British. Although he wrote dutifully enough, soon after his father's death, to the British political agent in Masqat that he wished to rule under Britain's protection and with her friendship, it was apparent that Faysal ibn-Turki contrived to be an independent monarch in fact as well as in theory.[80]

From the first, the sultan displayed an independence that vexed the Anglo–Indian government. As one Anglo–Indian official, the chronicler J. G. Lorimer, wrote: "[Faysal's] natural impatience of restraints and obligations reacted unfavourably on his relations with Great Britain."[81] The venerable British resident in the Persian Gulf, Sir Edward Ross, a man who

[79] *Précis Maskat*, p. 9; Lorimer, I, 532, 546, 556; *Admin. Rpt.: 1901-1902*, p. 7; Al-Salimi, II, 303-304; Bent, *Southern Arabia*, p. 58.

[80] *Admin. Rpt.: 1888-1889*, pp. 23-24.

[81] Lorimer, I, 533.

had been on close and friendly terms with the new sultan's father, remained quite reserved toward the son. Although Ross forwarded the Zanzibar subsidy without delay, he held up formal recognition of Faysal ibn-Turki as sultan until April 1890.[82] The delay may have been a ploy to facilitate the negotiations Ross was conducting with the sultan. These resulted ultimately in the Anglo–Omani Commercial Treaty and Non-Alienation Agreement of 1891, which bound the Omani ruler not to cede any of his territories to any power without first receiving British approval. Also the Anglo–Indian government was rethinking the nature of its connection with Oman. The delay in recognition and the tone of the negotiation generally may well have chagrined the sensitive sultan (how much angrier he would have been had he known that British officials were discussing the possibility of proclaiming a formal protectorate over his realm), but no open Anglo–Omani disagreements took place until after Colonel Ross retired as resident in 1892.

While Edward Ross's skill as a diplomat neutralized some of the impatience that Faysal ibn-Turki felt toward his British protectors, the surface calm in Anglo–Omani relations that prevailed until 1893 also benefited from the fact that during the early years of the sultan's reign he was preoccupied with Omani domestic politics. Initially, Sultan Faysal attempted an aggressive forward policy designed to increase Masqat's control over Oman's interior and tribal regions. Very soon after his accession Faysal ibn-Turki concluded an agreement with Salih ibn-'Ali which freed a royal army of 3,000 to launch an attack on Ibrahim ibn-Qays' stronghold at al-Rustaq in September 1888. The attack was an utter failure and brought a serious setback to the prestige of the new ruler. The resistance of al-Rustaq, led by the late Imam 'Azzan ibn-Qays' second son, Sa'ud ibn-'Azzan, was so strong that it even inspired the long quiescent Al Sa'd tribe of al-Batinah to rise

[82] *Admin. Rpt.: 1889-1890*, p. 5; *Précis Maskat*, p. 2.

up, temporarily cutting off the sultan's army from its coastal operating base at Barka. It was not long before the sultan abandoned the attack. Probably even more damaging than his failure to take al-Rustaq (considered a very strong fortress), was that during the course of the campaign Sultan Faysal ran out of money and gave up the adventure without paying his army. In many ways Faysal ibn-Turki never really recovered from the failure of this his initial undertaking as sultan.[83]

The debacle before al-Rustaq and its revelation of Faysal ibn-Turki's lack of capacity inspired the formation of a new antigovernment coalition which combined the small forces of 'Abd al-'Aziz ibn-Sa'id—Faysal's uncle and Sultan Turki's half brother, ex-wazir, and longtime tormentor—as well as Sa'ud ibn-'Azzan and Hamud ibn-'Azzan, both nephews of Ibrahim ibn-Qays and sons of 'Azzan ibn-Qays. But Sultan Faysal reacted quickly to counter this combination and organized a new force some 2,000 men, plus some adherents from the Nu'aym tribe under the command of his younger brother, Fahd ibn-Turki, to deal with it. Throughout most of the winter of 1888-89 Prince Fahd scoured the mountains in search of the elusive leaders of the coalition with no success. In one way the expedition did record a large success, however—it convinced 'Abd al-'Aziz ibn-Sa'id that he did not have any chance of displacing Faysal ibn-Turki as sultan. Wearied by 15 years of wandering through interior Oman unsuccessfully trying to organize a movement which might make him sultan, 'Abd al-'Aziz ibn-Sa'id in March 1890 accepted an offer of a subsidy to be supplied by the rulers of Oman and Zanzibar and voluntarily went into exile. He lived in Bombay until his death in 1907 and never saw Oman again.[84]

The sultan's lack of military success and his ever dwindling revenue supply persuaded him in 1890 to give up his attempts to impose himself forcibly on the interior and to utilize instead another tactic to affirm his influence in Oman. This was to

[83] Al-Salimi, II, 283-84; Lorimer, I, 526-28; *Précis Maskat*, pp. 1-2.
[84] Lorimer, I, 528; *Précis Maskat*, pp. 1-2.

nurture the understanding he had reached with Salih ibn-'Ali and to try to improve his reputation among conservative Ibadis. The good relations between the sultan and Salih ibn-'Ali lasted as long as it suited the old shaykh's desires—that is, until 1894—and apparently as long as the Masqat government kept up its deliveries of large subsidies to him. Faysal ibn-Turki was far more solicitous of conservative sensibilities than was his father, and he tried mightily during the early part of his regime at least, to gain the favor of conservative opinion. One indication of this attempt to conciliate the conservatives and his sympathy for some of their views was the sultan's attitude toward the slave trade and slave-holding. Unlike Sultan Turki, who went out of his way to cooperate with the British on the slave trade issue and who solidified British friendship by doing so, Sultan Faysal did no more than to live up to the letter of his treaty obligations. He let it be known that he shared the common Omani attitude of supporting the institution of slavery by owning slaves and by acquiring more when he could. He made no pretense of cooperating with the British in preventing the traffic in slaves and volunteered no information or aid to help in its suppression. Whereas in 1890 Faysal ibn-Turki's kinsman, the sultan of Zanzibar, initiated legal steps that eventually caused domestic slavery to die out in that country, British officers in Oman stated that the sultan's attitude as well as the growing disorder in the countryside would preclude Britain from pressing for any limitation of domestic slavery there.[85] Indeed, the British commonly, and undoubtedly correctly, believed their efforts to curb the slave trade were held against them by rulers such as Faysal ibn-Turki and by the Gulf's inhabitants generally.[86]

Seemingly, Faysal ibn-Turki believed that if he did not have the raw power to impose unity on Oman then possibly he could gain influence by aligning himself with local opinion and local prejudice. Also, it seems that Sultan Faysal had de-

[85] *Précis Slave*, pp. 45-47; Lorimer, I, 2,505, 2,513.
[86] "Hamilton to Curzon, 7 Nov. 1901," India Mss.–2, Vol. III.

signs on acquiring the style of "imam" as well as that of sultan. He used both titles on the few coins he minted.[87] Non-Omani Ibadis—mainly those in north Africa and in their small colony in Egypt—referred to him as "Imam of Masqat and Oman" and he was listed by them as a leader of the faith in Oman along with such conservative stalwarts and religious scholars as Salih ibn-'Ali, Sa'id ibn-Nasr, 'Ali ibn-Muhammad, Hilal ibn-Zahir, and 'Abdallah ibn-Humayd al-Salimi.[88] Still, Faysal ibn-Turki's flirtation with the conservatives was never carried to the point where he abandoned the basically moderate Ibadi stance of his regime. It is likely that he was trying to attract all shades of Ibadi opinion rather than set himself up as a champion of any one faction.

Whatever Sultan Faysal's reasons for adopting the policy he did in regard to the interior and the conservatives, in the long run it collapsed—because he miscalculated his financial and military resources and mismanaged his political and diplomatic moves. By the end of 1890, as a result of the remarkable about-face in his policy regarding the affairs of interior Oman, he gave up any idea of increasing his administrative involvement there and even declined requests to arbitrate tribal disputes. It is not entirely clear why Sultan Faysal abdicated his responsibilities in the interior although probably it was due to a combination of a growing lack of money and an attempt to build his popularity among conservative elements. It was not long, however, before the sultan's new laissez-faire treatment of interior tribal disagreements allowed the rivalries to become red hot.[89] In 1891 disorder erupted in Wadi Sama'il between Hinawi and Ghafiri elements. Because the sultan did nothing to pacify this strategic district, the trouble grew worse. Eventually an al-Hirth caravan bringing al-Shar-

[87] Lorimer, I, 491, note.
[88] Al-Miṣri, *Kitāb al-Hadīyah*, p. 82.
[89] "Memorandum, Mockler to Government of India, Feb. 1891," *Précis Slave*, p. 45; *Admin. Rpt.: 1889-1890*, p. 24; *Admin. Rpt.: 1893-1894*, p. 19; *Précis Maskat*, p. 2; Lorimer, I, 526-28.

qiyah dates to the coast for export was raided and very heavy fighting developed.[90] The hostilities continued to escalate to the point where by 1892-93 it raged not only in Wadi Sama'il but in Ja'lan and al-Batinah, and even Salih ibn-'Ali requested that the sultan do something to end the disorder. All roads between the coast and the interior were cut and the trade of Masqat and Matrah dropped precipitously.[91] It is probable that the sultan's lack of energy in dealing with the spreading anarchy in the interior was due to his rapidly shrinking revenue supply. This suspicion is supported by the fact that in 1894 Faysal ibn-Turki failed to deliver the customary subsidies to the Ghafiri shaykhs of Wadi Sama'il, an action which predictably had dire consequences.[92] Masqat's control even over coastal districts declined at the same time since the sultan was unable to maintain his steamships. The *Dar al-Salam* was sold in Bombay while the *Sultani* simply rotted to pieces. By late 1894 the sultan's seeming indifference to their problems had estranged many of the tribes traditionally friendly to the moderate government.[93]

Another dimension was added to this alarming situation as a result of Sultan Faysal's encouraging arms traders to use Masqat as a center for the import and distribution of modern weapons throughout southern Asia. By 1895 Omani tribes began to acquire stocks of modern rifles and ammunition, and by 1900 the inhabitants of the port of Sur, as well as many of the tribes of Ja'lan, al-Sharqiyah, al-Jabal al-Akhdar, and al-Zahirah, were all too strong for the sultan to overawe with the usual military forces he could raise in times of emergency.[94] In 1902 the situation had developed to the point where a British military expert warned that no more would a few shells fired from a gunboat suffice to protect Masqat but that a costly

[90] *Admin. Rpt.: 1890-1891*, p. 15.

[91] *Admin. Rpt.: 1892-1893*, pp. 19-20; Lorimer, I, 528-29.

[92] *Admin. Rpt.: 1893-1894*, pp. 19-22.

[93] Lorimer, I, 530-32.

[94] "Curzon to Hamilton, 3 Jan. 1902, no. 5: Viceroy," Public Records Office Mss., F.O. 60/622; Lorimer, II, 1,390; *Précis Trucial Chiefs*, p. 71.

campaign including the landing of Anglo–Indian troops would be necessary to deter future assaults by the sultan's enemies.[95] The expert's words were to prove prophetic during World War I when Masqat was next attacked.

The deterioration of Anglo–Omani relations, however, accelerated between 1893 and 1895 to the point where no longer could it be a foregone conclusion that the British would be willing to use their military forces to uphold Sultan Faysal. The dissipation of the friendly climate which traditionally distinguished the relations between the sultanate and the Anglo–Indian government was the result of a fortuitous mixture of circumstances including Sultan Faysal's desire to lessen his dependence on the British, the unskilled, uninformed and overbearing actions of the post-Ross generation of Anglo–Indian officials in the Gulf, and the opportunity for diplomatic adventuring presented by the Persian Gulf's inclusion in the 1890s within the sphere of great power imperial clashes. Sultan Faysal was particularly impatient with the extraterritorial status that British Indian subjects sometimes abused within his realm. His protests did little, however, except irk the British officials to whom they were directed. The 1893 relations between Sultan Faysal and Major Hayes-Sadler, the British political agent in Masqat, deteriorated to the point of insult.[96] When the collision of rival great power imperial ambitions took concrete form after the opening of a French consulate in Masqat in 1894, Sultan Faysal quickly realized that he had gained an opportunity to strike against the British.[97] By 1895 the sultan had started playing the game of trying to balance the French against the British. Whether his grievances against the British were just or not, Sultan Faysal succeeded in provoking the displeasure of the Anglo–Indian government at the same time his influence among the Omani tribes was collapsing.

[95] "Colonel C. E. Yates to Government of India, Foreign Department, 5 May 1902, no. 5," Public Records Office Mss., F.O. 60/622.
[96] Lorimer, I, 535-36, 555.   [97] *Précis Maskat*, p. 61.

The situation exploded in February 1895. The immediate cause of the blow-up was the alienation of Salih ibn-'Ali by Sultan Faysal. During 1894 the fact that the sultan was extending aid to an al-Hirth shaykh who was seeking to displace Salih ibn-'Ali as the tribe's leader became known to the old shaykh. When the sultan did not answer Salih ibn-'Ali's letters concerning the affair, the old warrior set out once again to forge an antisultanate coalition.[98] The situation was not entirely dissimilar to that of 1868 when Sultan Salim's alienation of Salih ibn-'Ali set the stage for the overthrow of the sultanate. Different, however, was the lack of a unified conservative movement led by many able men such as 'Azzan ibn-Qays or Sa'id ibn-Khalfan al-Khalili; Salih ibn-'Ali, himself, was a young man in 1868. But the leader was still able to attract numbers of Hinawi tribes to his banner, including al-Hirth, al-Hubus, Bani-Battash, 'Awamir, Bani-Ruwahah, and some lesser Hinawi forces from al-Batinah and the districts around Wadi Sama'il and al-Rustaq.[99] Aid was also extended to the coalition from an unlikely source, Sultan Hamud of Zanzibar, who had spent his boyhood in Oman and dreamed of re-creating a unified Omani–Zanzibari state. Sultan Hamud was visited during 1894 by a delegation of Omani conservative tribal leaders who returned to their country loaded with presents, including money, three cannon, and 300 barrels of gunpowder. When the British became aware of Sultan Hamud's intrigues they attempted to put an end to them by insisting that he disentangle himself from Omani politics, but this directive came too late to prevent the aid supplied by the Zanzibari sultan from reaching Oman.[100]

News of Salih ibn-'Ali's success in organizing a coalition to attack Sultan Faysal eventually reached him. Realizing he had neglected both his tribal allies and the defenses of Masqat itself, the sultan belatedly set about to halt the trend of events.

[98] Al-Salimi, II, 284; *Admin. Rpt.: 1894-1895*, pp. 15-18.
[99] Lorimer, I, 543.
[100] *Précis Maskat*, pp. 24-25.

But this effort did nothing to stop Salih ibn-'Ali's host of 2,000 men from descending through the undefended Wadi Sama'il passes into Masqat's suburbs in February 1895. Seizing what he thought was an opportunity to negotiate, Sultan Faysal welcomed 'Abdallah ibn-Salih, the old shaykh's son, representative, and field commander, to a parley. The negotiations were used by the conservatives to gather intelligence about the state of Masqat's defenses, but the sultan was led to believe that a bribe could buy his and his capital's safety. Accordingly, a gift of $MT 1,200 was sent to 'Abdallah ibn-Salih by the sultan who expected that his unwelcome guests would then depart. Instead of quitting Masqat, however, 'Abdallah ibn-Salih, late in the night of February 13, 1895, seized one of the city's gates and admitted a large group of coalition warriors that had hidden themselves outside Masqat's walls; he then took charge of this force as it occupied the key points in the city. Sultan Faysal only barely escaped to one of the harbor forts.

The aim of the attackers became clear when they hoisted the white standard of the imamate over the sultan's palace and declared Sa'ud ibn-'Azzan, son of the late imam, the titular leader of the movement. During the early stages of their occupation of Masqat the insurgents displayed great deference to the British, claimed that they wanted only the friendship of the Anglo–Indian government, and carefully restrained themselves from taking any plunder or from molesting any Indian merchants. Major Hayes-Sadler, the political agent, for his part, maintained a strict neutrality, although this posture was more a comfort to Salih ibn-'Ali than to the besieged sultan. But an essential weakness of the coalition, like others of the late nineteenth century, was that it contained no Ghafiri representation. Thus by March 1895 the sultan's frantic calls for aid and his promises of large gifts had attracted some 4,000 Ghafiri tribesmen who encamped in and around the city. Although 120 were killed and another 140 wounded in skirmishes, neither side had enough strength to push the other out of its positions and a stalemate developed.

At this point negotiations began, and on March 9, 1895 a peace was concluded in which Sultan Faysal pardoned Salih ibn-'Ali and his adherents, restored the subsidies he had been paying before the organization of the coalition, and delivered a special payment to Salih ibn-'Ali of between $MT 11,000 and $MT 17,000. Unfortunately, the discipline of the conservative tribesmen evaporated as they withdrew from Masqat. There was wholesale pillaging and the city was put to the torch. The Indian merchants suffered huge losses from the plundering and fire.[101]

Faysal ibn-Turki was shaken by his near escape and tried to profit from the lessons of the 1895 attack. He strengthened the long neglected defenses of Masqat and Matrah by mounting new 12-pound guns in his forts, reenlisting 40 African palace guards who had served his father, arming his palace guards with the newest rifles he could purchase, and restocking his munitions supplies. He also solidified alliances with al-Janabah, Bani-Bu-'Ali, Bani-Bu-Hasan, and Hajarayin—all southern tribes located mainly in Ja'lan—as well as with the Nu'yam tribe located on the northern borderlands of his realm.[102] Even more helpful to the sultan's efforts to recover some of his lost influence in the interior was a temporary disintegration of conservative cohesiveness that followed the evacuation of Masqat in March 1895. Salih ibn-'Ali's attack was the last flash of activity by the leaders who had dominated the conservative ranks since the mid-nineteenth century. Salih ibn-'Ali himself was cut down during a tribal war in 1896. When Ibrahim ibn-Qays died in 1898 all who had played a leading role in the affairs of the 1868-71 imamate were gone save the long inactive Faysal ibn-Hamud. With the passing of their old generation of sages, leaders, and warriors the con-

[101] For the attack on Masqat and its immediate aftermath see Al-Salimi, ii, 284-86; *Précis Maskat*, pp. 10-23; Lorimer, i, 536-43.
[102] Lorimer, i, 545; *Admin. Rpt.: 1895-1896*, pp. 13-15.

servative ranks found themselves temporarily without established leaders. The death of 'Abdallah ibn-Salih in 1895 deprived the conservatives of a potential chief and it took some years to develop new directors, but when they finally emerged in 1900-10 they were to prove themselves even more able than their predecessors. At any rate, as early as 1896 Sultan Faysal raided some of the conservative tribes—now divided and leaderless—that had combined against him in 1895.[103]

After surviving the crisis of 1895 some observers surmised that Sultan Faysal might move, as his father had done in 1875, to reconstruct his regime on a sound and realistic basis. This was not to be the case, however, because Faysal ibn-Turki in 1895 was face to face with a severe revenue crisis and because his displeasure with the British was greater than ever since they had given him no special help during the February 1895 attack on his capital.

Since the closing of the Indian mints to the free coinage of silver in 1893 the sultan's government had been trying unsuccessfully to cope with an ever-deepening financial crisis. Of course, an undercurrent of financial stringency had vexed the Omani authorities since Sayyid Sa'id's death in 1856, and the treasury had for a long time operated on a hand-to-mouth basis. But the financial difficulties of the 1890s were of an especially urgent nature. In many ways the sultan was powerless to deal with his embarrassment because he was squeezed between a relatively constant level of income and a situation of rising prices. Also, the distress in Oman was just one expression of a worldwide economic phenomenon in which silver-based coinages everywhere fell in value. But the sultan's fiscal ignorance also contributed to his woes. In 1898 the customs was leased by Faysal ibn-Turki for a fee of $MT 140,000 to a concessionaire who netted $MT 214,000 from farming this tax. At the same time, Sultan Faysal was running a deficit in his treasury of $MT 700 per month, a large deficiency in the

103 Al-Salimi, II, 286-88.

Omani perspective but one that would have been erased easily if the sultan had been receiving all the customs proceeds.[104]

The Omani government's solvency was destroyed during the aftermath of the 1895 attack on Masqat. The Ghafiri shaykhs, whose affirmative answer to Sultan Faysal's appeal for aid in February 1895 may well have saved his throne, converged on the monarch begging special presents and increased subsidies in return for their help. In addition, the British presented a bill of $MT 77,895 to the sultan to indemnify those Indian merchants who suffered losses during the pillaging which climaxed the conservative occupation of Masqat. The Indians originally calculated that their losses totaled $MT 206,000 but many of their claims proved to be excessive or fraudulent. In presenting his demand Major Hayes-Sadler originally requested that the sultan assure the payment of the indemnity by levying a punitive tax on all goods that came from the interior regardless of whether or not the commerce belonged to tribes guilty or innocent of the pillaging of Masqat. This was undoubtedly an expression of Hayes-Sadler's dictum that "one Arab is about as untrustworthy as another." Ultimately, the British agent accepted the proposition that only the offending tribes should indirectly pay the indemnity through a 20 percent punitive tax on all their exports, but he was unwilling to promise to support the sultan if disorders broke out because of the imposition of the levy. This hard line angered the sultan to the extent that his distaste for Britain reached a new high and pushed him even closer toward France. The fact that in 1896 Whitehall directed that this tack be abandoned did not repair the damage done by Hayes-Sadler in the sultan's hour of need. The punitive tax netted only $MT 20,000 in 20 months of application largely because it, like the customs, was farmed out to the sultan's chief creditor, Ratansee Purshotam.[105]

After 1895 the sultan fell more and more heavily in debt

[104] Lorimer, I, 546; *Précis Maskat*, p. 134.
[105] *Admin. Rpt.: 1895-1896*, pp. 13-15; *Précis Maskat*, pp. 22-23, 36.

to Purshotam and his Hindu business associates. Sultan Faysal began to rely on the dangerous practice of borrowing from one banker to pay back the interest on loans he received from others. To save the government from bankruptcy the Anglo–Indian authorities loaned Sultan Faysal 60,000 rupees in 1895 and extended the same courtesy again in 1897. These credits helped the sultan to pay off the very high interest loans he had contracted, but they were granted on the condition that he would borrow from no other foreign power. In 1897 Faysal ibn-Turki owed about $MT 130,000 to Hindu and Arab bankers. Typical of the deals Sultan Faysal arranged was one with an Arab banker who extended a credit of $MT 30,000 but which carried with it a 24 percent interest charge. By 1898 the sultan's indebtedness had jumped to $MT 190,000 and during that year it was discovered that Faysal ibn-Turki had misused half of the 1897 loan from Britain. Sultan Faysal, nevertheless, continued to refuse to consider reforming his financial apparatus. Complete collapse seemed imminent during the aftermath of the French coaling station concession crisis of 1899 when the British stopped delivery of the Zanzibar subsidy.[106]

The explosion of Faysal ibn-Turki's pretension that he was his own master was inevitable once he crossed the British. It has been pointed out that even before 1895 the sultan had earned the dislike of Britain's representatives in Masqat despite the realities that made their good will vital to his continuation on the throne. It is true that the policy carried out by these British representatives in Oman was equally blundering and that the arrogance of these agents irritated the sensitive sultan and only encouraged the "uncommendable" attitude which was said to characterize his feelings toward the British.[107] After the February 1895 assault on Masqat Anglo–Omani relations deteriorated very rapidly. The sultan considered that the policy of "strict neutrality" enunciated by Hayes-Sadler after

[106] Lorimer, I, 572-73; *Précis Maskat*, p. 66.
[107] *Admin. Rpt.: 1895-1896*, p. 1.

Salih ibn-'Ali occupied his capital, to be a British failure to live up to their obligations toward him.[108] Sultan Faysal failed to realize that his sullen attitude in respect to his dynasty's longtime friend and protector had undermined his claim to British aid, aid which was, after all, only an implied not an explicit responsibility of the British.

Into this breach Ottavi, the wily consul who landed in Masqat in 1894 to advance French influence there, moved adroitly to encourage Sultan Faysal's resolve to resist British paramountcy. The rise of French influence in the sultan's court was facilitated when Faysal ibn-Turki appointed a certain 'Abd al-'Aziz of the Bani-Ruwahah tribe as his secretary, a post 'Abd al-'Aziz was also filling for Ottavi himself. This man had far more influence with the sultan than the wazir, Sa'id ibn-Muhammad, pro-British as he was, and the latter eventually was dismissed in 1898.[109] The fact that Ottavi was more concerned with swaying the sultan's conduct of his foreign relations than he was with affecting internal events did not assuage injured British pride at all. But it does appear that some in the Anglo–Indian government realized that the alarming deterioration in Anglo–Omani relations was due, in some measure at least, to the British failure to assist Sultan Faysal during the 1895 crisis. Consequently, some attempts to appease the sultan were made, including the grant of loans and military aid to help suppress a rising in Dhofar. Crowning these conciliatory efforts was the issuing of an ultimatum in 1896 to the Omani tribal shaykhs that Britain would not tolerate any more attacks on the Masqat–Matrah district, a pronouncement similar to that issued in Sultan Turki's behalf in 1886. But Faysal ibn-Turki reacted coldly to these gestures which he considered as being prompted only by British fears that their ascendancy would give way to that of France and that, in any case, they had been extended after the real need for them had passed.[110] The sultan went on being difficult

---

[108] *Précis Maskat*, pp. 16-22; Lorimer, I, 551. [109] Lorimer, I, 556.
[110] *Précis Maskat*, pp. 21-22; Lorimer, I, 551-55.

and aggravated the bad situation in many ways such as insisting that the claims of Indian merchants for indemnity of the losses they had sustained in the attack of 1895 should receive no preference over the claims of native Omani merchants. Whether they were just or not, the British viewed such tactics as proof of Sultan Faysal's "obstinate" posturing.[111]

The denouement came in 1898. It started when Faysal ibn-Turki refused to fire the customary salute on Queen Victoria's birthday. Next, one of the sultan's slaves insulted a party of visiting British naval officers. Apologies for both lapses were delivered but to the Anglo–Indian authorities the incidents were taken as more indications of Sultan Faysal's basic hostility toward Britain.[112] But it was the announcement that Sultan Faysal had granted the French a concession to establish a coaling station in the vicinity of Masqat that was the last straw. This was taken as a grave and direct threat to Britain's position in the Gulf and to the security of her Anglo–Indian empire. From the secretary of state for India in Whitehall right down to Her Majesty's political agent and consul at Masqat responsible British officialdom resolved to end the defiance of "this petty prince."[113] Coincident as it was with the Fashoda crisis, the "Masqat crisis" of 1898-99 was viewed by British public opinion as just one more aspect of a worldwide Anglo–French imperial confrontation. Thus most Britons were happy to bring things to a head, for it was believed a "sharp action" was necessary "to improve an otherwise almost intolerable position." Under Lord Curzon's direct instructions Major Fagan, the agent at Masqat, Colonel Meade, the resident in the Persian Gulf, and Admiral Douglas, the East Indies station commander, publicly humiliated the sultan and ultimately forced him to capitulate and cancel the concession on the decks of a British warship whose guns were aimed at the sultan's palace. At the same time the Zanzibar subsidy was withheld from the bankrupt sultan and the law officers of the

---

[111] *Précis Maskat*, p. 23.   [112] *Ibid.*, pp. 63-64.
[113] "Hamilton to Curzon, 10 Mar. 1899," India Mss.–2, Vol. I.

British crown issued statements to the effect that Britain would be justified in punishing or even in deposing any Omani sultan who broke his solemn engagements with the Queen-Empress.[114] The "Masqat crisis" of 1898-99 was in one sense a tombstone which memorialized the death and the ceremonial burial of Faysal ibn-Turki's "independence" policy. Ottavi's intrigues and Curzon's severity had brought France to the point where she either had to resist British determination to neutralize French influence in Oman or back down. Although Lord Salisbury intervened in time to prevent the crisis from worsening and softened the implications of the confrontation somewhat, a choice could not be avoided and France backed down. The French retreat left Faysal ibn-Turki to face the full brunt of Curzon's wrath; the unfortunate sultan could do nothing but surrender meekly to all British demands and hope to preserve his title. While attending what might be regarded as his own political funeral on the deck of Admiral Douglas's flagship, Sultan Faysal expressed a hope that the British government would afford protection if the French tried to punish him for abrogating the coaling station concession.[115] Faysal ibn-Turki still had an instinct for survival.

The revival of Anglo–Omani cooperation, 1899-1903. The institution of the sultanate was in a very weak condition in February 1899. Sultan Faysal's attempts to extend his power in Oman's interior during the early part of his reign coupled with his subsequent withdrawal from participation in tribal affairs had only stimulated disorder in Oman's rural areas. His courtship of the conservatives ended with Salih ibn-'Ali's attack on Masqat in 1895. His annoyance with the weight of the British presence in his country angered those whose good will was necessary if his rule was to endure. His attempt to balance British power with that of France ended in the debacle of 1899. Moreover, his government was bankrupt. Only the fact that Faysal ibn-Turki was still Sultan of Masqat and

[114] *Précis Maskat*, p. 77. [115] *Ibid.*, pp. 73-74.

Oman, still a legally independent monarch, stood between him and total failure. Between February and October 1899 the future of the British–Omani connection—indeed, the future of the sultan himself—was clouded with uncertainty.[116] The atmosphere eventually cleared in October 1899 when Major Percy Cox replaced Major Fagan as political agent at Masqat. Within a few months of his arrival Cox's sympathetic treatment of Faysal ibn-Turki had softened the sultan's hostility toward Britain to the point where the ruler began to move toward a close reliance on the new political agent's advice. Meanwhile, the pro-British Sa'id ibn-Muhammad, who became wazir once again in 1899, began to restore some of the practices he had supervised during Sultan Turki's reign. By the end of 1899 Sultan Faysal took the step of requesting that the British protest in his behalf to the French government concerning the matter of those Omani dhows which had adopted the practice of sailing under the French flag. This move signaled the sultan's intention to rely almost exclusively on British advice in matters of foreign affairs.[117]

In domestic politics, too, Sultan Faysal returned to the way charted by his father. When Sa'id ibn-Muhammad retired as wazir in 1902 he was replaced by another old stalwart of the moderates, Sulayman ibn-Suwaylim.[118] The sultan was able to restore some temporary stability to his finances by accepting more British loans and by halting the practice of selling the right to farm the customs. After establishing a government customs administration in 1899 the sultan received an average of $MT 80,000 more per year between 1899 and 1904 than he netted during the last five years of private customs farming.[119] The absence of a united conservative opposition also allowed Sultan Faysal, using techniques similar to those practiced by his father, to reestablish his regime's influence in the

[116] "Hamilton to Curzon, 30 June 1899," India Mss.–2, Vol. I.
[117] "Hamilton to Curzon, 5 Jan. 1900," India Mss.–2, Vol. I.
[118] Lorimer, I, 525.
[119] *Ibid.*, pp. 571-73, 584-86; *Précis Maskat*, p. 134.

interior. By 1903 his sway was greater in the rural parts of his domain than in any previous year during his reign, and he even controlled some points, such as Nazwa, where his father's rule was minimal at best. In 1903, too, the sultan purchased an armed steamer, which increased Masqat's power over the coastal districts of the sultanate.[120]

The years 1899 to 1903 also mark the beginning of a new phase in the fortunes of the conservative Ibadis of Oman. With the death of Ibrahim ibn-Qays at al-Rustaq in 1898 the last of the old leaders of the 1868-71 imamate who was still active politically passed away. 'Azzan ibn-Qays' son Sa'ud ibn-'Azzan then attempted to revive and reorganize the conservative movement later in 1898 when he called a conclave at al-Rustaq to investigate the possibility of reviving the imamate with himself at its head. For a short time it appeared that Sa'ud ibn-'Azzan's cause might succeed, but the younger chiefs who had inherited the conservative leadership had not yet developed the poise, experience, and prestige to provide the political and religious cohesion needed to bring about the restoration of a fundamentalist government at that juncture.[121] In 1899 the murder of Sa'ud ibn-'Azzan ended a promising career. But in time other young leaders did mature. Salih ibn-'Ali's place as the most important among the tribal chiefs supporting the conservative cause was taken by his son 'Isa ibn-Salih. Also, the need for a commanding religious and intellectual leader to rally conservative opinion, a function that had not been performed by an obviously able man since the death of Sa'id ibn-Khalfan al-Khalili in 1871, eventually showed signs of being fulfilled by 'Abdallah ibn-Humayd al-Salimi, a person destined to become a noted theologian, lawyer, and historian of the conservative movement. Another significant occurrence during the first years of the twentieth century came when some of the tribes of al-Sharqiyah and 'Uman began to shut themselves off from outsiders. In 1902 'Isa ibn-Salih of al-Hirth tried to

[120] Al-Salimi, II, 291-95; Lorimer, I, 583-84.
[121] Al-Salimi, II, 289-91.

prevent some British scientists from investigating the extent of certain coal deposits located inland from Sur. When Percy Cox tried to facilitate a meeting that would open the area peacefully to scientific investigation 'Isa ibn-Salih dismissed the idea with the words "I will not see him and he will not see me."[122] These words were to prove prophetic when, after a conservative imamate was recreated in Oman's interior in 1913 with 'Isa ibn-Salih as one of its founders, its official policy ultimately reflected this isolationist attitude.

But the revival of conservatism did not command in 1903 the loyalty and popularity that it would have a decade later and so Faysal ibn-Turki could enjoy his title. But the realities of his power were very apparent in 1903 when Lord Curzon visited Masqat and Sultan Faysal during the course of a vice-regal tour of the Persian Gulf which was being made to emphasize British predominance in the region. Curzon reported after his visit to Oman that Sultan Faysal had adopted the tone of a "loyal feudatory of the British Crown rather than that of an independent sovereign." The viceroy also made allusions to the fact that the sultan occupied a place vis-à-vis Britain similar to that of the Indian princes who had ranged themselves alongside the British raj. To compensate Sultan Faysal for his submissive posture, Lord Curzon assured the ruler that Britain would uphold his rule by force if necessary.[123] Ten years later Britain had to do just that.

But if Faysal ibn-Turki after 1899 was willing to act as a "loyal feudatory" should, he was not too pleased with his role. He became despondent on occasion, and in 1903, the very year he deferred to Lord Curzon so convincingly, Sultan Faysal talked seriously of abdication.[124] Faysal ibn-Turki's personal sense of failure, isolation, and bewilderment must have been acute. He was accused by his countrymen of being a tool of foreigners, yet his wish to identify himself with Oman and its traditions is symbolized well by his continued use of the

122 *Ibid.*, p. 301; *Précis Maskat*, p. 115.
123 Lorimer, I, 2,634-36.   124 *Ibid.*, p. 587.

title "imam" on his coins. Although he realized after his humiliation in 1899 that he lived in a world where modern power counted for much, Faysal ibn-Turki did not really understand the workings of that power and seemed to dread the changes the future might bring. It is little wonder that a man who once tried to affirm the independence of his office and his country did not want to lead that country away from its traditions.

CHAPTER 9

Epilogue: Oman in the Twentieth Century

DURING the first half of the twentieth century events in Oman continued to develop within the context that had been established there between 1862 and 1903. The interests of the seaboard townsmen and moderate Ibadism were represented by the sultan's government in Masqat, a regime shielded and assisted by the British. The moderates were opposed by parochially oriented conservative Ibadi groups entrenched in the country's interior who sought to preserve a congenial religious–political environment in Oman. Meanwhile, the economy of the country—already stagnant in 1903—continued to deteriorate. These characteristics, variously expressed according to changing circumstances, continued to summarize Omani realities until 1955. Since that year, the first signs that fundamental changes in the basic context were imminent have appeared. Now, it seems almost certain that Oman is ready to embark on a new era in its history and that we are witnessing the beginning of the end of the country's hundred year long ordeal as an economic and political backwater of little importance and even less influence in the world at large.

DIVIDED OMAN—SULTANATE AND IMAMATE, 1913-55

For most of 1900-10 Sultan Faysal ibn-Turki appeared to be strengthening his position within Oman. In retrospect it is clear that the apparent growth was largely chimerical. Sultan Faysal never really recovered from the shock of 1899 when his dreams of independence were shattered and he was publicly humiliated on the decks of a British warship. While Sir Percy Cox was political agent—from 1899 to 1904—the chastened sultan readily followed his lead. Thus, with the aid of Anglo–Indian government loans and the advice of "the uncrowned king of the Gulf," Faysal ibn-Turki temporarily restored some health to the Masqat exchequer.[1] Also, he regained some influence among the interior tribes by reinstituting as best he could the policies and techniques utilized by his father, Sultan Turki, whereby the ruler served as a peacemaking balance in the highlands and inland districts. But much of Sultan Faysal's relative success in the years immediately after 1903 was due not so much to his own actions as to the energetic efforts undertaken in his behalf by Sulayman ibn-Suwaylim, the ex-slave who was the wazir of the Masqati government from 1902 to 1907. The fact that the several conservative Ibadi leaders remained divided and suspicious of one another until they finally joined together in 1913 meant the sultan was not faced with the necessity of coping with a strong opposition to his rule, a circumstance which also contributed to the aura of relative calm which prevailed. In 1906 the sultan was able to establish—officially at least—friendly relations with Shaykh 'Isa ibn-Salih—who had succeeded his father, Salih ibn-'Ali, as tamimah of the al-Hirth of al-Sharqiyah and as the leading Hinawi tribal figure among the conservatives—at a time when Shaykh 'Isa was seeking allies in a dispute with Shaykh Himyar ibn-Nasir of Bani-Riyam.[2]

In the realm of Oman's foreign affairs the years 1904-14 were ones of increasing calm in contrast to the agitated maneuverings of the previous decade. There was a settlement of the outstanding Anglo–French disagreements concerning Oman, as well as a general recognition among the great powers of British predominance in southeastern Arabia. The forging of the Anglo–French Entente in 1904 was followed a year later by the settling of the "Muscat dhows–French flags case" by the Hague Tribunal. Next, between 1908 and 1914 energetic British efforts to obtain the suppression of the Masqat munitions trade were successful and Britain gained international

[1] "Curzon to Cox, 22 Jan. 1917," quoted in Graves, *Life of Cox*, p. 230; the phrase was used by Curzon to describe the status Sir Percy had attained in the Persian Gulf region during the course of his labors there.

[2] Al-Salimi, II, 302-303; Arabian American Oil Company, *Oman*, p. 52.

recognition of her right to exercise a "free hand" in controlling the Omani arms commerce. Initially, the French resisted these moves which they regarded as a British stratagem designed to strike at France's right of guaranteed free access to Omani markets, but eventually Paris gave in to Whitehall's offer of compensation. The year 1914 marked the close of a 20-year period in which France had asserted her treaty rights and ambitions in Oman. Following the French retreat no other great power came forward to challenge Britain's preeminence in the sultanate. Moreover, since Ibn-Sa'ud was only beginning his distinguished career that was to lead to the reestablishment of a strong Sa'udi state, no immediate problems were posed for Oman's leaders or for her British protectors from that quarter.

Oman's fleeting moment of internal order ended early in 1907. Sulayman ibn-Suwaylim was murdered passing through the territory of the al-Siyabiyin tribe in Wadi Sama'il, while returning from a visit to 'Isa ibn-Salih's seat at al-Qabil in al-Sharqiyah. The slaying of the strong-willed wazir was apparently the fruit of a growing resentment in some tribes against Sulayman's readiness to "meddle" in their internal affairs. The violence also presaged trouble for the sultan in the vital pass district. Sultan Faysal organized an expedition to punish al-Siyabiyin, which, while it gained some measure of vengeance against the guilty, did little of a permanent nature to strengthen the ruler's position in Wadi Sama'il. It also proved to be virtually the last instance of Faysal ibn-Turki asserting himself decisively in the interior. Without the astute Sulayman ibn-Suwaylim to assist him, the bewildered sultan's government lapsed back into disorganization. The precarious financial equilibrium reached between 1899 and 1904 was an early casualty, as the sultan, despite promises he had made to consult the British concerning his financial dealings, secretly secured large new loans from local Hindu merchants, from the customs administration, and even from M. Goguyer, the most important of the French arms dealers in Masqat. The government's financial embarrassment intensified in 1910 following a steep decline in customs revenue after Britain established a naval blockade in the Gulf to halt the reexport of arms from Masqat to other regional ports. In 1911 the Anglo–Indian authorities rescued Faysal ibn-Turki from impending bankruptcy only by advancing a large, interest-free loan to him, but the sultan's lethargic administration continued to lack any real direction.[3]

This situation of uneasy drift exploded in 1912 when the Anglo–Indian government convinced Sultan Faysal to set up a warehouse in Masqat to supervise the import and export of all weapons and ammunition in and out of Oman. Since 1898 the British had been pressing the sultan to exercise stricter control of the munitions trade. Also, the British government had forced most of its own subjects—including Indians—to abandon the commerce in firearms so that by 1912 the trade contributed mainly to the profits of French and German interests. Although Sultan Faysal had signed some innocuous control measures he had resisted previous British efforts to limit stringently the arms trade, because the business contributed significantly to Masqat's commercial activity and so to his impoverished treasury. For instance, in 1907 the sultan collected £14,500 in arms import duties. He was induced to restrict the traffic only after the Anglo–Indian authorities pledged to increase the annual "Zanzibar subsidy" by a lakh of rupees (100,000 rupees or £6,666) in order to compensate him to some degree for the customs revenues he would give up by agreeing to a trade limitation. For the British, the 1912 arms trade agreement put an end to the security problem caused by "gun-running" in the Persian Gulf, but for Sultan Faysal and his government the conclusion of the agreement precipitated one of the most dangerous crises ever faced by an Al Bu Sa'id regime.[4]

[3] Al-Salimi, II, 303-305; "Arms Trade—1913," India Records–5.

[4] Wilson, *Persian Gulf*, p. 271; Arabian American Oil Company, *Oman*, p. 53; "Arms Trade—1913," India Records–5; "Muscat Trade Reports, file 1917: no. 234, 1911/12, 1912/13, 1913/14," India Records–6.

To many in Oman the sultan's signature on the arms agreement was the final proof of his total subservience to Christian foreigners and of his heretic tendencies. The sultan's reliance on British military aid and his acquiescence—grudgingly given though it was—to British views in regard to the slave trade were well known. Indeed, in 1901 'Isa ibn-Salih had addressed a strong letter to Faysal ibn-Turki protesting the freeing of escaped slaves by the British.[5] In 1912 Shaykh 'Isa also protested against the barriers being erected to block the arms trade. But other conservative figures went even further than writing letters of protest. By the winter of 1913 conservative Ibadi leaders and preachers had roused much of 'Uman, al-Sharqiyah, and al-Jabal al-Akhdar by speeches in which they pictured the arms warehouse scheme as a British device to deprive the people of Oman of modern weapons. It is true that once Sultan Faysal established the warehouse he thought that he would benefit politically because he could prevent the interior tribes from arming themselves with guns that could be turned against him. The only thing wrong with this assumption by the sultan was the fact that the Omani tribes had been acquiring stocks of new, serviceable rifles and ammunition for some 20 years. The tribes were armed to the teeth already; the door had been closed too late.[6]

In the spring of 1913 sundry conservative chiefs, faced with what they conceived as a threat to them all, began to join together. At the time, there were three main conservative factions. The most doctrinaire group in the sense of being inspired by the vision of reestablishing an ideal Ibadi state in the classical mold was that grouped around Shaykh 'Abdallah ibn-Humayd al-Salimi, a blind religious scholar well versed in Omani history and conservative Ibadi ideology. Al-Salimi was strongly supported by his son-in-law, Shaykh Salim ibn-Rashid

[5] Graves, *Life of Cox*, p. 63.

[6] G. Bell, *The Arab War: Confidential Information for General Headquarters from Gertrude Bell: Being Despatches Reprinted from the Secret "Arab Bulletin"* (London, 1940), p. 21.

al-Kharusi of the Bani Kharus, a Ghafiri tribe that provided many Ibadi imams in medieval times. The champion of the conservative Hinawi tribes was 'Isa ibn-Salih, tamimah of al-Hirth, the martial tribe that supplied the hard core of conservative military strength after Salih ibn-'Ali helped to proclaim the imamate of 'Azzan ibn-Qays in 1868. Shaykh 'Isa was a forceful and intelligent leader whose orientation, like that of his father, was basically political. He was inspired by a desire to assure the autonomy of his tribe, its supremacy among the Hinawis, and his personal leadership in conservative councils. Not as doctrinaire as al-Salimi, 'Isa ibn-Salih, although he took his religious views seriously, was willing to consider expedient political compromises. Another among the major conservative chiefs, and a new source of strength for fundamentalist Ibadism, was Shaykh Himyar ibn-Nasir al-Nabhani, tamimah of the Ghafiri Bani-Riyam. The Bani-Riyam, whose chief town, Tanuf, was perched on the slopes of al-Jabal al-Akhdar overlooking 'Uman province, had remained aloof from 'Azzan ibn-Qays' imamate and the conservative cause generally until the early twentieth century. Fears that his autonomy and the Ibadi faith were being threatened by increased foreign meddling in Oman undoubtedly caused Shaykh Himyar to embrace the conservative program. The motives of the Bani-Riyam shaykh were more conditioned by family ambitions than were those of the other founders of the 1913 imamate. The Nabhani branch of the Bani-Riyam furnished several of the rulers who dominated interior Oman between the twelfth and seventeenth centuries.[7]

The conservative coalition was forged in two stages. First, Himyar ibn-Nasir, al-Salimi, and Salim ibn-Rashid al-Kharusi joined forces, engineered al-Kharusi's election as imam at Tanuf in May 1913, and set out to attract the rest of the Ibadi community to the newly restored imamate.[8] The conclave of

[7] B. Thomas, "Arab Rule under the Al Bu Sa'id Dynasty of Oman," *Proceedings of the British Academy*, xxiv (1938), 47; Arabian American Oil Company, *Oman*, pp. 53, 75-82.

[8] Saudi Arabia, *Memorial*, i, 318; Bell, *Arab War*, p. 21.

religious scholars who ratified the restoration of the imamate also declared that Sultan Faysal ibn-Turki was deposed, that he was "dissociated from the affairs of the Muslims [the Ibadis] and deprived of any role in their realm, his decrees becoming null and void."[9] Thus, it is clear that originally the new regime aimed at establishing an imamate like that of 1868-71 which would include all Oman—Masqat and the coast, as well as the interior. At first, 'Isa ibn-Salih held himself aloof from the new conservative combination, doubtless because of his well-known enmity toward Himyar ibn-Nasir, his antagonism toward 'Abdallah ibn-Humayd al-Salimi, and his practical political sense that prompted him to wait and see how the newborn authority was received. He did not have to wait long. In June 1913 Nazwa was taken; in imitation of its ancient status it became the imam's capital. Then in July the neighboring 'Umani town of Izki capitulated. Meanwhile, most of the tribes of 'Uman—both Ghafiri and Hinawi—offered their allegiance to the new imam. The fact that Ghafiris as well as Hinawis were attracted to al-Kharusi's white banner and that they were among the leaders and organizers of the imamate was most significant because one of the main reasons for the failure of 'Azzan ibn-Qays' government and the subsequent lack of permanent conservative successes against the moderate sultans in Masqat was the absence of extensive Ghafiri participation in the fundamentalist movements. 'Isa ibn-Salih, after reading the signs, joined with the imamate in July 1913 and immediately became one of its most influential figures. His adherence solidified a conservative Hinawi–Ghafiri alliance of formidable proportions which remained strong for over 40 years under the unifying aegis of the imams.[10]

By July 1913 the British political agent in Masqat, Major S. G. Knox, became so alarmed at the possible consequences of the progress of the imam's cause that he sent a letter to Nazwa

[9] Saudi Arabia, *Memorial*, I, 320-21.

[10] Thomas, "Al Bu Sa'id Dynasty," *Proceedings of the British Academy*, XXIV (1938), 47; Bell, *Arab War*, p. 21.

stating that the Anglo–Indian government would not allow Masqat and Matrah to be captured. The imam's reply was hardly one to comfort Major Knox since it warned that the British should not interfere in the affairs of the Ibadis and that they "must not commit aggression against us."[11] Under the circumstances it was only prudent to land a small Indian Army detachment at Matrah in July to signal the Anglo–Indian government's resolve to live up to its commitment to defend Sultan Faysal. Nevertheless, in August the sultan's position deteriorated dangerously because the Wadi Sama'il passes and the town of Sama'il itself were overrun by the imam's adherents. Now Masqat and Matrah were directly menaced by a regime whose declared intention was to depose the sultan. Accordingly, in September 1913 the Anglo–Indian troop strength was doubled and the soldiers moved into entrenchments at Bayt al-Falaj at short distance inland from the twin port cities.[12]

On October 4, 1913, as his hold over his realm continued to evaporate, the unfortunate Faysal ibn-Turki died. He was succeeded by his eldest son, Taymur ibn-Faysal, then 27, who had taken an increasingly active role in his father's government. Inheriting a nearly empty treasury as well as a shaky throne, Sultan Taymur tried as best he could to reverse the tide of events by inviting his old acquaintance 'Isa ibn-Salih to Masqat in December to parley with him. The talks were inconclusive, however, and in the spring of 1914 the imam was gaining adherents even among the coastal tribes. After the seaport towns of Barka in al-Batinah and Quryyat, about 40 miles south of Masqat, were taken over by conservative forces, Sultan Taymur ibn-Faysal controlled little more than Masqat and Matrah, Sur, Suhar, and a few small al-Batinah ports. But in April 1914 the conservatives received their first check when gunfire from *H.M.S. Fox* and *Dartmouth* drove them from Barka and Quryyat. Following century-old policy the

[11] Saudi Arabia, *Memorial*, I, 319.
[12] Bell, *Arab War*, p. 21.

British would tolerate no threat to their hegemony over the Gulf's shores. But the outbreak of World War I in August 1914 meant that British ships and military forces would no longer be available to support the sultan on a few hours' call. Meanwhile, German propaganda reputedly filtering into Oman via Zanzibar and German East Africa (Tanganyika) was spreading the message that British dominance in the Persian Gulf region would soon be a thing of the past. Nevertheless, in August 1914 more Anglo–Indian soldiers arrived to defend Sultan Taymur. When Imam Salim and 'Isa ibn-Salih made their long-heralded assault upon the capital in January 1915, Masqat's defenses were ready.[13]

The attack was made by 3,000 men against 700 well-entrenched Anglo–Indian soldiers. The imam's confident army fell on its outnumbered but well-trained, disciplined foe in a frontal charge in full daylight. This lack of any semblance of martial guile resulted in so terrible a slaughter that the imam's now discouraged army withdrew into the highlands and Masqat has not had to endure any attacks since.[14] The coastal regions were cleared of remaining imamate forces when Sultan Taymur led a force against the previously troublesome Bani-Battash tribe in July 1915 and forced them to surrender their tribal seat, Hayl al-Ghaf, as well as the port village of Daghmar, a place located south of Masqat, where a fortified outpost was constructed. Despite rumors that a conservative thrust against Sur was imminent in October 1915, the sultan did not have to contend with any more moves toward the coast.[15]

Meanwhile, following the failure of the conservative effort to drive Taymur ibn-Faysal into the sea, a five-year-long succession of half-hearted negotiation attempts started between the sultanate and imamate. These began on the initiative of India's viceroy, Lord Hardinge, who during a visit to Masqat

---

[13] *Ibid.*, pp. 21-23; Arabian American Oil Company, *Oman*, p. 54.

[14] Thomas, "Al Bu Sa'id Dynasty," *Proceedings of the British Academy*, XXIV (1938), 48.

[15] Bell, *Arab War*, pp. 25-27.

in February 1915 offered the services of the British political agent as a mediator. While the sultan eagerly accepted Lord Hardinge's suggestion, the imam's followers looked on the British overtures as a sign of the sultan's weakness and forthcoming collapse; moreover, they apparently wondered how impartial a mediator any British officer would be, given the fact that scores of their comrades had been killed by Anglo-Indian troops just a month earlier. Nevertheless, formal contacts began in April 1915, followed in May by talks between 'Isa ibn-Salih and the political agent. These contacts continued sporadically throughout the summer of 1915 when, after it became clear agreement was impossible at the time, they were shelved.[16]

The conservative demands put forth during the course of the negotiations are interesting because they throw light on the aims of the Salim al-Kharusi regime, and also because many of them were incorporated subsequently into the Treaty of al-Sib of 1920 which ended hostilities between the sultanate and imamate. At various points in the negotiations the conservatives argued that they were not opposed to a British presence in Oman but that they did wish all British troops removed from the country. Also, they said that they regarded the sultan as a heretic because he did not conform to their version of Ibadi practice, and they maintained that the British should not support him in matters contrary to religious truth. A general complaint against the British from the Ibadi point of view was that the Westerners permitted the forbidden, such as the import and sale of wine and tobacco, but forbade the permitted, such as the trade in slaves and arms. Further, the conservatives denied the right of the British to claim the command of the sea, which, they said, should be open to all, and attacked the practice of forcing all ships engaged in overseas journeys to go first to Masqat to pay duties. The conservative negotiators also alluded to the fact that the people of Oman were suffering from the continued fall in the value of the dollar and the con-

16 *Ibid.*, pp. 21-23.

current increase in the price of food and cloth. These conditions, of course, had been developing over many decades, but the general economic dislocations that resulted from World War I heightened the distress; the British and the sultan were blamed for the difficulty in any case. This complaint also shows that the blockade that had been imposed on all imports into the interior was causing hardships there. Another economic criticism of the conservatives was that members of interior tribes—particularly al-Hirth—who owned property on the coast and in Zanzibar, or who were owed money by people who lived in these places were unable to supervise their business interests or settle claims. As might be expected, the right to trade in slaves and arms was defended. Specific complaints against the sultan's government, besides that of general irreligiousness, were that its justice was corrupt, that favoritism was shown to friends of the palace, that Ibadi religious law had been abandoned, and that the ruler's income, largely mortgaged in advance to Hindu businessmen, was used to support a large and unnecessary list of officers, relatives of the sultan, and various hangerson. Despite this catalogue it was stated that the conservatives were willing to regard the sultan "as ruler of Oman" if the imam actually administered the country according to religious law either personally or through a representative at Masqat. Thus, it appears that the conservatives were willing to "compromise"—to the extent of leaving the sultan on his throne if he were willing to become a puppet of the Nazwa authorities.[17]

For his part, Sultan Taymur rejected the conservative demands and became convinced that the imam did not want peace because he refused to return the Wadi Sama'il forts even though 'Isa ibn-Salih seemed ready to do this in the interests of securing peace. In any event, the sultan and his British allies adopted a defensive stance along the coast while the imam proceeded to consolidate his grip on interior Oman. In August 1917 young Ahmad ibn-Ibrahim, a nephew of the last

[17] *Ibid.*, pp. 23-24.

imam, 'Azzan ibn-Qays, but also a cousin and a friend of the sultan, was forced out of al-Rustaq by Imam Salim ibn-Rashid as the climax of a conservative drive which secured the Hajar mountain valleys north of Wadi Sama'il. Once again 'Isa ibn-Salih disagreed with the imam, the shaykh preferring to leave Ahmad ibn-Ibrahim in al-Rustaq. The expulsion served to heal once and for all the century-old breach between the Qays ibn-Ahmad and Sultan ibn-Ahmad branches of the Al Bu Sa'id family, and Ahmad ibn-Ibrahim fled to Masqat where he became a trusted aid of the moderate regime.[18]

Between 1913 and 1920 life in Oman's coastal and interior provinces was disrupted by the combined effects of the civil war inside the country and the general dislocations that disturbed the entire Persian Gulf region during World War I. In Oman's inland districts, the expansionist energy of the al-Kharusi imamate was spent by 1917 as the Nazwa leaders found that they lacked resources sufficient to unseat the British supported sultan. With trade links between the ports and the inner hinterland cut and high prices prevailing, the scarcity of money in areas controlled by the conservatives was so acute in 1916 that property belonging to Al Bu Sa'id partisans was seized, a measure followed in 1918 by the prohibition of coin exports. The misery caused by civil war was more than matched by that brought by the worldwide influenza epidemic of 1918-19 which killed an estimated 20,000 Omanis, hit the inland provinces particularly hard, and prompted Imam Salim to designate a special day of prayer.[19] On the coast, the effectiveness of the Masqat government progressively deteriorated as the emergency continued. Sultan Taymur, although well meaning, was not a skilled administrator, did not understand

[18] *Ibid.*, p. 28; Arabian American Oil Company, *Oman*, p. 64; "Bushire Residency Monthly Reports, file 1919: no. 2,297," India Records–6. Some sources claim al-Rustaq fell in July 1916, but most official British records agree that the date of the stronghold's capture by the imam was 12 August 1917.

[19] *Admin. Rpt.: 1918*, p. 47; "Bushire Residency Monthly Reports, file 1919: no. 2,297," India Records–6.

finance, and did not possess a character stern enough to reverse the tide of chaos that was engulfing his realm. Nor did he receive competent administrative help from his Al Bu Sa'id relatives, most of whom were content to pocket their allowances without providing much service in return. Tribal support evaporated as the money available to subsidize the great shaykhs disappeared; the bulk of the Hinawi tribes joined the imam while the Ghafaris either followed the same course or, at best, adopted neutrality. By 1918 a disastrous trade depression combined with the high costs of waging war and with governmental incompetence to produce a situation in which the sultan, already owing over 750,000 rupees, was falling ever-deeper into debt to Masqat's Hindu bankers who charged the monarch 40 percent interest for their loan services. Preoccupied with their own war, the British were content to keep the Masqat government barely afloat by forwarding periodic doles to the sultan in the form of interest-free advances on his subsidy. Meanwhile, after 1913 Masqat's business fell into a depression rivaling that of the 1860s. This decline was due to the cumulative effects of the end of the munitions trade, the civil war's stoppage of most traffic between inland and seaboard Oman, the increasing competition from the rising port of Dubayy on the Trucial Coast, and especially to World War I which disorganized steamer services and caused commodity shortages throughout the Persian Gulf. In 1917–18 the value of Masqat's trade dropped to £323,815, almost half its normal prewar total. The only bright spot in this otherwise dismal picture was the boom enjoyed by Omani shipowners who were able to recapture some of the regional carrying trade temporarily abandoned by steamers and to take advantage of wartime smuggling opportunities.[20]

Clearly, the country could regain some measure of stability only if peace were restored, the relationship between conserv-

[20] *Ibid.*; "Personalities—Arabia, 1917, pp. 71-72," India Records–5; "Muscat Financial Affairs, file 1914: no. 1,173," "Muscat Trade Reports, file 1917: no. 234, 1917/18," India Records–6.

ative and moderate Ibadis reconstructed, and the badly worn Masqati administrative machine that had received few repairs since the days of Sultan Turki overhauled. The British were aware that the country's depressing predicament was due in no small part to the weakness, corruption, and unpopularity of the Masqat government. Also, they recognized that because their money, troops, and effort kept the moderate regime alive, Masqat's failures necessarily reflected discredit on Britain. As early as 1914 Sir Percy Cox, the resident, advanced a scheme to revitalize the creaking Masqat government by seconding a British "confidential advisor" and an Anglo–Indian military officer to serve with the sultan's administration, but the plan was shelved when war broke out. Still, the British believed they could convince Sultan Taymur to accept a reform program when it suited them because of the perpetually precarious state of the sultan's treasury and his financial dependence on Britain. As Cox expressed it, ". . . if the Sultan is in our debt we are in a stronger position to guide Maskat affairs."[21] Ultimately, in the autumn of 1918 Major Haworth, the political agent in Oman, produced a plan to reorganize the sultan's "medieval" financial, administrative, and security apparatus and to introduce Anglo–Indian personnel into key posts in a reformed Masqat government. The idea was similar in its essentials to several projects the British had implemented or were discussing in connection with other areas they controlled in the Middle East. Despairing of curing his political impotence by his own efforts, Taymur ibn-Faysal agreed to Haworth's proposals, received a 650,000-rupee loan sufficient to settle his debts, but surrendered to the British considerable de facto control over the day-to-day conduct of the central Masqat government.[22]

Between 1919 and 1921 Haworth's successor at Masqat, Ma-

[21] "Cox to Viceroy, enclosure in telegram viceroy to secretary of state, 20 Nov. 1916, in Muscat Financial Affairs, file 1914: no. 1,173, "India Records–6.

[22] "Bushire Residency Monthly Reports, file 1919: no. 2,297," "Muscat Financial Affairs, file 1914: no. 1,173," India Records–6.

jor R. E. L. Wingate, initiated the reform program. In 1920 Captain McCollum, who had been serving as political agent in Kuwait, became the first of a succession of British wazirs and financial advisors who have headed the Masqati sultans' government. Stringent financial controls were established: the spending of the sultan and his family was curtailed severely, the customs service was overhauled completely, with new posts imposed on outlying ports such as Sur and Suhar, and British-trained Egyptians replaced Masqati Indian officials in the central treasury. Executive departments that later evolved into finance, port and customs, interior, foreign relations, and military offices were created, while the heads of these offices and other senior aides of the sultan were formed into a council of state empowered to act for the ruler in his absence. In 1921 a British officer of the Indian Army, Captain E. V. McCarthy, was seconded to Masqat, where he became the organizer and first commander of a small but well-drilled military formation, "The Muscat Levy Corps." Originally composed of Persian mercenaries but later recruited locally and in Makran, the Levies replaced the Anglo–Indian detachment that had saved the Al Bu Sa'id dynasty during the 1913-20 war with the imamate. Also in 1921, the purchase of two powerful motor launches signaled a revival of Masqat's determination to control its coastal waters. The law courts, whose corruption was often publicized by the conservatives, were revamped to apply an Ibadi version of Islamic law, while a "chief court" at Masqat, whose decisions could be appealed to the sultan, was created.[23]

The British realized that a successful reorganization of the moderate regime depended on ending the drain on the sultan's scarce resources caused by the war with the imam. Thus, in September 1919, in the same month the Haworth reforms

[23] Thomas, "Al Bu Sa'id Dynasty," *Proceedings of the British Academy*, XXIV (1938), 49-52; the appointment of a British wazir, in theory a temporary expedient, in practice has been a permanent change; "Muscat Levy Corps, file 1920: no. 6,818," "Muscat Financial Affairs, file 1914: no. 1,173," India Records–6.

were inaugurated, Wingate also approached the imam in an effort to revive peace negotiations. But the austere Imam Salim would not agree to the terms presented to him. Consequently, in an effort to increase the pressure for a compromise of the factional strife the sultan's government increased penal taxes on imamate-produced commodities up to 50 percent of the value of some classes of goods.[24] Nevertheless, not until after the murder of Imam Salim ibn-Rashid al-Kharusi in July 1920 by a disgruntled Al Wahibah tribesman did a climate emerge conducive to reaching an agreement. An election for a new imam was held without delay after the assassination, the choice being Shaykh Muhammad ibn-'Abdallah al-Khalili, a member of the Hinawi Bani-Ruwahah tribe, a confidant of 'Isa ibn-Salih and a grandson of Sa'id ibn-Khalfan al-Khalili, who was the chief organizer and advisor of the imamate of 'Azzan ibn-Qays 50 years earlier. The election of Imam Muhammad ibn-'Abdallah signaled a shift to the more conciliatory posture that had been favored by 'Isa ibn-Salih, and negotiations between the imamate and sultanate were soon resumed. On September 25, 1920 the two regimes, utilizing the mediation of Major Wingate, signed the Treaty of al-Sib by which the governments of the imam and the sultan agreed that they would coexist in peace and the tribes and shaykhs of Oman agreed not to attack the coastal towns.[25]

---

[24] "Bushire Residency Monthly Reports, file 1919: no. 2,297," India Records–6.

[25] The text below is translated from an Arabic version distributed by the Political Department, League of Arab States:

Treaty of al-Sib

(In the name of God, the Compassionate, the Merciful)

This is the peace concluded between the government of Sultan Taymur ibn-Faysal and Shaykh 'Isa ibn-Salih ibn-'Ali al-Harithi on behalf of the Omanis whose names are signed hereto, through the mediation of Mr. Wingate I.C.S., political agent and consul of the government of Great Britain in Masqat, who is empowered by his government in this matter to be an intermediary between them.

And as for the conditions set down below, four pertain to the government of the sultan and four pertain to the Omanis.

Those pertaining to the Omanis are: First, that not more than five

The treaty is vague in several instances. For example, the exact nature of the sultan's rights of sovereignty in Oman is not detailed nor is the imam specifically granted independence. Nothing was said concerning the right of the imam to carry on relations with foreign powers although one authority mentions a secret pact that forbade any requests for foreign intervention.[26] Yet much was set down concerning the extradition of criminals and free exchange of peoples and goods between the territories controlled by the two governments. In summary, the two signatories seem to have recognized each other's mutual autonomy within their respective spheres and avoided specific mention of the thorny questions of sovereignty and precedence. An imprecise document, unlike a modern Western treaty in its construction, the Treaty of al-Sib is something more than an armistice but something less than a

---

percent shall be taken from anyone no matter what his race coming from Oman to Masqat or Matrah, or Sur, or the other towns of the coast.

Second, all Omanis shall enjoy security and freedom in all the towns of the coast.

Third, all impediments on anyone entering or leaving Masqat, or Matrah, or the other towns of the coast shall be lifted.

Fourth, the government of the sultan shall not grant asylum to any lawbreaker escaping from the justice of the Omanis and it shall return him to them if asked. It shall not interfere in their internal affairs.

The four conditions pertaining to the government of the sultan are:

First, all the tribes and shaykhs shall be at peace with the government of the sultan, and they shall not attack the towns of the coast nor shall they interfere in his government.

Second, all travelers going to Oman on lawful business and for commercial affairs shall be free and there shall be no impediments on trade and they shall be under protection.

Third, they shall expel and give no asylum to any wrongdoer or lawbreaker fleeing to them.

Fourth, the claims of merchants and others against the Omanis shall be heard and judged on the basis of justice according to shari'ya law.

Written in the town of al-Sib on the eleventh day of the month of Muharram in the year 1339 [25 Sept. 1920].

See also, "Muscat and Oman," *Middle East Journal*, Vol. xi, no. 3 (Summer 1957), pp. 282-84, for a critique of the treaty.

[26] R. Vadala, "Mascate," *L'Asie Française*, Vol. xxiii, no. 211 (May 1923), p. 135.

definitive, clear settlement of all the issues that clouded relations between the two branches of Omani Ibadism. Wingate acted for the sultan and 'Isa ibn-Salih spoke for the imam in the successful dealing. Later the treaty was ratified by the imam and some 15 major shaykhs who supported him.

Between 1920 and 1955 the two governments that administered Oman went their not quite separate ways. In the sultan's dominions two serious problems presented themselves—how to deal with the continued depression of the coastal economy and how to restore confidence in the government's ability to rule effectively. The economic troubles faced by the Masqat regime were not new ones; rather, they were the same ones that had been vexing sultans since the 1860s, although after 1912 they reached a more critical stage. Following World War I commerce revived temporarily, but in the mid-1920s another recession began which left the economy without sufficient strength to resist the crippling blows of the world depression of the early 1930s. Dates remained Oman's chief export, but new plantations in Iraq and the United States captured almost all of the American market supplied by Omani produce before the mid-1920s. The total value of Masqat's trade was £575,603 in 1919-20, £637,817 in 1925-26, £474,202 in 1926-27, and £364,905 in 1933-34—a figure which rose again into the mid-£400,000 bracket after the worst stage of the 1930s depression ended. Emphasizing the continuing malaise of the seaboard economy is the fact that these totals are in the same range as those recorded in the 1875-1900 period. As in the pre-World War I years imports continued to exceed exports in value and the same variety of products were exchanged, with the exception of weapons and ammunition—items whose market was destroyed by the arms warehouse agreement of 1912. Too, by the 1930s inexpensive Japanese goods began driving some British products such as cotton cloth out of favor. The Maria Theresa dollar continued to be subject to the rise and fall of world silver prices, and in general continued its long slide in value relative to both the rupee and the pound sterling. In the early 1930s, especially, the worth of the Maria Theresa dollar dropped precipitously, though it later recovered somewhat. The continued flight of trade from Masqat—a trend intensified by the growth of Dubayy on the Trucial Coast as an exchange center for large areas of southeastern Arabia once supplied via Masqat—prompted most of the Indian community of Masqat either to emigrate out of Oman or move to Matrah, a mart whose business recovered following the restoration of communications between Oman's interior and the coast. By the mid-1920s Masqat's population had fallen nearly to the 4,000 mark. The city lost most of its economic functions to Matrah, but retained its rather shopworn political significance.[27]

For a few years in the 1920s the possibility that there might be commercial deposits of oil in the sultanate gave some hope that a way out of the long and ever deepening economic depression might be found. In 1923 Sultan Taymur promised the Anglo–Indian government that no concessions for exploiting possible oil deposits located in his territory would be given without first consulting the British political agent and receiving New Delhi's approval. This agreement was similar to others made by the Trucial shaykhs in 1922.[28] In 1925 the sultan's promise was followed up by a grant permitting the D'Arcy Exploration Company to look for oil, gas, and other minerals.[29] A geological expedition into the western Hajar was not successful in finding anything of commercial value, however, and the concession lapsed three years later.[30] In

---

[27] Great Britain, Department of Overseas Trade, *Economic Conditions in the Persian Gulf, April 1929,* ed. Lt. Cmdr. Forester (London, 1929), pp. 16-18; *Economic Conditions in the Persian Gulf, October 1934,* F. H. Gamble, ed. (London, 1935), pp. 24-26; *Report on Economic and Commercial Conditions in the Persian Gulf, December 1936,* F. H. Todd, ed. (London, 1937), pp. 13-15; "Muscat Trade Reports, file 1917: no. 234, 1919/20," India Records-6.

[28] Aitchison—1933, XI, 216, 319.   [29] *Ibid.,* p. 284.

[30] C. J. Eccles, "The Sultanate of Muscat and Oman," *Journal of the [Royal] Central Asian Society,* Vol. XIV, part 1 (1927), pp. 28-29; Arabian American Oil Company, *Oman,* p. 68.

1937, Sultan Taymur's son and successor, Sa'id ibn-Taymur, gave a new 75-year concession for exploration, production, and transport to Petroleum Development (Oman and Dhofar) Ltd., then a subsidiary of the Iraq Petroleum Company; later the Dhofar rights were given up by the concessionaire and were taken up by American interests.[31]

The economic woes of the sultanate contributed to the considerable difficulty in applying its reform program. When the customs service was reorganized it had to contend with the initial hostility of the Hindu business community, since the Indians had controlled and profited from the old system. Also, when new customs posts were set up in Sur, Suhar, and several small al-Batinah ports in 1920 the government faced not only tribal resistance but also obstruction from nearly autonomous Al Bu Sa'id walis such as Prince Hamad ibn-Faysal at Suhar, who went so far as to threaten customs officers with beatings if they intruded into his preserve. Hamad ibn-Faysal and the other Al Bu Sa'id princelings eventually had to surrender and even accept the indignity of having to limit their personal expenditures to the narrow limits set in the civil list instituted by the new British wazir. The habitually troublesome Al Sa'd tribe of al-Batinah successfully defied Masqat's efforts to establish customs houses in their midst for two years, until November 1922 when the tribe's resistance crumbled before a coordinated attack by British gunboats and the recently organized Muscat Levy Corps. But in the south Masqat was not quite so successful in imposing its authority. Although in 1920 British gunboats forced the important port of Sur to capitulate to the new order, in the interior province of Ja'lan more determined resistance was encountered. There, the Bani-Bu-Ali tribe moved from a posture of noncompliance with the sultan's regulations to one of de facto independence by the

---

[31] Arabian American Oil Company, *Aramco Handbook* (1960), p. 116. Petroleum Development Limited's concession in Oman was reorganized in 1960 so that ultimately 85 percent ownership was vested in Shell Petroleum Ltd., British subsidiary of Royal Dutch Shell, and 15 percent was controlled by the Gulbenkian interests.

late 1920s, when the tribal shaykh began to call himself "amir of Ja'lan."[32]

In the main, the Masqat authorities succeeded in building up the government's efficiency, financial standing, and prestige during the 1920s. Although many of the old forms within the state, especially in local administration, were retained despite the reorganization, the newly installed European officials certainly brought a new style to the Masqat government. Also, the trend toward direct British involvement in the internal affairs of the sultanate that had started in the time of Lewis Pelly reached its logical conclusion. British influence in Oman reached its peak during the reign of Taymur ibn-Faysal who was content to leave the details of government to his advisors, to the extent that he took frequent trips to India and even visited Britain and Europe in 1928. Administrative reorganization implied the beginning of a new concept of government in the sultan's dominions—a slow cautious change toward Masqat's assumption of a more direct and influential administration within the country. This trend has continued since the 1920s although the "Sultanate of Muscat and Oman" is today still governed according to the same basic principles established in Sultan Turki's reign, and exerts its influence in most areas indirectly and through the intermediary of tribal authority. Nevertheless, tribal shaykhs since 1920, although they are still responsible for governing their people, have been more and more often placed in a position of having to carry out policies decided on by Masqat officials rather than being able to apply policies born during bargaining between individual shaykhs and the sultan.

But the stability that slowly spread through much of the sultanate during the 1920s was threatened anew by the disastrous effects of the Great Depression of the 1930s on the weak Omani economy and fiscal system. As trade fell so too did the value of the Maria Theresa dollar. The inability of the government to cope with the new economic crisis and its political

[32] "Persian Gulf Residency Diaries, file 1921: no. 1,749," India Records–6.

ramifications finally led, in November 1931, to the abdication
of Sultan Taymur ibn-Faysal—officially for reasons of poor
health—and to the nearly simultaneous resignation of the
British wazir, Bertram Thomas. Sultan Taymur, like his grandfather, Sultan Turki, half a century earlier, had tried to halt
the deterioration of Al Bu Sa'id rule in Oman by his open and
extensive reliance on British aid and advice. In a sense, Taymur ibn-Faysal's political realism was rewarded; his dynasty
was saved even if he could not avert his own premature retirement to a retreat in India.

Sultan Taymur was succeeded early in 1932 by his oldest
son, Sa'id ibn-Taymur, then 21, and educated in India at a
school for princes conducted by the Anglo–Indian government.
Sultan Sa'id, like his father, received British recognition as
heir-apparent during his father's reign, a practice which, in
effect, established the principle of primogeniture as the guide
for selecting the Masqati sultan. Although Sa'id ibn-Taymur
continued to rely on several British and other foreign advisors,
a hallmark of his reign was his emphasis on restoring the freedom of action and de facto as well as de jure independence of
his sultanate. The new sultan realized that a prime reason for
the erosion of his country's independence was its chronic in-
solvency and consequent dependence on British support. Therefore, Sultan Sa'id developed a talent—rare among his recent
forebears—for husbanding his government's scarce financial resources without harming its effectiveness. Also, in time he established his ascendancy within his government by actively supervising the decision-making process. Thus the sultan steadily reasserted his legal rights, affirmed his determination to be master
in his own house, and prompted the British to relax many of the
unofficial supervisory practices they had employed in Oman
since 1899. Still, during World War II the sultan cooperated
readily with the British and several Royal Air Force landing
fields were constructed between Salalah in Dhofar and Masqat.
These airfields continued to be useful after the war as occasional civil flights were introduced.

In the interior of Oman the imamate of Muhammad ibn-'Abdallah al-Khalili was developing along more isolationist and less elaborate lines. Until the 1940s the conservative regime was dominated by three personalities—Imam Muhammad ibn-'Abdallah al-Khalili, 'Isa ibn-Salih, and Sulayman ibn-Himyar, who apparently succeeded his father as tamimah of Bani-Riyam a short time before the Treaty of al-Sib was signed.[33] The imam was about 35 when elected to lead the conservatives. An isolationist, Imam Muhammad resisted the growth of all but the most necessary contacts between his community and foreigners and was content to see his state restrict its sway to interior Oman. Until his death in 1946, 'Isa ibn-Salih was the leading military, diplomatic, and political power in the imamate. A dignified, quiet man, Shaykh 'Isa was an astute, respected, and practical leader. Sulayman ibn-Himyar was a powerful but rather self-seeking, swaggering individual. While he served Imam Muhammad loyally and well, he also was fond of styling himself "malik" or king of the Nabhaniyah or as "amir" of al-Jabal al-Akhdar—the Green Mountain. Interested in modern gadgets, Shaykh Sulayman sought to acquire such things as radios and automobiles. After 'Isa ibn-Salih's death Sulayman ibn-Himyar became the leading secular figure in the conservative regime.[34]

The dedication of Muhammad ibn-'Abdallah al-Khalili's imamate to Omani particularism was emphasized many times. In 1925, when he feared that 'Abd al-'Aziz ibn-Sa'ud—the unifier of Saudi Arabia who was fresh from his triumph over the Hashimite kingdom of the Hijaz—was about to expand eastward in the direction of al-Buraymi, al-Zahirah and Oman, the imam ordered a drive northward from 'Uman to occupy the endangered localities before they were annexed to the Sa'udis. An Ibadi army composed of both Hinawi and Ghafiri units, led by 'Isa ibn-Salih, and accompanied by Sulayman ibn-Himyar, marched as far as the al-Zahirah town of 'Ibri where

---

[33] Shaykh Sulayman was one of the witnesses to the treaty.
[34] Arabian American Oil Company, *Oman*, pp. 70-82.

a conservative governor was installed after the towns of Dariz and Dank tendered their submissions to the imam. At that point, Shaykh 'Isa fell ill, the expedition distintegrated, and the disappointed imam offered his resignation because of his failure to secure al-Buraymi. But the resignation was not accepted and despite the visit of a Sa'udi party to al-Buraymi and some correspondence between a Nu'aym shaykh and the Sa'udi amir of al-Hasa and the eastern provinces, 'Abdallah ibn-Jiluwi, King 'Abd al-'Aziz was too occupied reordering his new conquests to divert himself in al-Buraymi at the time. Nevertheless, it seems that the Sa'udi king believed he was justified in claiming as his any territory over which his predecessors had ruled or enjoyed a "sphere of influence" during the nineteenth century. Such a definition certainly encompassed al-Buraymi, and even included Oman itself, since the sayyids at Masqat had paid "protection money"—zakat—to the Sa'udis for 60 years prior to 1868. Imam Muhammad remained wary of possible Sa'udi moves into southeastern Arabia throughout his life although his successor established warm relations with al-Riyadh during the tense days of 1954.[35]

With its incorporation of 'Ibri into its territories, the twentieth century imamate reached its territorial limits. Although these boundaries were never plotted exactly, generally they included in the south the oasis of Bilad Bani-Bu-Hasan, the seat of a Hinawi tribe of the same name. In the east the crest of the Hajar chain was regarded as the frontier although Sama'il in the Wadi Sama'il and al-Rustaq on the seaward slopes of the Hajar above al-Batinah were ruled by the imam, too. In the north 'Ibri was the last firmly held outpost of the conservative government; in the west the sands of al-Rub' al-Khali marked the limits of Nazwa's influence. Thus the provinces of 'Uman, al-Sharqiyah, the Wadi Sama'il and al-Jabal al-Akhdar districts, the northern part of Ja'lan, and the

[35] *Ibid.*, pp. 67-68; Saudi Arabia, *Memorial*, I, 343-44; Eccles, "Muscat and Oman," *Journal of the [Royal] Central Asian Society*, Vol. xiv, part 1 (1927), p. 40; Kelly, *Eastern Arabian Frontiers*, pp. 118-19.

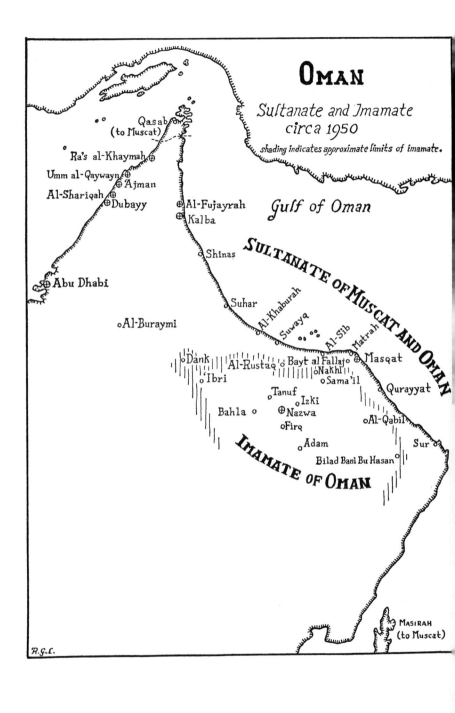

OMAN

Sultanate and Imamate
circa 1950

shading indicates approximate limits of imamate.

Gulf of Oman

SULTANATE OF MUSCAT AND OMAN

IMAMATE OF OMAN

Qasab
(to Muscat)

Ra's al-Khaymah

Umm al-Qaywayn
Ajman
Al-Sharigah
Dubayy
Al-Fujayrah
Kalba

Shinas

Abu Dhabi

Suhar

Al-Buraymi

Al-Khaburah
Suwayq
Al-Sib
Matrah
Dank
Al-Rustaq
Bayt al-Fallaj
Masqat
'Ibri
Nakhl
Sama'il
Qurayyat
Tanuf
Izki
Bahla
Nazwa
Al-Qabil
Firq
Adam
Sur
Bilad Bani Bu Hasan

MASIRAH
(to Muscat)

R.G.L.

extreme southern area of al-Zahirah were all dominated by the imam.[36]

Under Muhammad ibn-'Abdallah al-Khalili's direction the office of imam was carried on in unostentatious yet effective fashion. While conducting the affairs of the conservative Ibadi community the imam, quartered in the great round citadel which dominates Nazwa, sat in his council chamber on a rug since the use of a chair would have been too reminiscent of a king upon his throne. The imam kept his own financial records in account books and his treasury was located in a Nazwa house. In handling correspondence the thrifty imam used the blank portion of the incoming message to write his own reply or had the answer penned by the chief qadi of Nazwa, who for many years was Mansur al-Farisi, a man who served the imam as a chief secretary, wazir, and general advisor. Files of petitions and correspondence were maintained. Since he was the religious as well as political head of his community —a man above the Hinawi-Ghafiri split which sometimes agitated his people—much of the imam's time was spent in judging or reviewing legal cases and in arbitrating tribal disputes, all of which were settled according to conservative Ibadi precedents. Although he kept his distance from foreigners, the imam was accessible to petitioners and others in the Ibadi community who wished his services.

In his administration the imam was aided by qadis and other appointees directly responsible to him, as well as by the great factional magnates such as 'Isa ibn-Salih or Sulayman ibn-Himyar and by lesser tribal chiefs. In addition to the walis and qadis appointed to the more important towns, local administration was carried on by tax collectors and tribal shaykhs. All of these officials, including the shaykhs, were confirmed in their offices by the imam. The zakah, which in the imamate was a true Muslim property tax somewhat analogous to a tithe, was the chief source of state revenue, although doubtless it was supplemented by monies diverted occasionally

[36] Arabian American Oil Company, *Oman*, pp. 7-9.

from various leaders' private incomes to public purposes. Although military requirements were discharged by tribal levies the imam maintained a small standing force of 400 or 500 men. The imamate flew its own flag—a white banner on which was displayed in red a straight sword under an Arabic inscription meaning "Victory is from God and triumph is near."[37]

Besides its relations with the sultan in Masqat and with the Sa'udi authorities in al-Riyadh the other most troublesome problem faced by the conservative community during the 1920s, 30s, and 40s, was the great drought which desiccated al-Sharqiyah's once lush date groves. In the late 1940s many villages were deserted; even al-Qabil, the chief oasis and seat of the tribe of al-Hirth, was almost depopulated. Imports of salt fish brought in from Masqat allowed many of al-Sharqiyah's date cultivators to survive. These people also had to endure the consequences of absentee landlordism because many of al-Sharqiyah's plantation owners preferred to live in Zanzibar. Commonly, these absentee landlords used to have most of the date harvest carried to Matrah for sale where larger profits could be made than was possible if the produce was sold in the interior.[38] Doubtless the killings and expulsions of Arabs from Zanzibar following the revolution there in 1964, which overthrew its Al Bu Sa'id sultan, have prompted many landowning families to return to Oman and al-Sharqiyah.

THE REUNIFICATION OF OMAN UNDER MODERATE RULE

As long as Muhammad ibn-'Abdallah al-Khalili was imam the situation in Oman remained stabilized in accordance with the understanding reached at al-Sib in 1920. But the death of the old imam in May 1954 was followed in December 1955 with the occupation of Nazwa by soldiers of Sultan Sa'id ibn-Taymur and the eclipse of the imamate. This unheralded

[37] *Ibid.*, pp. 70-74. The imamate flag, whose sword-and-inscription design may be of rather recent origin, was shown to the author at the Imamate of Oman Office, Zamalik, Cairo, U.A.R. in July 1959. Transliterated the inscription reads: "Naṣrun min Allahi wa fatḥun qarībun.

[38] Arabian American Oil Company, *Oman*, p. 82.

event was a product of the mixing of many complex factors, not the least of which was the combination of the century-and-a-half-old Sa'udi effort to control at least the inland districts of southeastern Arabia, with the new and conflicting ambitions of international oil interests. This latter development began in the Arabian peninsula in May 1933 when the Standard Oil Company of California received a concession to exploit any petroleum deposits that might be buried under the eastern provinces of the kingdom of Saudi Arabia. Initially modified in 1936, the concession ultimately was exploited by the Arabian American Oil Company, an operating company jointly owned by Standard Oil of California, Texaco, Standard Oil of New Jersey, and Socony–Mobil. The fortunes of Saudi Arabia after the early 1930s were inextricably bound to the success of Aramco in tapping the kingdom's petroleum resources.

To gain their 1933 concession the Americans had beat out the British-dominated Iraq Petroleum Company. In order to restore its competitive position, Iraq Petroleum—with some British governmental support—directed various subsidiary firms to secure concessions in Qatar (1935), the Trucial Coast (1937), and Oman (1937). The Omani concession, signed by Sultan Sa'id, did not differentiate between his and the imam's territory. It also included Dhofar until Petroleum Development (Oman) Ltd. decided to abandon this seemingly unpromising area, a circumstance that led the sultan to grant in 1953 a new concession to the Dhofar–Cities Service Petroleum Corporation, a partnership of the American Cities Service Company and the Richfield Oil Corporation.

There was one major difficulty about all of these concessions —with the possible exception of the one held by Cities Service. Since the exact borders between Saudi Arabia and the various British-protected states of south and southeastern Arabia had never been determined there was also no way of knowing the exact limits of the various oil concessions. From 1933 on it was a race between the oil technicians and the diplomats to see if oil fields would be brought in before or after it was legally determined in what country the field was located. In any event, the oil riggers moved much faster than the foreign offices. In 1934—a year after an oil concession involving eastern Arabia was signed—negotiations started between the British Foreign office and the Saudi Arabian Ministry of Foreign Affairs in an attempt to settle definitively the boundaries of the southeastern portion of the Arabian peninsula. These talks sputtered on until 1938 and nothing had been settled when World War II intervened.[39] Only after Petroleum Development Ltd. resumed its search for oil during 1947-48 in the Trucial Coast and al-Buraymi districts—areas whose exact boundaries were still unclear—was the oil race and the border dispute revived. Not wanting to be shut out of a possible producing area of undetermined sovereignty, Arabian American Oil Company survey teams began moving into the regions along the eastern limits of al-Rub' al-Khali and into places adjacent to the Trucial Coast. Once again it was time for political authority to attempt to catch up to the fast-moving survey crews. The inevitable occurred in April 1949 when the British political officer in Abu Dhabi ordered an Arabian American Oil Company survey party to leave a place he claimed was part of Abu Dhabi. The British authorities were particularly disturbed because this party was accompanied by armed Saudi Arabian soldiers and were evidently unaware that such an escort was standard on all Aramco survey operations in Arabia wherever these happened to be located.[40] As a result of the expulsion, the Saudi Arabian government protested to the British embassy at Jiddah on April 26, 1949 and presented a counter claim that the point from which the survey team had been ejected was in fact Saudi Arabian territory. In this way the so-called Buraimi Dispute began, an argument which actually involves a complex set of disagreements concerning many

[39] Saudi Arabia, *Memorial*, I, 400-18; Kelly, *Eastern Arabian Frontiers*, pp. 123-29.

[40] Arabian American Oil Company, *Instructions, Field Parties in Saudi Arabia*, n.d. (1949 ?), pp. 14-17.

thousands of square miles in eastern Arabia and not just one cluster on oasis villages.[41]

It was into this wide-ranging disagreement that the destinies of the sultan of Mascat and Oman and the imam of Oman were drawn. Moreover, there were many who believed the future of Great Britain itself could well be affected by the outcome of this dispute, not only because much of British and Western European industry was powered by Persian Gulf oil, but also because of the financial benefits—particularly in regard to the availability of new investment funds—that would accrue if sterling bloc companies and local princes friendly to Britain dominated any major new oil fields in the Persian Gulf.

Although British and Saudi Arabian diplomats reopened negotiations on the frontier question in 1949 and even agreed to establish a frontier commission, the results of these deliberations were no better than those of the 1934-38 talks. Meanwhile, both sides were pushing survey parties and troops into various disputed areas while both Saudi troops and the British-led Trucial Oman Levies occupied posts within al-Buraymi. In October 1952 both Imam Muhammad and Sultan Sa'id became convinced that the Sa'udis were going to try to take all of al-Buraymi by force, so the two Omani rulers prepared to counter this eventuality with their own military forces. The British restrained the sultan, however, and the imam did not move alone. Thus the intrigues and diplomacy continued to boil despite an arbitration attempt that began in the summer of 1954. In May 1954, as explosive tension built up, Imam Muhammad ibn-'Abdallah died.

---

[41] The respective positions of the Saudi Arabian, British, and British allied Arab governments in regard to the frontier are set forth in Saudi Arabia, *Memorial*; and Great Britain, *Arbitration Concerning Buraimi and the Common Frontier between Abu Dhabi and Sa'ūdi Arabia; Memorial submitted by the Government of the United Kingdom of Great Britain and Northern Ireland* (London, 1955). See also Kelly, *Eastern Arabian Frontiers*, chap. 5, for a pro-British view of the dispute as it developed to 1954.

In the election that followed the sultan, who had been cultivating conservative opinion for some time, was a candidate, but predictably he lost. Yet, so did the two preelection favorites, a son of the late Imam Salim ibn-Rashid al-Kharusi and the intellectual Muhammad ibn-'Abdallah al-Salimi, son of the religious scholar so instrumental in establishing the 1913 imamate. The victor was Ghalib ibn-'Ali of the Hinawi Bani-Hina, who gained the crucial support of both Sulayman ibn-Himyar, and Salih ibn-'Isa, the young shaykh who had emerged as the successor of his father, 'Isa ibn-Salih. The new imam was an unknown quantity in the highly volatile political climate of southeastern Arabia and was immediately beset with all manner of pressures. A glimpse of what the future held for Imam Ghalib appeared in September 1954 when the British and Sultan Sa'id became convinced that the new ruler was receiving Sa'udi gold and arms and was about to become al-Riyadh's pawn in the matter of oil concessions. If true, this could prove very troublesome since the British were sinking test wells at Fahud in country between that occupied by the imam and the unmarked al-Rub' al-Khali border of Saudi Arabia. It was also believed that both Sulayman ibn-Himyar and the imam's energetic brother, Talib ibn-'Ali, were the real powers in the Nazwa government and that both men would not hesitate to aid the Sa'udis if it could bring them private benefit. In September 1954, acting on these convictions, capitalizing on anti-imamate intrigues in al-Zahirah, and in concert with detachments from the tribe of al-Duru', the Muscat and Oman Field Force occupied 'Ibri in Sultan Sa'id's behalf. This action was very important because it drove a wedge between the imam's territory and the Sa'udi outpost at al-Buraymi. If Imam Ghalib had not been in contact with the Sa'udis before the occupation of 'Ibri, a town held by the imams since 1925, it would have been surprising if he had held aloof from them after the incident.[42] On November 25,

42 Arabian American Oil Company, *Oman*, p. 74; Kelly, *Eastern Arabian Frontiers*, pp. 185-86.

1954 the imam took a momentous step when via his brother, Talib ibn-'Ali, he forwarded a request for full membership to the Arab League. Apparently he was seeking a more solid diplomatic platform from which to operate and hoped to identify his cause with the general struggle of Arab nationalism against the vestiges of British imperialism, a drive then entering a crisis stage. In his application the imam stated that the Imamate of Oman was a free and independent stage governed according to Islamic law.[43] The Arab League authorities were evidently somewhat uncertain how to proceed concerning the communication from the little known imamate and in December 1954 they asked for advice from Saudi Arabia and Yeman about the matter. Finally, the council of the Arab League decided to postpone action on the application pending more study. In October 1955 the League let it be known that it "welcomes the application of the Imamate of Oman for membership" but took no final action.[44] Before the League's machinery produced a final decision the imamate had been occupied. Ghalib ibn-'Ali's application for Arab League membership reopened the whole question of the meaning of the Treaty of al-Sib of 1920, especially in regard to the autonomy or independence of the imam and his right to conduct foreign relations.

Events moved rapidly toward a climax in 1955. After the breakdown of the Anglo–Sa'udi arbitration efforts in Geneva in September 1955 amidst a flurry of charges and countercharges that each side was trying to prejudice the deliberations of the arbitration tribunal, the British decided to act. On October 26, 1955 the Trucial Oman Levies, on behalf of Sultan Sa'id and Shaykh Shakbut of Abu Dhabi, occupied al-Buraymi and expelled the Sa'udi police detachment located there. At the same time the British government announced that because the effort to reach an impartial settlement of the

[43] League of Arab States, Political Department, "A Note from the Secretary General On the Question of the Imamate of Oman," mimeographed background paper (Cairo, 6 August 1957), p. 9.
[44] *Ibid.*, p. 10.

frontier dispute had been undermined by Saudi Arabian intrigue, they were imposing a solution of the border question. This solution was based on the 1937 "Riyadh Line" and left practically all of the contested territory in the hands of Abu Dhabi or the sultan of Muscat and Oman.[45] The status of the frontier has remained at this unresolved stage since 1955 because, naturally, Saudi Arabia refused to recognize the validity of the British actions or its version of the frontier. With the British determined to use whatever force was necessary to maintain their paramountcy in southeastern Arabia, little hope was left for an imam who was identified—rightly or wrongly—with the Sa'udi cause.

Up to the fall of 1955 Sultan Sa'id ibn-Taymur had been more a spectator than initiator of events in this frontier dispute. By that time, however, it seems he became convinced that Imam Ghalib had violated what the sultan conceived as the imamate's autonomous—but not independent—status. Also, he feared that if indeed Nazwa had become a puppet of Riyadh then his own rule could be undermined. Consequently, during November 1955 the sultan mobilized a surprise strike against the imamate. Already, Sa'id ibn-Taymur, with the aid of oil concession payments, had built up his armed forces to a point where they consisted of four separate British-trained and led units—the Dhofar Force stationed at Salalah, the motorized Muscat and Oman Field Force based at the Petroleum Development Ltd. oil camp at Fahud, the Batinah Force stationed at Suhar, and the old Muscat Levies based at Bayt al-Falaj near the capital. In December the sultan's army moved. Advancing in their motorized transport, the Field Force quit their advanced post at 'Ibri and on December 15 they rolled into 'Uman province, occupied Nazwa, and scattered the imamate's leaders—all at a cost of one rifle shot fired at the advancing convoy. Two days later the Batinah Force stormed al-Rustaq

[45] Kelly, *Eastern Arabian Frontiers*, pp. 202-206; Arab Information Center, *British Imperialism in Southern Arabia* (New York, 1958), pp. 76-78. These works give conflicting versions of the reasons for the breakdown of the arbitration.

after some determined resistance by Talib ibn-'Ali. Shortly after these lightning blows, Sa'id ibn-Taymir arrived in Nazwa to take possession of his new provinces after enduring an unprecedented overland truck trek of 600 miles from Salalah in Dhofar. The sultan defended the annexation of Oman's inland provinces by asserting that Ghalib ibn-'Ali had broken the Treaty of al-Sib by plotting with the Sa'udis to create a completely sovereign imamate which must inevitably have become only a creature of the al-Riyadh regime.[46]

For a time things were quiet in Oman as Sulayman ibn-Himyar and Imam Ghalib both made their peace with the sultan and were allowed to return to their homes. The defiant Talib ibn-'Ali, however, escaped to Saudi Arabia where he set up headquarters in Dammam. The Saudi Arabian government, after considering the possibility of charging Great Britain with aggression before the United Nations Security Council, dropped the idea and instead continued diplomatic relations with London—a posture perhaps encouraged by American diplomacy. But Anglo–Saudi Arabian relations deteriorated to the point of diplomatic rupture following the Suez crisis of 1956. Meanwhile, Talib ibn-'Ali, together with two sons of 'Isa ibn-Salih, established in Cairo an 'Imamate of Oman Office" which carried on a campaign to publicize the point of view that the British and the sultan had occupied an independent Arab country.

During early 1957 Talib ibn-'Ali arranged for the smuggling of arms and conservative refugees into Oman's interior. Then in June 1957 Talib rejoined his brother who proclaimed the reactivation of the imamate and conservative bands occupied Nazwa. By July all of the major towns of 'Uman, as well as the al-Jabal al-Akhdar districts controlled by Sulayman ibn-Himyar, were flying the white banner of the imamate once again. The sultan was unable to suppress the restored conservative government so he called for British aid which was forth-

---

[46] J. Morris, *Sultan in Oman* (New York, 1957), contains an entertaining yet thoughtful account of these events.

coming in the late summer. The sultan called the movement a revolt, while the imam said he was fighting a war to regain the independence that had been taken from Oman in 1955. Although the Sa'udis and the Arab League supported the imam's actions with some aid and much publicity, by September Nazwa and 'Uman were reoccupied by the sultan's forces. But the fighting went on until the sultan's troops and 300 British soldiers stormed up the slopes of al-Jabal al-Akhdar to dislodge the stubborn conservative warriors. By January 1959 Imam Ghalib, Talib ibn-'Ali, Sulayman ibn-Himyar, and other conservative notables had fled to Dammam where they set up a government in exile. In Oman, minings, sniping, and other guerrilla activity continued.[47]

The upheaval had the effect of hardening the sultan's opinion against accepting Sa'udi offers to reopen the arbitration, a position supported by the British Foreign Office. But in September 1959 United Nations Secretary-General Dag Hammarskjöld took up the question informally, and a year later the "Question of Oman" was placed on the General Assembly agenda. In January 1963 Britain and Saudi Arabia finally restored diplomatic relations and agreed to discuss the border question under United Nations auspices and that is where the issue rests today. For their part, the imam and his followers still issue defiant statements and promise an eventual triumphant return.[48]

Meanwhile, Sa'id ibn-Taymur was occupied with less spectacular problems, although they were ones of more long-range import. With the reunification of Oman into a single political unit, a condition that had not existed in a practical sense since the fall of 'Azzan ibn-Qays' government in 1871, the sultan found himself coping with the dilemma of trying to meet the insistent demands of a country seeking to catch up with a world that had passed it by. At the same time he was trying to control all change and preserve the existing regime.

In the late 1950s the pace began to accelerate as the oil

[47] Kelly, *Eastern Arabian Frontiers*, pp. 284-85.   [48] *Ibid.*, pp. 266-68.

crews—relatively free to go about their business since the events of 1955—pushed their explorations and tests. Camel tracks were replaced by truck routes connecting Masqat and al-Sharqiyah via Wadi Sama'il. Nazwa, in turn, was linked with Fahud and with al-Buraymi via 'Ibri. Also a road up the al-Batinah coast was pushed from Masqat toward Suhar and al-Shariqah on the Trucial Coast. A state Development Department, largely financed by British money, was organized in 1959 to expand the agricultural, transport, health, and educational resources of the sultanate. Under these auspices agricultural experiment stations were opened at Suhar and at Nazwa to improve Omani irrigation, fertilizing, and crop cultivation techniques.[49] But all these activities did not change the sad facts that decreed that Oman must remain a region of subsistence agriculture and of depressed seaboard trade and fishing activity unless basic innovations change the country's resource base.

For instance, in the early 1960s the economy of Oman was still essentially a stagnant one as it had been for a hundred years. While Gulf Aviation Ltd. ran scheduled air flights between Bahrain and Masqat, Oman's main window on the world remained the British India Steam Navigation Company or Strick Line steamers that called at the capital as they did in the 1890s. While the figures indicated that the value of Masqat's trade had jumped compared to the trade totals of the 1930s—imports were valued at £3,700,000 and exports at £700,000 in 1962—currency inflation and devaluation as well as rising price levels account for much of the seeming rise in trade values. While the imports included items such as vehicles, machine parts, and cement—all things that were used in oil exploitation—as well as the traditional grain, coffee, sugar, and cotton goods, exports still consisted largely of the ancient standby commodities produced by Oman—dates, fish,

[49] Europa Publications: "Muscat and Oman," *The Middle East and North Africa, 1964-1965* (London, 1964), pp. 440-41.

and fruits. The Maria Theresa dollars and the local small coins in circulation were still pegged to the freely circulated Indian rupee which was itself tied to sterling.[50]

But the breakthrough took place in 1963. Petroleum Development (Oman) Ltd.—which had been reorganized in 1960 on the basis of 85 percent ownership by Shell Petroleum Ltd. —finally made a major oil strike. Three fields were brought in at Fahud and two nearby points, Natih and Yibal, which together were estimated to be capable of producing up to 10,000,000 tons of oil a year. In 1964 plans for building a pipeline from the Gulf of Oman to tap the new fields were announced. Meanwhile, the Cities Service–Richfield group, which had struck some oil already, and a new Pure Oil Company effort organized in 1962 were hopeful of finding other major deposits in Dhofar. Clearly, capital would be forthcoming to begin to develop the sultanate into a modern state.[51]

Undoubtedly the sultan's political apparatus will be one of the first of the local institutions to be altered. Although a tendency toward more active administration had been developing in the sultanate since the governmental reorganization of 1919-21, the necessity to control the impending modernization of Oman implies a need for a much larger corps of government officials and experts—many of whom undoubtedly will have to be foreigners. In 1963 the sultan's government operated on a modest budget of approximately £1,000,000 a year, and the sultan's administrative apparatus still looked much as it did in 1921. His personal advisor, the wazir, was still a Britisher—Major F. C. L. Chauncy. His minister of the interior, and the virtual viceroy of the newly annexed interior districts, was the Al Bu Sa'idi prince, Ahmad ibn-Ibrahim, who became the sultan's confidant after being dispossessed of al-Rustaq by the Imam Salim in 1917. A secretary for external affairs, a military secretary, and a port and customs director made up the other top posts in the central administration.[52]

[50] *Ibid.*   [51] *Ibid.*   [52] *Ibid.*

424

Oman in the 20th Century

As FOR THE FUTURE, it seems certain that major changes will occur in a short time in Oman. Already the preconditions that determined the trends of the past century have been irreparably altered. The isolation of the interior, the environment of economic stagnation, British political predominance over the Indian Ocean basin—each is passing. Mineral exploitation will bring secondary economic growth and perhaps even a revival of Masqat as a shipping center or at least as the home of a modern fishing fleet. The problems of political reconstruction undoubtedly will be most difficult to cope with and will be complicated by Sultan Sa'id's instinctive Ibadi suspicion of innovation and all but the most necessary foreign contacts. The split between conservative and moderate Ibadism must be compromised, although Omani conservatism has been an extremely resilient ideology. Also, the 160-year-old problem of Oman's relationship with the Sa'udis must be faced, as must the question of the future design of Anglo–Omani relations. The fact that since 1951 the British representative has been referred to as the consul-general instead of the political agent mark the transformation of tutelage into alliance, but, nevertheless, the sultan still leans heavily on British military aid. An Indian consul-general has been stationed in Masqat since 1947, and undoubtedly stronger ties with the United States and other nations will be necessary in the future. Finally, the Omani sultanate will have to come to terms with the new forces of modernism and nationalism that are revolutionizing the Arab world. To accomplish this a number of alternatives—none very likely at present—might be considered in the future. These include federation with other Persian Gulf or even South Arabian principalities, federation into a greater state of Arabia embracing the entire peninsula, and federation or incorporation into a large pan-Arab state. In a few years a takeover by a revolutionary modernizing regime might come. A more likely prospect is an accommodation with modern realities led by a new generation of Al Bu Sa'id leaders such as those personified by the Sandhurst-educated heir to the throne, Prince Qabus ibn-Sa'id.

Leaving speculation aside, it is clear that, come what may, Sultan Sa'id ibn-Taymur, because of his involvement, however reluctant, in Oman's emergence into the modern world, has been the most important ruler produced by the Al Bu Sa'id dynasty since the reign of his illustrious namesake, Sayyid Sa'id ibn-Sultan, over a century ago.

Bibliographical Notes

Index

Bibliographical Notes

SINCE the history of Oman has attracted only a small number of students this bibliography will not reveal a large number of important secondary works. Moreover, only a small number of Arabic works devoted to Oman's history are presently available to non-Omani scholars. Even among those books and articles which contain significant material dealing with Masqat, Oman, and the Persian Gulf, it often seems that such information was included by the writer as an afterthought or as something subsidiary to another, more central concern. In the following listings a few works that do not appear in footnotes but which give useful background information are included.

A. OFFICIAL AND PRIVATE UNPUBLISHED ARCHIVAL SOURCES

The major archival collections consulted during the preparation of this work are those of the Public Record Office, the India Office Library, and the Foreign Office Library—all in London—as well as the records of the French Ministry of Foreign Affairs in Paris. Of these, the India Office Library records and manuscripts proved to be the most useful because of the wealth of their information on internal events in Oman. The collections in these archives most useful in preparing this study were:

France, The Archives of the Ministy of Foreign Affairs, Paris. The nonpolitical dispatches of M. Ottavi, vice consul and French representative in Masqat in the 1890s, are in "Correspondance Commerciale—Muscate, 1894-1901," and contain much specific economic information and some background material on political and social conditions. Ottavi's political dispatches were not open for public use during 1959 when the author used the Quai d'Orsay records, but when these are available we will have a much clearer picture of domestic events in Oman during the 1890s and of the details of the French effort to detach Sultan Faysal from his ties to Britain.

Great Britain, Foreign Office Library. Contains material useful in reconstructing the events leading up to the definitive "Lansdowne Declaration" of May 1903 and to Lord Curzon's tour of the Persian Gulf in the same year. These marked Britain's determination to retain her monopolistic political position in the Gulf. See the documents in "Private Papers of Lord Lansdowne as Foreign Secretary, vol. XXIX."

Great Britain, India Office Library. The following collections among the library's "European Manuscripts" are indispensable for tracing the development of Anglo–Indian policy in the Persian Gulf and Oman during the late nineteenth century. Also the material occasionally treats internal events in the area's principalities: "Elgin Collection, Papers of the Ninth Earl of Elgin and Kincardine, Letters from and to the Secretary of State for India." "Hamilton Collection, Private Correspondence India, Lord George Hamilton to Lord Curzon, no. C 126." "Hamilton Collection, Private Correspondence India, Lord Curzon to Lord George Hamilton, no. D 510." "Lansdowne Correspondence, Correspondence of Lord Lansdowne to and from the Secretary of State for India, no. D 558." "Lansdowne Correspondence, Selections of Despatches to Her Majesty's Secretary of State for India, no. D 558." "Wood (Halifax) Collection, India Office Correspondence, Correspondence of Sir Charles Wood with Sir Bartle Frere, 1859-1865."

————. The "India Office Records," especially those of the Indian Foreign Department's Political and Secret Department, are one of the most important sources for the internal history of the various districts of the Persian Gulf, as well as for the details of Britain's and India's connection with the region. Much in the way of source material indigenous to the Gulf states, such as letters and decrees, are contained as enclosures in the correspondence sent by British representatives in the area to their superiors in India and Britain. There are often at least four copies of a single letter available since a copy was retained in the Gulf in the files of the originating office and many of these files are now stored in the Indian archives in New Delhi; a copy was kept in the Anglo–Indian government files also located in New Delhi; another information copy was forwarded to the India Office in London and later was placed in that agency's library; and since many British officials in the Gulf held dual Indian and Foreign Office appointments, still another copy often would be sent on to the Foreign Office in London from whence it eventually was put in the archives in the Public Record Office. Normally, records in the India Office Library are released for public use 56 to 60 years after the events they describe. Among the specific "Political and Secret Department Records" collections containing important data on happenings in late nineteenth and early twentieth century Oman are: "Political and Secret Proceedings (External)." "Letters from the Persian Gulf." "Political and Secret Department Memoranda." "Secret Letters from India." "Political and Secret Department Files." "Secret Letters Received, Various." The early phases of Britain's connection with the Gulf are detailed in "Factory Records—Persia and the Persian Gulf."

Great Britain, Public Record Office. Among the manuscript documents in the Foreign Office Archives, series 27 (France), 54 (Masqat), 60 (Arms Trade), 78, 364 (Ottoman Empire), and 84 (Slave Trade), are important for this study. The collections of the Foreign Office Archive are better sources for the twentieth century history of the Persian Gulf than are those in the India Office Library. But for the nineteenth century the Foreign Office Archives is useful, mainly for clarifying questions dealing with the external relations of the various Gulf states. Even in this regard, however, the India Office materials often touch on matters not treated with much detail in the nineteenth century Foreign Office material. While they were not used in this study, the "Admiralty Archives" also contain information on Persian Gulf naval arrangements.

Bibliographical Notes

The richest and most complete collection of material dealing with Persian Gulf events prior to 1947 reputedly is in the National Archives of the Government of India in New Delhi. For Persian Gulf affairs consult the "Proceedings of the Government of India in the Foreign Department." The "Proceedings" supposedly contain much material sent as enclosures that was never forwarded to London. Also, some original residency and Masqat political agency archives reportedly are stored in New Delhi. Since 1947 Indian consuls have been stationed in various Persian Gulf locations including Masqat, so new material dealing with the region is still being filed at New Delhi.

In the United States archival material on Persian Gulf affairs, including those of Masqat, are deposited in the National Archives in Washington, in the collections of consular reports maintained there. The Dutch Reformed Church of America stores the records of its various Persian Gulf missions, including those of the Masqat–Matrah mission and hospital station, at its New Brunswick, New Jersey seminary library; there is undoubtedly much information touching on social and health conditions in Oman in this collection. Among private business concerns the files of companies such as the British India Steam Navigation Company, its parent concern— the Peninsular and Oriental Steam Navigation Company, Petroleum Development (Oman) Ltd., the Iraq Petroleum Company, Shell Petroleum Ltd., and Dhofar–Cities Service Oil Company undoubtedly will yield much economic and other data on Oman when scholars gain access to them. Among the oil companies, the Arabian American Oil Company research library at Dhahran contains a unique gathering of Arabic chronicles and materials dealing with various parts of Arabia, including Oman, which are not available elsewhere. Finally, it is known that the Sultanate of Muscat and Oman maintains a governmental archive that includes correspondence, since material from this source was presented as evidence in the Buraimi Arbitration of 1954-55. Moreover, Sultan Saʻid ibn-Taymur reportedly is most interested in his country's history and it is rumored that he owns a fine collection of manuscripts and other material dealing with Omani history.

Listed under this category are a number of works which, although printed, were prepared originally for restricted use within the confines of a small number of government departments. Thus many of the books cited are very often as difficult to consult as unpublished sources because of their extremely limited availability. Again, the India Office Library and, undoubtedly, the National Archives in New Delhi, are virtually the only places where all of these materials are stored. Other, newer published sources touching on Omani and Persian Gulf history similar in nature to many listed in this category reportedly exist and will become available as the need to maintain restrictions on their use passes.

Carnegie Endowment for International Peace. J. B. Scott, ed. *The Hague Court Reports.* New York, 1916. A work that contains a copy of the "Masqat dhows arbitration" award.

Crawford, D. G. *Roll of the Indian Medical Service, 1615-1930.* London, 1930. This has information on Anglo–Indian personnel who served in the Persian Gulf.

Foster, W., ed. *Letters Received by the East India Company from its Servants in the East.* London, 1900. A compilation that throws light on early European contacts with the Persian Gulf.

France, Chamber of Deputies. *Le Journal Officiel, Débats de la Chambre des Députés.* Paris, annual.

France, Ministry of Foreign Affairs. *Annuaire Diplomatique et Consulaire de la République Française.* Paris, annual.

France, Ministry of Foreign Affairs. *Documents Diplomatiques Français, 1874-1914.* Paris, 1929-54. While this is an admirable compilation in most respects, the editors did not include many significant documents concerning French activities in Oman and the Gulf during the 1890s and 1900s.

Gooch, G. P. and H. Temperley, eds. *British Documents on the Origins of the War.* London, 1926-38. See Vol. I for material on the Masqat crisis of 1899.

Government of Bombay. C. P. Rigby. "Report on the Zanzibar Dominions." *Selections from the Records of the Bombay Government.* new Series. no. LIX. Bombay, 1861. An interesting account of Zanzibar just at the time it was separated from Oman.

———— R. H. Thomas, ed. *Selections from the Records of the Bombay Government. Historical and other Information, Connected with the Province of Oman, Muscat, Bahrein, and other Places in the Persian Gulf.* new Series. no. XXIV. Bombay, 1856. One of the main sources for Persian Gulf and Omani history for the first half of the nineteenth century, most of the separate articles are from the pens of British officials serving in the region and many are of considerable quality and touch on several aspects of the local scene.

Government of India, Foreign Department. C. V. Aitchison, ed. *A Collection of Treaties, Engagements, and Sanads Relating to India and Neighbouring Countries.* 3rd ed., Calcutta, 1892, vols. IX-XII. 4th ed., Calcutta, 1909, vol. XII. 5th ed., New Delhi, 1933, vol. XI. An indispensable collection of treaties and engagements detailing the relations of the various Persian Gulf principalities and Iran with the British home and Indian goverments. The more important treaties between Persian Gulf governments and non-British states are also included. The fifth edition was the last in this series, which is always referred to as "Aitchison" in commemoration of the first editor and the founder of this remarkable compilation. While the volumes are most valuable as sources of treaty texts, the historical narrative which gives the background for the documents is useful also.

————. J. G. Lorimer, compiler. *Gazetteer of the Persian Gulf, 'Omân and Central Arabia.* Calcutta, 1908-15. A monumental and indispensable digest of information on the Persian Gulf from the beginning of the European penetration until 1904. The first volume contains the results of Lorimer's historical researches among the records of the Anglo–Indian government. Although this history emphasizes the story of the British connection with the Gulf states and is written from a pro-British imperialist point of view, the author treated the internal history of the many principalities in the region as completely as possible. Volume II contains two parts, a painstakingly prepared geographic and social summary of the area as it was in 1904, and a separate section of maps, charts, and genealogical tables. A photo copy of the first volume of this work in the Princeton University Library is one of the few copies of Lorimer in the United States.

———. *Report on the Administration of the Persian Gulf Political Residency and the Masqat Political Agency.* Calcutta, annual between 1873 and 1904. One of the primary sources for late nineteenth century Persian Gulf and Omani history, the Administration Reports contain year-by-year summaries of happenings inside the various Gulf principalities and on the Iranian coast, detailed trade and shipping figures, and occasional articles on aspects of the regional history, geography, tribes, economy, flora and fauna, etc. The reports were continued as a secret series after 1904 and copies are in London's Public Record Office. The New York Public Library has a virtually complete file of the 1873-1904 series reports.

Government of India, Political and Secret Department. *Précis of the Affairs of the Persian Coast and Islands, 1854-1905.* Simla, 1906. Details the rebirth of Teheran's control over Iran's Persian Gulf coastal areas. This, like the other *Précis* listed in these notes, is based on the Indian archives and was written as part of the preparatory process of compiling Lorimer's monumental digest of Persian Gulf information cited above. Because they often contain direct references to or in many cases lengthy quotes from the raw correspondence in the files of the Anglo–Indian government, many times the *Précis* provide information not found in Lorimer and also give clues for searches into the archives.

———. *Précis of Correspondence on International Rivalry and British Policy in the Persian Gulf, 1872-1905*. Simla, 1906. Rather more far-ranging than its title implies.

———. *Précis of Correspondence Regarding the Affairs of the Persian Gulf, 1801-1853*. Simla, 1906. An excellent and extensive source for the establishment of British supremacy in the Persian Gulf. There is also considerable material on the internal history of the various principalities of the region.

———. *Précis of Correspondence Regarding the Trucial Chiefs*. Calcutta, 1906.

———. *Précis of Nejd Affairs, 1804-1904*. Simla, 1906. Records the fortunes of the Sa'udis during the nineteenth century, and the rule of the Rashidis.

———. J. A. Saldanha, ed. *Précis on Commerce and Communications in the Persian Gulf, 1801-1905*. Simla, 1906. A mine of economic information, this *précis* summarizes and presents in a convenient form much of the data included in the yearly Administration Reports during 1874-1904.

———. J. A. Saldanha, ed. *Précis of Makran Affairs*. Simla, 1906. One of the very few sources available concerning this coastal area in southern Iran and western Pakistan.

———. J. A. Saldanha, ed. *Précis on Maskat Affairs*. Simla, 1906. One of the very few sources available concerning this coastal area in southern Iran and western Pakistan.

———. J. A. Saldanha, ed. *Précis on Maskat Affairs, 1892-1902*. Simla, 1906. The most complete work on Oman in the 1890s.

———. J. A. Saldanha, ed. *Précis of Naval Arrangements in the Persian Gulf, 1862-1905*. Simla, 1906. Details how British paramountcy in the Gulf was asserted. It also provides data on maneuverings and disagreements in Anglo–Indian and British official circles concerning British commitments in the Gulf.

————. J. A. Saldanha, ed. *Précis on the Slave Trade in the Gulf of Oman and the Persian Gulf, 1873-1905.* Simla, 1906. A major source for the history of the east African slave trade and its Arabian extensions.

————. J. A. Saldanha, ed. *Précis of Turkish Expansion on the Arab Littoral of the Persian Gulf and Hasa and Katif Affairs.* Simla, 1906. This work constitutes a history of virtually the entire period of Ottoman occupation of Arabia's east coast from Kuwait to Qatar. There is also considerable material on Ottoman–British diplomatic relations during the post-1871 period.

Great Britain, Admiralty, Naval Staff, Naval Intelligence Division Geographical Section. *A Handbook of Arabia.* Vol. i (General), London, 1916. Vol. ii (Routes), London, 1917. Still stands as a very useful publication in many respects. Much of its data on the Persian Gulf evidently was based on Lorimer but it is more generally available.

Great Britain, Admiralty, Naval Intelligence Division. *Iraq and the Persian Gulf.* London, 1944. Similar to the Arabian handbook listed above but with some newer information and a different geographic emphasis. Although the Persian Gulf proper receives considerable attention there is no treatment of Muscat and Oman.

Great Britain, *Arbitration Concerning Buraimi and the Common Frontier Between Abu Dhabi and Saʻūdi Arabia: Memorial Submitted by the Government of the United Kingdom of Great Britain and Northern Ireland*, London, 1955. This work contains a considerable amount of information about Omani affairs.

Great Britain, Foreign Office, Historical Section. *Persian Gulf.* Peace Handbook no. 76. London, 1920. A guide produced for the use of treaty negotiators after World War I, this work is rather slim and presents the Persian Gulf solely from the perspective of Anglo–Indian and British imperial interests.

Great Britain, Department of Overseas Trade. *Economic Con-*

ditions in the Persian Gulf. "Apr. 1929 edn.," Lt. Cmdr. Forester, ed. London, 1929. "Oct. 1934 edn.," F. N. Gamble, ed., London, 1935. "Dec. 1936 edn.," F. H. Todd, ed., London, 1937, issued as *Report on Economic and Commercial Conditions in the Persian Gulf.* These occasional reports supply some of the information that before 1904 was more systematically presented in the annual Administration Reports. Since World War II reports similar to the ones cited above have appeared at uneven intervals. Evidently, there is now a special annual series of mimeographed reports on Masqat trade.

Great Britain, Foreign Office. *Muscat Dhows Arbitration, in the Permanent Court of Arbitration at the Hague.* Vol I (Case). Vol. II (Counter-Case). Vol. III (Argument). London, 1905. Contains some material on the slave trade and internal events in Oman, as well as on the Anglo–French dispute over Oman and the issuing of French flags to Arab captains.

Great Britain, India Office. *The India List and the India Office List.* London, annual to 1947. A source for information about British personnel serving in the Persian Gulf; since 1947 such data has been in *The Foreign Office List.*

Great Britain, *Parliamentary Debates, House of Commons.* London, annual. See 1899 volume for debate on the Masqat crisis.

Great Britain, *Parliamentary Debates, House of Lords.* London, annual.

Great Britain, *Parliamentary Papers.* London, annual. This series has many valuable reports touching on Persian Gulf matters. Especially useful in the preparation of this study were: "Report Addressed to the Earl of Clarendon by the Committee on the East African Slave Trade, no. C 203." *House of Commons Sessional Papers.* Vol. LXI (1870). "East Coast of Africa, Correspondence on Slave Trade, no. C 340." *House of Commons Sessional Papers.* Vol. LXII (1871). "Report on the Condition and Prospects of British Trade in Oman,

Bibliographical Notes

Bahrein, and Arab Ports of the Persian Gulf, no. Cd 2281." *House of Commons Sessional Papers.* Vol. LXXXV (1905).

The Hague Permanent Court of Arbitration. *Recueil des Actes et Protocoles concernant la différence entre France et Grande Bretagne . . . Boutres de Mascate.* The Hague, 1905.

Hurewitz, J. C. *Diplomacy in the Near and Middle East, a Documentary Record.* Princeton, 1956. Vol. I (1535-1914), Vol. II (1914-1956). This important, carefully prepared compilation gathers together many treaties and documents that would be impossible for most researchers to consult in ordinary circumstances. The perceptive introductions and bibliographies that precede each document add immeasuraly to the value of the work.

Iran, Ministry of Customs and Posts. *Tableau Général du Commerce avec les Pays Étrangers.* Teheran, 1902.

Lepsius, J., A. M. Bartholdy, and E. Thimme, eds. *Die Grosse Politik der Europäischen Kabinette, 1871-1914.* Berlin, 1922-26. There are a few references to Oman in this collection.

Saudi Arabia. *Memorial of the Government of Saudi Arabia: Arbitration for the Settlement of the Territorial Dispute between Muscat and Abu Dhabi on one side and Saudi Arabia on the other.* Cairo: A.H. 1374/A.D. 1955. A major source for the modern history of eastern Arabia, based on Arabic as well as European materials. This memorial, although written to support a Saudi political position, contains much unique information on the economic and social, as well as political structure, along Oman's borderlands. It is especially good for nineteenth and early twentieth century history and Sa'udi–Omani relations.

Sultanate of Muscat and Oman. G. C. L. Bertram. *The Fisheries of Muscat and Oman.* No date or publisher; probably written in the late 1940s.

———. C. S. Fox. *The Geology and Mineral Resources of Dhofar Province, Muscat and Oman and other parts of the Sultanate of Muscat and Oman, Southeast Arabia.* Calcutta, 1947.

Bibliographical Notes

C. BIBLIOGRAPHICAL MATERIALS

There are no bibliographies specifically devoted to Omani matters known by the author but there are a number of books that together constitute an extensive guide to Western literature on the country and even contain some references to Arabic sources on the subject. By all odds the most extensive bibliography concerning the Persian Gulf and Oman is contained in Lorimer, *Gazetteer of the Persian Gulf, Oman and Central Asia*, cited above. This work's bibliography contains hundreds of titles of books and articles published prior to 1904. Another fairly voluminous bibliography, and one more available than Lorimer, is appended to A. Wilson, *The Persian Gulf* (London, 1928). Probably the best bibliography of published materials on the Arabian Peninsula is American Geographical Society, H. Hazard, ed., *Bibliography of the Arabian Peninsula* (New Haven, 1956). This was compiled for the Human Relations Area Files and contains some descriptive comments of the publications cited. J. C. Hurewitz, *Diplomacy in the Near and Middle East*, cited above, a document collection, introduces each entry with a short but well-chosen list of references. Another difficult to find but excellent source on Oman and one that lists a number of Arabic as well as Western sources is Arabian American Oil Company, Relations Department, Research Division, *Oman and the Southern Shore of the Persian Gulf* (Cairo, 1952). Individual articles in the *Encyclopaedia of Islam* and entries in J. D. Pearson, *Index Islamicus, 1906-1955* (Cambridge, England, 1955), and its supplement, issued in 1962, also contain useful bibliography on Oman. Two works with a great amount of anthropological information of Oman and other Persian Gulf districts are H. Field, *Ancient and Modern Man in Southwestern Arabia* (Coral Gables, Fla., 1956); and *Anthropological Bibliography of the Persian Gulf Area* (Washington, D.C., 1952).

D. SELECTED LIST OF ARABIC AND WESTERN PUBLICATIONS

Adamiyat, F. *Bahrein Islands: A Legal and Diplomatic Study of the British–Iranian Controversy.* New York, 1955. This work contains some factual information on nineteenth century history but it concentrates mainly on the twentieth century.

al-Akkad, S. "La Rivalité Franco–Britannique dans le Golfe Persique et les Dependances de l'Oman, 1798-1862." Unpublished Thèse compl. lettres. University of Paris, 1952.

Anderson, J. N. D. *Islamic Law in Africa.* London, 1954. Has a short treatment of east African Ibadi practices.

Anspach, A. *La Russie Economique et l'Oeuvre de M. Witte.* Paris, 1904.

Anstey, V. *The Economic Development of India.* 4th ed. London, 1952. A well-known treatment of the subject that provides background for research on non-Indian trading partners of the subcontinent.

———. *The Trade of the Indian Ocean.* London, 1929. Concentrates on the modern period but indicates the central position occupied by India in the economies of the entire Indian Ocean basin.

Arabian American Oil Company. *Aramco Handbook.* Haarlem, 1960. A well-illustrated introduction to Saudi Arabia and Muslim religion and culture intended for new employees of the oil company, which gives a good summary of oil operations in Saudi Arabia and the Persian Gulf.

———. *Instructions, Field Parties in Saudi Arabia.* No place, no date [1949 ?]. Indicates the practices followed by Aramco survey teams in Saudi Arabia, including instructions for handling military escorts.

———. *Oman and the Southern Shore of the Persian Gulf.* Cairo, 1952. Arabic and English texts. One of the few really important secondary works on Oman. In some ways the book is a primary source since part of the information about tribes was derived from interviews with tribesmen from the vicinity. Although prepared in the early 1950s when the dispute over eastern Arabia's frontiers was heating up, this book is remarkably free of bias and argumentative statements. It is the authors' point of view that Oman historically is divided into two separate political entities, a coastal sultanate centered at Masqat and an interior Imamate of Oman. Includes historical, geographic, tribal, religious, political, and economic material about southeastern Arabia.

Arab Information Center. *British Imperialism in Southern Arabia.* New York, 1958. Gives the Arab League viewpoint on the Buraimi dispute, the imamate of Oman, and the British role in Aden and the South Arabian Federation.

Argyll, Eighth Duke of. *Eighth Duke of Argyll, Autobiography and Memoirs.* London, 1906. Includes some information about the Duke's term as Secretary of State for India during the late 1860s and early 1870s.

Auber, J. *Histoire de l'Ocean Indien.* Tananarive, 1955. A thoughtful and unusual work that treats the Indian Ocean region as a unit.

Aubin, J. "Les Princes d'Ormuz du XIIIᵉ au XVᵉ siècle." *Journal Asiatique.* Vol. cdxii. Paris, 1953.

Auzoux, A. "La France et Mascate au xviiiᵉ et xixᵉ siècles." *Revue d'Histoire Diplomatique.* Vols. xxiii-xxiv. Paris, 1909-10. A good summary of Franco-Omani involvements.

al-Balādhuri, Abu al-'Abbās. *Kitāb Futūḥ al-Buldān.* M. de Goeje, ed. Leiden, 1866. Contains an account of Oman's annexation by the Islamic state in the seventh century.

Barbosa, D. *The Book of Duarte Barbosa.* M. L. Dames, translator. London, 1918.

Barnes, J. "Indigenous Politics and Colonial Administration." *Comparative Studies in Society and History.* The Hague, 1960. Vol. ii.

Barney, F. J. and A. Mason. *History of the Arabian Missions.* New York, 1926.

ibn-Baṭṭuṭah, Muḥammad. *Voyages d'Ibn Batoutah.* Defremery, C. and Sanguinetti, eds. and trans. Paris, 1854.

Beckingham, C. F. "Baḥr Fāris." *Encyclopaedia of Islam.* New ed. Vol. i. A good summary of Persian Gulf history.

———. "The Reign of Ahmad ibn-Sa'id, Imam of Oman."

Bibliographical Notes

Journal of the Royal Central Asian Society. Vol. xxviii. London, 1941.

Belgrave, J. H. D. "A Brief Survey of the History of the Bahrein Islands." *Journal of the Royal Central Asian Society.* Vol. xxxix. London, 1952.

Bell, G. *The Arab War : Confidential Information for General Headquarters from Gertrude Bell; Being Despatches Reprinted from the Secret "Arab Bulletin."* London, 1941. Outlines the formation of the twentieth century imamate in 1913 and follows the course of the struggle between the sultan and imam up to 1916.

Bent, J. T. "Muscat." *The Contemporary Review.* Vol. lxviii. London, 1895.

Bent, J. T. and M. *Southern Arabia.* London, 1900. The Bents visited Masqat in 1889 and 1890 and give vivid descriptions of Sultan Faysal and the declining city.

Brinton, J. Y. "The Arabian Peninsula: the Protectorates and Sheikhdoms." *Revue Egyptienne de Droit International.* Vol. iii. Cairo, 1947.

Buckland, C. E. *Dictionary of Indian Biography.* London, 1906. Useful for information on important Indian figures in the late nineteenth century including Britons serving or living there.

Burton, R. *Zanzibar.* London, 1872. A typically well-written, interesting, and generally accurate Burton account.

Cambridge History of India. Cambridge, 1922-37. A standard history of India most notable for its coverage of the European-dominated period of Indian history.

Carruthers, D., ed. *The Desert Route to India, 1745-51.* London, 1929. Contains material on the Persian Gulf in the eighteenth century.

Caskel, W. "Al-'Arab." *Encyclopaedia of Islam.* New ed. Vol. i.

Chesney, F. R. *The Expedition for the Survey of the Rivers Euphrates and Tigris.* London, 1850. This multivolume publication treats the Persian Gulf as it was in the mid-nineteenth century in considerable political and economic detail.

443

Chirol, V. *The Middle Eastern Question or Some Political Problems of Indian Defense*. New York, 1903. The imperial challenge to the British position in the Persian Gulf at the beginning of the twentieth century as seen by a follower of the school of Curzon and Cox.

Columb, J. C. R. *Slave Catching in the Indian Ocean*. London, 1873. A lively account of the British naval crackdown on the east Africa slave trade in the 1860s. The book contains a great deal of illustrative information on many aspects of slaving operations, and is especially good in its descriptions of Arab slave ships. When Columb discusses treaties and historical questions he sometimes makes factually inaccurate statements. The author's pictures of Zanzibar and Masqat are quite vivid.

Costes, E. "The Present Situation in the Persian Gulf." *Contemporary Review*. Vol. LXXXV. London, 1904. One of many similar articles which warned Britain of the designs of other imperial powers on the Persian Gulf.

Coupland, R. *East Africa and its Invaders from Earliest Times to the Death of Seyyid Said in 1856*. Oxford, 1938. This standard work includes an account of the growth of the Omani presence in East Africa as well as of the slave trade.

Coyajee, J. C. *The Indian Currency System (1835-1925)*. Madras, 1930. Affords background data for the currency crisis which vexed Oman after 1873.

Cuinet, V. *La Turquie d'Asie*. Paris, 1892-94. A statistical description of the Ottoman provinces in Asia, including those in Iraq and on the western shore of the Persian Gulf.

Curzon, G. N. *Persia and the Persian Question*. London, 1892. Written from the viewpoint of an unashamed champion of British imperialism, this work is a classic. Curzon published it while still young but it is a clear indication of how he would view Indian defense, Iranian and Persian Gulf problems when he achieved high office. The book contains much factual data valuable for reconstructing the late nineteenth century situation in Iran and its borderlands.

Bibliographical Notes

Dadachanji, B. E. *The Monetary System of India*. Bombay (1955?).

Danvers, F. C. *The Portuguese in India*. London, 1894. Still a standard work.

Daud, M. "British Relations with the Persian Gulf, 1890-1902." Unpublished Ph.D. thesis, University of London, 1957. An encyclopedic compendium that gives equal attention to events of great and little consequence. Although the author is able to use sources in Middle Eastern languages, the work is based almost exclusively, it seems, on official British and Anglo–Indian sources.

De Goeje, M., ed. *Bibliotheca Geographorum Arabicorum*. Leiden, 1876-1906. Arabic texts of the Arab geographers, many of whom report on medieval Oman.

Dougherty, R. *The Sealand of Arabia*. New Haven, 1932. The ancient Persian Gulf.

Dugdale, B. *Arthur James Balfour*. London, 1936.

Eccles, G. J. "The Sultanate of Muscat and 'Oman, with a Description of a Journey into the Interior Undertaken in 1925." *Journal of the [Royal] Central Asian Society*. Vol. XIV. London, 1927. An excellent description of the central western Hajar Mountain region, with interesting political information included.

Encyclopaedia of Islam. 1st and new editions. Leiden.

Europa Publications. "Muscat and Oman." *The Middle East and North Africa, 1964-1965*. London, 1964. This authoritative series of yearbooks contains much hard-to-find contemporary data on all manner of things pertaining to Oman today.

Ewart, E. A. (Boyd Cable, pseud.). *A Hundred Year History of the P. & O. Peninsular and Oriental Steam Navigation Company*. London, 1937. A "company history" commissioned for the one hundredth anniversary of the P. & O., which has some information on the start of British India Steam Navigation Company sailings on the Persian Gulf.

445

Bibliographical Notes

Faroughy, A. *The Bahrein Islands, 750-1951.* New York, 1951. A pro-Iranian discussion of Iran's claim to Bahrain.

Fraser, L. "Gun Running in the Persian Gulf." *Proceedings of the [Royal] Central Asian Society.* Vol. xxx. London, 1908.

————. *India under Lord Curzon and after.* London, 1912. Both of these works by Fraser, editor of *The Times of India,* incorporate valuable material on the Persian Gulf during the first decade of the nineteenth century.

Galbraith, J. S. "The 'Turbulent Frontier' as a Factor in British Expansion." *Comparative Studies in Society and History.* Vol. ii. The Hague, 1960.

Goldsmid, F. J. *Telegraph and Travel, a Narrative of the Formation and Development of Telegraphic Communication between England and India.* London, 1874. An exhaustive account of the building of the Indo–European Telegraph.

Graves, P. *The Life of Sir Percy Cox.* London, 1941. A biography of one of the great figures in the history of British involvement in the Persian Gulf, which contains valuable material on the history of the region.

Guillain, G. *Documents sur l'Histoire, la Géographie et le Commerce de l'Afrique Orientale.* Paris, 1856. Contains material on Oman during the early nineteenth century based on Arabic sources found in Zanzibar.

Hakima, A. Abu. *History of Eastern Arabia, The Rise and Development of Bahrain and Kuwait.* Beirut, 1965.

Hamilton, A. *A New Account of the East Indies.* Edinburgh, 1722. The first volume of this interesting and varied account includes information on early eighteenth century Masqat and the Ya'aribah imams.

Harrison, P. W. *Doctor in Arabia.* New York, 1940. Based on the author's career as a medical missionary in Oman.

Harrison, P. W. and W. Storm. "The Arabs of Oman." *Moslem World.* Vol. xxiv. New York, 1934.

Hay, R. *The Persian Gulf States.* Washington, D.C., 1956. A valuable book by a former political resident.

446

Bibliographical Notes

Hazard, H., ed., Human Relations Area File. *Eastern Arabia.* New Haven, 1956. A useful summary of information on all aspects of life in Oman and the Persian Gulf, which treats interior Oman as a historically distinct country.

Heyd, W. *Histoire du Commerce du Levant au Moyen Age.* Leipzig, 1885-86.

Hogarth, D. G. *The Penetration of Arabia, a Record of the Development of Western Knowledge Concerning the Arabian Peninsula.* London, 1904.

Hornell, J. "A Tentative Classification of Arab Seacraft." *Mariner's Mirror.* Vol. xxvii. London, 1942.

Hoskins, H. "The Background of the British Position in Arabia." *Middle East Journal.* Vol. i. Washington, D.C., 1947.

———. *British Routes to India.* New York, 1928. A very convenient account with much of value concerning the Persian Gulf in the nineteenth century and the transportation schemes that affected the region.

Hourani, G. F. *Arab Seafaring in the Indian Ocean in Ancient and Early Medieval Times.* Princeton, 1951. A fine piece of economic history that also contains useful political and cultural information.

Huart, C. "Sīrāf." *Encyclopaedia of Islam.* 1st ed. Vol. iii.

Ivanov, M. S. *Babidskie Vosstaniya v Irane.* Leningrad, 1939. A valuable treatment of the Babi movement and the economic dislocations in mid-nineteenth century Iran that fed it.

Kajare, F. *Le Sultanat d'Omân: Étude d'Histoire Diplomatique et de Droit International. La Question de Mascate.* Paris, 1914. A study of the legal aspects of Anglo–French differences over Oman by an Iranian prince.

Kelly, J. B. "British Policy in the Persian Gulf, 1813-1843." Unpublished Ph.D. thesis. University of London, 1956. An excellent study of the growth of British involvement in the Persian Gulf and the establishment of the trucial system there. This thorough, perceptive work is based on official

British and Anglo–Indian archival materials and deserves to be more widely read than it can be in its present form.

―――. "The Legal and Historical Basis of the British Position in the Persian Gulf." *St. Antony's Papers. Number IV. Middle Eastern Affairs.* London, 1958. A short but well-presented summary of the growth of the British position in the Gulf.

―――. "Sultanate and Imamate in Oman." *Chatham House Memoranda.* London, 1959. A pro-sultanate interpretation of the differences between these two institutions as they have developed since 1913.

―――. *Eastern Arabian Frontiers.* London, 1964. A book that takes such a determinedly pro-British stance in regard to the Buraimi dispute that it can stand as an unofficial British "counter argument" to the position presented in the Saudi Arabian *Memorial* which was prepared for the abortive 1954-55 arbitration of the southeastern Arabian border dispute. There is some useful historical information, particularly on nineteenth century events, but the work's essentially argumentative nature is patent.

Kucchal, S. C. *The Industrial Economy of India.* Allahabad, 1963. A most useful discussion on the growth and organization of the Indian economy.

Langer, W. L. *The Diplomacy of Imperialism, 1890-1902.* 2nd ed. New York, 1951.

Lee, S., ed. *Dictionary of National Biography.* London, 1895, and after.

Lewicki, T. "Les Premiers Commerçants Arabes en Chine." *Rocznik Orientalistyczny.* Iwow: 1935. Vol. xi.

Liebesny, H. J. "International Relations of Arabia: the Dependent Areas." *Middle East Journal.* Vol. i. Washington, D.C., 1947.

Lockhart, L. "The Menace of Muscat and its Consequences in the late Seventeenth and early Eighteenth Centuries." *Asian Review.* New series. Vol. xlii. London, 1952.

―――. "Nadir Shah's Campaign in 'Omān 1737-1744." *Bulle-*

tin of the School of Oriental [and African] Studies. Vol. VIII. London, 1935.

————. "Outline of the History of Kuwait." *Journal of the Royal Central Asian Society*. Vol. XXXIV. London, 1947.

Longrigg, S. L. *Oil in the Middle East: Its Discovery and Development*. London, 1954. A detailed study by a former consultant to the Iraq Petroleum Company.

Low, C. R. *History of the Indian Navy, 1613-1863*. London, 1877. A publication containing much information useful for understanding the growth of British influence in the Gulf.

Martin, B. *German–Persian Diplomatic Relations, 1873-1912*. The Hague, 1959. Contains an account of the growth of German interests in Iran and the Middle East.

Martineau, J. *The Life and Correspondence of Sir Bartle Frere*. London, 1895. A valuable work, in that it treats Frere's relations with Pelly and his reasons for wanting a new type of British regime in the Persian Gulf after 1862.

Mason, P. (P. Woodruff, pseud.). *The Men Who Ruled India —The Guardians*. London, 1954. A readable account of the varying styles of British rule in India as they developed before the twentieth century.

Maurizi, V. *History of Seyd Said, Sultan of Muscat; Together with an Account of the Countries and People on the Shores of the Persian Gulf, Particularly of the Wahabees*. London, 1819.

Melamid, A. "The Political Geography of Trucial Oman and Qatar." *Geographical Review*. Vol. XLIII. New York, 1953.

Metcalf, T. R. *The Aftermath of Revolt, India, 1857-1870*. Princeton, 1964. A valuable account which provides a familiarity with the post-Mutiny climate in India which so affected the work of Pelly in the Persian Gulf between 1862 and 1872.

Miles, S. B. "Across the Green Mountains of Oman." *The Geographical Journal*. Vol. XVIII. London, 1901.

————. *The Countries and Tribes of the Persian Gulf*. London, 1919. Written in Miles's old age, this work makes up in valuable data for what it lacks in organization. A major source of information on the Persian Gulf by one who shaped its modern history.

————. "Journal of an Excursion in Oman, in South-east Arabia." *The Geographical Journal.* Vol. VII. London, 1896.

————. "On the Border of the Great Desert: a Journey in Oman." *The Geographical Journal.* Vol. XXXVI. London. August, October 1910.

————. "On the Route between Sohár and el-Bereymí in 'Omán, with a note on the Zatt, or Gypsies in Arabia." *Journal of the Asiatic Society.* Vol. XLVI. London, 1877.

————. "Sketch of the life of Seyyid Sultan bin Ahmad." *Persian Gulf Administration Report: 1887-1888.* Calcutta, 1888.

————. "A Biography of the Late Seyyid Said." *Persian Gulf Administration Report: 1883-1884.* Calcutta, 1884.

Misra, S. C. *Muslim Communities in Gujarat.* New York, 1964. Provides background information on the formation and organization of various Khoja communities, one of which is present in Masqat-Matrah.

al-Miṣri, Muṣṭafa. *Kitāb al-Hadīya al-ūla al-Islāmīya lil Mulūk wa al-Umarā' fi al-Dā' wa-al-Dawā'.* Cairo, ca. 1903. A book by a north African Ibadi settled in Cairo, calling for a Pan-Islamic type of solution for the Islamic world's turn-of-the-century problems; briefly mentions Oman and some of its leading Ibadi figures.

Moore, A. "Notes on Dhows." *Mariner's Mirror.* Vol. XXVI. London, 1940.

Morris, J. *Sultan in Oman.* New York, 1957. A well-presented, interesting and thoughtful account of the reunification of Oman under moderate Ibadi rule and of future possibilities for the country. The few minor historical inaccuracies in the book do not detract from its value as a firshand description.

Bibliographical Notes

Nambudiripad, K. N. S. *A Short History of Indian Currency.* Poona, 1955.

Newton, Lord. *Lord Lansdowne, a Biography.* London, 1929.

Osgood, J. B. F. *Notes of Travel or Recollections of Majunga, Zanzibar, Muscat, Aden, Mocha, and other Eastern Ports.* Salem, 1854. An informative account by a New England traveler.

Palgrave, W. G. *Narrative of a Year's Journey through Central and Eastern Arabia.* 3rd ed. London, 1866. Palgrave's comments on Masqat and the coast of Oman just after the partition of the Omani empire are very informative. His information about the interior must be treated with more caution.

Pelly, L. "The Persian Gulf as an area of Trade." *Proceedings of the Royal Geographical Society.* London: 1863-1864. Vol. VIII.

———. "Remarks on the Tribes, Trade, and Resources around the Shore Line of the Persian Gulf." *Transactions of the Bombay Geographical Society.* Vol. XVII. Bombay, 1863. An important 80-page article that details much of Pelly's thinking about the Persian Gulf of the 1860s.

———. "A Visit to the Wahabee Capital, Central Arabia." *Journal of the Royal Geographical Society.* Vol. XXXV. London, 1865.

Philby, H. St. J. B. *Sa'udi Arabia.* London, 1955.

Porter, C. *The Career of Theophile Delcassé.* Philadelphia, 1936.

Prasad, B. *The Foundation of India's Foreign Policy.* Calcutta, 1955.

Rees, J. D. "Russia, India and the Persian Gulf, or the Western Frontiers of India." *Asian Review.* Vol. XXXIV. London, 1903.

Rentz, G. "Djazīrat al-'Arab." *Encyclopaedia of Islam.* New ed. Vol. I.

———. "Muḥammad ibn 'Abd al-Wahhāb (1702/03-1792) and the Beginnings of Unitarian Empire in Arabia." Unpublished Ph.D. thesis, University of California, Berkeley, 1947. An important study of the beginnings of the Sa'udi state by a leading student of Arabia.

Ronaldshay, Earl of. *The Life of Lord Curzon, Being the Authorized Biography of George Nathaniel, Marquess Curzon of Kedelston, K.G.* London, 1928. A three-volume study of a figure who determined much of the Persian Gulf's modern history.

Ross, E. C. "Memorandum on the Tribal Divisions in the Principality of Oman." *Transactions of the Bombay Geographical Society.* Vol. XIX. Bombay, 1873.

———. "Outlines of the History of 'Oman from A.D. 1728 to 1883." *Report on the Administration of the Persian Gulf Political Residency: 1882-1883.* Calcutta, 1883.

———, trans. *Annals of 'Omān by Sirhán-bin Sa'id-bin Sirhán of the Benú 'Ali Tribe of 'Omān.* Calcutta and Bombay, 1874, as reprinted in *The Journal of the Asiatic Society of Bombay.* Part I, No. 2. A translation of an important anonymous chronicle, *Kashf al-Ghummah,* whose author is erroneously identified.

Ruschenberger, W. *A Narrative of a Voyage round the World including an Embassy to Muscat and Siam, in 1835, 1836, and 1837.* Philadelphia, 1838.

Ibn-Ruszayq, Ḥumayd ibn Muḥammad. *Al-Fatḥ al-Mubīn fī Sīrat al-Sādat al-Bu-Sa'īdīyīn.* G. P. Badger, ed. and trans. *History of the Imāms and Seyyids of 'Omân by Salîl-Ibn-Razîk, from A.D. 661-1856.* London, 1871. A major source for Omani history; written from the moderate Ibadi viewpoint favorable to the Al Bu Sa'id dynasty and the commercial groups at Masqat. The Badger translation is faulty in several respects, especially its dating. His notes increase the value of the work considerably and bring the story down to the late 1860s.

Said-Ruete, R. *Said bin Sultan (1791-1856), Ruler of Oman and Zanzibar: His Place in the History of Arabia and East Africa.*

452

Bibliographical Notes

London, 1929. A biography written by Sayyid Sa'id's grandson.

Salem, E. A. *Political Theory and Institutions of the Khawarij.* Johns Hopkins University Studies in Historical and Political Science. Vol. LXXIV, No. 2. Baltimore, 1956. A detailed, useful, well-presented study of Khawarij beliefs and practices.

al-Sālimi, 'Abdallāh ibn-Ḥumayd. *Tuḥfat al-Aʿyān bī-Sīrat Ahl ʿUmān.* 2nd ed. Cairo, 1931. A history written by one of the founders of the conservative Ibadi imamate in 1913. A major source for Omani events prior to 1910, this work reflects the outlook of fundamentalist Ibadi groups bent on establishing their idealistic vision of right conduct in practical life and politics in Oman. Like the Ibn-Ruzayq history listed above, *Tuḥfat al-Aʿyān* is most useful as a source for the period after the mid-eighteenth century. Interestingly enough, large parts of the texts of both works are nearly identical in the sections that deal with Oman's history prior to the eighteenth century. Evidently both authors drew on a third source—most likely the anonymous *Kashf al-Gummah.* In the first edition of this work the title evidently was written with the phrase "fī-Sīrat" rather than the "bī-Sīrat" of the second edition.

al-Sālimi, Muḥammand ibn-'Abdallah. *Nahḍat al-Aʿyān bī-Ḥurriyyat ʿUmān.* Cairo, 1380/1961. A sequel to *Tuḥfat al-Aʿyān* by the elder al-Sālimi's son, which tells the story of the 1913-55 imamate and the continuing efforts of conservative Ibadis to reestablish their state in interior Oman. Reportedly, the original manuscript of this work was extensively edited by Arab League officials before its publication.

Sanger, R. H. *The Arabian Peninsula.* Ithaca, 1954. Includes descriptive chapters on the several Persian Gulf principalities.

Sauvaget, J. "Sur d'Anciennes Instructions Nautiques Arabes." *Journal Asiatique.* Vol. CXXXVI. Paris, 1948.

Schwarz, P. "Hurmuz." *Zeitschrift der Deutschen Morgenländischen Gesellschaft.* Vol. LXVIII. Berlin, 1914.

453

Bibliographical Notes

Satoudeh, H. O. *L'Evolution Economique de l'Iran et ses Problèmes.* Paris, 1936.

Storm, W. H. *Whither Arabia? A Survey of Missionary Opportunity.* New York, 1938.

Streck, M. "Ķais." *Encyclopaedia of Islam.* 1st ed. Vol. III.

Strenzoik, G. "Azd." *Encyclopaedia of Islam.* New ed. Vol. I.

Stübe, R. "Hormuz." *Encyclopaedia of Islam.* 1st ed. Vol. II.

Sumner, B. H. *Tsardom and Imperialism in the Far East and Middle East, 1880-1914.* London, 1942. A short but excellent survey of Russian imperialism's aims, practices, and limitations in the pre-World War I period.

Sykes, P. *Sir Mortimer Durand, a Biography.* London, 1926.

Tarling, N. *Piracy and Politics in the Malay World.* Melbourne, 1963. The Introduction contains interesting observations about "pirate societies" and thus has something to say to a student of the premodern Persian Gulf.

Thesiger, W. *Arabian Sands.* New York, 1959.

Tūrān Shah. "Chronicle of the Kings of Hormuz." Appendix to *Travels of Pedro Teixeira.* W. F. Sinclair, trans. London, 1902.

Thomas, B. *Alarms and Excursions in Arabia.* Indianapolis, 1931. Records some experiences of the author while he served as wazir to Sultan Taymur.

Thomas, B. "Arab Rule under the Al Bu Sa'id Dynasty of Oman." *Proceedings of the British Academy.* Vol. XXIV. London, 1938. A useful presentation of the general trends of modern Omani history.

Vadala, R. *Le Golfe Persique.* Paris, 1920.

Vadala, R. "Mascate." *L'Asie Française.* Vol. XXIII. Paris, 1923.

Veccia Vaglieri, L. "L'Imâmato Ibâdita dell' 'Omân: La Ricostituzione dell' Imâmito Ibâdita nell' interno dell' 'Omân." *Annali dell' Istituto Universitario Orientale di Napoli.* New series. Vol. III. Naples, 1949.

Wadia, R. A. *The Bombay Dockyard and the Wadia Master Builders.* Bombay, 1955. A very illuminating book which sheds light on the types of ships used in the Persian Gulf and other parts of the Indian Ocean after the mid-seven-teenth century.

Wahbah, H. *Jazīrat al-'Arab fī al-qarn al-'Ishrīn.* Cairo, 1354/ 1930. A standard Arabic account of Arabian events during the early twentieth century. Translated into English as *Arabian Days,* London, 1964, with the author identified as H. Wahba.

Wagner, R. "Deutschland und England am Persischen Gulf." *Duetsche Kolonialzeitung.* Vol. xviii. Berlin, 1901.

Wellsted, J. R. "Narrative of a Journey into the Interior of Oman." *Journal of the Royal Geographical Society.* Vol. vii. London, 1837.

———. *Travels in Arabia.* London, 1838. An interesting travel account that includes an extensive description of coastal and interior Oman in the 1830s.

———. *Travels to the City of the Caliphs, along the Shores of the Persian Gulf and the Mediterranean.* London, 1840. Most of the material on Oman is actually by Lt. H. A. Ormsby and edited by Wellsted.

Wilson, A. T. *The Persian Gulf.* Oxford, 1928. The classic account of Gulf history. The narrative stops just prior to World War I and emphasizes the British role in the region.

Winder, R. B. "A History of the Su'ūdi State from 1238/1818 until 1308/1891." Unpublished Ph.D. thesis. Princeton University, 1951. Revised and republished as *Saudi Arabia in the Nineteenth Century.* New York, 1965. A detailed, well-written account that will doubtless become a standard on the subject.

Zwemer, S. M. *Arabia: the Cradle of Islam.* Edinburgh, 1900.

455

Index

Index

Index

Index

arms manufacture, 146, 153
arms trade, 99, 138, 148, 152-54.
See also munitions trade
army: in Oman, 354-57
around-Africa route, 20
artillery, 279, 377. See also cannon
artisans, 140, 146
Asia, 14, 241, 257-58
'askari ('askarī): a soldier, 355
assistant resident, 172
Atkinson, Capt. G.A.: political
agent at Masqat 1867-69, 196, 288
attack on Masqat in 1877, 336; in
1883, 375-77; in 1895, 375-77
Australia, 91
autonomy, 357-62, 404, 419
al-'Awamir (al-'Awāmir) tribe, 36,
375
Azdi (Azdī): "southern" Arabs, 34
'Azzan ibn-Qays ibn Ahmad ('Azzān ibn-Qays ibn-Aḥmad Āl Bū
Sa'īdī): Lord of Suhar early 19th
century, 273
'Azzan ibn-Qays ('Azzān ibn-Qays
ibn-'Azzān Āl Bū Sa'īdī): imam
1868-71, 201, 204, 218, 272; genealogy, 273, 278; becomes leader
of Qays branch, 282-83; struggle with Sultan Thuwayni, 283;
joins coalition against Sultan Salim, 292-93, 295; elected imam,
296; character, 298-99; consolidation of rule, 300-307; captures al-
Buraymi, 302-305; government of,
307-13; foreign policy failures,
312-17; collapse of regime, 316-
20; death in battle, 319; 324-25,
333, 335, 336, 340, 370, 375, 385,
393-94, 399, 403, 422

"bad dollar," 128
Badger, Rev. G.P., 275n
Badr ibn-Sayf (Badr ibn-Sayf ibn-
Ahmad Āl Bū Sa'īdī): regent
1804-1807, 273
Badr ibn-Sayf (Badr ibn-Sayf Āl Bū

Sa'īdī): military commander and
official, 328-29, 344-46, 355, 368
baghala (baghalah): sailing ship,
120, 122
Baghdad (Bagdād), 14, 103-104
Bahla (Baḥlā'): fortress, 305
Bahrain (al-Baḥrayn) Island: principality, 6, 15; late 18th century
commercial challenge, 62; failure
of 1828 Omani invasion, 69; value
of exports 1830, 97n; trade with
Lingah, 101; 134, 147, 166-69,
172; maritime disorders 1867-68,
191, 198, 214-15, 218-19, 221, 232,
423. See also Anglo-Bahrain Exclusive Agreement
balance of power, 171
Balfour, Arthur J.: British prime
minister 1902-1906, 264
Balkans, 257
Baluchis, see al-Balush
Baluchistan (Balūshistān): province, 101, 103, 152, 171, 347, 355,
363
al-Balush (al-Balūsh): tribe, 34, 36
Bandar 'Abbas (Bandar 'Abbās):
seaport, 71; as steamer port, 101,
115, 164, 217-19, 288-89, 293; restoration of Iranian administration, 313-14, 317
Bandar Jissah (Bandar Jiṣṣah): cove
near Masqat, 248-49, 251
Bani- 'Ali (Banī- 'Alī) tribe, 36
Bani- 'Amr (Banī- 'Amr) tribe, 36
Banians: Hindu traders, 131-44
Bani-Battash (Banī-Baṭṭāsh) tribe,
36, 375, 396
Bani-Bu- 'Ali (Banī Bū 'Alī) tribe,
36, 284, 293, 302, 306, 318-19, 360,
377, 407
Bani-Ghafir (Banī-Ghāfir) tribe, 35-
36
Bani-Ghayth (Banī-Ghayth) tribe,
36
Bani Bu Hasan (Banī Bū Ḥasan)
tribe, 36, 290, 295n, 318-19, 377

460

Index

Index

Index

Index

Index

Index

Index

ture of hegemony, 241, 256, 259-68, 287, 312; decline of power, 321-22, 332, 364, 395-96

political supervisory regime, involvement in internal politics of Persian Gulf states, 157-60, 162-67, 171, 175-79; development of ties with local rulers, 187-95, 197-205; extraterritoriality in Oman, 192-93, 194-95, 202, 203, 218-20, 349-50, 374; anti-slave trade drive, 197-200, 207-10; Omani financial dependence on Britain, 198-99, 220-33; Curzon's humiliation of Sultan Faysal, 241-56, 280-83; compromise of Omani independence, 254-55, 274-76, 279, 284-85, 288, 290-91, 314, 316-20, 330-31, 337-38, 364-65, 375, 380-83, 386; intervention in 1913-20 Oman Civil War, 394-405; directs reconstruction of Omani sultanate, 400-405, 408; Buraimi dispute, 418-22; suppression of imamate, 421-22

political supervisory regime: conduct of local foreign affairs, 157-63, 164, 165-67, 179, 197-205; countering Ottoman and Qajar expansion, 212-19; Anglo-Bahrain Agreement of 1880, 215-16; Exclusive Agreements of 1887-1892, 220-23; nature of control over Omani foreign affairs in 1892, 220-23, 230-34, 340, 364; French flags affair, 384; Buraimi dispute, 418-22

political supervisory regime, Political Agency, Masqat: medical facilities, 154-55; establishment, 165, 172; subordination to residency, 194-97; situation in late 19th century, 211, 224-28; extraterritoriality, 229-30; fall in quality of personnel, 236-40; Pengelly as agent, 281; Atkinson as agent, 288, 291, 310, 323, 327-28;

Miles as agent, 342, 344, 349-50, 374-83; Cox as agent, 384, 394-406, 425

political supervisory regime, Political Residency in the Persian Gulf: encouragement of modernization, 92-94; laissez-faire role until 1860s, 85-96, 171-73, 103; early residency, 164-65; shift to Bahrain, 165; reorganization of 1820s, 167-69; reorganization of 1862-72, 177-205; critique of office of resident, 184-85; Ross as resident, 205-33; late 19th century structure, 210-11, 230-33; fall in quality of personnel, 235-40, 374, 379-80, 256-68, 326, 330-31, 368, 382

Omani relations: military aid to sultanate, 169, 209, 224-26, 228, 231, 237, 247, 285, 325, 330-31, 337-38, 381, 395-96, 407, 421-22, 429; financial aid to sultanate, 224-25, 228, 231, 235, 247, 325-53, 365, 380, 384, 388-89, 391, 400-401, 423; diplomatic aid to sultanate, 169, 224, 363; political support to sultanate, 70, 113, 154-57, 157, 169, 201-205, 209, 222, 226, 229, 247, 267, 274-75, 290-91, 301, 313-20, 323, 327-28, 330, 334, 339, 364-65, 401-402, 407, 409; question of declaring a protectorate over Oman, 221-23, 247, 252, 256, 275, 369; British subjects in Oman, 218, 230, 292, 330-31, 349-50, 425. See also Anglo-Oman relations

resident at Baghdad, 165

resident at Basra, 165

Royal Air Force, 409

Royal Navy: anti-slave trade operations, 63-65, 69, 121-22, 149-51, 192, 207-10, 392; anti-munitions trade measures, 153-54, 391-92, 173, 187, 190-92, 197, 209-12, 225-27, 241-42, 245, 252, 284, 330-31, 382, 395-96

Index

Index

Index

Index

Index

land, state owned, 352
Lansdowne, Lord: viceroy of India and foreign minister, 221-22, 265
Lansdowne Declaration of 1903, 266
law, 203, 230, 402
R.I.M.S. Lawrence: dispatch ship, 211
Lawrence, Sir John: governor general and viceroy of India, 1864-69, 185-86, 189, 191, 193-94, 287-88
lease, 218
Lebanon (Lubnān), 81
Levant, 21, 174
liberalism, 180
lighthouses, 15
limes, 146
Lingah (Bandar-i-Langah): port, 101, 172, 219
liquor, 308
Livingstone, David, 92, 187, 208
Liwa (Liwā'): town, 347
loans, 232, 235, 288, 312, 353, 388-89, 391
local rulers, 230-232
Lohania Wania subcaste, 131
London, 63, 97, 122, 193-94, 238, 275, 421
H.M.S. London: cruiser, 210
J. G. Lorimer: Anglo-Indian official, 368
Lynch Bros. Inc., 85, 89
Lynch Road, 102
H.M.S. Lynx: gunboat, 192
Lytton, Lord: governor general and viceroy of India 1876-80, 208, 257

al-Ma'awil (al-Ma'āwil): tribe, 36
Mackenzie, Robert: Indian shipping owner, 88-89
Mackinnon, Sir William: founder of British India Steam Navigation Company, 88-92, 95, 276
Madagascar, 243-44
magic, 344

H.M.S. Magpie: gunboat, 192
al-Mahariq (al-Maḥārīq) tribe, 36
Majid ibn-Sa'id (Mājid ibn-Sa'īd Āl Bū Sa'īdī): sultan of Zanzibar 1856-70, 272; genealogy, 273; asserts independence of Zanzibar, 274, 276, 285, 288; finances unseating of Imam 'Azzan, 315-18; his death, 318
Makran (Makrān): Iranian province, 71, 103, 121, 289, 299, 313, 355
Malacca: Malaya port, 62-63
malik (mālik): king, 49
Mamluks (Mamlūk): rulers of medieval Egypt, 21
managing agent system, 135-38
Manah (Manaḥ): fort and town, 305
al-Manasir (al-Manāṣīr) tribe, 36
Mansur al-Farisi (Manṣūr al-Farīsī): wazir to Imam Muhammad, 413
al-Maraziq (al-Marāzīq) tribe, 36
marine technology in Oman, 111
maritime peace, 26, 116-18, 165, 168
maritime truce and treaty system, see Great Britain, Anglo-Indian Government
Masirah (Jazīrat Maṣīrah) Island, 30
al-Masna'ah (al-Maṣna'ah): town, 127, 291, 300, 330-31, 360
Masqat (Masqāṭ): seaport and capital, 3-5, 11-12, 23-24, 31-32, 37; expulsion of Portuguese, 53-54; rise as entrepôt, 54-55, 59; trade and shipping 1750-1800, 60-63; start of decline, 64-65; city in 1830s, 65-66, 71, 123; 1862-72 economic depression, 79-108, 111-123; shipping late 19th century, 117-119, 142; trade late 19th century, 123-25; population changes, 124-26, 126-27; dominance of Indian merchants, 131-44; slave trade, 148-

Index

Index

Index

Index

intellectual, ideological, religious organization, 109-113, 154-56, 158, 346, 423. *See also* Ibadi sect

politics: coastal provinces, 37-39, 51-52, 55-56, 60, 72, 109-13, 226-27; dismemberment of Omani Empire, 276-77, 279, 286, 287n; collapse of moderate regime, 290-95; unpopularity of 1868 imamate, 298, 305, 308-13, 320; British policy toward, 336-37, 356; Sultan Faysal's loss of control, 373; restoration of control, 385, 388; 1913-1920 civil war, 395-405; reorganization, 405-10

politics: finances, 61, 69; revenues in 1856, 72, 130, 143-44, 153, 159, 201, 208-09, 230; revenues in 1861, 276-78, 281-82, 288; finances of 1868 imamate, 299, 307, 310-13, 324-30, 340, 363n; crisis of 1890s, 370, 372-73, 376, 378-80; temporary reform, 383-84, 388-89; renewed crisis 1907, 390-91; bankruptcy caused by 1913-1920 Civil War, 400-401; reorganization of 1920, 401-402, 407; Sultan Sa'id restores solvency, 409; 1913 imamate financial system, 413-14, 420; 1963 budget, 424

politics: history, 3-4; period of supremacy in Persian Gulf, 20-25, 29-39, 53-74; importance in 1856, 71-75, 109-113; decline summarized, 157-59; succession crisis of 1856-68, 199-201, 272-94; conservative uprising of 1868, 294, 320; events 1871-1903 summarized, 321-22; 20th century summarized, 388; creation of 1913 imamate, 392-95; civil war of 1913-1920, 394-405, 411, 421-25

politics: interior provinces, 37-39, 51-52, 54-55, 60, 72, 109-13, 227; affect of split of Omani Em-

pire, 277, 286-87; dominate Oman 1868-71, 294-313; loss of enthusiasm for 1868 imamate, 306-307, 316-20, 336, 359; extent of Sultan Turki's influence, 362-63; Sultan Faysal's abortive attempt at strong control, 366, 369-77; stability of 1899-1907 period, 388-90; establishment of 1913 imamate, 391-95; civil war against coastal regime, 395-405; center of imamate, 410-14, 420, 424

politics: structure of institutions: unity and diversity, 37-39; political apparatus 1856, 72, 74, 203, 271; official creation of sultanate 1861, 275, 276, 278, 285; structure of 1868 imamate, 296-313, 314, 322-23, 328-333, 336-38; reconstruction of political apparatus under Sultan Turki, 339-64; role of British as advisors, 340; theory of sultanate, 341, 342, 344, 346; central political apparatus, 341-46; lack of Omani advisors of quality, 342-46; provincial apparatus, 346-50; town apparatus, 346-50; police and judicial structure, 346-50; tribal government, 347-49; prisons, 349; revenues, 350-53, 362; expenditures, 354, 358-61; tribal politics, 357-63; overseas dependencies, 363; British aid, 363-65, 367-68, 376-77, 379, 394; reform of administration, 401-406; Anglo-Indian personnel join administration, 401-402, 407-408; 1913 imamate apparatus, 411-14; organization of sultanate in 1963, 424

politics: techniques and conduct, 130, 157-58, 174-75; importance of British recognition, 201-202, 203; attitude toward moderate rulers, 204-205, 208-10, 223-30, 272, 275-76, 323; dynastic rivalries, 278-81, 294, 325; consoli-

478

Index

479

Index

Index

481

Index

Index

Index

Index

DATE DUE

FEB 9 '8			
FEB 15 1982			
OCT 1 4 1985			
NOV 4 1985			

GAYLORD   PRINTED IN U.S A.